# Encouragement Daily

Soli Deo Gloria     Glory to God alone

Encouragement Daily

# What are people saying about Encouragement Daily?

We spend our lives searching for answers, wondering what our purpose is and what this crazy thing called life is all about. Yet, the answers have been around for thousands of years. Scripture provides the guidance and wisdom we seek to live our best life. My good friend Bob Springer has compiled fantastic examples of Scripture that will inspire you on a daily basis. Coupled with his personal wit and keen insight, Bob provides the foundation for you to start your day with faith, hope and courage. Sit and listen - let God (through Bob) do the talking. There is no better way to start your day than with God's word and *Encouragement Daily!*

As someone who has struggled with faith for most of his life, I have learned that daily, consistent time with the Lord provides the safest and sturdiest place with which to build a foundation for a happy, productive, and Christ-like existence.
Thomas S. Russo, Jr.
Editor, *Encouragement Daily*
Author, *There Are No Politics In Heaven*

As I read these letters from God through you, I can imagine what burden or praise you were carrying when you wrote. Your examples can be followed by many. I found the index of devotions on Encouragement Daily very helpful. Your personal stories are always helpful. This is the way to start my day!
Brock Dutton
TWA Pilot, Retired

My most favorite author, next to Bob of course, is Kyle Idleman, and in his books, he often refers to things in his own family, which helps us relate to the fact that here is this Pastor and he is quick to confess that he also is human. My thought is that you've approached that humanness and it makes a great personal connection for your readers with you, the author.
Phil Juntti, Retired

Encouragement Daily is Chock full of poignant "truth" pictures worth pondering for spiritual growth. Biblical truth is drawn from the common and ordinary experiences of our lives, much the same way Jesus used illustrations and metaphors from the common experiences of his day to share his good news.
Scott Taylor, General Manager
Star 99.1 FM Radio

I believe Encouragement Daily will help people to understand God in a more down to earth way.
Rev. Anne K. Havrilla, Associate Pastor,
Liberty Corner Presbyterian Church

Encouragement Daily

# Encouragement Daily

## *Hope For Today and Beyond!*

## 366 Daily Christian Devotionals

By Robert "Dr. Bob" Springer

Edited by Thomas S. Russo, Jr.
Author of
*There Are No Politics in Heaven*
Public Servant, Author, Professor, Coach and Man of God

Double R Ministres, LLC
2019

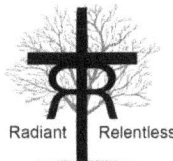

Radiant  Relentless

# Encouragement Daily
## *Hope For Today and Beyond!*
Copyright © 2019 by Robert H. Springer

Robert H. "Dr. Bob" Springer
bob@calldrbob.com
www.EncouragementDaily.us
908.625.8149

Printed in the United States of America

Scripture Verses

ISBN: 978-1-7339296-0-8

# DEDICATION

First and Foremost; To the Lord my God
be all glory and honor.
Pray for me also, that whenever I write,
You will give me the words.

Proverbs 31 (NKJV)
> [10]A wife of noble character who can find? She is worth far more than rubies. [11]Her husband has full confidence in her and lacks nothing of value. [12]She brings him good, not harm, all the days of her life.

A Woman of valor. Without My woman of valor and wife, Jean, none of these things I have done would be possible. Jean is my incredible support; she has always made it possible for me to go to Honduras, on youth Mission trips, to Habitat Projects and on Boards of local organizations. She is the one who supports me in all my efforts of faith. Her selflessness sends me places and allows me to help those Jesus calls me to help.

Thanks, also, to my family who has been my constant support. They allow me to go although they miss me. My assurance to them is let me go and know I will return. They share me with you too. Thank You Father for my family and the love I have for them. And the love You have for them and me!

Also, Tom Russo is the one who made this grammatically correct and understandable. Tom honored the fact that these devotionals are Spirit inspired and could not be changed. He understood the works had to stand as written. Tom asked questions and helped clarify these stories so they make sense to those who may not know me personally. Tom is the "that" patrol. He eliminated more "thats" than I ever imagined possible. We should have had a contest where readers could guess how many times I used the word "that" and a prize for the winner. Next time!

Thanks to Stefanie Lesnik for her sunrise mountain scene photograph which she has allowed me to use to grace the covers of Encouragement Daily and the website.

Thanks to Aaron Anderson for his skillful design and layout of the book cover.

Thanks to David Schroeder for his insight into Encouragement Daily in his Foreword. I am humbled by his assessment.

Caution – writer! *Anything you say or do may end up in one of my stories.* Thanks to all the people in my life whose stories fill these pages. I would say the names have been changed to protect the innocent but there *are no innocent*. You may recognize yourself in these stories and wonder if I wrote about you. Maybe. We all face the same challenges. I want you to know you are not alone.

May God bless each of you with His magnificent Grace and may you be blessed by these writings. In Jesus name I pray!

# INTRODUCTION

Welcome to Encouragement Daily. Why am I writing this? I am inspired to do so! I write because there are too many people unhappy and unfulfilled. Are you one of them? Walk with me as we learn, together, how much we are loved and how wonderfully we were made!

I wanted to encourage you at a time when many need encouragement. Also, I read them myself. When I write down these thoughts which are given me, it helps me clarify my thinking. I am reminded of who I am and *whose* I am and what He wants for and from me. If you are like me (and you probably are), you are too critical of yourself. You have a tendency to forget your successes and amplify your shortcomings. Well, be encouraged! As Ethel Waters said, "God don't make no junk!" You are fearfully and wonderfully made. I hope this helps you live with abandon and be a light in this dark world. Let me know how you do. I know you can, and will, do marvelous things.

This is a daunting endeavor. I feel the call, but I am not always sure I am up to the task. Pray for me also, that whenever I write, words may be given me that I might fearlessly proclaim the Gospel. Pray I might be equipped, strengthened and empowered to run this race and manage to accomplish the task to which I am being called. Let me know if and how these words are helping you. Be blessed!

In Him,
Robert "Dr. Bob" Springer
908.625.8149
bob@calldrbob.com
www.EncouragementDaily.us

## Personal Mission Statement
### Glorify God ♦ Build Relationships
### ♦Benefit People♦
### Teach ♦ Inspire ♦ Encourage

# FOREWORD

Thanks for inviting my participation. I hope several or many other friends will also contribute. Here is my response and endorsement:

Quite likely "Dr. Bob", as he is known, (and self-confessed not to be a medical doctor) has never taken the Hippocratic Oath, but if there is a spiritual version of it, Bob Springer abides by it. He is all about bringing health into your life on a daily basis. Unlike the medical prescriptions of most doctors, which are given in 30- or 90-day doses, *Encouragement Daily* is a whole year's supply of healthy supplements that will energize, inspire, equip, and even heal you for abundant living for here and now and eternal living for then and there.

Changing the metaphor from medicine to food, "Dr. Bob" is also a nutritionist who provides a balanced menu of biblical meals that touch on thirteen timely topics that are parts of everyday life for everyone. I am amazed by the biblical breadth found in *Encouragement Daily*. For example, randomly selecting one week, August 1-7, meals are served up from Jonah, Isaiah, Deuteronomy, Ecclesiastes, Acts (twice), and Galatians. Checking the menu for another week, April 7-13, I found nutrients on Relationships, Quality of Life, Attitudes, Encouragement, and Faith (from Psalms, Luke, Isaiah, Romans, Matthew (twice) and Titus).

Bob spices the entrees with stories from many of the interesting people he has met over the years, but especially edifying is his own transparency. He and I share a personal challenge which he reveals in one of the daily doses; we are both critical thinkers — that's a good thing — but the dark side of that is being critical judgers of other people. So, imagine how blessed I was to turn to my birthday article and find "Be an Encourager," based on Hebrews 10:24-25. Thanks, Dr. Bob. It's the right prescription for me! And you will thank Dr. Bob, too, as your daily doses of *Encouragement Daily* bring blessing into your life.

Cordially,

David E. Schroeder, Ed. D.
President, Pillar College,
President, MasterWorks, Inc.

## JANUARY 1   MOVING FORWARD
### Quality of Life

Philippians 3:12-14 (NKJV) Pressing Toward the Goal

*12 Not that I have already attained, or am already perfected; but I press on, that I may lay hold of that for which Christ Jesus has also laid hold of me. 13 Brethren, I do not count myself to have apprehended; but one thing I do, forgetting those things which are behind and reaching forward to those things which are ahead, 14 I press toward the goal for the prize of the upward call of God in Christ Jesus.*

Welcome to a New Year! How was last year? Was it all you hoped it would be? How will you approach this year? What are your feelings about what is coming? Have you been trying to go it alone in the past? Is that the way it was meant to be? Are things going your way or does every day seem like a struggle? It was not meant to be. God created the world and all that is in it including a paradise garden called Eden. Then, He created Adam and Eve and placed them in that garden. They walked with Him in the cool of the afternoon. All was well. But things went awry! At present, we have challenges. The world is a dark place. Sometimes, it can be overwhelming. We need to remain focused. But focused on what? What do you see when you watch the news? We need to be focused on Him!

When we focus on Jesus, shadows disappear. Things become possible! Hope is renewed! We go forth into the future with a positive attitude and a feeling we can make a difference. And it is true. You can make a difference. You were anointed, equipped and empowered by your Creator. He asks you to remain in faith, to press on toward the future. The past can hinder us! Will you let last year's difficulties block the blessing God has for you in the New Year by not pressing forward towards the goal of the upward bound call of Christ Jesus? He calls you to faith, to love and to His call. What is His call? He calls you to Love Him with all your heart, soul, mind and strength and to love your neighbor as yourself.

This year, learn to love yourself as God loves you! Then, go out and love your neighbor as yourself.  If you don't like the condition of the world, go out and change your little corner. Make me proud of you! Receive and use the Blessings!

Thank You Lord for granting us a New Year. Be with us as our guide so we can live Your way, love others and glorify You. In Your name we pray!

# JANUARY 2 IT'LL BE OK

### Encouragement

Romans 8:18-25 (NIV) Present Suffering and Future Glory

*18 I consider that our present sufferings are not worth comparing with the glory that will be revealed in us. 19 For the creation waits in eager expectation for the children of God to be revealed. 20 For the creation was subjected to frustration, not by its own choice, but by the will of the one who subjected it, in hope 21 that the creation itself will be liberated from its bondage to decay and brought into the freedom and glory of the children of God.*

*22 We know that the whole creation has been groaning as in the pains of childbirth right up to the present time. 23 Not only so, but we ourselves, who have the first-fruits of the Spirit, groan inwardly as we wait eagerly for our adoption to sonship, the redemption of our bodies. 24 For in this hope we were saved. But hope that is seen is no hope at all. Who hopes for what they already have? 25 But if we hope for what we do not yet have, we wait for it patiently.*

Everyone and everything are under the weight of sin. Our world is far from perfect. People are short-tempered and mean. It seems like it is only getting worse. But is it? Has the world gotten worse? Did not Cain kill Able? So, what do we do? Do we give up and give in to the negativity? Or do we live with hope for a better world to come?

As for me, I choose to live in hope. I try to filter out the bad stuff. My knowing about it is not going to help. Sometimes I feel a little ill-informed but that is better than being burdened with bad things I cannot change. I figure I should focus on things I can change. I would like to focus on the people around me and build relationships. Perhaps I can make someone's day a little brighter. I learn and use the name of our waiter or waitress. I compliment people every chance I get. If we can concern ourselves with our own corner of the world and work toward shining our light in that corner, then the world will improve.

How will you live today, tomorrow and into the future? Do you have hope? If not, shouldn't you? All of creation is waiting to be redeemed. Creation cannot redeem itself. Only you can go to God and ask for forgiveness and redemption. Then, all of creation can be redeemed with you! And if God would redeem you, He would redeem others with you. *"9 "The Lord is not slow to fulfill his promise as some count slowness, but is patient toward you, not wishing that any should perish, but that all should reach repentance."* (2 Peter 3:9). God is wanting and waiting to bless you. Will you receive those blessings? A lot depends on your faith, but God will make it happen!

Lord, thank You for the gift of all creation. It is magnificent. Help us to walk in Your ways. You gave us Your Word to guide us to the destiny You prepared for us. In that Word You teach us to love one another. Help us to shine Your light into our dark world bringing it back to Your original design. In Your name we pray! Amen!

## JANUARY 3    BEING CONTENT
Attitude

Philippians 4:11-12 (NKJV)
*¹¹ Not that I speak in regard to need, for I have learned in whatever state I am, to be content: ¹² I know how to be abased, and I know how to abound. Everywhere and in all things, I have learned both to be full and to be hungry, both to abound and to suffer need.*

Do you complain about everything or have you learned to enjoy what you have? Have you learned to appreciate things? Joni Mitchell wrote a song called *Big Yellow Taxi*. The words are as follows:

> Don't it always seem to go
> That you don't know what you've got till it's gone?
> They paved paradise, Put up a parking lot

Do you appreciate what you have? Do you appreciate those around you? If so, do they know? How many times do people never tell others how much they mean to them? I appreciate you!

Whenever I hear the aforementioned verse, I think of my Dad. My father was the picture of contentment. He was almost always happy except when he couldn't find the TV Guide. One time, my wife Jean cooked "Award Winning Chicken" from a recipe she got from the newspaper. Jean is a really good (make that great) cook! In our almost 40 years of marriage, she has had only one failure in the kitchen and that was it! The chicken was awful! We all sat down to eat. Nobody wanted to be the one to tell Jean it was awful. Jean broke the silence! Meanwhile, Dad was still eating. I asked him what he thought of the chicken. Dad said it was interesting and continued eating. My Dad would never ever say anything bad about Jean's cooking. I learned something that day! I learned to be content whatever my situation. You see, my Dad led by example. Whether in need or blessed, I have learned to be content from him.

Are you happy? I am not suggesting that you not strive for better. You should always try to be all God has planned for you to be. He has put dreams in your heart and you should reach for them. But please enjoy things along the way. Life is a journey, not a destination. It is all about relationships! Don't worry, be happy! Be content! Smile more! Thank people for what they do! Live each moment! Enjoy your blessings and your life will be a blessing to you and others! Tell them you care! Tell them!

Lord, teach us to be happy with what we have while listening to You for Your guidance. Your plan for us is perfect. You have given us all we need to be who You created us to be. Let an attitude of gratitude flavor everything we do and let that bring glory to You. In Your name we pray! Amen!

## JANUARY 4   LET GO
Attitude

Isaiah 61:1-3 (NIV) The Year of the LORD's Favor

*The Spirit of the Sovereign LORD is on me, because the LORD has anointed me to proclaim good news to the poor. He has sent me to bind up the brokenhearted, to proclaim freedom for the captives and release from darkness for the prisoners, ²to proclaim the year of the LORD's favor and the day of vengeance of our God, to comfort all who mourn, ³and provide for those who grieve in Zion— to bestow on them a crown of beauty instead of ashes, the oil of joy instead of mourning, and a garment of praise instead of a spirit of despair. They will be called oaks of righteousness, a planting of the LORD for the display of his splendor.*

Are you looking forward to the New Year with eager anticipation? Are you expecting God's blessings in the coming year? Remember, you bring about what you think about! What are you thinking about?

Isaiah was a prophet of God and said a lot of things that God told him to say. He lived 750 years before the birth of Christ. He conveyed messages God wanted us to understand. He told us God *wants* to bless us! If we follow God's ways, we will be blessed. But there *is* a catch! Actually, there are several catches. You see, we have to first believe in God. Second, we have to believe He wants to bless us. Third, we have to believe that He has the power to do so. In Matthew 9:29, Jesus said "According to your faith let it be done to you...". Do you believe these things?

Also, there is another principle at work here. It is the principle of exchange. A crown of beauty *instead* of ashes, the oil of joy *instead* of mourning. In other words, you give God your ashes and He will give you His crown. You give Him your mourning and He will give you joy. It doesn't sound like a bad deal to me. You have to be willing and take the action step of letting go of ashes and mourning. You have to let go of the hurt, let go of the shame, let go of the mourning and whatever else you are holding which keeps you from His blessings.

I heard a story of how trappers catch monkeys in Africa. They fill a barrel with bananas and drill a hole in the side of the barrel only big enough for a monkey's open hand. When the monkey reaches in and closes his hand around the banana, he cannot withdraw his hand through the hole. At that point, the trapper approaches and throws a net over the monkey. You see, the monkey is not willing to let go of the banana so he can escape. He is caught by refusing to let go of that which traps him. Is that how you are? Are you unwilling to let go of the hurt of the past? People fear change. Is that why you want to remain where you are? The devil you know is better than the devil you don't know.

Do you believe God wants to bless you? Do you feel worthy of His blessings? A long time ago, God told Abram that God will bless you! In Genesis 12:2, God said ²"I will make you into a great nation, and I will bless you; and all peoples on earth will be blessed through you." All peoples on the earth! Huh! That includes you and me.

So, go out and live blessed, love blessed and be blessed! Let others see your good works and praise your Father in heaven.

Lord, You said You would bless us all. Help us to have faith that You will do just that. Remind us of the many stories throughout the Bible where You made a promise and then kept it. If You were faithful then, help us to understand You will be faithful now. Help us to let go of that which binds us and trust You for our future. In Your name we pray! Amen!

## JANUARY 5   BE STRONG AND COURAGEOUS
Attitude

Joshua 1:9 (NIV)

*⁹ Have I not commanded you? Be strong and courageous. Do not be afraid; do not be discouraged, for the LORD your God will be with you wherever you go."*

We face a new year with new challenges. Some of them are daunting. In many cases, you seem to face these challenges alone. Or do you? Do you ever walk alone? If you are a person of faith, you never walk alone. The Lord your God goes with you wherever you go. He makes the crooked places straight. He levels out the peaks and valleys. He watches your back. Just as He promised Abraham, Isaac and Jacob, He will go with you. He loves you. He wants what is best for you.

Joshua was Moses righthand man. He was faithful to Moses and did everything that was in his power to support God's chosen leader. At the end of his life, God told Moses he would not enter the Promised Land. Moses had led the Children of Israel (Jacob) for 40 years but it was time to prepare a new leader. Joshua was that leader. As Joshua stepped into the role of leading more than two million people, I am sure he was a little nervous. The Lord God spoke with him to reassure him. If you listen carefully, He still speaks today.

The Lord wants to lead and guide you. He wants to go with you. But first, you have to invite Him in. He is a gentleman. He would not enter your life without an invitation. Revelation 3:20 says *"Here I am! I stand at the door and knock. If anyone hears my voice and opens the door, I will come in and eat with that person, and they with me."* God will abide with you. That means He will live in your heart! If God be for you, who dares be against you? Now go out there and face the world knowing who you are and whose you are! Be strong and courageous!

Lord, You promised to go with us. At times, we are scared. We can't see You nor feel You. By Your Spirit, make Your presence known. Give us the confidence to be strong and courageous. Help us to walk in Your ways shining Your light into the darkness. Cause us to be a blessing to those we meet. In Your name we pray! Amen!

Christ before me; Christ behind me; Christ beside me; Christ within me!

## JANUARY 6   BE A FRIEND

Quality of Life

Ecclesiastes 4:9-10 (NIV)
*9 Two are better than one, because they have a good return for their labor:*
*10 If either of them falls down, one can help the other up.*
*But pity anyone who falls and has no one to help them up.*

### Proverbs 17:17 (NIV)

*A friend loves at all times, and a brother is born for adversity.*

Do you have a lot of friends? Are they true friends? What is a true friend? Isn't that someone who will be there in the difficult times? Someone who has seen you at your worst and not run away? Someone who knows you, warts and all.

In Ecclesiastes, Solomon tells us we are better off with a friend. He tells us of the synergy that comes from working with someone else. There is also protection and profit in a partnership. God told us "it is not good for man to be alone. God always knows best.

Almost everyone wants good friends but not everyone knows how to find them. Zig Ziglar offered the secret! He said "when you go out looking for friends you can't find them anywhere. When you go out looking to **be** a friend, you will find them everywhere!" What do you do? How do you go out to be a friend? By thinking of others.

In John 15:12, Jesus says *"My command is this: Love each other as I have loved you. 13 Greater love has no one than this: to lay down one's life for one's friends."* Does he mean I actually have to die to gain a friend? Nah! But it does mean that you have to put the needs of others first many times. You have to die to self. Do you call people you haven't spoken to in a while or do you always wait for them to call you? Do you remember the birthday of others? Do you send cards or e-mails just because? Do you follow up with others who have had some challenges in their lives? Greater love has no one than this, than to lay down his life for his friend.

Our first foster son did not want to make any friends when he came to live with us. He had been through the pain of making friends and then losing them when he moved. He could not understand that it was possible to maintain friendships over many years. I explained I have been friends with (Uncle) Carmen for 58 years. That does not happen by accident. It takes work. Carmen and family moved several times. Our parents had to transport us many days. But we worked at that friendship and held it together to this day. One time when I called Carmen, he picked up the receiver before it rang and was shocked to hear my voice. He was getting ready to call me. We are kindred spirits who have shared agape love for more than half a century. It is even hard for me to fathom.

Are you happy with the friends you have? Are they with you in the good times and the bad? Are you with them when they need you? How do they make you feel? Do you bring out the best in each other? Can you say "I like me best when I am with you?" Go out today intending to shine God's light and BE a friend. See who you attract!

One word of caution! This can be problematic. You can become resentful if you always put others first. You do need to have proper boundaries. Boundaries will help you establish guidelines for taking care of yourself. You cannot help others if your life is compromised. Ask God to help you establish these boundaries, so you can be the person He designed you to be. Work in and through Him to be a friend to yourself and your family as well as to others you will meet. In Jesus name I pray! Amen!

## JANUARY 7   BE TRANSFORMED AND TRANSFORMING
### Quality of Life

Romans 12 (NIV) - A Living Sacrifice
*12 Therefore, I urge you, brothers and sisters, in view of God's mercy, to offer your bodies as a living sacrifice, holy and pleasing to God—this is your true and proper worship. ² Do not conform to the pattern of this world, but be transformed by the renewing of your mind. Then you will be able to test and approve what God's will is—his good, pleasing and perfect will.*

You are going into a New Year. Are you going to be the same old you or are you looking for a change? Are you different than the world around you? If not, are you ready to be transformed? What example do you want to set? Will people see you and say, "I want to be like them"? I want what they have.

In Romans, Paul urges us to live lives unto the Lord. He tells us not to be like the world around us. He asks us to be transformed in our minds. The only way that will happen is if we live according to God's will. To do that, we must know what God's will for us is. Studying His Word will reveal God's will.

Do you live by a higher standard? In 1960, Hebrew National launched an ad campaign which said they answered to "a higher authority". Can you guess who that authority was and is? It is the Lord *your* God. Do people see you as answering to a higher authority? Are you the one in your corner of the world who sets the higher standard? At this time of year when others are setting resolutions, you could be setting the standards. Zig Ziglar used to say, if you go around setting the example (or, in this case, the standard), you won't have to do so much about setting the rules.

How will you live in the coming year? Leader or follower? Standard setter or lowerer? Are you going to follow God's good, pleasing and perfect will? Look to Him and be the leader He has called you to be! Set the example. Shine the light. Integrity is doing what you know is right even when you think no one is looking. Now is your chance to brighten your corner of the world in His name.

Thank You Lord for the chance to brighten the world in Your name. Transform us into who You want us to be. Let us live in a way that is pleasing to You. Help us to know and do Your will. In Jesus name we pray! Amen!

## JANUARY 8    RUN YOUR RACE

Faith

Hebrews 12: 1-3 (NIV)

*Therefore, since we are surrounded by such a great cloud of witnesses, let us throw off everything that hinders and the sin that so easily entangles. And let us run with perseverance the race marked out for us, ²fixing our eyes on Jesus, the pioneer and perfecter [finisher] of faith. For the joy set before him he endured the cross, scorning its shame, and sat down at the right hand of the throne of God. ³Consider him who endured such opposition from sinners, so that you will not grow weary and lose heart.*

Ready, Set, Go! Are you ready to run the race? We are at the beginning of a New Year and it is time to run the course that is set out before us.

Who are these witnesses? The book of Hebrews tells us that life is a race set before us in which we are to compete. Jesus is the goal on which we should fix our eyes. He is the finish line. We are told He endured the cross all for us so that we should be encouraged and strengthened to press on in the face of opposition. All the world are witnesses who will see whether we will glorify Him who gave it all for us. Will they see us persevere?

There are things we must do first:

We must know the course and which way to go.

> How do you know which way to go? If you are heading to Boston, you can use Google Maps or your GPS. What if you want to take a spiritual journey and go to the place of Rest across the Jordan? How do you get directions? You read God's Word, the Bible (**B**asic **I**nstructions **B**efore **L**eaving **E**arth). Do you know which way to go? If not, ask directions!

We must keep our eye on the prize.

> Fixing our eyes on Jesus, the author and finisher of our faith will give us direction and focus. Jesus will never leave nor forsake you. He will be encouraging you along the route and there, at the finish line, waiting to say, "well done thou good and faithful servant!"

We must understand what it takes to start and finish the race.

Luke 14:27-30 (NKJV)

> ²⁷*And whoever does not bear his cross and come after Me cannot be My disciple.* ²⁸*For which of you, intending to build a tower, does not sit down first and count the cost, whether he has enough to finish it— ²⁹lest, after he has laid the foundation, and is not able to finish, all who see it begin to mock him, ³⁰saying, 'This man began to build and was not able to finish'?*

> Without planning, you cannot know all that is involved in the course you have set. If you don't finish, your effort may be wasted. There are other consequences as well as mentioned in the Luke passage.

We must know why we run.

John 10: *¹²But a hireling, he who is not the shepherd, one who does not own the sheep, sees the wolf coming and leaves the sheep and flees; and the wolf catches the sheep and scatters them. ¹³The hireling flees because he is a hireling and does not care about the sheep. ¹⁴I am the good shepherd; and I know My sheep, and am known by My own.*

You must know the WHY of everything you do. If not, you are just a laborer who will give up too easily if things get tough. There is little invested. It seemed like a good idea at the time of inception. I like to use the word "motive". Are you embarking on this course because parents or friends said you ought to try this? Why are you doing this? What do you hope to accomplish?

I am in the business of changing lives! That may sound arrogant. I don't mean it to be that way but if I cannot improve your life somehow, why enter into a relationship? I want people to feel better for having known me. I want to brighten my corner of the world! I like the expression "I like me best when I am with you!" I want to bring out the best in others. I want to teach, inspire and encourage.

Joel Osteen says, "You should live is such a way as to cause others to win!"

We must train so we have the stamina needed to finish.

James 4:2 says *You lust and do not have. You murder and covet and cannot obtain. You fight and war. Yet you do not have because you do not ask.*

Will you have the resources to finish the race? What resources are needed? If you look to Jesus, He will give you what you need. God doesn't call the equipped; He equips the called! Ask Him!

Many start a race; not all finish. Are you a finisher? Do you have what it takes? Do you know *why* you are running? Do you know the One who calls you to the race? Are you running your race or His? His race will be more rewarding.

Lord, please reveal to us the race You have marked out for us. Teach us why we run and show us to where we should run. Let us always run to You! Teach us Your ways so we might know You better and understand why You call us to this particular race. And equip us to succeed and finish the race, bringing glory to You in the process. In Your name we pray! Amen!

# JANUARY 9    BE STRONG AND COURAGEOUS

Support

Joshua 1:5-9 (NKJV) God's Commission to Joshua

*⁵ No man shall be able to stand before you all the days of your life; as I was with Moses, so I will be with you. I will not leave you nor forsake you. ⁶ Be strong and of good courage, for to this people you shall divide as an inheritance the land which I swore to their fathers to give them. ⁷ Only be strong and very courageous, that you may observe to do according to all the law which Moses My servant commanded you; do not turn from it to the right hand or to the left, that you may prosper wherever you go. ⁸ This Book of the Law shall not depart from your mouth, but you shall meditate in it day and night, that you may observe to do according to all that is written in it. For then you will make your way prosperous, and then you will have good success. ⁹ Have I not commanded you? Be strong and of good courage; do not be afraid, nor be dismayed, for the LORD your God is with you wherever you go."*

What if you knew you had a Champion that was always looking out for you? No matter where you go, no matter what you do, this champion would watch your back. Someone who would support and encourage you in all ways. Someone who would believe in you. What if that someone knew things about you that you did not even know yourself and knew what you were capable of doing?

Now that Joshua has taken the lead of Israel, God is speaking to him about what Joshua is to accomplish. Joshua has to lead two million unruly people who each think they know what is best. God's purpose here is to strengthen Joshua and assure him the Lord will be with him and not to be afraid. The Lord also tells Joshua he will be successful and prosperous.

Well you *do* have that Champion. He loves you and knows how you were made and what you are capable of doing. He has a plan for your life. He has resources to put at your disposal. He has everything you need to succeed in the mission He set out before you.

Are you being all you were created to be? As God was with Moses and Joshua, He is with you! Nothing has changed. He is the same yesterday, today and forever. If you follow His ways, He will make your way prosperous and give you good success. Your Champion asks you to be strong and courageous because He knows the plans He has for you and they are plans to prosper you. To give you hope and a future! Be strong and courageous! Walk in His ways. Your Champion has your back!

Lord, You said You would always be with us. I believe you. Sometimes, we lose sight of You and draw back into fear. At those times, send Your Spirit to reinforce our faith. We know of Your great plans for us. Help us to live into those plans and be who You have called us to be. In Your name we pray.

# JANUARY 10    ALL IS NOT LOST
Grief

1 Thessalonians 4:13-17 (ESV)

*But we do not want you to be uninformed, brothers, about those who are asleep, that you may not grieve as others do who have no hope. For since we believe that Jesus died and rose again, even so, through Jesus, God will bring with him those who have fallen asleep. For this we declare to you by a word from the Lord, that we who are alive, who are left until the coming of the Lord, will not precede those who have fallen asleep. For the Lord himself will descend from heaven with a cry of command, with the voice of an archangel, and with the sound of the trumpet of God. And the dead in Christ will rise first. Then we who are alive, who are left, will be caught up together with them in the clouds to meet the Lord in the air, and so we will always be with the Lord.*

I always wonder how people without faith handle loss and other difficult situations. Without faith, you have no hope for a future. Death is the end for people without faith. For me, it is just the beginning!

I lost my Dad in December 22, 2003. It was customary to bury him the next day. By the time he was transported up from Florida, the funeral fell on Christmas Eve. It was an awful day with pouring rain. Fred did not want to be buried on Christmas Eve. Nothing went according to plan; at least not our plan. He ended up being temporarily stored in a mausoleum until we were actually able to inter him in the family plot the next week. We ended up with two funerals as if one was not difficult enough.

> Psalm 16
>
> [8]*I have set the LORD always before me. Because he is at my right hand, I will not be shaken. [9]Therefore my heart is glad and my tongue rejoices; my body also will rest secure, [10]because you will not abandon me to the grave, nor will you let your Holy One see decay.*

We were very close and a lot alike. We did many things together. My Dad taught me the basics of how to live, how to act and how to fix things! He was a good man! He set a fine example of what it means to be a man of God, a faithful husband and loving father and always put his family first. You may not have had such a father. My father was the closest thing I could see to my Heavenly Father. He loved us no matter what. When I messed up, he would say "you'll do better next time." I was devastated when he passed. He was only 82. I thought I would have him for many more years. I was raised Jewish. In our faith, it is customary to light a candle on the Yahrzeit or anniversary of a loved one's death. I was not so thrilled about Dad's death. It seemed to me his life was much more important. I light my Memorial Candle on Dad's Birthday. I want to be reminded of his presence rather than his absence. In a way, he is still here. I remember his love and his teachings as I go through my days. I prayed for many years that God would bring me a child I could love as my Dad loved me. The example of my Parents marriage of 58 years has helped my brother and me to understand marriage is for life.

Celebrate the life of people you have loved and lost! If you are a person of faith, you will see them again. They will be there to greet you when you pass into His Rest. If you were nice to them, they may even save you a seat.

From the Mourner's Kaddish (Prayer or hymn of praise)

*May He who establishes peace in the heavens, grant peace unto us and unto all Israel; and say ye, Amen.*

Lord, thank You for those You have put in our lives to lead and guide us. They are a blessing to us. Thank You that You never leave us and give us the strength to endure loss and grief. Help us to honor our grief and mourn this loss while remembering the hope we have in You! In Your name we pray! Amen!

## JANUARY 11    BE AN ENCOURAGER
### Quality of Life

Hebrews 10:24-25 (NIV)

[24] *And let us consider how we may spur one another on toward love and good deeds,* [25] *not giving up meeting together, as some are in the habit of doing, but encouraging one another— and all the more as you see the Day approaching.*

We need to work with each other. Gen 2 says [18] And the LORD God said, *"It is not good that man should be alone."* I believe two people working together can accomplish as much as five people working alone. There is a synergy that happens when people work together. If you look at that synergy, there is something there that makes things go better. Could it be that the people involved encourage each other? Are you an encourager? Do you encourage others to be their best? Paul asked us to consider how we can spur one another on towards love and good deeds. Can you think of a better mission? If you are always alone, who can you encourage? If alone, who will encourage you? As you can see, it is not good for man to be alone.

With that in mind, we are called to build relationships. It is only in relationships that we grow. We are called to love one another. We need to be in relationship to love. What better way to love someone than to encourage them? As a parent, this is even more important. Some parents rant at their kids that "they will never amount to anything" because they did not follow instructions. If God, through Paul, tells us to encourage, why would we say something like that? You mission, if you choose to accept it, is to live in such a way as to cause others to win! Whom will you inspire? How will you do that? Will you use your words to encourage and inspire? I hope so. Don't wait! Do it now!

Lord, help us to be encouraging. Give us the words we need to say to build others up. Let us share the love You have given us with those we meet. Let Your glory shine forth from us in word and deed. In Your name we pray!

# JANUARY 12   PREPARE FOR THE HARVEST
Encouragement

John 4:34-38 (NKJV)
*[34] Jesus said to them, "My food is to do the will of Him who sent Me, and to finish His work. [35] Do you not say, 'There are still four months and then comes the harvest'? Behold, I say to you, lift up your eyes and look at the fields, for they are already white for harvest! [36] And he who reaps receives wages, and gathers fruit for eternal life, that both he who sows and he who reaps may rejoice together. [37] For in this the saying is true: 'One sows and another reaps.' [38] I sent you to reap that for which you have not labored; others have labored, and you have entered into their labors."*

Many say the Bible is no longer relevant. The stories don't make sense in today's world. Today's passage is an example where Jesus talks about the harvest and few of us are farmers. What is Jesus talking about when He says the fields…" are already white for harvest"?

The harvest is the gathering of souls into faith in Christ. The time is now. Our world is full of people who live without hope. They see nothing but darkness and despair. The outlook is bad for them. But as Zig Ziglar used to say, "when the outlook is bad, try the up-look. It is always better!" It goes on to talk about sowing and reaping. What do you sow in your daily life? Do you sow (plants seeds) of encouragement? Do you sow joy? Do you sow peace? And what is the confusion about the sower and reaper and who gets what? Just because you plant a seed of encouragement into someone does not mean you will reap the benefit. Encouraging a stranger will not benefit you directly but it will improve the world.

There is the concept of unintended consequences. Many times, actions we take (sowing) bring results or consequences we would *not* have chosen. For example, God tells us He hates divorce. In a divorce, two adults come to an impasse and can no longer continue their lives together. A seed of discord has just been sown. It is their intention to go their separate ways. But what happens? Those who were once supportive become adversaries. Love turns to hate. Relationships are broken. Friends are forced to take sides. If there are children, their loyalties are stretched. Respect turns to rudeness and competition. It sets up an atmosphere that is caustic. And it affects that family for generations. Both my brother and I have been in marriages for 40 years. Do you think that has anything to do with our parent's example of 58 years of marriage until my Dad's death?

What about the harvest? Are you reaping what you sow? Do you want a better world? Are you sowing love, joy, peace, patience, kindness, goodness, faithfulness, [23] gentleness and self-control (Galatians 5:22, Fruits of the Spirit)? You may not be a farmer, but you can sow good seeds! Are you intentional in your actions? Do you weigh the consequences both intentional and unintentional? What are you sowing?

Our world is a dark place. It is time for us to shine our lights. You have the power to change the world in the words you use. Will you sow light or darkness? Or maybe, you will reap the seeds of light someone else has sown. Is there someone you know who needs a relationship of unconditional love; a relationship with Jesus? Are you receiving wages for eternal life? Revival begins with you! Will you begin the Harvest? Are you prepared? Do you need help?

Father lead us to the person to whom You wish to speak today and give us the words they need to hear. Help us to plant joy, peace and goodness in Your vineyard. May we bring You glory in the way we live today. In Your name we pray!

## JANUARY 13    REST FOR THE WEARY
Support

Matthew 11:28-29 (NIV)

28 *"Come to me, all you who are weary and burdened, and I will give you rest.* 29 *Take my yoke upon you and learn from me, for I am gentle and humble in heart, and you will find rest for your souls.*

Are you overwhelmed? Are you tired? Are you stressed? Are there too many things on your plate? Why do you think that is? Have you set boundaries that would limit things in your life to make them manageable? Sometimes, we tend to overcomplicate things. We take on too much! We over commit! Instead of prayerfully considering what we take on, we often just go ahead with whatever comes our way.

But is that the way Jesus wanted us to live? No, it's not. In fact, Jesus wants you to rest. He asks you to come to Him and he will give you that rest. During Biblical times, there were over 600 laws the people were obligated to follow, and the burden was great. Most of those laws were actually traditions established by the Pharisees. They used those "laws" to control the people. Jesus wanted to free us from many things including reducing our burdens. You see, He wanted us to give Him our burdens. He wants us to lay them at the foot of the cross. One thing more. Many of us lay them down only to return shortly to pick them back up again. Remember, once you give things to God, they are His. Do not try to take them back. Let go and let God!

What does this all mean? It means we need to go to Jesus with our life plans while we are still in the planning stage. If we go to Him, He will stop us from taking on too much, going the wrong way and being overburdened. When we follow His plan for our lives, He will make the path easier and our burdens lighter. Will you follow Jesus? He is your Rest!

Lord, thanks that You offer us rest in many ways. Help us to find our strength and rest in You. We have everything we need in You. Let us take time to be quiet and hear Your voice. In Jesus name we pray!

# JANUARY 14  ARE YOU DIFFERENT

Grace and Mercy

Matthew 5:17-18 (NIV) The Fulfillment of the Law

*17 "Do not think that I have come to abolish the Law or the Prophets; I have not come to abolish them but to fulfill them. 18 For truly I tell you, until heaven and earth disappear, not the smallest letter, not the least stroke of a pen, will by any means disappear from the Law until everything is accomplished.*

The Ceremonial Law was given in Leviticus. Through these ceremonies, God taught us about sin, how sin offended Him and how we could sacrifice in certain ways to bring us back to relationship with Him. *"...and without the shedding of blood there is no forgiveness of sin."* (Heb 9:22b). "Jesus fulfilled every part of the ceremonial law and we do not have to repeat these offerings today. However, the principles of the offerings reflect God's character and remain valuable today." BSF

To fulfill the Law took perfection. *"Be perfect as your heavenly Father is perfect."* (Matthew 5:48b) Be holy as God is holy. Is that something anyone besides the Son of God could do? Certainly not! What do you do? How are you supposed to live? Is perfection, which is following all the Laws, the goal? I have heard perfection is the enemy of greatness. One of the kids in the Confirmation Class I taught in 2007 wrote the Message on Perfection based on God's Word in Genesis. She said it was inconsistent for us to strive for perfection and give 110% when God called His best creation, man (Adam in Hebrew), very good. If very good was God's rating, where do we, as the created, come off trying to go beyond that level to perfection? The only perfect One was Jesus and they hung Him on a tree! My Study Bible tells me the purpose of the ceremonial law was to help us love God and teach us of His character. Jesus tells us the two laws we need (the summation of all the laws and the prophets) are to love God and love our neighbors as ourselves. Is that what the world teaches, to love our neighbor?

First, God gave us only one law, don't eat from THAT tree. Then, He gave us ten laws. The religious leaders expanded that to 600+ laws. What has been our track record with the law? How do you want to live? Do you think you can keep the law?

When people see you, what do they see? Are you just like everybody else or is there something special about you? Jesus was the reflection of God's character. Our calling is to live according to God's perfect will for us. Jesus clarified that to us teaching that it was the Spirit of the Law and not the letter of the Law that mattered. It was a new way of understanding the Law to bring us back to the original purpose of loving God. We are to reflect the fruits of the Spirit. What are you reflecting? Whom do you follow? What light do you cast into the dark places? Are you different?

Father, we cannot be perfect on our own by following the Law. It is hopeless if that is our way. But Your way is better. You gave us the gift of Grace in Your Son. Help us to follow Him the best we can and remind us of Your grace which takes us where we cannot go on our own. It takes us to You! Thank You for that grace and Your love for us. In Jesus name we pray! Amen!

# JANUARY 15   WHAT YOU SAY CAN HURT THEM AND YOU
## Quality of Life

Matthew 15 (NIV) Selected Verses

*[10] When He had called the multitude to Himself, He said to them, "Hear and understand: [11] Not what goes into the mouth defiles a man; but what comes out of the mouth, this defiles a man." [16] So Jesus said, "Are you also still without understanding? [17] Do you not yet understand that whatever enters the mouth goes into the stomach and is eliminated? [18] But those things which proceed out of the mouth come from the heart, and they defile a man. [19] For out of the heart proceed evil thoughts, murders, adulteries, fornications, thefts, false witness, blasphemies. [20] These are the things which defile a man, but to eat with unwashed hands does not defile a man."*

In the Old Testament, there were the dietary or Kosher laws which had a lot of restrictions about what you could and could not eat (Leviticus 11). There was a great deal of information about what to do and how to do it. People were so concerned about what they ate. They were concerned that something could make them unclean. Jesus spoke to us about the purpose of the Law which was to bring us to love God. He spoke about the Spirit rather than the letter of the Law.

In Acts 10, Peter had a vision. It was about what you could eat.

Acts 10:11-15 (NIV)

*[11] He saw heaven opened and something like a large sheet being let down to earth by its four corners. [12] It contained all kinds of four-footed animals, as well as reptiles and birds. [13] Then a voice told him, "Get up, Peter. Kill and eat."*
*[14] "Surely not, Lord!" Peter replied. "I have never eaten anything impure or unclean."*
*[15] The voice spoke to him a second time, "Do not call anything impure that God has made clean."*

God was telling Peter that anything that God created was clean. God had just overwritten the ceremonial law, or had He? You see, Jesus sacrifice of Himself was the final sacrifice needed under the ceremonial laws, so it was not important what you ate.

The real thing is not what goes in your mouth but what comes out. Leviticus 19:14 says "'Do not curse the deaf....'" Why not, they can't hear you anyway. Your curse will fall on you because you heard it. Words have power. What do you say about yourself? What do you say about or to others? Do you criticize or praise? Do you look for good or find fault? Do you lift up or tear down? Do you use your words to bless your family, friends and others? Your words can bless others! Go out and bless someone today!

Lord, thank You for Your grace by which we all live. And it is Your grace that points us to Your love rather than ceremonial laws. Remind us of Your love and that it is more important than rules. Your grace is sufficient for all our needs. Help us to accept and live within that grace. In Jesus name we pray!

25

# JANUARY 16   WHAT IS YOUR MOTIVE
## Attitude

Hebrews 10 (NIV) Selected Verses - Christ's Sacrifice Once for All
*10 The law is only a shadow of the good things that are coming—not the realities themselves.*
*........4 It is impossible for the blood of bulls and goats to take away sins.*
*5 Therefore, when Christ came into the world, he said: "Sacrifice and offering you did not desire, but a body you prepared for me;*
*6 with burnt offerings and sin offerings you were not pleased.*
*7 Then I said, 'Here I am—it is written about me in the scroll— I have come to do your will, my God.'"*
*16 "This is the covenant I will make with them after that time, says the Lord.*
*I will put my laws in their hearts, and I will write them on their minds."*

Why do you do the things you do? One of my favorite words is motive. In today's context, it sometimes has a bad connotation. It is often related to a crime. But there are good motives. It relates to one of my Life Verses which is Matthew 12:34b, *".... For out of the abundance of the heart the mouth speaks."* What does that mean? It means what is in your heart will eventually come out of your mouth. Motive speaks to what is in your heart. It relates to the "why" of your life. You can't be one kind of person in business and another kind of person at Church. You are who you are no matter how you try to hide things.

God made it clear He looks at the heart which is the source of our motives to see the why. Many people are just going through the motions. They are trying to get by with the least possible to satisfy a requirement. Is that you? Do you do the least you can get away with or do you do things as if unto the Lord? Why do you do what you do? Is it out of the overflow of your heart that you want to bless others? At BNI (Business Networking International), you are taught the motto "Givers Gain". I think this comes from Zig Ziglar's statement that "you can have everything you want out of life if you will just help enough other people get what they want." If you go out intending to love and serve others, you will be blessed in the process of blessing them!

So, what's your motive? What is in your heart? Are you loving your neighbor as yourself? What's the "why" of it all? Will you ask God to fill your heart with His love, so you can go out and bless others?

The lyrics from the song "Write Your Story" express how we might want to live. It is what I ask Jesus to do! I want Him to change me from the inside out.

FRANCESCA BATTISTELLI LYRICS "Write Your Story"
> I'm an empty page I'm an open book
> Write Your story on my heart
> Come on and make Your mark
> Author of my hope Maker of the stars
> Let me be Your work of art
> Won't You write Your story on my heart

Will you ask God to write His story on your heart? Do you want to live the life He has designed for you? Then do everything as if it were a testament to its creator and yours!

Lord, please write Your story on our hearts. Mold us into the kind of people You want us to be. In Your name we pray!

## JANUARY 17    DON'T WORRY, BE HAPPY
Faith

Philippians 4:6-7 (NIV)

*⁶ Do not be anxious about anything, but in every situation, by prayer and petition, with thanksgiving, present your requests to God. ⁷ And the peace of God, which transcends all understanding, will guard your hearts and your minds in Christ Jesus.*

What is the strongest nation in the world? It is the imagination! And worry is a waste of the imagination. Jesus says (Matthew 6:27) *"Which of you by worrying can add one cubit to his stature?"* Worrying does you no good. In fact, it distracts you from the real task at hand. You cannot fully concentrate on God's plan for your life if you let worry interfere. Where does worry come from anyway? It comes from the deceiver, the father of doubt and lies and it is a way to prevent you from following God's will and plan for your life. You see, God's plan is to prosper you and not to harm you. If God be for you, who can stand against you? So why worry?

Dale Carnegie wrote a book called *Stop Worrying and Start Living* in which he said that 99% of the things we worry about never happen. If that is true, and I believe it is, we spend 99% of our worry time for nothing. What if we applied that time to creating new and better things?

Last April, I went to Honduras on a Dental Mission Trip. During a quiet time alone there, God spoke to me and said, "Trust Me!". My Pastor Don did a Sermon series where he interviewed people about challenges they faced and how they got through them. Each person told how God had spoken to them. Two of them resonated especially with me and I added them to my Word from the Lord!

Here is how they fit: Trust Me! I am all around you! It'll be OK!

Why worry? The Lord of all Creation promised to never leave nor forsake you. He has spoken to your contemporaries. He promises to be with you and He who promises is faithful. Remember the Footprints poem; "It was then that I carried you." God will bring you through the valley to the table He has set before you on the other side. Remember things are not happening to you, they are happening for you! God has a plan for your good. Trust Him! When things look bad, look to Jesus and it will always look better!

> Turn your eyes upon Jesus,
> Look full in His wonderful face,
> And the things of earth will grow strangely dim,
> In the light of His glory and grace.  Helen H. Lemmel, 1922

Lord, You said You would never leave nor forsake us. I believe You! Help us to remain in You and not worry. Your plans for us are great. Lead us in the way You would have us go. In Your name we pray!

## JANUARY 18   HOW'S YOUR FAITH
Faith

Hebrews 11 (NIV) Selected Verses
*Now faith is confidence in what we hope for and assurance about what we do not see. ² This is what the ancients were commended for.*
*³ By faith we understand that the universe was formed at God's command, so that what is seen was not made out of what was visible.*
*⁶ And without faith it is impossible to please God, because anyone who comes to him must believe that he exists and that he rewards those who earnestly seek him.*

Seeing is believing or is it? Have you ever been to a magic show? I saw Lance Burton, the magician, in Las Vegas once. He made a car disappear. Were you aware they are called illusionists? Do you believe in magic? I don't! But I do believe in the magic of believing. You see I don't understand how a brown cow can eat green grass and give white milk, but I know it does. When we enter a highway where the sign says 287 North, do we believe it will take us to our destination? How do we know?

God promised Abram (Abraham) he would be the father of many nations when Abram and Sarai were childless. Would you have believed God? It took 25 years for the "Promise" to come to fruition. Sarai laughed at the possibility. Abram and Sarai wavered in their faith during that time. What would you have done? Do you believe in God? Do you believe He will keep his promises? Really?

Do you think you deserve what God has promised? Do you understand how marvelous He has made you? Do you worry even though God says, "fear not"? How's your faith today? Do you focus on your problems rather than your Creator?

Well I have good news! You are fearfully and wonderfully made. You are made in God's image and likeness. He is mindful of you. You are a masterpiece; God called you very good. In fact, that was His highest rating for all of His creation. He has great plans to prosper you. You are holy, righteous and redeemed by the blood of the Lamb. He will uphold you with His righteous right hand!

I am learning to believe and trust God. He made promises thousands of years ago to Abraham and his sons. God reminded the sons of the Promise. The Bible chronicles the promises and their completion. He was trustworthy then and He is trustworthy now! Why not dig deep into His Word and learn the character that is in His heart. You will see promises made and answered. Unlike the financial advertisements, *past performance IS an indication of future behavior.* But first, you must believe. Why not trust God, walk in His ways and allow Him to prosper you today?

Thank you for your faithfulness Lord! You made promises that were Yours alone to keep and You have always kept them. Help us to trust and believe. In Your name we pray!

# JANUARY 19 MINDFUL OF GRACE
### Grace

Jeremiah 31:33 (NKJV)
*33 But this is the covenant that I will make with the house of Israel after those days, says the*
*LORD: I will put My law in their minds, and write it on their hearts; and I will be their God, and*
*they shall be My people.*

In Evangelism Explosion, a course I took to learn how to make disciples, it taught that head knowledge of Jesus alone was not good enough. You had to accept Jesus into your heart. I have done that with great results. But I have discovered, heart knowledge alone is also not enough. I have Jesus in my heart now. It is time to get Him back into my head. Grace needs to be in your head as much as in your heart. You'll see why in a little bit.

Many of us, me included, do not achieve all they could because of head trash. Head trash like I'm not worthy. I'll never be able to do that. I don't have the talent. The accuser tells you that you don't have what it takes. You're not smart enough. You're not good enough. You're too far behind and many, many more. If you are truthful you do not deserve God's grace. That is why it is called Grace! Grace is unmerited favor. You have the favor of God upon you and in you. You should be able to accomplish all things!

The Lord says He will write His law in our minds and on our hearts. Why did He say He would put His law in our minds? God's law was given because of His love for us. His Grace is why He wants the best for us and His law is how He guides us to that best. God's law is Grace. Therefore, He puts His Grace in your mind if you will let Him. We need to accept His grace into our minds to force out the head trash! Only when we believe we can in our minds, will we achieve the dreams God has put in our hearts. Believe and achieve!

Lord, it is by Your grace we grow into who You designed us to be. It is by Your grace the we live. By Your Spirit, guide us into the destiny You planned for us. Write the story of Your love on our hearts and let that story bring glory to Your Holy Name. In that name we pray!

# JANUARY 20     THE DEVIL MADE ME DO IT

Faith

Luke 10:17-20 (NIV)

*17 The seventy-two returned with joy and said, "Lord, even the demons submit to us in your name." 18 He replied, "I saw Satan fall like lightning from heaven. 19 I have given you authority to trample on snakes and scorpions and to overcome all the power of the enemy; nothing will harm you. 20 However, do not rejoice that the spirits submit to you, but rejoice that your names are written in heaven."*

Who knows who Flip Wilson is? If you said yes, you have just dated yourself as older (like me). Flip Wilson was a comedian who played Geraldine Jones on the show. This was a huge part of *The Flip Wilson Show* and was played by Wilson wearing women's clothing. Some of "Geraldine's" most famous quotes are, "The devil made me buy this dress!

Do you believe in Jesus? Do you trust Him? If Jesus tells you something, are you going to believe it?

Do you believe in Satan? Some of you don't believe in Satan and that he exists. In fact, a pastor of a Church I attended told me they did not believe Satan existed.

In our conversation, when I mentioned that bad things often come from Satan, I could sense these people backing away from me, even though not physically, because they did not believe Satan exists. Many ask why bad things happen to good people. Why do you suppose that is? God has a plan for good for you. Who is it that has bad things in mind for you? If Jesus said He saw Satan fall, shouldn't you believe Him? Therefore, Satan is someone real and present and causes bad things in your life. It is his job to distract you from the plan God has for you. He causes you to doubt. He is probably responsible for most of your head trash. Do you have head trash? What do you think would help overcome your doubts? Focus on the Author and perfecter of your faith and His plan for your life so you can avoid distraction. He will take you places you never imagined possible.

Lord, please wrap Your hedge of protection around us to keep away the evil one! You said You had a plan to prosper us. Please work Your plan for our good. Remind us of who we are in You. Our names are written in Your book of life by Your grace. Thank You! In Your name we pray!

# JANUARY 21    IF GOD BE FOR US....

Faith

2 Kings 6:16–18 (NKJV) Elisha Captures Blinded Syrians

...*16So he answered, "Do not fear, for those who are with us are more than those who are with them." 17Then Elisha prayed and said, "O LORD, I pray, open his eyes that he may see."* And the LORD opened the servant's eyes and he saw; **and behold, the mountain was full of horses and chariots of fire all around Elisha**. *18When they came down to him, Elisha prayed to the LORD and said, "Strike this people [the Syrians] with blindness, I pray."* So, He struck them with blindness according to the word of Elisha....

Have you ever come up against a challenge that looked overwhelming? You were afraid of failure because the odds looked heavy against you. In the natural, there was no way you could succeed. In your own power, it looks impossible. They key is you are not in your own power! You are not alone if you put your trust in God. In fact, you are never alone because He walks with you.

In the story about Elisha, a Prophet of God, the King of Syria wants to capture Elisha to prevent him from giving details of the Syrian attack plan to the king of Israel through his prophecy. There was a mighty force sent to capture Elisha. They were greatly outnumbered in the natural and it looked bad for Elisha and the city of Dothan. But Elisha had faith. He trusted God to care for him and God is faithful. Elisha's servant was terrified, but Elisha calmed him asking the Lord to truly open the servant's eyes. When God did open his eyes, the servant saw "the mountain was full of horses and chariots of fire all around Elisha". God had His legions of Angels at the ready to attack the Syrians to defend Elisha because Elisha belonged to the Lord.

To whom do you belong? Are you a child of the Most High God? If so, don't you think God will defend you? Why are you afraid? Throughout the Bible, in each story, it tells of God's character and faithfulness. God always protects His own. Do you want that kind of power on your side? You may not see it, but God is always working for good of those who belong to Him. He is making a way where you don't see a way. He is leveling the hills and valleys. You will still face challenges, but they will not overwhelm you.

Lyrics from the Mercyme song Greater:

'Cause I hear a voice and He calls me redeemed when others say I'll never be enough

And greater is the One living inside of me Than he who is living in the world

"Fear not, for I am with you." Says the Lord! Move ahead with confidence for God has your back! God is for us! Greater is He who is in you than he who is in the world.

Those who are for you are more powerful that those who are against you. Lord, thank You that You are our protection. Thank You that You are on our side. Better yet, that we can be on Your side. Thank You that Your angels watch over us standing ready to defend us at Your command. And we know that Your command is always to protect Your own. Thank You that You call us Your own. In Jesus name we pray!

# JANUARY 22   IS YOUR LIGHT SHINING
Attitude

Matthew 5:14-16 (NIV)

[14] *"You are the light of the world. A town built on a hill cannot be hidden.* [15] *Neither do people light a lamp and put it under a bowl. Instead they put it on its stand, and it gives light to everyone in the house.* [16] *In the same way, let your light shine before others, that they may see your good deeds and glorify your Father in heaven.*

The world is a dark place. Watch the news and see one bad thing after another. If you look at the darkness, it can become overwhelming. You can develop a hopeless demeanor from too much negative input. But we cannot ignore the evil that comes from sin. We are a fallen people, so what to do? Do we ignore all the bad? Not hardly! But better to set a good example.

Jesus was teaching His disciples about how they should live. He went up the side of a mountain and sat down to teach. He shared what is now known as the Beatitudes in this Sermon on the Mount. Instead of living the way the world lives, Jesus taught how we should live and that we should set the example. Right living will bring glory to God.

Imagine you are in a totally dark room. There is no light, so you cannot see anything. Now imagine you light one candle in that room. What happens? That one candle adds enough light to the room, so you can see. The light dispels the darkness. What do we learn from this? That adding just a little light to a dark place changes things. It dispels darkness. It gives back hope. One of the plagues in Egypt was darkness; it was a darkness you could feel. Sometimes, while watching the news, I can feel the darkness. I see the evil one causing doubt and despair and feelings of hopelessness. You can change all that with your light. Be an encourager.

Instead of giving in to the darkness, light your light. Jesus called you the light of the world. Don't hide it but let your light be seen by all. Your light comes from the true Light of the World. Let His glory shine out through you to brighten up your corner of the world. If each of us shines our light, the darkness would be pushed back, and the world will be a bright place of hope. God's love is that light. He asked us to love one another like He loves us. Do that and you can push back the darkness. Do random acts of kindness today to shine your light!

Lord, You said we are to shine our light! Our light is but a reflection of You, the Light of the World! Help us to be bold and shine into the dark places. Strengthen our resolve to shine for You. Lead us to the places of darkness so that we can share Your love and light with all who live in darkness that we might bring them to You. In Jesus name we pray!

"This little light of mine, I'm going to let it shine."

# JANUARY 23   THIS IS TOUGH
## Quality of Life

John 16:33 (NIV)
*"I have told you these things, so that in me you may have peace. In this world you will have trouble. But take heart! I have overcome the world."*

Did you think everything would go your way as soon as you turned over your life to God? Many Christians think everything should be easy for them. After all, they are following Jesus. Won't He pour out blessings upon them? Jesus warned us that it would not be easy.

James 1:2-4 says of Trials and Temptations, *"² Consider it pure joy, my brothers and sisters, whenever you face trials of many kinds, ³ because you know that the testing of your faith produces perseverance. ⁴ Let perseverance finish its work so that you may be mature and complete, not lacking anything.*

Is that the attitude you take toward trials? Do you consider it pure joy? I know I don't. I am just learning to accept challenges as lessons. I ask what God is trying to teach me through this event? After all, it is not happening to me; it is happening for me! In Romans 5, it says *³ Not only so, but we also glory in our sufferings, because we know that suffering produces perseverance; ⁴ perseverance, character; and character, hope.* God uses these challenges to refine us. A kite only flies high when it flies against the wind. Only in adversity are we strengthened. If everything is easy, we do not build strength, skill and persistence. God disciplines those He loves. If He did not care about you, He would let you do whatever you want because He doesn't care how it turns out. By caring, He wants what is best for you and will lead you in the narrow way which will bring you good things.

I am not yet at a place where I can consider it pure joy. I don't know if I will ever be at that place. But I am learning to look for the lesson, the silver lining in the rain cloud. I think that is what God wants us to do. He wants us to stay in faith through the trial and learn something from the challenge. What do you face today? Did you lose something you needed? Have you been overlooked for a promotion? Did someone else get an opportunity you thought should be yours? Ask God to show you why this was not His timing. Be patient. God has something far better in line for you. Remain calm and wait for the good He is longing to bring to you! He has overcome the world all for you!

Lord, You said we would have trouble in this world. Help us to recognize the trouble in this world prepares us for the blessing in Your Kingdom. Show us the lesson You are trying to teach us. Refine us to be who You designed us to be. In Your name we pray! Amen!

# JANUARY 24   BE PREPARED TO STAND

Support

Ephesians 6:10-18 (NIV) The Armor of God

*[10] Finally, be strong in the Lord and in his mighty power. [11] Put on the full armor of God, so that you can take your stand against the devil's schemes. [12] For our struggle is not against flesh and blood, but against the rulers, against the authorities, against the powers of this dark world and against the spiritual forces of evil in the heavenly realms. [13] Therefore put on the full armor of God, so that when the day of evil comes, you may be able to stand your ground, and after you have done everything, to stand. [14] Stand firm then, with the belt of truth buckled around your waist, with the breastplate of righteousness in place, [15] and with your feet fitted with the readiness that comes from the gospel of peace. [16] In addition to all this, take up the shield of faith, with which you can extinguish all the flaming arrows of the evil one. [17] Take the helmet of salvation and the sword of the Spirit, which is the word of God.*
*[18] And pray in the Spirit on all occasions with all kinds of prayers and requests. With this in mind, be alert and always keep on praying for all the Lord's people.*

The Boy Scouts motto is "be prepared". When you are facing a challenge, it is always good to be prepared. How strong are you? What training do you have in self-defense or military tactics? If you need to defend yourself, how prepared are you? Can you take care of yourself and your family? Can you face the evil one in your own power and prevail?

If you think you have everything it takes to prevail over the dark forces that permeate our world, you are fooling yourself! What will you do? Is it hopeless? On your own, you cannot succeed but you are not on your own. If fact, you are never alone. You don't have to do these things in your own power. The Lord your God goes before you making the crooked places straight and leveling the peaks and valleys. He gives His angels charge over you to protect and deliver you. He gives you everything you need to prevail if you will stand your ground. How can you do that? By using the tools, He has provided. He gives you the belt of truth, the breastplate of righteousness, the shoes of peace, the shield of faith, the helmet of salvation and, the most powerful of all, the sword of the Spirit which is the Word of God. When you face evil, all you need to combat it is the Word. "Get thee behind me Satan." Resist the devil and he will flee from you. When Jesus was in the desert for 40 days being tempted, the only weapon He used was the Word of God. In Matthew 4, Jesus used three passages of Scripture to resist the devil and he fled!

Do you want the power to resist evil? It is available to you. The full armor of God is available to any who seek the Lord for those who seek Him will find him. Are you wearing your full armor? Are you prepared to stand? Stand firm then in your armor! Be God's warrior.

Lord, please provide us Your full armor so we will be able to stand for You. Guide us in Your ways. Let Your glory shine out from us to those in peril as a beacon of hope. You are our hope and shield. In You, we put our faith and trust. In Jesus name we pray!

# JANUARY 25   HELP ME TO STAND TOO
## Quality of Life

Ephesians 6:18-20 (NIV)

*[18] And pray in the Spirit on all occasions with all kinds of prayers and requests. With this in mind, be alert and always keep on praying for all the Lord's people. [19] Pray also for me, that whenever I speak, words may be given me so that I will fearlessly make known the mystery of the gospel, [20] for which I am an ambassador in chains. Pray that I may declare it fearlessly, as I should.*

Many years ago, I attended a men's Bible study held at a local restaurant. The owner was a devout Christian who wanted to do his part in leading people to Christ, so he opened his restaurant at 6:30 in the morning so we could meet. His name was Jack and he was an amazing man. He opened the meeting with a joke and then he would ask for prayer joys and concerns. He never wrote any of them down but touched upon each item during his prayer time. It was a special time for me and taught me how to pray. With Jack, it was just a chat with God. Wow! You mean I could talk to God?

There were men of all ages there. There were fathers who brought their sons. Some had grandchildren there. One of the older men, Leif, had a long spiritual journey and used his knowledge and experience to encourage those newer to the faith. I was new to my faith then. Leif suggested we all have a Life verse; a verse to which we could turn when we face a challenge that would remind us of God's care and concern for us. Something that could strengthen us in our faith. My first Life Verse was Matthew 12:34b "Out of the overflow of the heart, the mouth speaks." I remembered that good should come out of my mouth. Whatever came out was a reflection of what was contained within me. I wanted to be good from the inside out and follow my newfound Savior.

Later, I discovered that I could have more than one Life Verse. As I read through the Bible, another verse spoke to me. I chose Ephesians 6:19 which reads "Pray also for me, that whenever I speak, words may be given me so that I will fearlessly make known the mystery of the gospel,". It opens a new phase of my life. I came to understand that God, by His Holy Spirit, could and would speak through me if I am open to His lead. Now, I am open! When in a conversation, I pause to allow the Spirit to speak through me. Pray for me also, that the Spirit will continue to speak to me and through me in these daily devotionals. Pray I continue to share the Good News. Pray the words given me are the words you need to hear. The words I need to hear! When I write these things, I read them for myself. God speaks to me, so I can speak to you. Please ask Him to continue.

Lord, thank You that You speak to me. Help me to be quiet and listen. Your word is everything to me. Give me the words You want to say to those to whom I speak and write. May Your words bless all who read them. In Your name I pray!

# JANUARY 26   WHY CAN'T I FORGIVE MYSELF
## Grace and Mercy

Leviticus 16 (NIV) Selected Verses

[11] *"Aaron shall bring the bull for his own sin offering to make atonement for himself and his household, and he is to slaughter the bull for his own sin offering.......* [14] *He is to take some of the bull's blood and with his finger sprinkle it on the front of the atonement cover; then he shall sprinkle some of it with his finger seven times before the atonement cover.*

[15] *"He shall then slaughter the goat for the sin offering for the people and take its blood behind the curtain and do with it as he did with the bull's blood: .......* [16] *In this way he will make atonement for the Most Holy Place because of the uncleanness and rebellion of the Israelites, whatever their sins have been. ...., having made atonement for himself, his household and the whole community of Israel.*

[20] *"When Aaron has finished making atonement for the Most Holy Place, the tent of meeting and the altar, he shall bring forward the live goat.* [21] *He is to lay both hands on the head of the live goat and confess over it all the wickedness and rebellion of the Israelites—all their sins— and put them on the goat's head. He shall send the goat away into the wilderness in the care of someone appointed for the task.* [22] ***The goat will carry on itself all their sins to a remote place***, *and the man shall release it in the wilderness.*

You've confessed your sin, repented from it and you are still hounded by guilt. Why? The person you have harmed has said they forgive you. God has offered you forgiveness. What is it going to take to get out from under this dark cloud? If God can forgive you, why can't you forgive yourself? Because you don't think you are worthy of His forgiveness, that's why. What is it about us that we struggle so much with letting go?

When God's presence rested over the Atonement cover in the Most Holy Place (Leviticus 16), He looked down on the Ark of the Covenant which contained the Law God Himself carved into the two tablets. As He looks down, He sees that we have broken His Law. When Aaron sprinkles the blood of the sacrifice on the atonement cover, it covers the sins of the people. God now sees the Law through the blood of the sacrifice. Just as many years later, God sees us through the blood of the perfect sacrifice, Jesus the Christ.

God created the sacrificial system for us to be able to atone for our sins. The second goat was supposed to carry our sins off into the wilderness and remove them from us. This goat was to carry the guilt and shame away. Without the shedding of blood, there is no forgiveness of sin. Jesus, the perfect sacrifice, shed His blood once for all. He did that for you and for me. John 15:13 says *Greater love has no one than this: to lay down one's life for one's friends.* Jesus calls you His friend. You are holy righteous and redeemed by the blood of the Lamb. The One who formed the universe calls you the apple of His eye and a masterpiece. It is time to stop listening to those voices in your head telling you that you are not good enough. It is time to listen to the voice of Truth, the voice of God who tells you that you are His beloved child. Let go and let God. Accept His Word and His Truth and say Amen!

Thank You Lord that Your forgiveness is complete. By the sacrifice of Your Son, we have all been cleansed and can now stand before You dressed in His robe of righteousness. It is only by the blood of the Lamb that we can come before You. By His stripes we are healed. Thank you for healing us. In Your name we pray!

# JANUARY 27   GOD WANTS TO BE GOOD TO YOU

Support

Isaiah 30: 18-20 (NIV)

*18 Yet the LORD longs to be gracious to you; therefore he will rise up to show you compassion. For the LORD is a God of justice.  Blessed are all who wait for him!*

*19 People of Zion, who live in Jerusalem, you will weep no more. How gracious he will be when you cry for help! As soon as he hears, he will answer you. 20 Although the Lord gives you the bread of adversity and the water of affliction, your teachers will be hidden no more; with your own eyes you will see them.*

"Yet the Lord longs to be gracious to you" There it is in print. The Lord *longs* to be good to you. And yet we mess that up! We let things get in the way. Usually, we are what gets in the way. Do you block the things God wants to do for you?

Isaiah also says God will be gracious to you when you cry for help. Do you cry out to God for help? Or do you think He is too busy with important things to listen to your little concerns. God cares about everything that concerns you. It says, *"As soon as he hears, he will answer you."* As soon as he hears! How can He hear if you don't speak? You matter to Him. Matthew 10:29-30 (NIV) says *29 "Are not two sparrows sold for a penny? Yet not one of them will fall to the ground outside your Father's care. 30 And even the very hairs of your head are all numbered."* Someone who knows how you were formed and the number of hairs on your head must care about you. You are His masterpiece.

Since we now know how much God cares about us, how will we live? Will we speak to Him about all of the things that are going on in our lives or will we only go to God as a last resort? Don't you think it would be better to ask God what His will is for us than to make our decisions and then ask God to bless them after the fact? Some people have come to a place in their Spiritual Journey where they have conversations with God and He answers. I am one of those people and I am willing to admit it. Isaiah says He will answer you! Why would you be surprised? Does God speak to you? He does me. Most of the time, it is through my subconscious; I don't know what to do and then all of a sudden, I have the answer. Once in a great while, I hear a clearly audible voice. I heard God last April in Honduras. I believe Isaiah! How about you?

One last thought. I try to use these words to encourage you. Sometimes, people think encouraging messages leave out the full truth of the Bible. I do not want you to think that. You will still see the bread of adversity and the water of affliction, but they will not overwhelm you. God uses these things to refine you, not to harm you. Speak to Him. Ask for His favor. You are the apple of His eye and he wants to bless you. Why not let Him bless you today? Out of the overflow of those blessings, you can bless others. Thank you, Lord!

# JANUARY 28 ARE YOU LISTENING
Faith


1 Kings 19:9-13 (NIV)The LORD Appears to Elijah

*And the word of the LORD came to him: "What are you doing here, Elijah?"*

*[10] He replied, "I have been very zealous for the LORD God Almighty. The Israelites have rejected your covenant, torn down your altars, and put your prophets to death with the sword. I am the only one left, and now they are trying to kill me too." [11] The LORD said, "Go out and stand on the mountain in the presence of the LORD, for the LORD is about to pass by."*

*Then a great and powerful wind tore the mountains apart and shattered the rocks before the LORD, but the LORD was not in the wind. After the wind there was an earthquake, but the LORD was not in the earthquake. [12] After the earthquake came a fire, but the LORD was not in the fire. And after the fire came a gentle whisper. [13] When Elijah heard it, he pulled his cloak over his face and went out and stood at the mouth of the cave.*

*Then a voice said to him, "What are you doing here, Elijah?"*

Did you hear that? I could have sworn I heard someone speaking but there's no one around. It must be my imagination.

Elijah had just come off one of the biggest victories of his career. The Lord God Almighty had just proven Elijah to be correct in his prophecy that the Lord was more powerful than the Priests of Baal. In fact, the Lord sent down fire which burned up the sacrifice Elijah had doused in water and vaporized the 400 Priests of Baal. Now he was cowering in a cave because Jezebel threatened his life. Did he forget what just happened? Now God wanted to speak with him. Uh Oh, Elijah is in trouble with the big Guy.

You would think the all-powerful Creator of the universe would come with thunder and lightning and the blast of a trumpet. But that is not always the case. In Isaiah, it says "after the fire came a gentle whisper...." Did you hear that? God's voice came in a gentle whisper. If you're not careful, you could miss it.

In the Day of Atonement (Yom Kippur, Leviticus 16) service, one of the things I remember most from the prayers is "A Still Small Voice was heard". Not a great thunder or bright flash but a still small voice. While God is all powerful, He most times is gentle. He does not want to terrorize us. He wants to love us. How do you know it is God speaking? When I was in turmoil about which path, I should be taking in life, there was too much going on. I have trouble quieting my mind and listening. I went to Honduras with the Dental Team for their yearly visit. I was completely out of my comfort zone in many ways. I had few electronics and they only worked at times in certain places. I was able to be quiet and open my heart to listen. I was lying in a dental chair waiting for Ernesto, the Honduran dentist on the team. I heard God say, "Trust Me!" It was a clear voice but a whisper. I looked around and no one was there. How do I know it was God? Who else could throw their voice into that room and speak to me? Who else would ask for my trust? I am not even sure what He wanted me to trust him for or with. I just knew in my spirit He was speaking to me.

God still speaks to His children today. How do I know? Many times, I struggle with challenges to which I have no solution. When the answer comes, it has all the details, so I know it was not of my own doing. I am not that wise. If I listen for that still small voice and wait patiently, at the right time, the solution always comes.

Recently, Pastor Don Feuerbach did interviews of people who had gone through or were going through adversity. Two of those people were Helen Hoines and Linda Downey. I take notes from the messages, so I can use what I learn at a later time. After listening to Linda Downey say God told her it would be OK, I remembered what He told me. Pastor Don reminded me of what Helen said she heard. I put those together and this is what I discovered. "Trust Me! I am all around you. It'll be OK!" My, Helen's and Linda's words from the Lord.

Do you have trouble quieting your mind? Are you too busy to slow down and listen? Do you have so much going on that you don't leave room for quiet time with God just in case He wants to speak with you? I am asking you now to free up some time in your schedule. Do a few less things. Set aside time to pray and just listen. I bet you will find God still speaks and He would like to speak with you!

Listen!

Thank you, Lord for your Word and Spirit! Speak to us. We know You have good plans for us. Reveal Your plans to us in Your timing and Your gentle way. In Your name we pray! Amen!

## JANUARY 29   HELP US TO CHANGE
Relationships

Revelation 21:5 (ESV)

*5 And he who was seated on the throne said, "Behold, I am making all things new." Also, he said, "Write this down, for these words are trustworthy and true."*

God tells us that He makes all things new. When He enters your heart, things are supposed to change. If we have anger issues, Christ's influence should change us for the better. 2 Corinthians 5:17 says *"17 Therefore, if anyone is in Christ, the new creation has come: The old has gone, the new is here!"* What is your life looking like?

There is a song that asks, "When they see me, do they see you?" What do people see in you? Are you setting the example you want to set? People learn more about you by what you do rather than what you say. Would you want others to behave as you behave? Do you want others to catch what you have? When you accept Christ as your Lord and Savior, things are supposed to change; not immediately but over time. He will change you for the better from the inside out. He will open your heart to see what he sees. He sees us as His beloved children. He sees what we can become. He knows how you were made since He made you. And when He made you, He destined you for great things. But to get to your destiny, you will need to change and grow.

God can renew you through the transforming of your mind and your heart. Day by day, there are little changes. What used to upset you doesn't matter anymore. Your focus is on Jesus and how He asked you to live. You can endure the challenges more easily. It is not what happens to you that determines how far you go in life; it is what you do about what happens to you. Do you react or respond? Today, will you pause and think about what is happening and decide how you will respond, or will it be the same old, same old? What example will you set? Whose light will you shine? Thank you, Lord that we are being transformed by You.

Lord, change us from the inside out! Let us show the world we belong to you by the way we love. Let us love others as You have loved us! In Your name we pray!

# JANUARY 30 I NEVER SAID IT WOULD BE EASY
## Quality of Life

John 16:33 (NKJV)

*33 These things I have spoken to you, that in Me you may have peace. In the world you will have tribulation; but be of good cheer, I have overcome the world."*

In this world you will have trouble. There you have it. Not you might have challenges; you *will* face challenges. Nobody said change would be easy. The world is a difficult place and there are many things that come against us. But is that a bad thing? What would life be like if everything went our way? I know you would like to try that for a while, wouldn't you? Truth is, it would be boring after a while. Also, we would not grow in our walk with God. When things come against us, they refine us or make us change direction. God can use adversity to lead you to your destiny. Adversity can be a roadblock that forces you to go a different way. We don't like roadblocks, though.

When things don't go your way, how do you take it? Do you take your bat and ball and go home? Do you become grumpy like me? Well there are other options. These days, when it doesn't go my way, I tend to look for reasons why. I ask God "what are you trying to teach or show me?" I am learning that it is not happening to me, it is happening *for* me! Some of the worst times in my life are not so bad when I look back on them. If this had not happened, I might never have moved from where I was. The saying is every cloud has a silver lining. I will go even further. The cloud itself may have shielded you from being burned by the sun.

I have a hat that says, "Attitude is Everything!" Why would attitude be important? When things happen, do you react or respond? What is the difference? React is an almost automatic reaction to stimulus. There was not careful thought and planning. Response implies thought and consideration. It allows time for understanding the situation and giving a good and appropriate reply. You have thought about it and this would be the best reply. Attitude (peaceful or angry) determines response. What is your attitude? Do you always have to be right? Do you think you know more about the situation than others? Even if you have more experience, will the other person listen to you if you have a superior attitude? No, they won't. If you can be open to learning, God can teach you through every situation. Let him teach you. He will lead you to your best!

Thanks for Your warnings, Lord. When trouble comes, please help us to be prepared. Give us Your peace so that we can respond rather than react! Remind us that You have already won and that You give us victory in You. In Your name we pray. Amen!

## JANUARY 31   THE PAUSE THAT REFRESHES! ; ;

Relationships

James 1:19 (NIV) Listening and Doing
*19 My dear brothers and sisters, take note of this: Everyone should be quick to listen, slow to speak and slow to become angry,*

When programming a phone number with and extension into a cell phone the ";" is a two second pause which allows the phone number to be dialed and then pause for you to signal when to dial the extension. If you don't enter the number this way, the phone system gets confused and tells you that you have dialed a non-working number. It is that pause that makes everything work better or even work at all. How about that? A little pause for the system to dial the number makes the call go through.

I wonder if life isn't just like that. I wonder if a little pause before responding would not help the "call" go through. Communication seems to be the most difficult part of relationships. People have different communication styles and words have different meaning depending on how they are used and their tone. Since relationships are the most important things in life, shouldn't we work toward improving them through better communication? James tells us to be quick to listen. If you immediately gave someone your full attention when they approached you, would that make them feel important to you? If you listened carefully, how would that make them feel? Would these feelings improve relationships? The answer is yes! How do you listen?

James goes on to say you should be slow to speak. Does that meeeaan thaaaat yoooouuu shoooouuuuld stretch out your words? Nah! It means you should listen to learn and not listen preparing to offer a rebuttal. Really listen! What are the words but also, what is the thought behind those words? Why did this person come to you? Do they have needs you could address? Are they upset and why? If you could just insert a ";" into the response to allow you to think through the reason for the conversation, would you be able to give a better response? When you listen, do you listen to gain understanding or to form a reply? Stephen Covey said, "seek first to understand; then to be understood." No one will fault you for saying "I need to think about that. Can I get back to you?"

Finally, James goes on to say be slow to become angry. Are you defensive in your conversations? When someone asks, "Did you leave this here?", do you bite their head off for accusing you? I have a tendency to use an accusatory tone when asking that type of question which makes others defensive. How could you better ask a question? Maybe, "I was wondering how this item got here? Do you know?" What was the purpose of the question? Did you want the person that left the item to know where it is usually kept so they can put it away next time? Anger clouds thinking. It makes us react rather than respond. It damages relationships. Since all of life is about relationships, shouldn't we try our best to build up rather than tear down?

I have a document that contains "`;.;`' (Semicolons) in the format of a 3x5 card. Write to me and request the document. Then, print them out, cut them apart and place them in locations to help you to remember to pause. The next time you have conversation with someone, why not try a short pause before responding? It may just improve that relationship! This won't be easy but keep trying.

Lord, help us to keep trying! Give us the patience to be slow to respond so there is time for You to give us the right words. May Your Spirit guide us to build others up through our conversation. May our speech bring glory to You and edify those who hear. In Your name we pray!


Mercyme Song "Greater" refrain:
There'll be days I lose the battle, Grace says that it doesn't matter, 'Cause the cross already won the war
He's Greater, He's Greater
I am learning to run freely, understanding just how He sees me And it makes me love Him more and more
He's Greater He's Greater
'Cause I hear a voice and He calls me redeemed When others say I'll never be enough
And greater is the One living inside of me Than he who is living in the world

# FEBRUARY 1   YOU ARE AMAZING
Faith

Philippians 4:12-13 (NIV)

*¹² I know what it is to be in need, and I know what it is to have plenty. I have learned the secret of being content in any and every situation, whether well fed or hungry, whether living in plenty or in want. ¹³ I can do all this through him who gives me strength.*

If someone told you that you would be asked to do certain things for which you have no training, you would tell them it is impossible. You would deny the ability to accomplish that goal or task. After all, you don't know how to do what you have been asked to do.

My best friend is in the end stages of ALS. His wife (who is probably tied with my wife for second best friend because we have known each other since we were sixteen) is his primary care giver. She is doing things that amaze me. Things for which she has no training. Things she would deny the ability to do; yet, they are getting done. And no one is more shocked than she is.

We all have a tendency to doubt what we are able to accomplish because we believe we do things in our own power. Well, we don't do things in our own power. It took me a long time to figure that out. I used to think everything was up to me but with power comes responsibility. I thought I was in control and I was the one that made things happen. When I became aware of the power all around me that was really behind me, things became easier and better. I thought it was my responsibility to make things happen. When it did not go the way I planned, I felt badly as if I had failed. Each time I looked at the darkness of the world, I was ashamed I had not cleaned up my corner of the world as if that were possible. Well I am not in control now and never was. What a relief! It's not my fault!

There are two extremes playing out here. One is not feeling capable and the other is believing you are in control. Neither is good for us and both are unbelief. If you don't think you can do it, you are not seeing things in the Spiritual realm. You are not seeing the horsemen and chariots of fire the Lord has sent to your aid. If you are believing you are a self-made man or woman, you are missing the Holy Spirit which teaches and guides you into all things. It is a delicate balance and it is best we not walk this tightrope alone. By walking with another person of faith, you can remind each other you are children of the Most High God and He will equip and guide you through all things. The Bible tells us we ought not think too highly of ourselves but it also says we are fearfully and wonderfully made. You are amazing. As dearly loved children of God, He will anoint, equip and empower us to do all things through Christ who gives us strength. Do not be afraid. Remember, Psalm 121:4 (NKJV) says *"⁴ Behold, He who keeps Israel shall neither slumber nor sleep."* He not only keeps Israel, He keeps you. You are never on your own! Listen for His word and act boldly in His name today!

Lord, thank You that You are always with us and provide all we need. Thank You for the gifts and talents You have given us. May we use them to Your glory and other's benefit. In Jesus name we pray!

# FEBRUARY 2    ASK AND YOU SHALL RECEIVE
Faith

James 4:1-3 (NKJV) Pride Promotes Strife
*Where do wars and fights come from among you? Do they not come from your desires for pleasure that war in your members? ² You lust and do not have. You murder and covet and cannot obtain. You fight and war. Yet you do not have because you do not ask. ³ You ask and do not receive, because you ask amiss, that you may spend it on your pleasures.*

Do you ask for the things God desires for you? Not for the things you want but the things God wants for you?

I had an e mail from someone on behalf of someone else who is no longer able to receive my devotionals because of the volume of e-mails they get. I don't know what made me ask her (actually, it was the Spirit) but I sensed she might like to receive them. The response was "Actually, YES! I didn't dare ask." She included the verse, "you have not because you ask not." Isn't that interesting? We know we could ask but don't. Why not? God wants us to be bold in our requests. He desires to bless us and yet we do not ask.

We go through life not getting things that would bless us and others around us because we do not ask for those things. You are a child of the Most High God. He has treasures stored up for you that are meant for your good. If He blesses you, chances are good those blessings will benefit those around you. It is like the H&R Block commercial with the warehouse of money just waiting for someone to claim it. Claim your blessings! Psalm 37:4 says *"⁴ Delight yourself also in the LORD, And He shall give you the desires of your heart."* That does not mean God will give you anything you desire. It means God will place desires in your heart that are His will for you; things that are good for you. You will want what God wants for you. You will be following His path for your life. When you follow His will, you will be blessed! Ask God to give you the desires of your heart and believe, boldly, that He will answer!

What is Your will for us? What blessings have You stored up for us that we do not yet have? We know You have great plans for us. Please help us to be bold in asking for these blessings in Your name. Amen!

# FEBRUARY 3 HIS GRACE IS SUFFICIENT

Grace and Mercy

2 Corinthians 12:7-10 (NKJV)

*[7] And lest I should be exalted above measure by the abundance of the revelations, a thorn in the flesh was given to me, a messenger of Satan to buffet me, lest I be exalted above measure. [8] Concerning this thing I pleaded with the Lord three times that it might depart from me. [9] And He said to me, "My grace is sufficient for you, for My strength is made perfect in weakness." Therefore most gladly I will rather boast in my infirmities, that the power of Christ may rest upon me. [10] Therefore I take pleasure in infirmities, in reproaches, in needs, in persecutions, in distresses, for Christ's sake. For when I am weak, then I am strong.*

Do you take offense when someone speaks badly to you? How about when they insult you? No one likes to be criticized, do they? Apparently, Paul had a different outlook toward insults. Paul thought it was a good thing. If you are not making a difference, no one notices you. It is only when you are on track and making a difference for God that you will fall under attack. Without the shield of God's grace, you are vulnerable.

Paul spoke about his shortcomings and how he was being blessed by God's grace in those shortcomings. He recognized he had faults and it was God's power and direction which led him to the places he needed to go to fulfill God's plan. Are you being led by God? When you are in God's power, you become strong beyond what you can imagine.

Do you work within God's grace? When you are working in His grace, things go well. Many times, we try to do things in our own power and that doesn't work out. When you are surrounded by the shield of God's grace, you are protected, strengthened and guided. Everything you need is given to you. His grace is truly sufficient for all your needs.

Lord, help us to live as one filled with, surrounded by and covered with Your grace! Let us work in Your power and not our own. By Your Spirit, guide us in Your ways today and every day. In Your name we pray! Amen!

# FEBRUARY 4   BE THANKFUL

Prayer

Philippians 4:4-7 (NIV) Final Exhortations

*⁴ Rejoice in the Lord always. I will say it again: Rejoice! ⁵ Let your gentleness be evident to all. The Lord is near. ⁶ Do not be anxious about anything, but in every situation, by prayer and petition, with thanksgiving, present your requests to God. ⁷ And the peace of God, which transcends all understanding, will guard your hearts and your minds in Christ Jesus.*

Do you rejoice always? Does your inward attitude always reflect your outward situation? When Paul wrote this, he was in prison. If anyone had reason to have a bad attitude, it was Paul. Yet he urged us to be joyful always. I have a hat that says "Attitude is Everything". It is true. It does not matter what is happening to you but how you respond.

What is true joy? True joy in knowing we rest in Christ Jesus and that He remains in us. If you remember Jesus is your Advocate and wants the best for you knowing He is capable of bringing it about, why worry? Things don't happen to you; they happen **for** you. You may have heard it said that worry is a waste of the imagination. Luke 12:25 (NIV) says *²⁵ Who of you by worrying can add a single hour to your life?* So, what will worrying do for you? Nothing!

Remember that part about praying unceasingly? Here it is again. "But in everything, by prayer and petition, with thanksgiving, present your requests to God." Not just the big things but all things; in everything. Don't forget to celebrate yourself. He does!

*"And the peace of God, which transcends all understanding, will guard your hearts and your minds in Christ Jesus."* Paul's advice is to turn our worries into prayers. Instead of worrying, pray. Do not be anxious. Be thankful for what you have knowing that God will provide all you need so there is no reason to worry.

How shall we live our days? In prayer with thanksgiving! Be thankful today!

Lord, thank You that You give us reasons to be thankful. Your protection should be enough to keep us from all anxiety. Help us to remain in Your peace with You the focus of our attention. In You, we find rest. In Your name we pray!

# FEBRUARY 5   DYING TO SELF

Grace and Mercy

John 12:24 (NIV)

*24 Very truly I tell you, unless a kernel of wheat falls to the ground and dies, it remains only a single seed. But if it dies, it produces many seeds.*

If a seed remains on the shelf, it suffers no distress. It also won't become anything other than the seed it already is. It doesn't give up anything but it doesn't gain anything either. There is always a sacrifice that needs to be made. If a seed is planted, it has to be placed in the dark place which loses all comfort. There are people walking on top of it. It is in the dark and the dirt. It appears as if it had died. One seed, once planted, can yield a plant that will yield 50-100 seeds so it can multiply immensely; but only if it sacrifices itself. Many people want the fruits but are not willing to go through the process. The process is important!

Jesus was in Bethany several days before Passover. As was His custom, He was teaching His disciples. Philip and Andrew asked Him if he would speak to some Greeks who requested to speak with Him. His answer did not exactly fit the question. It seems His speaking with them would plant seeds that would yield a great harvest. Are you speaking with people and planting seeds?

Jesus is the picture of a seed dying to itself and giving life to so many. He is the picture of the need for the perfect sacrifice to cover our sin. He was placed in the ground where he remained for three days. Then, he rose again showing the seed would blossom into many more seeds. The man who loves his life will lose it and the one who loses his life will keep it for eternal life. The seed of eternal life was planted more than two thousand years ago and still yields new life daily. What will He yield in you today?

Lord, thank You for Your sacrifice that is still producing new life to this day. Teach us to love You more than life itself and, in so doing, gain glory for You and eternal life for us. Also, let our life bring others to saving grace in You. In Your name we pray!

# FEBRUARY 6   GETTING TO KNOW YOU
Faith

2 Timothy 3:16 (NIV)

[16] *All Scripture is God-breathed and is useful for teaching, rebuking, correcting and training in righteousness,*

Why believe in and turn to God's Word? Most people in our current society say it is irrelevant. It was written thousands of years ago. How could it apply to our lives today? If the Bible was just a nice story, why would it include the failures and imperfections of its people? Wouldn't you make them all perfect and the story nice? In the first few chapters, we see disobedience and jealousy rear their ugly heads.

Firstly, we must address the authenticity of the Bible. Can we believe it is the inerrant Word of God? I do! I am not skilled in apologetics. Apologetics is the branch of Christianity that deals with the defense and establishment of the Christian faith. I just feel it in my bones. Peter told us (1 Peter 3:15) we should always be ready to defend our faith so here goes. The Bible was written (recorded) by 40 different people from diverse areas over 1500 years. They all wrote in their own way but recorded exactly what God intended. The message is the same even though recorded by 40 different people over 15 centuries. Moses told the story of Creation. How? He was not there. He recorded what God revealed to him. Everything lines up without contradiction. One challenge to this is the different genealogies in Matthew 1 and Luke 3. It is believed the Luke genealogy is of Mary, Jesus Mother, showing both sides of Jesus' line are through David. Have you ever played a game called telephone where each person whispers a phrase to the next person in the circle? Then, you compare the last person's take on the phrase to the first usually with hilarious results. If the Bible was not God-breathed, it would be like that game. Also, if it were purely a story, the authors would not have revealed all the faults of their characters. Archeology confirms the existence of many of the characters included in the Bible. Science again proves faith.

To read God's Word is to begin to understand the character of His heart. He walked with Adam and Eve in the garden He had created for them. Everything they needed was contained there. Right from the beginning, God showed His kindness, grace and compassion. He told them not to eat the fruit of the tree of the knowledge of good and evil because He knew what would happen to them; they would surely die (spiritually). God chose to lead by example. He walked with them in the Garden showing the proper way to go but they chose disobedience. He walked with mankind again in Galilee and tried to get people back on track with the Spirit of the Law rather than the letter of the Law. That ended badly; or did it? For those of us who believed in Him, it gave us back what was lost in the garden. God's glory was returned to us by the carpenter from Nazareth. We now have access to the Tree of Life! He has given us the right to become Children of God!

I call this *Encouragement Daily* so how should this be encouraging to you? If you read the Bible, you see, time and time again, mankind falling down in sin. You also see God picking them up each time, reviewing the lesson they should have learned and helping them to try again. My Dad must have learned that from God. I am from the "wait 'til your father gets home" generation. When I messed up as a kid, Dad's response would be "you'll do better next time." He verbally picked me up, dusted me off and said try again. That is what I would like you to see in the Bible. Your Heavenly Father always waiting to help you succeed wildly or do better next time. Failure is not fatal. He loves you beyond all you can imagine. ("For God so loved the world.....") If you delve into the Bible, you will learn God's heart. If you follow it, all will go well with you. Remember, you will still have difficulties but God will lead you through the valley (of the shadow of death) to the table He has prepared for you on the other side. The Bible and its truth can be the source of your strength. Dig into His Word and when you know Him, share Him with others!

Into Your Word we're digging deep to know out Father's heart.

Into the world we're reaching out, To show them who You are.

Thrive by Casting Crowns

Thank You Lord that You have given us Your Word to lead and guide us in the best way for us. Thank You that You redeem us and bid us, try again. Thank You for Your love, grace, compassion and mercy which surround us like a shield. In Your name we pray and give You praise!

# FEBRUARY 7   WHO'S LOOKIN' OUT FOR YOU   DO YOU HAVE PROTECTION   MY BIG BROTHER

Grief

Numbers 10 (NIV) Selected Verses - The Silver Trumpets

*The LORD said to Moses:* ² *"Make two trumpets of hammered silver, and use them for calling the community together and for having the camps set out.* ⋯⋯

⁸ *"The sons of Aaron, the priests, are to blow the trumpets. This is to be a lasting ordinance for you and the generations to come.* ⁹ *When you go into battle in your own land against an enemy who is oppressing you, sound a blast on the trumpets. Then you will be remembered by the LORD your God and rescued from your enemies.* ¹⁰ *Also at your times of rejoicing—your appointed festivals and New Moon feasts—you are to sound the trumpets over your burnt offerings and fellowship offerings, and they will be a memorial for you before your God. I am the LORD your God."*

Who is watching out for you? When you were a kid, did you have a protector? I became friends with Carmen DiCanto (Name was changed to protect the innocent. Who am I kidding; it is actually his real name because there were no innocent.) when we first entered Kindergarten just a few years back. At that time, Carmen was 1/3 larger than the next biggest kid in school. There was a sizeable difference. To us, he may as well have been Goliath! He had respect before he said a word. And I was lucky enough to be his friend and he, mine! That remained all through our lives until yesterday when, as they say "Until death do us part." Since I am still writing this, it is obviously Carmen who went to be with the Lord.

What if you could go through life knowing you had "protection"? I know, it sounds like the Godfather. Knowing that someone much stronger, wiser, smarter than you stood close behind ready to come to your aid at a moment's notice? Would you live more confidently? Would you be bolder? Would you try more things? What would you do if you knew you had all the support necessary to be successful?

The Lord your God is that protection. He goes before you leveling out peaks and valleys. He puts the right people in your path and gives you favor with them. His hedge of protection surrounds you like a shield. Speaking of a shield, a friend gave me a medallion about wearing the full armor of God. One of the pieces of armor is the shield of Faith. Maybe you don't have very much faith and you are worried you don't have enough. Maybe you don't believe in God. That's OK; He believes in you! No matter where you go, no matter what you do, God waits for you to sound the trumpet so He can come and rescue you. That should give you the confidence you need to live with excellence.

So today was not a great day for me. I am way behind in my writing. My mind is cloudy and my eyes are red and burning. I am suffering great loss! I'm not sure whether to blow the trumpet in need of support or for celebration that I had such a friend. But if you listen carefully, you can hear the trumpet blasts. The first is my cry for comfort for my deep personal loss and that of all who knew him. The second is for

53

the rejoicing of the angels about the arrival of my buddy. Thank You Lord for long term friendships.

Father, I thank You for a lifetime of friendship and love. Thank You that You gave me such a friend. Thank You for a lifetime of blessings and memories. Please walk with me and Christine, his wife (and best friend #2), as we grieve our loss. But, let Your Spirit remind us of our gain in having him to begin with. In Jesus name I pray.

# FEBRUARY 8   RELIGION VS. CHRIST
Relationships

Luke 10:25-37 (NIV) The Parable of the Good Samaritan

*25 On one occasion an expert in the law stood up to test Jesus. "Teacher," he asked, "what must I do to inherit eternal life?" 26 "What is written in the Law?" he replied. "How do you read it?"*
*27 He answered, "'Love the Lord your God with all your heart and with all your soul and with all your strength and with all your mind'; and, 'Love your neighbor as yourself.'"*
*28 "You have answered correctly," Jesus replied. "Do this and you will live."*
*29 But he wanted to justify himself, so he asked Jesus, "And who is my neighbor?"*
*30 In reply Jesus said: "A man was going down from Jerusalem to Jericho, when he was attacked by robbers. They stripped him of his clothes, beat him and went away, leaving him half dead.*
*31 A priest happened to be going down the same road, and when he saw the man, he passed by on the other side. 32 So too, a Levite, when he came to the place and saw him, passed by on the other side. 33 But a Samaritan, as he traveled, came where the man was; and when he saw him, he took pity on him. 34 He went to him and bandaged his wounds, pouring on oil and wine. Then he put the man on his own donkey, brought him to an inn and took care of him. 35 The next day he took out two denarii and gave them to the innkeeper. 'Look after him,' he said, 'and when I return, I will reimburse you for any extra expense you may have.'*
*36 "Which of these three do you think was a neighbor to the man who fell into the hands of robbers?" 37 The expert in the law replied, "The one who had mercy on him." Jesus told him, "Go and do likewise."*

Do you follow the letter of the Law or the Spirit of the Law? At that time, there were around 600 laws or traditions the people had to follow which was quite a burden. Most of these were man-made by experts in the Law. In the story Jesus told, a Priest and a Levite both passed by the injured man because, to touch him, would have made them unclean according to the ceremonial law. The next passerby was a Samaritan who stopped to help.

Was that the right thing to do in your opinion? Let's dig a little further. According to the Ceremonial Law, for either the Priest or the Levite to touch the man would have made them unclean and unable to perform their duties in the Temple. That would mean they were unable to serve God. What was more important for them; to serve God or this stranger by the side of the road? Now it seems a little more complicated. Maybe the two passers-by did what they thought was right. What does Jesus ask us to do? Here is the interesting part. Jesus said in Matthew 5:17 (NIV) *17 "Do not think that I have come to abolish the Law or the Prophets; I have not come to abolish them but to fulfill them."* Jesus should have said what the Priest and Levite did was within the Law and correct, but He didn't. He talked about loving your neighbor. Now I am really confused! Do I love God or do I love my neighbor? Yes!

Jesus came to fulfill the Law; the Ceremonial Law. The Law was provided out of love to guide us in the right path. If we take the loving path that God intended for us, all else will work out correctly. If you love your neighbor, you will not lie, cheat, steal, covet or any of the other bad things. Love comes first. Everything God has done for us is a result of His love for us. God created us for relationships with Himself and with each other. The Samaritan was more concerned about loving his neighbor than following a bunch of rules. That was what God really wanted to start with. We just became legalistic and tried to see who could be first in the Kingdom by following the Law.

Do you want to check off a box or do you want to live a life that makes a difference? The Lawyer in this story thought righteousness came from the Law. He was wrong. Righteousness only comes from trust in Jesus. We have none on our own. All we can do is love others as Jesus loved us. There are still Good Samaritans. My hope for you is you can be one of them. Look for someone to serve that can do nothing for you in return. Pay it forward! As Pastor Don Feuerbach said, put down religion and pick up life! Go now and be the blessing you are!

Father, we thank You that You are teaching us how to obey the Spirit of the Law rather than the letter of the Law. We thank You that You said love comes first. Help us to love as You love. In Your name we pray! Amen!

# FEBRUARY 9   JUST ASK FOR HELP

Quality of Life

Numbers 11: 10-17 (NIV) Selected Verses

*[10] Moses heard the people of every family wailing at the entrance to their tents. The LORD became exceedingly angry, and Moses was troubled. [11] He asked the LORD, "Why have you brought this trouble on your servant? What have I done to displease you that you put the burden of all these people on me?" [14] I cannot carry all these people by myself; the burden is too heavy for me....*

*[16] The LORD said to Moses: "Bring me seventy of Israel's elders who are known to you as leaders and officials among the people. ....and I will take some of the power of the Spirit that is on you and put it on them. They will share the burden of the people with you so that you will not have to carry it alone.*

Have you ever thought "I can't do this!" I know I have. I have a bad habit of not being able to say no. I want to do everything I see but I cannot. My friend Brock always asks me "what am I going to give up in order to be able to take on something new?" I know that question so well I ask it myself even before Brock gets his chance.

In the Book of Numbers, the Lord instructs Moses about how his burden can be reduced. James tells us "we have not because we ask not." Do you take on more than you should? Are you able to ask for help?

It seems it is human nature to take on too much or at least a part of our culture. But it is not always our decision. Moses carried this burden because the Lord called him to lead Israel. Either way, we were never made to carry these things all by ourselves. Back in Genesis, God said "It is not good for man to be alone." Because of that, God created a suitable helper because He did not want Adam to be overwhelmed. God wants to help. All you need do is ask. But if you're like me, you don't ask. Do you realize God will bring you help to share the burden? You are important to Him. He wants to make your burden easier and help you accomplish that which He has destined you to do. Go ahead, ask Him! He loves you and wants to help. He is waiting to hear from you. Ask Him!

Father, thank You that You always stand ready to come to our aid whenever we call. Help us to know when to call. You said You would never leave nor forsake us and You are faithful. But we must ask before You will come. Help us to include You in our lives and ask You to walk with us. In Jesus name we pray!

## FEBRUARY 10  BEING THAT HELP

Relationships

Psalm 69:13-16 (NIV) Selected Verses

*¹³But I pray to you, LORD, in the time of your favor; in your great love, O God, answer me with your sure salvation.¹⁴ Rescue me from the mire, do not let me sink;...*
*¹⁶ Answer me, LORD, out of the goodness of your love; in your great mercy turn to me.*

Are you afraid to ask for help? If you ask and they refuse, what would be the result? Would you be embarrassed? Probably. Is that a reason not to ask? Whom should you ask for help? Should you ask a difficult task of a stranger? Proverbs 18:24 says, *²⁴ "One who has unreliable friends soon comes to ruin, but there is a friend who sticks closer than a brother."* If you ask the wrong person, odds are it won't get done. Who is the one who sticks closer than a brother that you can always ask for help?

There are several answers that could fit here. Some of us have made friends that stick closer than a brother. I had such a friend. That takes time. You have to allow them time to prove their commitment over the years. Proverbs mentions "a" friend who sticks closer than a brother. That is the Lord. In Him, we can always put our trust because He will answer you out of the goodness of His love. Through His guidance, we can also find earthly brothers and sisters who will walk with us and share blessings and burdens. That is important. While we all want someone to share a burden, it is very disappointing when we have great success and no one is there with whom we can celebrate. Either way, we were never meant to walk alone. Some people say they are self-made. That is another way of saying lonely. Do you walk alone? In whom do you put your trust? What if you knew one who was always ready, willing and able to share burden and blessings? You do!

Last night when I came out from my Bible Study, there was a man scraping the ice off my windshield. I had not asked him for help yet there he was doing me a good service. WOW. A random act of kindness! I thanked him and received the blessing. I am not good at receiving so this was special for me. What if you could give that feeling to others? What if you could lend assistance to someone before they even ask? That changes everything. Here is what I am suggesting. Look for people you can help. Be a friend to those around you. Shine your light in the dark places. Someone you meet today will be lonely and need a friend, a kind word, a thoughtful deed. Maybe they just need someone to listen. You have those blessings in you; why not let them out? Be a blessing today. Write me back and let me know how it goes!

Lord, thank You for the gifts and talents You give us. Help us to use them for the benefit of others and to Your glory. Make us bold to step out and share Your love. In Your name we pray!

# FEBRUARY 11  IS IT BLESSED TO RECEIVE, TOO
Relationships

Acts 20:35 (NIV)
*35 In everything I did, I showed you that by this kind of hard work we must help the weak, remembering the words the Lord Jesus himself said: 'It is more blessed to give than to receive.'"*

OK, Jesus said "It is more blessed to give than to receive." But I have always had a challenge with this verse. Let me tell you why. It sets us up to always want to give which is good. But no one has taught us to receive. If no one receives than no one would be able to give. There are many places in the Bible that talk about how we should help others and look out for the poor. Some of us are not poor but still need help. How will we learn to accept that help?

Receiving is an art in itself. A gift is not a gift until it is received. Another consideration is the joy of the giver is attached to the grace of the receiver. Yes, I said the grace of the receiver. About 20 years ago, I was in San Francisco on business. I drove to a downtown hotel to attend a gathering of clients and associates. I parked on the street outside the hotel. There was a homeless man camped in a doorway on the street where I parked. He offered to watch my car for me. Something made me decide to go into a local eatery to buy him a meal as thanks. I went and got a hamburger deluxe to go and brought it back to the man. Instead of receiving my gesture in the spirit in which I had offered it, the man abused me for not asking him what he wanted. I was furious! I was ready to take back the food and eat it myself in front of him. A simple thanks would have been better. That man did not know how to receive. But neither do I.

When someone tells you that you look well, how do you respond? If someone compliments your cooking, what do you say? Do you say I wish I had more time to prepare? Do you take compliments well? Why not? Can you just say thanks? Many of us try to do too many things on our own when it would go much better with other's help. I had some friends offer to help me with technical things in my business. They were doing it because they wanted to repay some of my kindnesses. They were clear they wanted to help me because they had seen me help others. It was my turn to receive. Receiving is a weak area for me. I am used to giving. Without the receiver, there can be no giver. Christ offers the greatest gift of all but it is of no use if we do not receive Him.

Is it more blessed to give than receive? I'm not sure. If you are reasonably well-off, you may have receiveaphobia. There is a cure. Just say thanks. I really appreciate you! Compliments wanted. God's favor rests upon you. There are those out there who want to help you in their own way. Let them!

Lord, teach us how to receive. You offer us grace and mercy. Both are ineffective if we cannot receive You. Let Your grace dwell richly in us so we can gracefully receive gifts others offer to us. Teach us to be thankful. In Your name we pray!

# FEBRUARY 12 I CAN'T DO THIS ALONE
## Quality of Life

1 Peter 5:6–9 (NIV)

*⁶ Humble yourselves, therefore, under God's mighty hand, that he may lift you up in due time. ⁷ Cast all your anxiety on him because he cares for you. ⁸ Be alert and of sober mind. Your enemy the devil prowls around like a roaring lion looking for someone to devour. ⁹ Resist him, standing firm in the faith, because you know that the family of believers throughout the world is undergoing the same kind of sufferings.*

Does it sometimes seem you have more things to do than you can manage? Sometimes we face challenges that are beyond the knowledge we have. You feel unable to manage. There is a voice in your head that tells you that you will never be able to accomplish your goal. It looks like more than you can do. At least, in your own power. But that's just it; you don't have to do things in your own power. You can cast your anxiety on Jesus. He loves and cares for you and will help you. You can do all things through Christ who gives you strength.

Peter is warning us about our enemy. He warns us the devil is on the prowl for someone whom he can devour. He tells you to resist the evil one. Do you think you have that power? If you do, you are mistaken. The only way you can resist is through Jesus' power. Ask Jesus to be your shield.

The biggest thing that prevents you accomplishing the things in front of you is you! Something in your mind tells you that you cannot do it. The enemy does everything in his power to distract you from your goals. All he needs to do is whisper and you begin to doubt. He does not have to prowl too far to make you think less of yourself. How will you handle him? Will you give in to doubt? You shouldn't! He that will help you with the challenges will give you the strength to stand your ground. Faith in God gives you His Spirit which can help you stand firm. God *is* for you. Who dares be against you? You are His Masterpiece. Let no one doubt you. Make sure you don't doubt yourself.

Lord, we look to You for our strength. Remind us You are for us and walk with us. Be our shield and protect us. When we doubt, remind us we are Yours made in Your image and likeness. Help us to be like You. In Your name we pray! Amen!

# FEBRUARY 13  WHO IS MY HELP

Support

Psalm 121:1-4 (NIV) A song of ascents.
*¹ I lift up my eyes to the mountains — where does my help come from? ² My help comes from the LORD, the Maker of heaven and earth. ³ He will not let your foot slip — he who watches over you will not slumber; ⁴ indeed, he who watches over Israel will neither slumber nor sleep.*

Sometimes it feels like we are all alone. The grind of daily life takes its toll on us. We feel battered and bruised. It seems like the whole world is against us. When you try to face the world alone, it seems impossible.

David reminds us we are never alone. The Lord is always there ready, willing and able to help. He never slumbers but watches to make sure you are protected. When things do happen, the Lord will use them for your good.

You are never alone! The Creator of the universe knows everything you face now and what you will face in the future. He promises He will never leave nor forsake you. He wants to help you. If you look to God, you will have more peace which lowers your stress. With lower stress, you can perform better. He watches over you looking out for your best interest. In fact, God watches over you at all times, waiting to help you with your needs.

Do you remember trying to learn to ride a bicycle? You had the concept of what to do but you needed those training wheels to keep the bike upright. They were your source of confidence while you mastered the steps needed to make riding possible. Then came the day you were going to forgo the crutch and really ride on your own. Your parent held on to you and ran alongside to keep you going. They were there to help you master the art of riding. They assisted as needed until they determined you were ready and then they let go. Often, they did not indicate they had let go giving you the opportunity to do it on your own. There came a point when you looked around to share your excitement to find you were riding on your own. With God, it is very similar. He is there when you need Him but He knows when to let go and let you ride on your own. He lets you use the talents He has given you.

God is with you in much the same way today. He is always there to lend assistance or answer a question. But He knows exactly when we should be riding on our own. It is a delicate balance to figure out when to ask for help and when to ride. How do you know? For me, I ask almost all the time. If a level of confidence develops in a decision, I know God has agreed. Otherwise, different thoughts come from my subconscious. At times, I formulate a plan and put it aside asking for input. I have been known to put a business plan in my Bible and wait on the Lord. If nothing comes, the plan is OK as it stands. The key may be the pause to allow God into the decision. Do you do that? Do you allow time for Him to speak? Maybe that pause would allow the One who neither slumbers nor sleeps to speak into your life. Today, be still and know He is God. He still speaks!

Lord, speak to Your children every day. Let us know Your will for our lives. Teach us Your ways and lead us down Your paths. Write Your story on our hearts You are our help! In Your name we pray.

# FEBRUARY 14 WHO LOVES YOU
### Grace and Mercy

1 Corinthians 13 (NIV) Selected Verses

*If I speak in the tongues of men or of angels, but do not have love, I am only a resounding gong or a clanging cymbal. ²If I have the gift of prophecy and can fathom all mysteries and all knowledge, and if I have a faith that can move mountains, but do not have love, I am nothing. ³If I give all I possess to the poor and give over my body to hardship that I may boast, but do not have love, I gain nothing. ⁴Love is patient, love is kind. It does not envy, it does not boast, it is not proud. ⁵It does not dishonor others, it is not self-seeking, it is not easily angered, it keeps no record of wrongs. ⁶Love does not delight in evil but rejoices with the truth. ⁷It always protects, always trusts, always hopes, always perseveres. Love never fails. ....¹³And now these three remain: faith, hope and love. But the greatest of these is love.*

What is love anyway? Can you define it? Thomas Jay Oord, Professor of Theology and Philosophy at Northwest Nazarene University, defines love as follows: "To love is to act intentionally, in sympathetic response to others (including God), to promote well-being." What does that mean? When I first heard this definition from Pastor Don Feuerbach in one of his messages, I was taken back. What a concept. Acting intentionally to promote well-being. Thomas Jay done good! It was a revelation to me. I made changes in my personal and business mission statements after hearing this definition.

Jesus said to love God and our neighbor. He said all else (the Law and the Prophets) hang on love. We are told we love because God first loved us. Think about it! If you love someone, you will not cheat, lie or steal where they are concerned. If you love someone, you will always do what is best for them, won't you? You will act intentionally to promote their well-being. Will you allow them to break rules which will cause harm? Will you remove house rules designed to teach them valuable lessons? Will you allow them to touch things that are hot? No, you will always do what is best for them even in the tough decisions.

Does love really mean never having to say you're sorry as it says in the movie *Love Story*? Of course not. I have been married almost 44 years. There have been a lot of "Sorry" in my career. Jean knows I am not perfect (I know that's hard to believe and all) but she still loves me. Just like my Heavenly Father. I fall down, He picks me up, dusts me off and says "Try again." Jean learned that from Him. She knows I will make mistakes but she loves me anyway. She loves me through and past those mistakes.

On this day dedicated to love, try to do things differently. Love! Do not be proud; do not be rude. Do not think of yourself. Be patient, be kind. Love and see the difference it will make!

Father, we love because You first loved us. Thank You for Your love which is so much more than we can ask or imagine. Greater love has no one than this. That He would lay down His life for His friends. It is hard to imagine You did that for us, but You did. Teach us to love like that. In Your name we pray.

# FEBRUARY 15  CAN WE TALK
## Prayer

Luke 11:1-13 (NIV) Selected Verses Jesus' Teaching on Prayer
*One day Jesus was praying in a certain place. When he finished, one of his disciples said to him, "Lord, teach us to pray, just as John taught his disciples." ² He said to them, "When you pray, say: "'Father, hallowed be your name, your kingdom come. ³ Give us each day our daily bread. ⁴ Forgive us our sins, for we also forgive everyone who sins against us. And lead us not into temptation.'" ...... ⁹ So I say to you: Ask and it will be given to you; seek and you will find; knock and the door will be opened to you. ¹⁰ For everyone who asks receives; the one who seeks finds; and to the one who knocks, the door will be opened. ¹¹ "Which of you fathers, if your son asks for a fish, will give him a snake instead? ¹² Or if he asks for an egg, will give him a scorpion? ¹³ If you then, though you are evil, know how to give good gifts to your children, how much more will your Father in heaven give the Holy Spirit to those who ask him!"*

What if I ask God for something and He doesn't give it to me? How do I ask? What do I say to Him? I don't really know how to pray. These are all things I have heard.

Jesus disciples were not really sure how to pray either. They saw Jesus take time regularly to pray to communicate with His Father. Jesus spent time speaking with His Father for guidance. It was a conversation with God. That is what God designed it to be; a conversation. God walked with Adam and Eve in the Garden in the cool of the afternoon. They spoke face to face. They had a relationship.

The disciples wanted to know how to have a conversation with God the Father. They wanted to better understand how to be close to God just as Jesus was. There is a formula for prayer called ACTS.

(1. Adoration, 2. Confession, 3. Thanksgiving, 4. Supplication) that comes from this prayer. If we follow this formula, it builds the relationship we are supposed to have with Him. He is your Heavenly Father and He wants to give you good things. Not necessarily what you want; but what you need and what is good for you. When you ask for something and you don't get it, go to number three and be thankful. If it was supposed to be yours, you would have it. God is never rejecting you; He is refining you. He is working all things together for your good. God's answers are yes, no or wait. They are all good answers for you. One more thing should be in here - not my will but Thy will be done. You have not because you ask not. When you ask, ask Him for what He wants for you. But ask!

Hello Lord! Thank You for listening to me and my rants. I love to speak with you. Thank You for caring and answering. Have I mentioned that I love You? Oh, and thanks for sending Your Son to redeem me. I don't deserve it but You give me grace anyway. Thank You! In Your name I pray!

# FEBRUARY 16  LIVE TO THE GLORY OF GOD
## Prayer

Deuteronomy 6:4-9 (NIV)

*⁴ Hear, O Israel: The LORD our God, the LORD is one. ⁵ Love the LORD your God with all your heart and with all your soul and with all your strength. ⁶ These commandments that I give you today are to be on your hearts. ⁷ Impress them on your children. Talk about them when you sit at home and when you walk along the road, when you lie down and when you get up. ⁸ Tie them as symbols on your hands and bind them on your foreheads. ⁹ Write them on the doorframes of your houses and on your gates.*

On what should we focus? There are so many things vying for our attention. Jesus said our focus should be on God first. From God, you will learn what else is important. We are to carry God's commandments in our hearts. If you have God's commandments in your heart (love Him), they are right there when you need them. Your motive will be right.

This portion of Scripture is called the Shema. The "Shema"—three biblical paragraphs (Deuteronomy 6:4–9; 11:13–21; Numbers 15:37–41), which starts with Judaism's defining statement: *Hear O Israel, the L-rd is our G-d, the L-rd is One.* Shema then discusses some of Judaism's basics: love of G-d, Torah study, the principle of divine reward and punishment, and our exodus from Egypt. {From chabad.org} These paragraphs are a central prayer of the Jewish faith.

Teaching others about God is important. What does it mean to impress them on your children? How do you "impress" others? I have friends who were raised in Church themselves but who never really impressed their children with the meaning and value of faith. At this point, their children do not have faith and they are regretting not having impressed them. God does not have grandchildren. Each generation must choose to build a relationship with God for itself. What is your relationship? Is it all you want it to be? There is still time to make it better.

How do you impress things on your children? One way is repetition. Zig Ziglar's mother used Sentence Sermons – short phrases that were easily repeated and remembered. An example was "People more attention pay to what you do than what you say!" Setting an example is a good place to start. Ask yourself, "Is this the example I want to set for my children?" You have heard it said that your life may be the only Bible some people get to read. They are watching your life to see what a follower of Jesus looks like. What are they seeing? What example does your life set?

This passage goes on to tell us to speak of God's commandments at all times, to tie them on our hands and forehead and write them on doorposts and gates. What does all that mean? The Tefillin go on our hands and forehead and the Mezuzah goes on doorways. They contain these scriptures on parchment and are used as reminders, helping us to keep God's commands on our hearts. You can Google these words and get more details. The point is to keep God in our hearts which will help us keep correct motives.

What does this all mean to you? It means you should live your life to the glory of God today! God has already given you all you need to live a victorious life. How will you use the gifts? Will you bring glory to Him today? I know you can! Let me know how it all works out for you.

Lord God may Your word be in our hearts so we can live lives that bring glory to Your Holy Name. Hear O Israel and the rest of us as well, the Lord Our God is One; Father Son and Holy Spirit. And He loves us too! Let's use His love to love one another.

# FEBRUARY 17  HOW SHOULD WE LOVE
## Quality of Life

1 John 4:7-11 (NIV)

*⁷ Dear friends, let us love one another, for love comes from God. Everyone who loves has been born of God and knows God. ⁸ Whoever does not love does not know God, because God is love. ⁹ This is how God showed his love among us: He sent his one and only Son into the world that we might live through him. ¹⁰ This is love: not that we loved God, but that he loved us and sent his Son as an atoning sacrifice for our sins. ¹¹ Dear friends, since God so loved us, we also ought to love one another.*

Jesus asked us to love our neighbor as ourselves. That pre-supposes you love yourself. How do we know how to love? Because God set the example. God entered the world as a man in the form of His Son Jesus and offered Himself in our place so we could have eternal life. That is the example of what love is and does. *"Greater love has no one than this, that he would lay down his life for his friends"* (John 15:13). Love is not just a feeling; it is also action. Remember the definition of love as "acting intentionally in sympathetic response to others, including God, to promote well-being." There is action involved.

How are we to love one another? Jesus told us to love our neighbor as ourselves. What actions do we take to love our neighbor? Do we need to listen better? Do we need to notice whether things are being done?  We have some elderly neighbors. One of the things that happened last winter was we noticed they did not clean their driveway after it snowed. That was very out of character. We also realized we had not seen them for a few days. Also, out of character. Clayton, our son, and I began the task of shoveling our way to their door to see if everything was alright. Thank God they were OK but just not feeling well enough to clean the driveway. It became apparent we needed to maintain their driveway. Most times, it is not apparent who our neighbor is and what their needs may be. It usually takes a deeper level of observation to see the needs of those who are our neighbors. Nevertheless, we need to be on the lookout for opportunities to love our neighbor.

In the movie "What Women Want" (2000) with Mel Gibson, Mel is suddenly able to hear what women are thinking. There is a girl in the office who feels invisible and unappreciated. She takes a sick day during which it seems she will take her own life. Mel remembers her internal conversations of despair and realizes something is amiss. He goes to her apartment to check on her. It is not actually stated but this move probably saved her life. Someone did notice her. Someone does care. That is an example (albeit Hollywood) of loving your neighbor.

Today, be more observant. Take action in love. Look for people who need a kind word. Commit random acts of kindness! Love with abandon! God has placed His love within you! Share it! Be the blessing I know you are today!

Father, You taught us how to love. Make us bold to share that love with those you put into our lives. Help us to see others through Your eyes and know their needs. Help us to listen between the words. Let us act out that love You showed us. In your name we pray!

# FEBRUARY 18  WHO IS THE GUY
## Grace

Mark 1:40-45 (NIV) Jesus Heals a Man With Leprosy

*40 A man with leprosy came to him and begged him on his knees, "If you are willing, you can make me clean." 41 Jesus was indignant. He reached out his hand and touched the man. "I am willing," he said. "Be clean!" 42 Immediately the leprosy left him and he was cleansed. 43 Jesus sent him away at once with a strong warning: 44 "See that you don't tell this to anyone. But go, show yourself to the priest and offer the sacrifices that Moses commanded for your cleansing, as a testimony to them." 45 Instead he went out and began to talk freely, spreading the news. As a result, Jesus could no longer enter a town openly but stayed outside in lonely places. Yet the people still came to him from everywhere.*

Why was Jesus indignant? Did He think the man doubted Him? The man knew Jesus was able to heal him. He knew he needed healing. He was not sure Jesus was willing to do the healing. Why not? Had Jesus not healed others? In John 5:6, Jesus asked a paralytic "Do you want to get well?" Interesting question, don't you think? Even more interesting was the excuse the man gave for an answer. I ask you, what are you carrying you know the LORD can remove? Are you willing to let go and let Him heal you?

I had a friend become ill with an incurable disease. I found a whole list of healing verses from the Bible I collected and gave to him. Ironically, the first verse was the one asking "do you want to get well?" My friend took no steps toward healing. It seemed to me he just gave up. Others had lived a long time with this disease. Why would he not take steps to maintain his health? It was a mystery to me.

When you're standing in the presence of God, do you ask Him for healing or do you wimp out and not speak? Do you give Him excuses or do you ask for His grace? Can you see Him? He stands just feet from you. If you could just touch the hem of His cloak, you would be healed! Will you reach out your hand now? Please? Reach out your hand!

Thank You Lord that you are willing and able. We don't deserve Your grace yet You lavish it upon us. You give it anyway. Give us the boldness to ask You for what we need. In Your name we pray!

# FEBRUARY 19 I KNOW WHAT YOU MEAN
## Grace and Mercy

Hebrews 4:15-16 (NKJV)

*15 For we do not have a High Priest who cannot sympathize with our weaknesses, but was in all points tempted as we are, yet without sin. 16 Let us therefore come boldly to the throne of grace, that we may obtain mercy and find grace to help in time of need.*

Have you ever been willing to lay down your life to save others? Have you ever been mocked or ridiculed for standing up for the truth? Is there anything you are now going through which He has not already experienced? How have you behaved in the toughest times of your life? Did you always show compassion, integrity and virtue? Jesus did! He endured humiliation and a brutal death just to secure your future life.

Jesus was tempted in every way that you are tempted. He has suffered every form of abuse. He doesn't have sympathy for you; He has empathy. He understands what it is like to face all these things personally. The Son of Man has been there. He knows what you mean.

In the Old Testament, the High Priest was the only person who could enter the Holy of Holies, which contained the Ark of the Covenant, to offer sacrifices for himself and for the people to atone for their sins. The sacrifice was the shedding of an animal's blood in place of the death sentence on people for their wrongdoings. Without the shedding of blood, there is no forgiveness of sin (Hebrews 9:22). Something had to die! For the wages of sin is death. The Perfect Lamb of God offered himself in your place. Let that sink it just a bit. He gave Himself up for you! Now that is a friend!

Sounds pretty heavy so far doesn't it? What's the encouraging part? Jesus opened a way for us to draw closer to God. He made a path through which we could return to fellowship with the Creator. He drew us back to Himself. How? At the moment of His death, there was a violent earthquake. It was so violent it tore the Temple Curtain from top to bottom opening a way for us to enter the Holy of Holies. This curtain was described as "the thickness of a man's palm" which could be 3-4 inches. What could tear that? What is important is it restored our path to return to God! God always wanted to be in fellowship with us. He walked with us in the Garden, didn't He? We sinned and were separated from Him. We left Him; He didn't leave us. He was always planning our return. And, at just the right time in history, Jesus entered our world and sacrificed Himself to open the door for our return. You now can draw near to God. Grace and mercy have been offered. Will you accept His gift?

Thank You Lord Jesus for the precious gift of grace through faith. Remind us your gift is for all people who turn to You. It is greater than we can ask or imagine and more than we deserve. Let us receive this grace with thanksgiving and praise. In Your name we pray!

# FEBRUARY 20 I FEEL SO ALONE
Loneliness

Matthew 27:46 (NKJV)
*⁴⁶ And about the ninth hour Jesus cried out with a loud voice, saying, "Eli, Eli, lama sabachthani?" that is, "My God, My God, why have You forsaken Me?"*

We all walk down paths that seem hard at times like we are walking all alone. We look around for comfort and support but it seems there is no one there for us. Sometimes it looks like the world is against us and we have nowhere to turn. Jesus felt that way on the cross as He cried out to God in His suffering.

In Matthew, Jesus is hanging on the cross enduring all the pain and embarrassment. He is feeling very alone because the Father is unable to look at him because of all our sin that Jesus has absorbed. Can you imagine how awful Jesus must have looked carrying all the sins of the world past, present and future? But He saw it through and finished the work the Father gave Him to our benefit.

Didn't God say He would never leave nor forsake us? Deuteronomy 31:6-8 (NKJV) says *"⁶ Be strong and of good courage, do not fear nor be afraid of them; for the Lord your God, He is the One who goes with you. He will not leave you nor forsake you."* Jesus was quoting Psalm 22 where it asks about being forsaken and abandoned. Later in the Psalm, it says "You have answered me..." It all works out and the Psalmist sings the praises of the Lord.

At times, we feel as if God does not care because we do not hear or see Him act at a given moment. We are not aware of all that is happening around us and we do not know the value and purpose of the trial we currently face. People of faith know that God works all things for the good of those who love Him. They are not always pleasant circumstances. These trials refine us in ways we need. God would not have allowed it if it would not ultimately be for your good. Do you remember the poem *Footprints*? In the poem, the person notes that at all the difficult times in their life, there were only one set of footprints in the sand making them think they were walking alone when things got tough. God answers them letting them know the footprints were His as He carried them through the times of trouble.

Are you facing difficult times? Do you feel alone? When Jesus felt abandoned, He cried out to God. Isn't that what we should do? And when we cry out, we can be confident He hears and will care for us. He has never failed in the past. He who promises is faithful. He will not fail now. He loves you more than His own life which He gave up on that cross to redeem you. God carries you in all you do. Lean on Him for your strength. He will never leave nor forsake you!

Lord, hear our cry when we call out to you. Come to us quickly. Show us Your kindness, mercy and grace. Walk with us in the difficult times. In Your name we pray.

## FEBRUARY 21  FOR JUST SUCH A TIME AS THIS

Love

Esther 4:14 (NKJV)

*"14 For if you remain completely silent at this time, relief and deliverance will arise for the Jews from another place, but you and your father's house will perish. Yet who knows whether you have come to the kingdom for such a time as this?"*

These are difficult times. The world is giving in to chaos. Terror groups flex their muscles, attack and murder innocent people. It has all the earmarks of the end times. However, man's inhumanity to man has gone on since Cain and Able. Jealousy caused the demise of Able. As we approach Easter, it is supposed to be a time of hope. Reading the newspaper could lower anyone's level of hope. The headlines can bring us down. What should we do about what is happening?

Esther became the Queen of Persia by an interesting turn of events with King Xerxes. She went from orphan to Queen. She was a Jewish woman and the King's top Advisor, Haman, had tricked the King into issuing an edict to kill all the Jews in Persia. She now had to choose to remain silent and survive or take a stand and try to stop the injustice. What would you do?

We are always called to make choices. Jesus came into the world to offer us a better way. We have to decide which course to take. Do we follow Him and do the things He teaches or do we take the easier way and go along with the ways of the world? At what point do you take a stand? Do you wait until chaos reigns before speaking up? Isn't that too late? Now is the time to decide.

Do you have a position of authority or influence in your work or neighborhood? Do you think God has led you to this place for some reason? I don't believe in coincidences. Things happen for a reason. Perhaps you are in the place you are so you can effect change. We are called to increase the Kingdom of God. In His Kingdom, people help each other. We are called to love our neighbor as ourselves. You can make a difference! You have been given everything you need to change your corner of the world. You are equipped! You are empowered! You are anointed! You are incredible! You are well able!  What will you do today with the gifts God has given you?

Lord, remind us of the gifts You have given us and of the Giver. We are called for times such as these. Help us to bring glory to You by using what You have given to the benefit of others. Teach us to walk in Your ways and love Your people. In Your name we pray!

# FEBRUARY 22 F.U.D.G.E.

### Encouragement

Isaiah 41:10 (NKJV)
*10 Fear not, for I am with you; Be not dismayed, for I am your God. I will strengthen you, Yes, I will help you, I will uphold you with My righteous right hand.'*

Fear Uncertainty & Doubt vs. Grace & Encouragement. What would you choose? What does God want for you? We read He is with us. He will strengthen us. He will help us. What does all that mean?

Isaiah was a Prophet of the Lord God Most High. He told people the things God spoke of to, and for, them. This is one of God's promises. The Lord God promised He would strengthen and uphold us. By His power we are strong. Are you strong in the Lord?

When Israel came out of Egypt, they wandered through the desert to Mt. Sinai where God gave them the Law. He told them, through Moses, to build a tabernacle where His Spirit would reside. God Himself would once again live among His people. In Exodus 40:34, when the tabernacle was completed, the cloud covered the Tent of Meeting and the glory of the Lord filled the tabernacle. Moses could not enter the Tent of Meeting because of God's glory. God was among His people leading and guiding them. God promises us to be with us, to strengthen us, to be our God, to help us and uphold us with His righteous right hand.

God doesn't want us to live lives of fear. His presence among us should give us the confidence we need to live as He designed. He has prepared things for us to enjoy. He gives us the strength we need for the tasks He has prepared for us to do. You are given the needed gifts to accomplish your destiny. You can do all things through Christ who gives you strength. With God as your helper, what will you do? Knowing that He is there for you, will you choose FUD or Grace and Encouragement? Choose wisely!

Lord God, thank You that You give us this choice. Reassure us that You will uphold us. Give us the confidence to choose Grace. In Your name we pray!

# FEBRUARY 23 THANK YOU FOR A SEAT AT YOUR TABLE
## Grace and Mercy

Luke 14:12-15 (NKJV)

*12 Then He also said to him who invited Him, "When you give a dinner or a supper, do not ask your friends, your brothers, your relatives, nor rich neighbors, lest they also invite you back, and you be repaid. 13 But when you give a feast, invite the poor, the maimed, the lame, the blind. 14 And you will be blessed, because they cannot repay you; for you shall be repaid at the resurrection of the just." 15 Now when one of those who sat at the table with Him heard these things, he said to Him, "Blessed is he who shall eat bread in the kingdom of God!"*

Sounds like what God does for us, doesn't it? He offers us a seat at His table for which we can never repay Him. His glorious riches are beyond all we could ask or imagine.

What does all that mean to us? God loves us so much that He wants us to sit at His table with Him. Think of it. We are invited to sit at the Captain's table so to speak. You have been invited to the feast. And what a feast it is! Please pass me another slice of grace. Can I have another piece of love? How about a bowl of care? For dessert, you have a choice of compassion, mercy, kindness or respect. OK, you can have some of each. He loves you! He cares for you! He wants to bless you! Will you accept the blessings?

Father, we thank you for a seat at your table. You give us more than we merit. We don't deserve it; we can never earn it and we can never pay you back. But we do accept Your gifts gladly. Help us to live in such a way as to bring glory to Your Holy Name. Help us to invite others to the table and make them feel welcome. Through Your grace and mercy, we live. Teach us to extend that mercy to others. In Your name we pray!

# FEBRUARY 24 YOU WANT ME TO DO WHAT

### Grace and Mercy

Luke 8:35-37 (NKJV)

*35 Then they went out to see what had happened, and came to Jesus, and found the man from whom the demons had departed, sitting at the feet of Jesus, clothed and in his right mind. And they were afraid. 36 They also who had seen it told them by what means he who had been demon-possessed was healed. 37 Then the whole multitude of the surrounding region of the Gadarenes asked Him to depart from them, for they were seized with great fear. And He got into the boat and returned.*

In this story, Jesus healed a demon-possessed man named Legion by transferring the demons within him to a herd of pigs nearby. The pigs ran down a cliff into the sea and were drowned. This was an awesome display of the Lord's power over demons which showed how He can heal people. Jesus had crossed the Sea of Galilee to the pagan side looking to bring healing to the people there. He only got to heal one man before the people put him out of town. Jesus brought incredible power to this town but the people were not ready to accept His grace. They were afraid of the power. They asked Jesus to leave them.

Many times, people are not ready to accept blessings because they don't think they are worthy. In Matthew 8:8 (NKJV) *8 The Centurion answered and said, "Lord, I am not worthy that You should come under my roof. But only speak a word, and my servant will be healed."* The Lord was willing to go and heal the Centurion's servant but the Centurion said he was not worthy of having Jesus in his home. What about you? Are you worthy? Why or why not? God says you are worthy by the blood of the Lamb. You are His masterpiece. You are fearfully and wonderfully made. It is because of God's grace that we are worthy. It is because He says so!

That one man, Legion, was important. Jesus only got to heal one person on this journey but each person matters. Legion, remained behind at Jesus' request and told the people of that region all Jesus had done for him. He gave his personal testimony and the people listened. When you have the greatest news in the world, people will eventually listen and accept. It takes time but God's plan cannot be thwarted. Be encouraged! The Good News will prevail.

Lord, thank You that, by Your grace, we are worthy because You say so! By Your stripes, we are healed. You gave us Your righteousness. Help us to accept the gift of Your grace. In Your name we pray!

# FEBRUARY 25 WHAT IS GRACE
## Grace and Mercy

Exodus 34:6-7 (NKJV)

[6] *And the* LORD *passed before him and proclaimed, "The* LORD*, the* LORD *God, merciful and gracious, longsuffering, and abounding in goodness and truth,* [7] *keeping mercy for thousands, forgiving iniquity and transgression and sin, by no means clearing the guilty, visiting the iniquity of the fathers upon the children and the children's children to the third and the fourth generation."*

Moses was up on Mount Sinai with the stone tablets that God commanded him to bring. He was in the presence of the Creator of the universe. God wrote the Ten Commandments on those tablets. This Law would show the people how far short of God's standards they had fallen. It is impossible to keep the Law in our own power. We need God's power here.

Moses did not know too much about God's grace at the point he led the Israelites out of Egypt. God knew the people would be difficult and He had plans to refine them. He always has plans to prosper us. He knew what it would take to make them into His people, a mighty nation. They had just made the golden calf and were worshipping it when God threatened to destroy them. Moses might be listed as one of the greatest salesmen in the world because of his efforts to convince God not to destroy Israel. He does punish sin. He showed His patience and mercy to Israel.

God showed His grace again hundreds of years later to an undeserving people. He sent His Son to seek and save the lost. I guess that is what God does. He forgives our iniquity and transgressions. Do you want justice or grace? People say life is not fair. If it was totally fair and you got what you truly deserved, would you be happy? I don't think so! But God is gracious, merciful and compassionate showing His love to a thousand generations. He loves you! You are His. Grace is undeserved favor. But it is of no value if you don't accept the offer. Open your heart to Him today and let Him bless you!

Lord, open our hearts to Your grace. Help us accept Your mercy. Show us that we fall short of the mark but You make up the difference. Give us Your righteousness by faith in You. In Your name we pray!

## FEBRUARY 26 BE AN ENCOURAGER
Love

Hebrews 3:12-14 (NIV)

*12 See to it, brothers and sisters, that none of you has a sinful, unbelieving heart that turns away from the living God. 13 But encourage one another daily, as long as it is called "Today," so that none of you may be hardened by sin's deceitfulness. 14 We have come to share in Christ, if indeed we hold our original conviction firmly to the very end.*

Do you ever get down? Do you notice some of your friends being a little negative or discouraged? Most of the world is discouraged. It is time we do something about that. It is time we encourage one another.

In our culture, it seems to be fashionable to denigrate one another. We use sarcasm and barbs in our conversation. We think it is funny but it does not build each other up as we are supposed to do. Hebrews tells us to encourage one another daily. Who was the last person you told how much you appreciate them? Did you thank the server when they brought your food? Did you take the time to listen to a friend who seemed a little down? Did you even notice?

One of the best things I have ever done is told my best friend I loved him before he passed away. He told me the same. Don't let opportunities slip away. Tell people you love them. Tell them you appreciate them. Tell them they matter. Tell them you believe in them. Take the time to notice those around you. Use your words to bless people. Speak blessings, love, encouragement, and every good thing into the lives of your family, friends and all those with whom you come in contact. Be a blessing. Be an encourager! Do it now while it is still today!

Lord, You always tell us how much You love us. Help us to tell others we love them. Teach us to lift others up in Your name. Give us the gift of encouragement. In Your name we pray!

# FEBRUARY 27 JESUS PRAYED FOR YOU

Prayer

John 17: 15-21 (NIV)

*15 My prayer is not that you take them out of the world but that you protect them from the evil one. 16 They are not of the world, even as I am not of it. 17 Sanctify them by the truth; your word is truth. 18 As you sent me into the world, I have sent them into the world. 19 For them I sanctify myself, that they too may be truly sanctified. 20 "My prayer is not for them alone. I pray also for those who will believe in me through their message, 21 that all of them may be one, Father, just as you are in me and I am in you. May they also be in us so that the world may believe that you have sent me.*

Do you ever realize how important you are to God? More than 2000 years ago, Jesus prayed for your protection. How does that make you feel? Who are we that He is mindful of us?

Jesus had just been telling the disciples what would be happening in the near future. He is preparing them for His departure from this world. He tells them He must go away in order for the Holy Spirit to come to be with us. The Holy Spirit will dwell within us. Jesus is praying for His own (you and me); that they would be safe and strong. He is asking God to protect them from the evil one. He also asked for us to be sanctified. That means to be set apart as or declared holy; consecrated.

But here is the thing that really stuck out for me. Jesus said "My prayer is not for them alone. I pray also for those who will believe in me through their message..." That's you and me! He that created everything seen and unseen prayed for us. We matter to Jesus. He is concerned with our welfare. He is asking God the Father to protect us and guide us.

Did you realize that you were that important? Did you know the Creator of the universe cares about you? You are special. You are a masterpiece. You were created in His image and likeness. You are well able. How does a person with all those qualifications live their life? Should you be bold? Should you be confident? Yes you should! What would you do if you knew you could not fail? If God be for you, who dares be against you? Step out in faith knowing Jesus intercedes for you that you may be one with Him and God the Father!

Father, give us a boldness in You! Help us live lives that bring glory to Your holy name. Make us aware of all we mean to You and let us live as heirs to the Kingdom and brothers and sisters of Christ. By Your will and power, let us live for and in You. In Your name we pray!

# FEBRUARY 28 HOW CAN I BE SURE

Faith

Isaiah 54:10 (NIV)

*¹⁰ Though the mountains be shaken and the hills be removed, yet my unfailing love for you will not be shaken*

*nor my covenant of peace be removed," says the LORD, who has compassion on you.*

Do you sometimes wonder if you really are going to heaven? Have you come to a place in your spiritual life where you know for certain that, if you were to die today, that you would go to heaven or would you say that is something you are still working on?

John 1:12 says *"¹² Yet to all who did receive him, to those who believed in his name, he gave the right to become children of God...",* How do we know if He has received us? Many people wonder if God's offer is to them and if He has accepted them. How do you know if you have your salvation?

God tells us if we receive Him, we *have* salvation. He knows whether you are sincere or if you are just saying the words. Romans 10:9 says *⁹ that if you confess with your mouth the Lord Jesus and believe in your heart that God has raised Him from the dead, you will be saved.* There it is! You will be saved. You cannot fool God about what is in your heart. He knows! The good news is He knows when you are sincere in acceptance and belief. And when you are, you become His child. His love for you is unfailing! His grace and mercy are unlimited! He adores you. Bask in the glow of His love. And while you are feeling that love, figure out how you can share it with those around you!

Father, I thank You that You are faithful to Your promises and it doesn't depend on me to earn my way to You. You promised that, in Your unfailing love, Your covenant of peace would not be removed. Help us to live in that peace knowing that He who promises is faithful. In Your name we pray.

# FEBRUARY 29 TAKE A LEAP OF FAITH
Faith

Hebrews 11:1-3 (NKJV)
*Now faith is the substance of things hoped for, the evidence of things not seen. ² For by it the elders obtained a good testimony. ³ By faith we understand that the worlds were framed by the word of God, so that the things which are seen were not made of things which are visible.*

Have you had opportunities to do something but hesitated because you were not sure of the outcome? Many times, we have ideas for inventions or business opportunities but procrastinate because we secretly don't believe we have what it takes to make it happen. Sometimes, we try to do things purely in our own power not putting our faith in our Lord. Many times, we put together our plan and then ask God to bless it. Wouldn't it be better to include Him in the design stage? Our ego leads us to believe we can do it on our own. A friend of mine said ego stands for "easing God out".

When we have faith, we believe God will bless us in our endeavors. If we trust in Him, we will let Him guide us in our efforts since He knows what is best. The world was formed at His word so He knows how it is all made. The Creator knows how the pieces fit. Why not ask Him what to do and how to do it? Follow His lead and watch the deliverance He will bring.

Thank You Lord for paving the way You would have us walk! Thank You that You always walk with us in the journey. You promised You would never leave nor forsake us. Help us to always feel Your presence. By Faith, lead us to our destiny which You established from before the beginning of the world. Hold us in Your everlasting arms! In Your name we pray!

# MARCH 1    WHAT, ME WORRY

Faith

Luke 12 (NIV) Selected Verses

²² *Then Jesus said to his disciples: "Therefore I tell you, do not worry about your life, what you will eat; or about your body, what you will wear.* ²³ *For life is more than food, and the body more than clothes.*

³² *"Do not be afraid, little flock, for your Father has been pleased to give you the kingdom.* ³³ *Sell your possessions and give to the poor. Provide purses for yourselves that will not wear out, a treasure in heaven that will never fail, where no thief comes near and no moth destroys.* ³⁴ *For where your treasure is, there your heart will be also.*

Worry is a waste of the imagination! Matthew 6:27 says ²⁷ *Which of you by worrying can add one cubit to his stature?* It is a complete waste of time as well.

Jesus was teaching His disciples not to worry. He tells them God the Father will provide. They are to live life by living each moment and not worrying about what happens next. You can't change the past. You can't change the future. All you have is now. Today is a gift. That is why they call it the present.

In our daily lives, things are very scary. We face challenges that stretch us beyond our comfort zone. In my work, issues arise I have never faced. In my writing, I sit with no ideas and a blank page. I looked at my computer screen for hours tonight with no ideas. In my spiritual walk, I have doubts and questions. How can I continue? I don't know what to do. I start to worry and then things spiral downward. I get to the "I'll never be able to..." statements. Hold the phone! I may never be able to, but He can. And He will!

You see, we were fearfully and wonderfully made. We are equipped, empowered, anointed and well able. We have been given the gifts we need to live the life for which we were destined. Worry gets in the way of using the gifts we have been given. Worry comes from the accuser. He says "You can't do that. You don't have the talent." That's a lie! You have been given everything you need. He says "you'll never be enough." Not true! You are a masterpiece! You are already enough even if you never do another thing. And it is not what you do but whose you are that matters.

Here's the thing. Whenever you think negative thoughts, they do not come from God. In fact, they show a lack of faith and that is a sin. Now no one wants to hear the word sin these days but worry shows a lack of belief that God will do what He promised. He who promises is faithful.

There is a song by Mercyme called Greater and it goes like this:

> Every day I wrestle with the voices That keep telling me I'm not right But that's alright
>
> Cause I hear a voice and he calls me redeemed When others say I'll never be enough
>
> And greater is the One living inside of me Than he who is living in the world

You see, you are holy, righteous and redeemed by the blood of the Lamb. The Spirit of the Lamb is within you. You are filled with power. You can do all things through

Christ who gives you strength. Therefore, why worry? Instead, trust God and let him lead you to your destiny. Your Father is pleased to give you the Kingdom. Worry will just delay the process. Be bold and step out in faith. Accept the gifts offered and say amen!

Take this Refrain any time you feel a doubt:

There'll be days I lose the battle Grace says that it doesn't matter Cause the cross already won the war

He's Greater He's Greater

I am learning to run freely Understanding just how he sees me And it makes me love him more and more

He's Greater He's Greater

And greater is the One who is living inside of me than he who is living in the world.

Thank You Lord that you live inside me and guide me today! Amen!

# MARCH 2    DON'T JUST SIT THERE, PRAY
Prayer

Philippians 4:5-7 (NIV)
*Let your gentleness be evident to all. The Lord is near. ⁶Do not be anxious about anything, but in every situation, by prayer and petition, with thanksgiving, present your requests to God. ⁷And the peace of God, which transcends all understanding, will guard your hearts and your minds in Christ Jesus.*

We have talked about worrying and why it is not good for you. Paul, the writer of Philippians, tells us not to be anxious about anything. That is easy for him to say. There is a whole lot about which to be anxious. We also spoke about not going it alone. There is no need. We have the option of relying on God in all things.

How do we ask for God's help? Paul tells us, in *every* situation, we should use prayer and petition to make our requests known to the Lord. It does not say in some situations but in every situation. Is Paul suggesting we take everything to God? Yes, he is. Not just the big things or the bad things but everything. If we fully rely on God (F.R.O.G.), we can have His peace. His peace is beyond our understanding. That means you can be at peace while in the middle of great turbulence, while others around you are struggling. That does not make sense, does it? When you are in the center of God's will, things go according to His plan and it all works out to your best interest. He loves you and wants what is best for you. What about the thanksgiving? You should approach God in prayer with a boldness thanking Him in advance that He has already made a way for good things to happen in your life. That is what His promises teach us. Hebrews 13:6b says *"The Lord is my helper; I will not be afraid..."*

What about the gentleness thing? Tell me, how do you want to be known? You can reason with people and persuade them of your case or you can bully them. There is an old expression which says "people convinced against their will are of the same opinion still." You can do a full-on frontal assault but the casualties are not usually worth the fight. What if you were able to share your viewpoint and show them you have a lot in common and could work together for the good of all? Would that be a better approach? With prayer, God will go before you paving the way and leading you to a win-win situation. God can give you favor with those with whom you did not have good rapport.

Finally, Paul tells us God's peace will guard our hearts and our minds in Christ Jesus. When you are at peace, will you think more clearly? When you are at peace, will you make better decisions? Will you be able to think win-win? When you focus on Christ, His light will shine through every good thing you do. It is out of the overflow of His love that your gentleness will be evident. When you hold Him near, He will influence you to be your best and others will notice! Live today as your best you and people *will* notice!

Thank you, Lord, that you are my Helper and will inspire me to be my best. I trust you will grant me favor with those I meet! Thank you for helping me write this devotion. Amen!

# MARCH 3     GOD LOVES YOU
Faith

John 3:16-17 (NKJV)
*[16] For God so loved the world that He gave His only begotten Son, that whoever believes in Him should not perish but have everlasting life. [17] For God did not send His Son into the world to condemn the world, but that the world through Him might be saved.*

With all the bad things going on in the world, do you ever question God's love for you? Is it hard to see beyond the troubles of the day? When you are going through a difficult time, are you able to focus on the goodness of God or would you say you have trouble remaining positive? Well, that's why we are writing Encouragement Daily.

John 3:16 is the most famous verse in the New Testament but many have trouble understanding the full breadth of its meaning. I cannot fully explain it here (or anywhere else for that matter with my limited knowledge) but there are some thoughts I would like to highlight for you now. God sent Jesus to atone for our sins because He knew we would never be able to make restitution for ourselves. There is basically no way we can be perfect as God's holiness requires to be in His presence. There is no way we can measure up. But before you get discouraged, God already knew that so He always had a plan by which we can be redeemed. (Redemption is a whole discussion by itself.) That plan was and is Jesus. Jesus is the perfect sacrifice, and what we could not do on our own, God already did for us through the perfect sacrifice of His Son. Think about that. The wages of sin is death. Therefore, God entered the world as a man, in the form of His Son Jesus, to offer Himself as a substitute for your death. Jesus gave Himself up for you and me!

For me, verse 17 is most important because it tells me God loves you and me so much that he already planned to come into the world not to condemn, but to redeem. He planned to offer you what was lost in the Garden with Adam and Eve. God wants a relationship with you and is willing to give Himself up to make that happen. My hope is you will begin to understand what it says in Ephesians 3 that you *[18] may have power, together with all the Lord's holy people, to grasp how wide and long and high and deep is the love of Christ, [19] and to know this love that surpasses knowledge—that you may be filled to the measure of all the fullness of God.* His love surpasses our understanding. Let His grace surround and redeem you!

Lord, thank you that you love us so much that you already gave Yourself up to redeem us. Help us to accept Your offer of grace and enter into a relationship with you. Walk with us please. Amen!

# MARCH 4     WHO ARE WE THAT YOU ARE MINDFUL OF US

Grace and Mercy

Psalm 8:4-5 (NKJV)

*4 What is man that You are mindful of him, And the son of man that You visit him? 5 For You have made him a little lower than the angels, And You have crowned him with glory and honor.*

In a lot of cases, I get the impression people don't really care about me. They seem to be wrapped up in their own concerns and don't have time to notice others. Do you feel the same way? What if there were someone who always cares for you? When you speak, they are attentive and listen. They pay attention to your moods and are helpful. What if they made you feel important? Would that make a difference? A person like that is usually called a friend.

Sometimes, it is hard to understand the all-powerful Creator of the Universe would want to listen to us and care for us. That He would want a relationship with us. That He would want to bless us. It is hard to understand but true! He is the One who decided to be mindful of us. He created us to be in relationship with Him. It is God's grace and mercy that leads Him to enter into that relationship.

What a Friend we have in Jesus, All our sins and griefs to bear!
What a privilege to carry, Everything to God in prayer!

Jesus is more than Lord and Savior. Jesus is also our friend. He is willing to listen. He cares. He is there for us in every situation. Why not speak with Him about how you are feeling. Ask Him to lead you today.

I thank You Jesus that You are willing to be my Savior, my Lord and my Friend! I thank You that I can bring all things to You and You will help me. I do not merit Your friendship and cannot earn it but I thank You that You are my friend by Your grace. I accept Your gift of grace gladly. Amen!

# MARCH 5     YOU CAN DO IT

Encouragement

Matthew 17:20 (NKJV)

²⁰ *So Jesus said to them, "Because of your unbelief; for assuredly, I say to you, if you have faith as a mustard seed, you will say to this mountain, 'Move from here to there,' and it will move; and nothing will be impossible for you.*

Every day, we are assailed by voices telling us we cannot manage the task in front of us. Sometimes, the voices are in your head. Sometimes they are your family, friends, co-workers or your boss. It is easy to listen to the voices. But there is One voice to whom you should listen. The Voice of Truth. That voice is the voice of Jesus.

Jesus tells us if we have even a little faith, nothing will be impossible for us. That seems too good to be true. He says we can move mountains. How's that? You see, He wants you to stay in faith and not get discouraged. Discouragement will lead you to give up. Faith gives you the hope you need to persist. If you persist, you will succeed. Here is a quote from Calvin Coolidge about persistence.

Nothing in the world can take the place of Persistence. Talent will not; nothing is more common than unsuccessful men with talent. Genius will not; unrewarded genius is almost a proverb. Education will not; the world is full of educated derelicts. Persistence and determination alone are omnipotent. The slogan 'Press On' has solved and always will solve the problems of the human race.     **Calvin Coolidge**

President Coolidge might have considered giving some credit to God for success, but he is on track when he says we must persist. When God sees your faith, He will intervene on your behalf. He will lead you on the right path.

You can listen to those negative voices either in your head or in your life. They can scuttle your destiny. Or you can listen to your God. He will lead you to do great things. You have to decide to whom you will listen! I suggest you listen to the voice of truth.

The Voice of Truth     Casting Crowns

But the voice of truth tells me a different story; And the voice of truth says, "Do not be afraid!"

And the voice of truth says, "This is for My glory"; Out of all the voices calling out to me

I will choose to listen and believe the voice of truth.

Lord, I thank You for Your voice that we hear. Help us to hear and distinguish Your Word and Your will for our lives. Blot out the other voices that tell us we can't and fill us with Your presence. Fill us with the voice of truth. Your word is truth (John 17:17).

# MARCH 6     WATCH WHAT THE LORD WILL DO

Encouragement

2 Kings 6:15-17 (NKJV)

*¹⁵ And when the servant of the man of God arose early and went out, there was an army, surrounding the city with horses and chariots. And his servant said to him, "Alas, my master! What shall we do?" ¹⁶ So he answered, "Do not fear, for those who are with us are more than those who are with them." ¹⁷ And Elisha prayed, and said, "LORD, I pray, open his eyes that he may see." Then the LORD opened the eyes of the young man, and he saw. And behold, the mountain was full of horses and chariots of fire all around Elisha.*

In this story, Elisha was being sought by the king of Aram for giving away his secrets. The king sent an army to surround the city of Dothan during the night and capture Elisha. In the morning, the servant goes outside and sees the vast army surrounding the city and he was freaked out. Elisha was not worried because he knew the Lord was with him. So much so, that the Lord sent horsemen and chariots of fire that were surrounding them on the mountains. They were ready to attack at the Lord's command. The servant lacked faith that God would continue His care for them and so he could not see their deliverance. Elisha didn't worry; he prayed! He remained in faith trusting God for the outcome. Do you trust God for the outcome?

I have a friend that is going through a tough time. She is facing challenges that can be overwhelming. When things get out of perspective, we tend to think they are impossible. In our conversation, she sounded discouraged. I am on a mission to encourage people. I want to remind them of all God has in store for them. I proceeded to share Elisha's story of how the Lord was watching out for His own with her and reminded her He is watching out for her as well. He is watching out for you, too!

We tend to forget God loves us and watches out for us. We need reminders. I am reminding you the mountains that surround you (challenges seem like mountains) are covered with the horsemen and chariots of the Lord. Do you see them? They are waiting to come to your aid at the Lord's command. Just ask Him for help. The army of the Lord is ready!

Lord, I thank You that You are always ready to come to our aid. I thank You that Your army is always close by in case we need help. I ask You would open our eyes to see the heavenly forces You call into existence on our behalf. Help us to live in confidence knowing that You go out before us in glory.

P.S. Here is one more little tip as a reminder of the power of God. Whenever you go somewhere when you face a challenge, find yourself some double doors through which you can walk. When you do, walk in the center pushing both doors open to make a wide passageway. You need to do that because the horsemen and chariots of the Lord will require a wide berth to go with you! You are not going alone and on your own! The Lord's army goes with you. He will work it all out for your good. Keep your eyes open and watch what the Lord will do.

# MARCH 7    HE HEARD YOUR CALL

Grace and Mercy

Jeremiah 33 (NKJV) Selected Verses

*3 'Call to Me, and I will answer you, and show you great and mighty things, which you do not know.'...... 6 Behold, I will bring it [Israel] health and healing; I will heal them and reveal to them the abundance of peace and truth. 7 And I will cause the captives of Judah and the captives of Israel to return, and will rebuild those places as at the first.*

Jeremiah was a Prophet of the Lord and told the people what God wanted to say to them. The people of Israel and Judah did not listen and chose to go their own way, not honor God by following His word. God had promised He would be with His people if they obeyed Him. They did not! Because of their disobedience, God scattered the people. The nation was split and Judah and Israel eventually fell to Babylon. Human nature is such that we turn to God when in trouble but turn to our own ways when all is well and prosperous as if we were the ones who improved our situation. Do you thank God in all things?

Even though God withdrew from His people (separation), He did not forsake them. He did incline His ear to them though scattered among the nations. For God still had good plans for His people. He knew they would return to Him once they saw how their own plans worked out. Like a good parent, God let them have their own way to see how things would work out. It is sort of like Dr. Phil's question - "How's that working out for you?" It was not working well at all. But God had plan B and C and D and so on!

Jeremiah told them what God said "Call to me, and I will answer you..." God heard their call, their cry and He answered. At that time in history, God gathered them back from Babylon after 70 years in captivity. However, the Bible speaks in many planes. It is a living, breathing document. Israel had gone through many cycles of disobedience. God also heard their cry at a later time in history. This time, He decided to write His laws on their hearts in a totally new way. This time, He would make a permanent way for His people to return to Him and keep the path open. This time, He would enter our world in human form and destroy sin and death forever. And He would do that by offering Himself as the ransom once and for all!

When you become fearful about your situation, remember, He heard you and came running to save and redeem you! He loves you beyond all you can ask or imagine. He loves you with an everlasting love. So much so that He tasted death on your behalf. He is coming again for you (us) to rebuild what was lost. Are you ready? Will you wait with me?

Thank You Lord that You love and care for us. Thank You that You are patient and offer us mercy instead of justice. Thank You that You are coming to us in our hour of need. Come Lord Jesus! Amen!

# MARCH 8     ARE YOU IN

Grace and Mercy

Luke 13:22-25 (NIV) The Narrow Door
*22 Then Jesus went through the towns and villages, teaching as he made his way to Jerusalem.*
*23 Someone asked him, "Lord, are only a few people going to be saved?"*
*He said to them, 24 "Make every effort to enter through the narrow door, because many, I tell you, will try to enter and will not be able to. 25 Once the owner of the house gets up and closes the door, you will stand outside knocking and pleading, 'Sir, open the door for us.' "But he will answer, 'I don't know you or where you come from.'"*

Who is the owner of the house? At what time will he close the door? Will we have any warning? What are the requirements to get in? Do I qualify? Am I in? Do I make the cut?

These are some of the questions raised by this passage. They are really about the Kingdom of Heaven. With that in mind, the owner of the house is the Lord. No one knows the day or hour of the closing of the door. The requirements are to believe in the Son. John 1:12 (NKJV) says *12 But as many as received Him, to them He gave the right to become children of God, to those who believe in His name.* As far as you qualifying, only you can answer that question. Have you received Him?

I have come to a place in my spiritual journey where I have come to understand relationships are the most important thing we can achieve. Take care of relationships and they will take care of everything else. The Ten Commandments are all about relationships: our relationship to God and to each other. What does it mean to believe in Jesus the Son? Revelation 3:20 says *20 Behold, I [Jesus] stand at the door and knock. If anyone hears My voice and opens the door, I will come in to him and dine with him, and he with Me.* In another translation, it says "I will abide with them and they with me." Abide implies more than just a meal and a limited time. Abide implies a relationship. Do you "know" Jesus? Are you in a relationship? What is written on your heart? Is Jesus' name there?

God has no grandchildren. It is not about your parent's relationship and them putting in a good word for you. It *is* all about whether or not you accept the offer. There is always discussion about faith vs. works. The only "work" you have to do is accept Jesus' offer. We don't deserve it, we can never earn it, we can never pay Him back. Nevertheless, the offer is always on the table!

Along the lines of qualifying, none of us "deserve" the offer. We don't qualify because of the Church to which we belong or the family we are in or how many good works we do. None of that matters. What does matter is you saying yes to Jesus. Do you hear Him knocking? Are you going to open the door and let Him in? He is a gentleman. He would never enter without your permission. He is waiting at the door to your heart. Will you give Him permission to enter and abide there?

Lord, I pray Your people will hear Your voice and open the door. It seems as it is not You who closes the door but we who do not open the door to You. There are those who are unsure. By Your Spirit, please give them the boldness to say yes to You.

Remind them of Your limitless love for them. And if they are not ready today, in Your patience, please continue to knock until they gain the courage to throw open the door. You said that You wish none should perish." In Jesus name I pray!

# MARCH 9    PAY IT FORWARD

Relationships

Matthew 25:35-40 (NKJV)

*35 for I was hungry and you gave Me food; I was thirsty and you gave Me drink; I was a stranger and you took Me in; 36 I was naked and you clothed Me; I was sick and you visited Me; I was in prison and you came to Me.' 37 "Then the righteous will answer Him, saying, 'Lord, when did we see You hungry and feed You, or thirsty and give You drink? 38 When did we see You a stranger and take You in, or naked and clothe You? 39 Or when did we see You sick, or in prison, and come to You?' 40 And the King will answer and say to them, 'Assuredly, I say to you, inasmuch as you did it to one of the least of these My brethren, you did it to Me.'*

Jesus told us to love our neighbor as ourselves. Here, He is describing what it looks like to do so. Sometimes, we go through our day not noticing the people with whom we come in contact. We pay attention to the important people but the rest seem to just pass by unnoticed. How about the server in the restaurant? Did you notice them? What was their name? What kind of day were they having?

Jesus is telling you every person is important, and you should care for them all. Jesus spoke to those on the margins of society that were not people of influence and these fisherman, tax collectors, prostitutes and other sinners took His message to the four corners of the world. He went to the little people to make sure they understood they mattered to Him. If we only care for the influential, the rich, those who can do things for us, of what merit is that? If these people mattered to Jesus, shouldn't they matter to us?

In a conversation with our son, I told him I am trying to raise him to be a contributing, productive member of society. I not only want him to take care of himself but I want him to look out and care for others. I want him to fight for the weak and stand up for justice and mercy. I want him to care for the least of these. Some have called that paying it forward. What do you call it? Is this something you want to undertake? Do you think it will improve our corner of the world?

Mother Theresa had a poem called *Anyway* on the wall of her home in Calcutta. It was written by Keith Kent and it is worth reading. Here is an excerpt from that poem which helps clarify the steps we should take.

> The good you do today, people will often forget tomorrow;
> Do good anyway.
> Give the world the best you have, and it may never be enough;
> Give the world the best you've got anyway.
> You see, in the final analysis, it is between you and your God;
> It was never between you and them anyway.

In the end, it is all between us and our God. If we do things for the least of these because our Lord asks us to do so, how will we be greeted when we arrive before Him? Will He be proud of us? Will He say "Well done good and faithful servant"? I think so. You are well able! Do good anyway!

Lord, please lead us to the people to whom You wish to speak through our lives today. Let our words be Your words. Guide us to be Your hands and feet. Help us to do justly, love mercy and walk humbly with You this day and every day. Amen!

# MARCH 10    LIVE CONFIDENTLY
Faith

Hebrews 13:5b – 6 (ESV)
*"Never will I leave you; never will I forsake you."*
*⁶ So we say with confidence, "The Lord is my helper; I will not be afraid.*
*What can mere mortals do to me?"*

I used to think I was in control of every situation. Boy was I mistaken. With control comes responsibility. I was very anxious because I felt the pressure of getting everything done by myself and in my own power. It was especially bad around the Holidays. I had to face God again and admit I had not cleaned up the world as if it were possible for me to do. What was I thinking? It was awful for me. Have you ever felt that way? Do you walk around with too large a burden on your shoulders? Are you trying to do things in your own power?

Well, we are not doing things on our own when we have faith in Christ. Sometimes, it sure feels that way though. Much has to do with whether we acknowledge God and His blessings in our lives. Our Heavenly Father knows what we need and will provide for us. He has said He will never leave nor forsake us. What does that mean? Have you ever had one of those days of blessing? A day where everything you touched turned to gold and everyone you met was pulling for you. People you don't even know were holding doors open for you. That is the Favor of God! God wants His favor to rest upon you always. He is right there looking to make your paths straight and your valleys not too low. He is your Helper! You and God are a majority. Are you living in the favor of God? Do you surround yourself with the hedge of His protection? Not sure how?

Be content! Do not fall in love with money. Know that God is your Helper and will provide all you need. He will NOT provide all you *want* but He will provide for your needs. Also, He has blessings stored up for you in His storehouse. They already have your name on them. The only thing standing between you and those blessings is *you*. That's right, you are blocking God's blessings by worrying, complaining and not listening to His still small voice when deciding how to live your life. Actually, you are living the life He gave you. You are a steward of that life. Why not live it to the glory of God? He will show you how. Go out today with confidence knowing the Lord is your Helper! Go out and love like you're not scared. Give when it's not fair. Fight for the weak ones. Fix your eyes on Him.

Lord, please go with my friends this day. Help them keep their eyes fixed on You. Help them live life with confidence knowing You go before them and will be their Shield and Protector and never leave nor forsake them. In Your name I pray. Amen!

# MARCH 11     BE BLESSED

Grace and Mercy

John 10:10 (NKJV)

*[10] The thief does not come except to steal, and to kill, and to destroy. I [Jesus] have come that they may have life, and that they may have it more abundantly.*

From the very beginning, God had good plans for us. In the beginning, He created the perfect garden for His children with everything they needed. Their only job was to tend the garden. It was called Paradise. They walked with God in the garden in the cool of the afternoon. They were in His presence.

The thief was in the garden posing as a serpent. He planned to steal the relationship from Adam and Eve. If he could just plant some doubt in their mind and get them to disobey God, he could break the relationship and rule over Paradise. It did not take too much convincing. Eve was an easy mark and Adam was little support. The evil one brought death into the world and destroyed what God had planned for His children. With one act, Paradise was destroyed. Adam and Eve were put out of the Garden and separated from God.

But God had another plan. You see, He always wanted great things for His most prized creation. He created Adam and Eve to rule over His creation. God would have to work things out another way. And that is exactly what He did. Way back then, God planned to redeem all of creation. He wants us to have an abundant life. He longs to give us great things. We are His masterpiece, His most prized possession. Jesus came that we could have that abundant life. Through Him, we are restored to God. We can enter back into His presence. Isn't that what this is all about; our finding a way back into the presence of God? Isn't that where you want to be? I know I do. Jesus has made and is making that possible. He has come that we can have life more abundantly! Praise God!

Thank You Lord, for my favorite two words, "But God". Lord, thank You for the abundant life You have given us. Thank You that You had a plan to redeem us even when we are disobedient. Thank You that no matter the tricks of the thief, You always make a way for us to return to You. Thank You for a seat at Your table!

# MARCH 12     FIRST THINGS FIRST

Encouragement

Matthew 6:33 (NIV)
*33 But seek first his kingdom and his righteousness, and all these things will be given to you as well.*

So many times, I meet with people who have great plans and wonderful ideas. They have the desire to improve their corner of the world. These dreams are much bigger than they are. Most often, if not always, these dreams are from God. Mostly, people don't realize that God is the one who gives them the dreams. The Lord says in Jeremiah 29:11, *"I know the plans I have for you. Plans to prosper you and not to harm you. Plans to give you hope and a future."* He *wants* to give you good things.

Many times, we work these plans as if they are our own doing. We get an idea to build a school or support facility. We do things in our own power. We struggle to make the plan come to fruition. It can be tiring and overwhelming when you try it all on your own.

Noah did not go out into the known world to capture and bring the animals to the ark. In Genesis 7:8, it tells how the animals *"came to Noah and entered the ark".* Could you imagine how difficult it would have been for Noah to have to find them and then get them into the ark? Do you think Noah could have convinced the elephant to get into the boat? Noah allowed God to work all things out through God's power rather than his own. The animals entered the ark.

What about you? Do you Fully Rely on God (F.R.O.G.) or do you try to do it on your own? Are you a self-made man or woman? Do you leave room for God to enter in to the process, the dream? Are you working in the Spiritual realm or in the secular world? All things are possible with Him who gives you strength.

Once upon a time, I used to think "If it's going to be, it's up to me!" That was before I realized things go much better and easier when you go God's way. Recently, I did a 10-Year Business Plan. I prayed about the plan asking God if He really wanted me to continue in the business. What did He see as the purpose of the business? What did He want me to accomplish? How should things be done? I asked the questions and tried to be quiet and listen for answers. He told me He wanted me to "change lives". Once I had formulated the plan and written it down, I placed it in my Bible. On a daily basis, I pulled it out after I prayed and asked God for His thoughts on what I had recorded and waited for other ideas. Sometimes, new thoughts would come and I would add them. Once the thoughts stopped coming, I realized the plan was according to God's will and He would make it come together. It is the same with these Devotionals. As I have told you, sometimes I do not have the next idea and I sit and ask for guidance. He always comes through for He is faithful. He called me to this task and He will bring it to fruition. He will never leave nor forsake me. By the way, I could still use your prayers that words are given to me.

We are told to seek first His kingdom and all the other things will come our way. You must work in the Spiritual realm allowing God to make things happen. Do you want God to bring the animals to you or do you want to go out looking for them? It is much better when God does the work. His plan and timing are perfect!

Thank You Lord that You have a great and perfect plan for our lives. I would ask You quiet our souls so we can hear Your voice and know Your plan for us. Thank you that Your plan is always perfect. Help us to be patient and wait for Your perfect timing. For we know Your plans will prosper us! Amen!

# MARCH 13    WHO DO YOU SAY I AM

Faith

Matthew 16:13-18 (NKJV)

*¹³ When Jesus came into the region of Caesarea Philippi, He asked His disciples, saying, "Who do men say that I, the Son of Man, am?" ¹⁴ So they said, "Some say John the Baptist, some Elijah, and others Jeremiah or one of the prophets."¹⁵ He said to them, "But who do you say that I am?" ¹⁶ Simon Peter answered and said, "You are the Christ, the Son of the living God." ¹⁷ Jesus answered and said to him, "Blessed are you, Simon Bar-Jonah, for flesh and blood has not revealed this to you, but My Father who is in heaven. ¹⁸ And I also say to you that you are Peter, and on this rock I will build My church, and the gates of Hades shall not prevail against it.*

How did Peter know that? Looking back from where we are, it is easy to compare all the things in the Gospel to the Old Testament prophecies and figure it out. Peter did not have that information at that time. As it says, it was revealed to him. Peter knew Jesus was the promised Messiah.

What about you? You have your own copy of the Bible including Old and New Testaments. You have all the evidence you need to understand who Jesus is logically. What about in your heart? Who is He to you? Is He your Lord? Savior? Friend? Or is He just a historical figure? Are you proud of who Jesus is in your life? Do you live in a way that shows He is inside you? Matthew 10:33 (ESV) says *³³ but whoever denies me before men, I also will deny before my Father who is in heaven.* Will Jesus be your advocate before God the Father? He will if you ask Him to be. He longs to build a relationship with you and reconcile you to the Father. Have you asked Him yet?

Our Church has a calling to make disciples who make disciples. That means we want to equip each person (The Saints) to go out following the Great Commission and make disciples of all nations. To do that, we must have a strong foundation built upon the Rock which is Jesus. It seems Jesus also founded a rock on which He would build His Church. He changed Simon's name to Peter which means rock and He told Peter that he would be the foundation of the Church. Jesus empowered Peter to be that strong foundation. Peter did fail several times but Jesus gave him another chance and Peter went on to success. We are the Church of Christ today because of what Peter did. In Peter's first speech at Pentecost, 3000 people became disciples. Peter knew how to make disciples. That same opportunity exists for us today and Jesus has given you that power.

How about you? Do you reach out to others with the Good News? Do you live in such a way as to draw others to you because they want the peace and the life that you have? If we are to make disciples, will we do it by preaching on street corners or by loving those whom God loves and encouraging them to draw close to us and thereby draw close to Him? If Jesus is in your heart, why not let His light shine out into this dark world in which we live? Are you afraid to speak to others about your faith? Why? It is Jesus who will build the Church by His Holy Spirit and through you. Be bold! Wait for the opportunity and speak out your faith. People want and need to hear the truth. 1 Peter 3:15 (NIV) says *"¹⁵ But in your hearts revere Christ as Lord. Always be prepared to give an answer to everyone who asks you to give the reason for the hope that you have. But do this with gentleness and respect....*" You have hope in Christ and the power of the Holy Spirit. Help others to find what you have found and enjoy the peace you have as well.

Father, I thank you that you have given us this hope. Help us this day to share You with those with whom we come in contact. Let the peace which we enjoy become available to others. Help us to make disciples who make disciples. Let Your light shine out and eliminate the darkness of this world. In your name we pray!

## MARCH 14    EITHER WAY
Prayer

Job 1:21 (NKJV)
*²¹ And he said: "Naked I came from my mother's womb, And naked shall I return there. The Lord gave, and the Lord has taken away; Blessed be the name of the Lord."*

When you pray, for what do you pray? Don't you usually ask for what you want? Do we think God is some kind of cosmic vending machine that we can ask for whatever we want? John 14:13 (NKJV) says *¹³ And whatever you ask in My [Jesus] name, that I will do, that the Father may be glorified in the Son.* What does it mean to ask "in My name"? It means to ask for things that are in God's will. Ask for things that will glorify God.

Job had it right! No matter what, blessed be the name of the Lord! Whatever the outcome, God will do what is in your best interest even if you don't like it. God gives what you need more than what you want. Since He knows the plan, He can choose more wisely.

What if we do not get that for which we prayed? Is God:

         a) not capable of delivering; or
         b) uncaring; or
         c) not listening; or
         d) other?

Certainly not! We have a finite capacity to understand an infinite universe. How could we possibly know what the best outcome in any situation should be? Do you think the Creator of that universe knows what would be best? I do! Job went through the loss of health, family and fortune. He was sitting in torn clothes but still in worship of God. He did not sin against God amidst all this calamity. He showed incredible faith. What would you do if you lost everything?

Stay in faith believing God will work all things for your good (Romans 8:28). This may be a test from God or it may be the work of the accuser trying to turn you against God. If you turn things around, I will give you praise Lord. And if it all remains the same, I am still going to give you praise.

"The Lord gives, the Lord takes away. Blessed be the name of the Lord." The Lord's name also means blessing for us as He longs to bless us in all things. Teach me your Word O Lord that I might know you better.

Lord, I thank You that You always have our best interest in mind. I thank You that You work all things for our good. Mostly, I thank You that You don't give us what we want but that You always give us what we need! In Jesus name!

# MARCH 15   HOW MUCH
Grace and Mercy

Luke 14:25-33 (NIV) The Cost of Being a Disciple

[25] *Large crowds were traveling with Jesus, and turning to them he said:* [26] *"If anyone comes to me and does not hate father and mother, wife and children, brothers and sisters—yes, even their own life—such a person cannot be my disciple.* [27] *And whoever does not carry their cross and follow me cannot be my disciple.*

[28] *"Suppose one of you wants to build a tower. Won't you first sit down and estimate the cost to see if you have enough money to complete it?* [29] *For if you lay the foundation and are not able to finish it, everyone who sees it will ridicule you,* [30] *saying, 'This person began to build and wasn't able to finish.'*

[31] *"Or suppose a king is about to go to war against another king. Won't he first sit down and consider whether he is able with ten thousand men to oppose the one coming against him with twenty thousand?* [32] *If he is not able, he will send a delegation while the other is still a long way off and will ask for terms of peace.* [33] *In the same way, those of you who do not give up everything you have cannot be my disciples.*

Do you think Jesus wants you to hate your family? He has spent so much time telling you to love your neighbor. Why would He ask you to hate your family? It doesn't make sense. When I see things like this, I ask myself what is He trying to teach us? He is teaching us to count the cost.

How much will it cost to complete a project? If you want to put an addition on to your house, you go out and get estimates. From those estimates, you can determine if you can afford the addition. Jean and I did that a few years back when we were considering an addition. What we found was the cost was too high for the benefit we would receive. We decided not to go ahead.

What is the cost of following Jesus? You cannot consider money alone. There are many things to consider. There are time, talent and treasure to consider. Time is something that once spent can never be retrieved, Time includes eternity. My friend Brock always asks me what I am willing to give up in order to begin a new undertaking. There are only so many hours per week available so it is a very valid question.

What does it mean to follow Jesus? Doesn't it mean that we are no longer going to live our lives for ourselves, but for Him? What does that look like? What would you be willing to give up in order to follow Jesus? It may cost you everything including your life. Is it worth it? Only you can decide. But for me, it is!

A number of years ago, I was at a Church meeting where we opened with some sort of devotional. We paired up and did the devotional. There is a method of asking the same question several times of a person to see the path the answers take. The question that night was "What would it grieve you to have to give up in order to follow Jesus?" I asked the question of my partner first. She gave me a long list of things like, her home, her education, her family and other things. When it was my turn, I said "Nothing!" I had come to a place in my spiritual walk where I knew everything I had was a gift from Jesus. I have come to trust Him. As a result of that trust, I know He would never take anything from me unless He was going to give me something better. He gave Jean to me. Why would He take her from me? It reminds me of the story of Abraham being asked to sacrifice his only son Isaac. Abraham went ahead with the plan and was about to follow through on God's request when the angel of the Lord called out to him to stop him. Isaac was the Promise God had given Abraham. God would not take away that Promise.

Our focus has been on giving things up to follow Jesus. Since He is the God of abundance and blessing, might we look at this differently? What if Jesus wants you to put Him first in all your thoughts and decisions? What if He wants to be Lord of your life? Maybe He wants to direct your steps and lead you to all the blessings He has stored up for you. Instead of giving up everything for Him, it seems to me He gave everything up for you because He loves you that much! How much? Enough that He gave His own life for you. You are that important to Him!

Lord Jesus, I thank You that You love us enough to give Yourself up for us! By Your Spirit, please guide us in Your ways that we might bring glory to Your Holy Name. Help us to live for You. In Your name we pray.

# MARCH 16 YOU LOVE ME THAT MUCH
## Relationships

John 15:12-16 (NIV)

*¹²My command is this: Love each other as I have loved you. ¹³Greater love has no one than this: to lay down one's life for one's friends. ¹⁴You are my friends if you do what I command. ¹⁵I no longer call you servants, because a servant does not know his master's business. Instead, I have called you friends, for everything that I learned from my Father I have made known to you. ¹⁶You did not choose me, but I chose you and appointed you so that you might go and bear fruit—fruit that will last—and so that whatever you ask in my name the Father will give you.*

How much does God love you? He loves you with a sacrificial love; a love strong enough that He laid down His life for you, literally. And He asks us to love one another as He has loved us. I don't know about you but I am not sure I am ready to lay down my life for someone else. Are you? Also, I don't think I am able to love as Jesus loved. I can try with His help.

What does it mean to lay down one's life for another? Does it mean I have to die to save someone else? Not necessarily. It means to "die to self". When we put the needs of others ahead of our own needs, we die to self or lay down our life for our friends. That is sacrificial love. There are many ways to help others. Listening to those who need to speak, helping someone, being kind, opening a door, encouraging someone and being patient are all ways of loving others. Love is one of the fruits of the Spirit. (Gal 5:22) Agape love is defined as "acting intentionally, in sympathetic response to others (including God) to promote well-being." How can you love someone today? Who is it God wants you to love? Will you keep your eyes open for opportunities?

How does it feel to know you are a friend of Jesus? Jesus chose you as His friend. He appointed you. He shared the "Master's business" with you so you know what He is about. He wants you to go and bear fruit that will last. Galatians 5 tells us *"²²But the fruit of the Spirit is love, joy, peace, patience, kindness, goodness, faithfulness, ²³gentleness and self-control."* These fruits will last! God does not call you to something for which He does not prepare you. He gave you all you need to accomplish the calling. You are appointed. You are called. You are equipped. You are empowered. You are well-able to go and bear fruit. He also gives you a promise! He says "Then the Father will give you whatever you ask in my name." For what will you ask in Jesus name? Will you bear fruit today?

Father I thank You that You love us so much that You laid down your life for us. Thank You for choosing us to bear fruit and giving us the chance to glorify You in that process. Lead us to the person to whom you wish to speak through our lives today!

# MARCH 17     I WANT YOU BACK

Grace and Mercy

Malachi 3:6-7 (NIV)

*6 "I the LORD do not change. So you, the descendants of Jacob, are not destroyed. 7 Ever since the time of your ancestors you have turned away from my decrees and have not kept them. Return to me, and I will return to you," says the LORD Almighty. "But you ask, 'How are we to return?'*

Malachi was written 430 BC. Even then, God had a plan. He always wanted to restore the relationship. God was just waiting for the right time and place. And that time was 463 years later and the place was Jerusalem.

We are reminded the Lord is always the same. That means He is faithful and keeps His promises. One of those promises was He would be our God and we would be His people. Even though we cannot uphold our side of the agreement and follow His decrees, God is patient not wanting any to perish. From the very beginning, God knew *we* could not keep the agreement and had another way to keep us close. His plan was to redeem us through His own sacrifice. We are separated from God when we sin. 1 John 1: 9 says "If we confess our sins, He is faithful and just to forgive us *our* sins and to cleanse us from all unrighteousness" but we do not want to admit our sin. Without that admission, we cannot return. Hence the question "How are we to return?"

Jesus came into the world to bring us back to a right relationship with Him. If we confess our sin and turn away from it, God will take us back. He will remove the sin completely and restore the broken relationship. Our repentance is our return to Him. His redemption could be seen as His return to us. I don't see it that way though. I believe that God is always with us just as He said "I will never leave nor forsake you." We have drifted away. God has never wavered!

Do you want to return to God? Do you want to grow into a deeper relationship with God? Now is the time. This is the season. Here comes the Lamb of God who takes away the sins of the world! Will you let Him take your sin away? Will you return to Him? He longs to take you back!

Thank You Lord that You always had a plan to draw us back to You. Thank You that You never left us. You knew we would stray so You made a way for us to return. Help us this day to return to You! In Your name we pray!

# MARCH 18    WHO WILL STAND UP FOR ME
## Support

Exodus 20 (NKJV) Selected Verses
*18 Now all the people witnessed the thunderings, the lightning flashes, the sound of the trumpet, and the mountain smoking; and when the people saw it, they trembled and stood afar off. 19 Then they said to Moses, "You speak with us, and we will hear; but let not God speak with us, lest we die." 20 And Moses said to the people, "Do not fear; for God has come to test you, and that His fear may be before you, so that you may not sin." 21 So the people stood afar off, but Moses drew near the thick darkness where God was........[The Lord said] In every place where I record My name I will come to you, and I will bless you.*

The Lord had just given the Israelites the Ten Commandments. You might want to go and read the whole chapter to understand the story better. You'll notice He did not call them the Ten Suggestions. After that, Moses came down to the people to share these commandments with the people. The people had seen His awesome power displayed and were terrified.

Why did God give us these Laws? Is it because He wanted to force us to live His way? There is a clue in the text. It says "In every place where I record My name I will come to you, and I will bless you." The Lord's name is recorded in these commandments. Therefore, since He is true to His word, we can know there are blessings in these commandments since the Lord's name is recorded there.

Jennifer Benson Schuldt said in Our Daily Bread "Because God is perfectly holy and we are desperately sinful, we cannot relate to Him. We need a go between, an Intercessor." Romans 8:34 (NKJV) says *"34 Who is he who condemns? It is Christ who died, and furthermore is also risen, who is even at the right hand of God, who also makes intercession for us."* Moses was the person who spoke for the Israelites. Jesus speaks for us now. We have an advocate who sits at the right hand of the Father and pleads our case. The Prosecutor is close to the Judge and the Prosecutor wants to help you and plead down the sentence. In fact, the Prosecutor is willing and has already paid the fine. You are forgiven. You are already justified. You are redeemed. You are blessed! Thanks be to God for His love of us! Go live as the Redeemed and see how you can lighten the load of another today. Will you share your story of redemption?

Thank You Lord for your intercession on our behalf. Thank You that You walk with us watching out for us at all times. Thank You that, wherever You record (or we speak) Your name that You will come and bless us! It is in Your name we pray! Amen!

## MARCH 19    HE IS RISEN SO WE CAN RISE
Faith

1 Corinthians 15:3-4 (NKJV)

*³ For I delivered to you first of all that which I also received: that Christ died for our sins according to the Scriptures, ⁴ and that He was buried, and that He rose again the third day according to the Scriptures,*

What do you fear most? The majority of people rank public speaking higher on the scale of fear even over dying. So, for arguments sake, let's rate dying as number two. Are you afraid of dying? What if I told you that you could overcome that fear and live forever? Would you want to know about it? Probably.

There is One who has overcome sin and death and lives to share that gift with you. Paul is the writer of this verse and the Book of Corinthians. Paul says what he received, he also delivered to us. So it is with Christ. What He received from the Father, the gift of forgiveness and eternal life, He also delivered to us. All we have to do is put our faith and trust in Him. In John 1:12 it says *"Yet to all who received Him...He gave the right to become children of God."* Are you a child of God? Do you want to be?

Hospitality was a big deal in ancient times. Greeting people and bringing them into your home was imperative. How do you greet people today? Jesus is coming. Will you receive Him? What stands in your way? Do you know how to receive Him? Is the house clean enough? On our fridge, we have a sign which says "Our House was clean last week; too bad you missed it!" Jesus doesn't care about your house. He only cares about your Temple and He is willing to clean the Temple up for you! He will clean the Temple in which His Holy Spirit will reside (your heart) if you will open the door to Him. Today, open the door. No excuses! Let Him come in and abide with you and love you. His love will make you feel better than you ever felt before!

Lord, You said You would abide with us if we invite You in. Help us today to overcome our fears and excuses and boldly throw open the door to our hearts. We know we will never be the same. Help us to be the people You called us to be. In Your name we pray!

## MARCH 20 SALVATION IS HERE.
## DO YOU SEE IT? DO YOU HEAR IT? DO YOU FEEL IT?

Faith

2 Corinthians 6:1-2 (NIV)

*As God's co-workers we urge you not to receive God's grace in vain.* [2] *For he says, "In the time of my favor I heard you, and in the day of salvation I helped you." I tell you, now is the time of God's favor, now is the day of salvation.*

Some people say seeing is believing but it ain't necessarily so. Illusionists show you things that are not real. Do you believe what you see? Do you believe things you cannot see? Are you aware that salvation is now here? At this time of year, we are reminded that God entered the world to reconcile us to Himself. The Kingdom of God is here and now in the spiritual sense. Zig Ziglar speaks of the way you look at things (attitude) making a difference. You can take the letters "n o w h e r e" and determine that the kingdom is "now here" or "nowhere" - you decide. Is your heart open to the kingdom? It can be seen through the eyes of faith.

My Pastor Don interviewed people who had heard God speak to them. I wrote down what they said. When I went to Honduras last year, I heard God speak to me. I put those things together and this is what we heard. "Trust me!" "I am all around you." "It'll be OK." He spoke these words and He is faithful. I choose to believe.

I know others have heard God speak but many are afraid to tell the story for fear others will think they are crazy. I maintain that God still speaks today. Write me if you have heard Him! I am going to tell those stories in my next book.

Now is the time of God's favor. He wants to be with you and He wants you to be with Him. Isaiah 55:6 says *"Seek the Lord while he may be found; call on him while he is near."* The Lord is always near. He is all around you. He stands ready willing and able to help you. A Leper asked Jesus if He was willing to make him clean. Jesus replied that He was willing. He is willing to help you too! Why not call on Him because He hears you too?

Father, we thank You that You hear us and are willing to help us. Open our hearts to Your presence. You said You would never leave us nor forsake us. You said You are willing to heal us! You said this is the time of Your grace and favor! Pour out that favor upon us and let us share it with those whom we meet. In Jesus name we pray.

# MARCH 21     WHAT DOES IT MEAN TO BE REMEMBERED BY JESUS

Failure

Luke 23 (NKJV) Selected Verses

[39] *One of the criminals who hung there hurled insults at him:* [40] *But the other criminal rebuked him [the first criminal]. "Don't you fear God?......* [41] *We are punished justly....* [42] *Then he said, "Jesus, remember me when you come into your kingdom."* [43] *Jesus answered him, "I tell you the truth, today you will be with me in paradise."*

Have you ever wondered if the things you have done would prevent you from being accepted by God? Many have said they have done bad things and God would never forgive them. Enter the thief on the cross. When Jesus was crucified, He was in between two criminals. We are not totally sure what these criminals did but some interpretations have said they were insurrectionists. Those are heavy charges deserving the death penalty. Crucifixion was the cruelest type of capital punishment that the Romans used to teach people a lesson about not defying the Roman Empire. These were bad guys.

The one thief understood who Jesus really was. How could he know Jesus was the Son of God? What had he heard? We do not know how but it could have been by faith through the Holy Spirit. Nevertheless, He knew and feared God. What do you think he felt about being forgiven for his sins? Since human nature is to compare ourselves to others, do you think your sins are worse than his? It is amazing he had a bold enough faith to even ask for forgiveness. But here is the thing. Because he was bold enough to ask, Jesus was bold enough to forgive. There is one more consideration. Jesus knows what is in your heart. The thief was repentant and contrite or he would not have been forgiven. He admitted he was being punished justly. 1 John 1:9 says "If we confess our sins, He is faithful and just and will forgive us our sins and cleanse us from all unrighteousness." Ask Him! It doesn't matter what you have done. He loves you for who you are. He knows how you were made. He knows what you can and can't do. He loves you anyway! Remember Him and He will remember you. Paradise awaits!

Thank You Lord that You love us anyway! You love us no matter what we have done. You said we are holy, righteous and redeemed by the actions You have taken. We are forgiven by Your grace! Thank You. Amen!

# MARCH 22     I FOUND IT (HIM)
## Grace and Mercy

Luke 15:1-7 (NIV) The Parable of the Lost Sheep

*¹ Now the tax collectors and sinners were all gathering around to hear Jesus. ² But the Pharisees and the teachers of the law muttered, "This man welcomes sinners and eats with them."*
*³ Then Jesus told them this parable: ⁴ "Suppose one of you has a hundred sheep and loses one of them. Doesn't he leave the ninety-nine in the open country and go after the lost sheep until he finds it? ⁵ And when he finds it, he joyfully puts it on his shoulders ⁶ and goes home. Then he calls his friends and neighbors together and says, 'Rejoice with me; I have found my lost sheep.' ⁷ I tell you that in the same way there will be more rejoicing in heaven over one sinner who repents than over ninety-nine righteous persons who do not need to repent.*

It has been said that the surest way to find something is to buy its replacement. That happened to me with a test meter. I finally bought the test meter I always wanted and misplaced it after a project. It was "lost" for 6 months. I needed to have one so I went on eBay and bought one similar to replace it. Shortly after, I was cleaning up my workshop and found the original. Boy was I happy! That which was lost in now found.

Who or what have you lost? Or is it you that feels lost and alone? You don't have to remain in those feelings. Some people may not even realize they are lost. They know something is missing but they are not really sure what it is. Do you feel something may be missing in your life? Jesus came to seek that which was lost. But more than just seek, He came to redeem that which was lost. Our world is a lost world. Communication is diminishing. People don't talk to each other, they text. We get so caught up in all our own things that we don't notice others. Relationships suffer. Many in busy metropolitan areas are lonely. Life expectancy is dropping in the U.S. because of the increase in suicide rates.

Relationships are of primary importance to God. He created this universe to facilitate fellowship with us. Relationships would restore what was lost. Do you want to be found? Do you have a relationship with Jesus? Does He call you friend? He is looking for you. He wants to build a relationship that can redeem that which was and is lost. There will be celebration in heaven for each relationship that is restored. Oh, that there would be celebration over you or one of yours!

What is the blessing here? You were not made to be alone. You were made to be in relationship and the primary relationship is with Your Creator. He stands close by ready to redeem and restore you. He wants to be your friend. He longs to bless you holding you in the center of His will. Will you let Him? He is even willing to hang out with sinners like you and me.

Lord, thank You that You care for us so much that You come searching for us. You said we are Your sheep and You are our Shepherd. As our Shepherd, guide us in Your ways. Lead us in Your pastures, beside still waters and restore our souls. Amen!

## MARCH 23    WHO IS THIS MAN
Faith

John 1:29-31 (NIV) John Testifies About Jesus

*29 The next day John saw Jesus coming toward him and said, "Look, the Lamb of God, who takes away the sin of the world! 30 This is the one I meant when I said, 'A man who comes after me has surpassed me because he was before me.' 31 I myself did not know him, but the reason I came baptizing with water was that he might be revealed to Israel."*

Have you wondered about the identity of Jesus? How could some people recognize Him while others denied who He was? John knew when he saw Jesus. How did he know? There are still doubts for many. How about you?

Here is the scene. John, this strange character (eats locusts and wild honey), is out in Bethany by the Jordon river baptizing people into the Kingdom of God. The Pharisees have sent a delegation to ask John if he is the Christ, the Anointed One. John says no. They press him for more details and He quotes Isaiah 40:3 saying "I am the voice of one calling in the desert, Make straight the way for the Lord." They ask him why he is baptizing and he replies "...among you stands one you do not know. He is the one who comes after me. The thongs of whose sandals I am not worthy to untie." Back in verse 15, John told them about the One who comes after him. In 14, he told them the Word became flesh. It was clear who Jesus was according to prophecy.

Have you ever known something and you just knew you were right? After investigation, you were correct. Sometimes, inside, you just know. I knew Jean would be my wife after first meeting her. There was just something special inside telling me to ask her. Of course, she had to think about it. She has never been one to decide anything quickly. I guess her reputation for making careful choices is a good thing as we have been together more than 40 years. If you have ever experienced something like this, you understand what happened next. John sees Jesus approaching and says *"29 Look, the Lamb of God, who takes away the sin of the world!"* There is significance to the "Lamb" part also. The Lamb points to the sacrifice that God ordained in the Old Testament (Leviticus) that people could offer in place of their own death for their sin; a substitution. Jesus also became the Paschal (Passover) Lamb that protected Israel from the Angel of Death during the Exodus from Egypt and still protects us today.

John goes on to say "...the reason I came baptizing with water is that he might be revealed to Israel." John's purpose was to reveal Jesus to Israel and us. John tells how he knew Jesus was the One. "He was told by the one who sent him to baptize 'The One on whom you see the Spirit come down and remain is he who will baptize with the Holy Spirit.' I have seen and I testify that this is the Son of God." Has He been revealed to you? Do you still have doubts? What will it take to convince you? You have heard from an eye witness.

John also tells us "12 Yet to all who believed in him, to those who believed in his name, he gave the right to become children of God...." That is an incredible offer. I have accepted it and hope you will too! Do you want to be a child of God? Ask Him! He is waiting for you. He wishes none to perish.

Lord thank You that You wait patiently for us to come to You in our own time. By Your Spirit, draw us to You. Prepare our hearts to receive You. May we hear John's voice preparing the way and leading us to the Lamb of God! In Your name we pray!

# MARCH 24    THERE'LL BE NO CONDEMNATION HERE
Grace and Mercy

John 8 (NKJV) Selected Verses

*3 Then the scribes and Pharisees brought to Him a woman caught in adultery. And when they had set her in the midst, 4 they said to Him, "Teacher, this woman was caught in adultery, in the very act. 5 Now Moses, in the law, commanded us that such should be stoned. But what do You say?".... 7 So when they continued asking Him, He raised Himself up and said to them, "He who is without sin among you, let him throw a stone at her first." ...And Jesus was left alone, and the woman standing in the midst. ...., He said to her, "Woman, where are those accusers of yours? Has no one condemned you?" 11 She said, "No one, Lord." And Jesus said to her, "Neither do I condemn you; go and sin no more."*

What is the worst thing you have ever done? Does anyone know about it? Have you kept the secret all these years? What if someone found out? Would it be embarrassing or devastating? It could be awful?

This woman's sin has just been made public! She stands before her accusers and they are ready to stone her to death for her crime. Adultery is a capital offense in that society. What do you think it should be today?

The Pharisees don't really care about this woman. There Law was clear. She was caught in adultery and should be stoned to death. By the way, where was the man with whom she was caught? Shouldn't he be there facing the music too? I digress. Why did they bring her to Jesus? They told about the Law and then said "...Now what do you say?" They were trying to trick Jesus into disagreeing with the Law. How did that work out for them? Jesus turned the whole thing around on them. They thought they would trick Him into breaking the Law to save this woman. He took it to a whole other level.

Jesus did not change the Law. He said in Matthew 5:17 that He had not come to abolish the Law but to fulfill it. He was not about to set the Law of His Father aside. The Law said she deserved death.  We all deserve death. But Jesus came that we might have life and have it more abundantly. He had a whole new plan. He would take the responsibility of the sin on Himself.

Jesus asked the accusers to go ahead and stone her if, they themselves, had no sin. One by one, they dropped their stones and walked away. There is none without sin for all have sinned and fall short of the glory of God. Instead of stoning her, they just learned of their own shortcomings. Not one of them was without sin and neither are we. Do you look down at other people in judgment? There is only one Judge and we are not Him. It is our job to love and leave the judging to God. Jesus asked her if there was anyone who condemned her. They all left her with Jesus alone. He said "Then neither do I condemn you...Go and sin no more." What an amazing gift! She was dragged there to be stoned to death and is given grace instead. Do you want grace? I do!

Lord, thank you for Your grace which is incomprehensible. We can never earn it or deserve it but You freely give us this gift. Guide us aright with Your good counsel but, when we do fail, quickly come to our aid and restore us to You. Lord, You make all things new. Renew our spirit today and help us to bring glory to You in word and deed. In Your name we pray.

# MARCH 25    HOW CAN I DO THIS
Faith

Hebrews 2:17-18 (NKJV)
*17 Therefore, in all things He had to be made like His brethren, that He might be a merciful and faithful High Priest in things pertaining to God, to make propitiation for the sins of the people. 18 For in that He Himself has suffered, being tempted, He is able to aid those who are tempted.*

Life is tough! Each day, many of us face challenges that seem beyond what we can bear. We wonder how we can get through these times. How can we live in this world and still be faithful to God's will? It seems impossible. If there was only someone who had already done it that we could ask for guidance. Why do we have to go through all this anyway?

We go through trials sometimes just to teach us what it is like to face a certain challenge. In 2000, I got fired from a job I should not have lost. I was hired by a Vice President who left the company. They replaced him with a much younger man who did not know the business. I won the Vice President's Award for Outstanding Service in January and was fired in July. I decided to sue the company for wrongful termination because I felt it was age discrimination and I was in a protected age class. Going through the process led me to depositions where I had to repeat the story many times. Each time I did, it was another blow to my self-esteem until I ended up in deep depression, the kind where you can't leave the house! I learned a lot about how debilitating that can be and how devastating to our lives. At that time, I would have given up altogether except for the glimmer of hope that was my faith. I had questions like "How could God let this happen to me?". It was only years later that I understood. I was not supposed to be working for a corporation. I could do more for the Kingdom on my own. Also, God wanted me to understand depression fully – from the inside – so I would know what it was like and how to help others. When I tell someone with depression "I know how you feel!", I really do understand. I learned many things which I have successfully used to help others through the darkness! I can help people back into the daylight because of what God has taught me through my own circumstances.

Hebrews 2 tells us about the One to whom we can turn who fully understands our plight. Jesus has been through every temptation that we face having been fully made like us so that He can understand what it is like. It is not sympathy, it is empathy! He knows what we are going through intimately.

What's more, He is our Faithful High Priest. As High Priest, He advocates for us with the Father. He is merciful and faithful. But the best part is that, not only will He help us through, He is willing to bear the burden and the costs of our sins and failures. He is ready, willing and able to aid us in the trials we go through. His mercy endures forever! Speak with Him. He understands.

Lord, we thank You that You fully understand our plight and come to our aid when we need You. Thank you that You are merciful and show us the way through the trials.

Give us strength for today and hope for tomorrow as we live our lives for and with You!

# MARCH 26    LEAVE ROOM FOR GOD – HE WILL MAKE IT ALL WORK

Faith

Numbers 14:39-45 (NIV) Selected Verses
*"We have sinned" they said. We will go to the place the Lord promised.".*[41] *But Moses said "Why are you disobeying the Lord's command? This will not succeed! Do not go up because the Lord is not with you. You will be defeated by your enemies..."*

The Israelites had just sent twelve spies into the Promised Land to see what it was like so they would know what they were up against. Ten of the twelve spies gave a negative report because they could not believe they could defeat the people living in the land. They disregarded God's promise to *give* them the land. God became angry with them for not believing His promise. When God threatened to destroy them, they half-heartedly said they would go up and take the land. At that point, God was not with them. They would have to go it alone and they were not able to accomplish the victory. Moses told them not to go but they went anyway and were repelled.

It always works best when we follow God's plan. To do that, we need to prayerfully discern the plan. When we try to do things in our own power, it does not work out well. When God goes before us, He makes crooked places straight. We can stand and watch what the Lord will do. God promised to give Israel the land and He is faithful. When Israel tried on their own, they were defeated. Later under Joshua, when they followed God's plan, the walls of Jericho fell at their trumpet blast because it was God's doing.

Are you doing things in your own power? What has the Lord called you to do? Are you following His will for your life and being blessed or do you feel it is an uphill battle? Do you think God has given you all the answers and you can do it on your own now? You may not like those results.

Ephesians 6:13 says *"Therefore, put on the full armor of God, so that when the day of evil comes, you may be able to stand your ground, and after you have done everything, to stand."* Have you heard the expression "Let go and let God."? You are to do all you can and let God do what you can't. When you are in the center of His will, He will fight your battles! He will give you the desires of your heart. He is known as Jehovah Jireh, the Lord our Provider.

Do you want success or defeat? When I was offered the opportunity to go to Honduras in 2014, I prayed for God's guidance about the trip. When I was still, I got the calling to go. I was going to a foreign country 3000 miles from home. I did not speak the language. I had never been out of the USA. I did not know any of the people on the trip. I did not know the job I would be doing. I was completely out of my comfort zone but not afraid. The whole time, I felt protected. Everything went well. The people were all wonderful and I felt comfortable like I was guided and loved. I knew God was with me. In fact, He said "Trust Me!" That is how I want all my life to be. I want to live as God wants me to live. How about you?

115

Father, I thank You for Your protection and grace. I thank You that You know what's best for us and You always lead us in the right path if we will just listen. Thank You for going before us making the paths straight and blessing us in our daily walk with You! Amen!

# MARCH 27     ONE WISH – WHAT IS YOUR REQUEST
Faith

Luke 18:35-43 (NKJV) Selected Verses A Blind Man Receives His Sight

*35 Then it happened, as He was coming near Jericho, that a certain blind man sat by the road begging. ····· 38 And he cried out, saying, "Jesus, Son of David, have mercy on me!" 40 So Jesus stood still and commanded him to be brought to Him. And when he had come near, He asked him, 41 saying, "What do you want Me to do for you?" He said, "Lord, that I may receive my sight." 42 Then Jesus said to him, "Receive your sight; your faith has made you well." 43 And immediately he received his sight, and followed Him, glorifying God. And all the people, when they saw it, gave praise to God.*

If you were face-to-face with Jesus, believing He could grant your wish and He asked what you wanted Him to do for you, what would you request? Do you know what you want? Would you even be bold enough to "cry out"?

One of the things that comes out in the story is the man's boldness. People tried to shut him up but he wouldn't have any of it. He continued to cry out. He had faith that could be seen or, in his case, heard! He knew this was "the Son of David" long prophesied. Do you believe Jesus can grant your request? Way down deep in your heart, is there faith that He can see? Many people say they believe but would they go out on a limb on that belief? Would you take the chance? This man believed down in his soul! 42 Then Jesus said to him, "Receive your sight; your faith has made you well." Jesus saw his faith and granted his request. He received his sight. The man was appreciative and followed Jesus, glorifying God!

Here is another important key. When God does something for you, do you glorify Him? Do you give Him praise? Our purpose is "to glorify God and enjoy Him forever"! Are you doing that? What have you done for Him lately? Have you pointed others to God with your praise?

Lord, thank You that You are willing and able to grant our requests. You said You will do anything we ask in Your name. By Your Holy Spirit, guide us in what to ask! Give us the desires of our hearts. In Your name and to Your glory, we go out to live this day! Amen!

## MARCH 28     SAVING SINNERS AND TAX COLLECTORS
### Grace and Mercy

Luke 19:1-10 (NKJV) Selected Verses - Jesus Comes to Zacchaeus' House
*Then Jesus entered and passed through Jericho. ²Now behold, there was a man named Zacchaeus who was a chief tax collector, and he was rich. ³And he sought to see who Jesus was, but could not because of the crowd, ⁵And when Jesus came to the place, He looked up and saw him, and said to him, "Zacchaeus, make haste and come down, for today I must stay at your house." ........⁷But when they saw it, they all complained, saying, "He has gone to be a guest with a man who is a sinner.".......⁹And Jesus said to him, "Today salvation has come to this house, because he also is a son of Abraham; ¹⁰for the Son of Man has come to seek and to save that which was lost."*

Parents sometimes say, when their child gets in trouble, the he or she just got mixed up with the wrong crowd. For we know the people with whom you associate have an effect on you. What about this Jesus character hanging out with sinners and tax collectors? What will people think? They all complained, saying "He has gone to be a guest with a man who is a sinner." *They* were unhappy. We know Jesus did not care what people thought but why would he associate with a *tax collector*? They were considered the worst of the worst.

You may have noticed Jesus did not go to the community leaders with His message of grace and forgiveness. Those leaders thought they already had God's favor. They were not interested in Jesus' message. "He came to that which was his own, but his own did not receive him." (John 1:11) God's message and Word will not be thwarted! If the leaders would not receive Him, someone would! So why did He come? He came to seek and save that which was lost. He came for you and me! Thanks be to God that He did!

Zacchaeus received salvation that day because he believed in Jesus. Salvation is available to you and me today as well because He came. He seeks you. There is no place where He cannot find you and He will search to the ends of the earth. You are that important to Him. You are his masterpiece. You, too, are a son of Abraham and a son (or daughter) of God! Will you receive Him today?

Lord, we thank You that You never give up on us. We thank You that You will search until you find us and we find You. We praise You because we are fearfully and wonderfully made. Bring Your salvation to our house this day. In Jesus name we pray!

# MARCH 29     IT'S RIGHT HERE

Encouragement

Luke 17:20-21 (NIV) The Coming of the Kingdom of God

*20 Once, on being asked by the Pharisees when the kingdom of God would come, Jesus replied, "The coming of the kingdom of God is not something that can be observed, 21 nor will people say, 'Here it is,' or 'There it is,' because the kingdom of God is in your midst."*

Sometimes, people are so busy looking for something they do not see what is right in front of them. They can't see the forest for the trees! Are you like that? Are you looking for the Kingdom? Where would be the best place to start looking?

I used to think the Kingdom of heaven was something I would see only after passing from this world. I thought I had to endure this life in order to earn my mansion in Heaven. I did not realize that, in God's realm, there are more dimensions than humans can see in our finite lives. There is more than meets the eye.

The Bible often speaks to us on different levels. We think it is talking about the physical level and it is in the spiritual realm. So it is with the Kingdom of Heaven. There is the real place and then there is the place in your heart. If you trust Jesus, He enters your heart and abides there. Any place where God has placed His name and resides is the Kingdom. Therefore, the Kingdom of God is here and now and living inside of you. If the Kingdom is inside you, how should you live? Should you live blessed? Should you live joyful? Should you have peace? Should you let the light of God's glory shine out from within? Yes, to all of the above. Live like a child of the King because that is what you are. Be bold. Enjoy God's presence. Let Him lead your life. Light up the room when you enter. Encourage others. Spread the good news that there is hope. Leave them wondering what is going on inside you!

Father, I thank you that you abide with us. I thank you that You are near and care for us. It is comforting to know that we are Yours and You are close. Help us to share the Kingdom and Your love with those we meet. In Your name we pray.

## MARCH 30    FAN THE FLAMES
Faith

Luke 24:13-35 Selected Verses (NKJV) The Road to Emmaus

*13 Now behold, two of them were traveling that same day to a village called Emmaus, which was seven miles from Jerusalem. 14 And they talked together of all these things which had happened. 15 So it was, while they conversed and reasoned, that Jesus Himself drew near and went with them. 16 But their eyes were restrained, so that they did not know Him...21 But we were hoping that it was He who was going to redeem Israel...28 Then they drew near to the village where they were going, and He indicated that He would have gone farther. 29 But they constrained Him, saying, "Abide with us, for it is toward evening, and the day is far spent." And He went in to stay with them. 30 Now it came to pass, as He sat at the table with them, that He took bread, blessed and broke it, and gave it to them. 31 Then their eyes were opened and they knew Him; and He vanished from their sight. 32 And they said to one another, "Did not our heart burn within us while He talked with us on the road, and while He opened the Scriptures to us?"*

Do you recognize the King of Kings? Does your heart burn within you when you think of Jesus? Is there a fire burning in your soul? Do you share that passion with those you meet? If you do, do you share that knowledge with others? Since you were made in the image and likeness of God, can people see the family resemblance? What do they see when they look at you?

I came to know Jesus in 1998. I was on the road to Basking Ridge when He got in the minivan with me. He spoke to me and it scared me. In fact, I drove 45 minutes past my exit trying to figure out what had just happened. I was a volunteer with a Church Youth Group but had not made a commitment to Christ as of yet. I decided to read the New Testament to see what all the ruckus was about. It is always good to know the opposing side, I thought. I have come to know there is only one side and it is God's side. The rest doesn't matter.

Wow! So that's what all those Prophets were talking about. Holy cow! This Jesus was and is amazing. Could all this be true? I was skeptical but I had to find out. I was a doubter at that point. Now, I know that doubters are *seekers* and it is good to doubt! Thomas doubted and discovered "My Lord and my God" (John 20:28). Thomas now believed. After Jesus entered the minivan, so did I believe! Now what? Who could I tell? Would they believe me? It took a month before I told anyone and it was my fellow youth worker that I told. She said what any good Presbyterian would say. She said "I think you should talk to the Pastor." And I did. That led to my Baptism.

Are you on fire for the Lord? The fire can start slowly and smolder for a long time or it can burst into flames. What would it take to get it to burst into flames within you? Does the Bible speak to you in ways you cannot explain? Does Jesus call out to you? Can you hear Him? Will you answer that call or will you ignore Him? He is coming! He is willing to walk with you on the road to Emmaus or Basking Ridge or anywhere else for that matter. He loves you! Are you ready? Put on your walking shoes and take the journey. I promise you won't be disappointed. Start a fire and fan the flames! Stir up the gift of God which is in you today.

Father thanks that You are sending Your Son to light the fire within us and fan those flames of Your gifts, love and mercy. Walk with us and teach us how we carry Your image within us. Teach us to be bold and use the gifts You give us to build the Kingdom. Teach us to shine Your light for others. Thank You that Your Kingdom is within us here and now. Help us to live lives as children of the King of Kings. In Your name we pray!

# MARCH 31    WHAT HE WOULDN'T DO FOR YOU

### Grace and Mercy

Isaiah 53:5 (NIV)

*5 But he was pierced for our transgressions, he was crushed for our iniquities; the punishment that brought us peace was on him, and by his wounds we are healed.*

When someone loves you, they do extraordinary things for you. What would you do for your family? What would you do for a stranger? How far would you go? We have heard stories of people who have donated kidneys to others or have taken a bullet for someone.

What kind of love makes someone go through crucifixion? The kind that wants to reconcile the whole world back to God. All of creation was separated from God by Eve's sin. There was a lot to reconcile. Jesus came to make a way for us all to return to God. You see, since the time of Adam and Eve, we had committed a lot of sins. There was a lot to reconcile.

Isaiah lived 750 years before the birth of Christ. He prophesied the events that would free us from sin and death. Jesus was pierced in His side by the Centurion. He was beaten and tortured and then crucified, all so He could take upon Himself our transgressions. He became the Passover Sacrifice that averted the Angel of Death from us. By His wounds we are healed. Because of what Jesus did, we are redeemed. He did all that for you and for me! He died so we can live. Incredible! How will you live?

Lord, we thank You for what You have done for us. You bought us back at a terrible price. How can we understand how much we mean to You that You would submit Yourself to this brutal death? You have redeemed us from sin and death. We can barely comprehend what You have done nor why You did it but we gladly accept Your grace! Amen!

# APRIL 1        ARE YOU KIDDING ME

Encouragement

1 Corinthians 1:18, 21 (NIV)

*18"For the message of the cross is FOOLISHNESS to those who are perishing, but to us who are being saved it is the power of God ... 21 For since in the wisdom of God the world through its wisdom did not know him, God was pleased through the foolishness of what was preached to save those who believe*

Easter time brings us once again to the celebration of the foolishness of the cross. YOU GOTTA BE A FOOL to believe the message of the cross and the message of the gospel – God coming to die on a cross for us. Yeah, right! Why would He do that? It seems utterly ridiculous. No one would do that, or would they?

It is incomprehensible that God would do what He did for us. But the proof is in the death and resurrection of Jesus. He did that for us. On this day of Pranks, I want you to know the message of the Cross and our redemption is No Joke! God loves you enough to give Himself up for you. He paid a painful price to ransom you from sin and death. You are *that* special and important to Him.

Then there is this story about the atheist holiday. An atheist became incensed over the preparation for Easter and Passover holidays and decided to contact the local ACLU about the discrimination inflicted on atheists by the constant celebrations afforded to Christians and Jews with all their holidays while the atheists had no holiday to celebrate. The ACLU jumped on the opportunity to once again pick up the cause of the godless. The case was brought before a wise judge who after listening to the long, passionate presentation of the ACLU lawyers, promptly banged his gavel and declared, "Case dismissed!"

The ACLU lawyer immediately objected and said, "Your honor, how can you possibly dismiss this case? Surely the Christians have many observances as do the Jews and yet my client and all other atheists have no such holiday!"

The judge leaned forward in his chair and simply said "Obviously your client is too confused to know about, or for that matter, even celebrate the atheists' holiday!" The ACLU lawyer pompously said: "We are aware of no such holiday for atheists. Just when might that be, Your Honor?"

The judge said, "Well, it comes every year on exactly the same date — April 1st! *"The fool says in his heart, "There is no God."* — Psalm 14:1

You've just been pranked but with some seriousness involved. I hope I got at least a little chuckle out of you. Enjoy the day, laugh a lot and be blessed. Share your joy with others. God loves you and so do I!

## APRIL 2    YOUR REDEEMER LIVES
Grace and Mercy

2 Corinthians 5:18-19 (NKJV)

*18 Now all things are of God, who has reconciled us to Himself through Jesus Christ, and has given us the ministry of reconciliation, 19 that is, that God was in Christ reconciling the world to Himself, not imputing their trespasses to them, and has committed to us the word of reconciliation.*

How does it feel to know God is willing to help you with the things that have gone wrong in your life? We have all gone our own way but yet He waits for us to return to Him. He wants us to be reconciled to Him. He never wanted us to be separated. We chose to disobey. In fact, He wants us to bring reconciliation to others as well. We are to lead by example.

Adam and Eve were expelled from the Garden and separated from God. Hell is described as separation from God. Jesus, while on the cross, spoke of being forsaken by God. We were made to be in His presence. Anything else is not good. Since we decided to go down a path that led away from God, He had to create a plan for our return. Jesus is that plan. God, in Christ, is working out our redemption and return to His presence. Since Christ accepted the burden of our transgressions upon Himself, redemption is through Him. Our trespasses are not imputed to us. They are upon Christ. We are now reconciled to God if we accept His grace.

What does this all mean? Imagine you are driving on the highway and there is a pile-up of cars in front of you such that you can't avoid. It looks like there is no way out. Suddenly, out of nowhere, a way opens up through which you are guided that takes you around the accident and you are completely safe on the other side. Someone or something has prevented what looked like serious injury or even death. What was that? That was the favor of God protecting you. God has redeemed you from this trouble. He wants the best for you.

God has made a way for you if you will just follow Him. 1 Corinthians 10:13 says "No temptation has seized you except which is common to man.... But when you are tempted, he will also provide a way out so that you can stand up under it." He is faithful to carry you through. Will you let Him? Do you complain when things go wrong or do you look for that "way out"? It is there. Keep your eyes and ears open and remain in faith. Your Redeemer lives!

Father, we thank You that You always provide a way out. Help us this day to remain in faith and look to you for the solution. We know you are there. Make Your presence and Your will known to us at each turn. Help us to live in such a way as to cause others to notice and be drawn to You. In Your name we pray. Amen!

# APRIL 3  HE IS RISEN INDEED

Grace and Mercy

1 Corinthians 15:12-20 (NKJV) Selected Verses - The Risen Christ, Our Hope

*12 Now if Christ is preached that He has been raised from the dead, how do some among you say that there is no resurrection of the dead? 13 But if there is no resurrection of the dead, then Christ is not risen. 14 And if Christ is not risen, then our preaching is empty and your faith is also empty. 15 Yes, and we are found false witnesses of God, because we have testified of God that He raised up Christ, whom He did not raise up—if in fact the dead do not rise. 16 For if the dead do not rise, then Christ is not risen. 17 And if Christ is not risen, your faith is futile; you are still in your sins!.........*
*20 But now Christ is risen from the dead, and has become the firstfruits of those who have fallen asleep [died].*

Do you believe Christ was raised from the dead? I do! That is one of the basic tenants of the Christian faith. There is a greeting on Easter Morning of "He is risen indeed." I serve a Risen Lord. I see myself as an Easter Christian. Many focus on Good Friday (Strange name for the day of death of our Lord) and cannot see the blessings to come. It may be called Good Friday because of all the good God worked for us in the death and resurrection of the Lord.

I know many bad things happened that lead to the death of Jesus. But my focus is beyond the death to the resurrection. I am an optimist. I always look for the good in every situation. Yea though I walk through the valley of the shadow of death, I don't intend to stop there. My Lord calls me to go through the valley, as He did, to the table He has prepared for me on the other side.

Are you walking? Will you continue through the valley? Do you see the table set before you? You have to look through your eyes of faith to see this table. If you look carefully, you will see Jesus at the head of the table and there is a place card with your name on it a few places away from Him. Do you want to sit on His right or His left? Look again. You will see Him beckoning for you to come, sit by Him. Go ahead! He has saved that place just for you. He is risen and waits for you!

Lord thank you that You are risen and offer us a seat at Your table. It is incomprehensible that You would save that place for us. Thank You that Your love for us knows no bounds. Help us to hear Your voice and answer the call to come to You. In Your name we pray. Amen!

# APRIL 4  IT IS FINISHED
Encouragement

John 19:28-30 (NKJV) It Is Finished

*28 After this, Jesus, knowing that all things were now accomplished, that the Scripture might be fulfilled, said, "I thirst!" 29 Now a vessel full of sour wine was sitting there; and they filled a sponge with sour wine, put it on hyssop, and put it to His mouth. 30 So when Jesus had received the sour wine, He said, "It is finished!" And bowing His head, He gave up His spirit.*

It is finished! What is finished? How could this happen? Wasn't He supposed to liberate Israel? What things were "now accomplished"? And now he is dead. What are we going to do now? I thought for sure He would free us from oppression! I am so disappointed. The two on the road to Emmaus echoed what many were thinking.

Most people thought that Messiah (Christ) would be a Mighty King that would come in power and liberate Israel from Roman occupation and restore the glory of the former kingdom. Isaiah 9:6 says *"6 For unto us a Child is born, Unto us a Son is given; And the government will be upon His shoulder. And His name will be called Wonderful, Counselor, Mighty God, Everlasting Father, Prince of Peace."* It is no wonder they would think Christ would be a conquering king since the Prophet Isaiah said the government would be upon His shoulder. But God had a different plan. He wanted to go another way. He was doing a new thing. God knew that Rome was a temporary problem for Israel. Sin, on the other hand, was a bigger issue!

God came to the weak to shame the strong and to the poor and uneducated to shame the wealthy and the religious leaders. He turned everything we know about wealth, strength and power upside down. This plan was inconceivable to us. God would take on human form and come to the lowly to spread His message to the ends of the earth. He would entrust the greatest news ever to a fisherman, a tax collector and others that society would never have chosen. And on top of that, he would offer Himself as the only sacrifice needed to redeem us. Aren't we supposed to serve Him? How is it that He came to serve us?

At this point, all the hopes and dreams of redemption seem dead along with Jesus. The religious leaders had struck the Shepherd and the flock had scattered as they predicted. Or did they? In hindsight, we see they stepped back to regroup. They had to have time to process what had just happened. Looking back from our vantage point, we know the "rest of the story" as Paul Harvey [a News Anchor from days gone by] would say. *We* have seen beyond the death to the resurrection. It looks totally different from here.

These twelve did take the message to the ends of the known world of their time and on to the whole world as we know it today. Some interesting circumstances precipitated the spread of the Gospel. Some were forced out of Jerusalem and had to find other places to live. Others went on a mission to share the story. Do you share the story? 1 Peter 3:15 tells us to *"...Always be prepared to give an answer to everyone who asks you to give the reason for the hope that you have. But do this with gentleness and respect....".* In other words, you are to share with others the reason for your hope as the gift it really is. That hope is the Risen Christ who redeems us. As Pastor Don Feuerbach says, "You are the bearers of the good news to the world." Things may seem dark as of today but Easter Sunday is always coming. And He is Risen! Go tell someone!

Father God, thank You for the gift of Your Son who brought a new covenant of love and redemption. You have shown us that, when things look their worst, You can bring out the best. Your power is made perfect in our weakness! Help us to walk in that power through the trials of every Friday but to remember that Sunday is coming! Help us to live lives as if every Sunday was Easter. Give us signs to remind us You always walk with us and will lead us to Your Rest if we would but follow. Thank you that, by Your Son's blood, we are Holy, Righteous and Redeemed! That we are loved more than we can fathom. In Jesus name we pray. Amen!

## APRIL 5    IT'S FRIDAY BUT SUNDAY IS COMING
Faith

Luke 24:1-12 (NIV) Selected Verses Jesus Has Risen

*On the first day of the week, very early in the morning, the women took the spices they had prepared and went to the tomb. ² They found the stone rolled away from the tomb, ³ but when they entered, they did not find the body of the Lord Jesus.... "Why do you look for the living among the dead? ⁶ He is not here; he has risen! Remember how he told you, while he was still with you in Galilee:" ......¹¹ But they did not believe the women, because their words seemed to them like nonsense. ¹² Peter, however, got up and ran to the tomb. Bending over, he saw the strips of linen lying by themselves, and he went away, wondering to himself what had happened.*

What just happened? Just hours ago, it looked like all our hopes and dreams were over! The One who was to redeem Israel was put to death by the Romans. The dream had just died along with Him. Now what?

Jesus had died on Friday and the religious authorities wanted His body down off the cross before sundown when the Sabbath began. Joseph of Arimathea had removed Jesus body, prepared it hastily and placed it in his own tomb. Now, on Sunday (the third day), after the Sabbath was over, Mary Magdalene, Joanna, Mary the mother of James, and the others with them came to the tomb to complete the task and give Jesus a proper burial. They were shocked at what they found or didn't find. Jesus was not in the tomb. Two angels told them Jesus was risen. In fact, they asked why the ladies were looking for the living among the dead. The two reminded them of what Jesus had said that He would rise on the third day. And now He has! He is risen!

The women went to tell the other the good news but no one believed them. Or did they? Peter decided to go look for himself. He wondered what had happened. He needed time to process all this and figure it out. It was too much to grasp at first. Could Jesus really have been raised from the dead? God is faithful. He did say He would rebuild His Temple in 3 days. Jesus was that Temple. God has decided to go one step beyond living among His people. He had now decided to live within His people. Peter, who had denied Jesus three times, now considered the thought the he would face Jesus again. What would he say? How would he tell Jesus that he had denied his Master three times? How can we face Jesus and explain how often we have denied Him?

Most times, we live our lives according to our own desires without consulting God. We make decisions and then ask God to bless them. Wouldn't it be better to invite God into the decision-making process so He can lead us to the blessings He wants for us? He gave up everything to redeem us. That shows how valuable we are to Him. Who are we that He is mindful of us? We are His children.

You have got to go through death to get to resurrection. Jesus went through an awful death. Once you pass from death to eternal life, you have overcome death. That is what Jesus did for us. He brought us from life through death and back to life again! Only this life is eternal. It has no end. Jesus stands ready to forgive our denials and other shortcomings. He knows how we are made and that we cannot manage without Him. He is with us now and will carry us through to life eternal. He is risen that you might rise!

Lord, we thank You that You are mindful of us and that You care so much for us. Thank you for opening the way for us to spend eternity with You in paradise! You have given everything that we might have life and have it to the full. Help us to live as redeemed people reflecting Your glory to a hurting world. In Jesus name we pray! Amen!

## APRIL 6    THE DREAMER LIVES OUT HIS DREAMS
Encouragement

Genesis 50:20 (NIV)
*20 You intended to harm me, but God intended it for good to accomplish what is now being done, the saving of many lives.*

There are many who will hold you back when you have large dreams. If you succeed, it may make them look bad. Many will do things to slow you down if not stop you from succeeding. My brother once said that the way my wife treated my Grandmother made the rest of us look bad. You have got to appreciate his honesty.

Joseph was the oldest son of Jacob by Rachel, his favorite wife. Joseph was Jacob's favorite son and he was not shy about letting others know. You need to be careful about playing favorites. It causes jealousy and that is why Cain killed Able. Do you set up jealousy in your family or beyond? Are you careful to make sure you are fair to others? It is normal for a person to feel closer to someone that is more like them but caution is needed. Be careful not to show favoritism because it destroys self-esteem and causes rivalry. Joseph was a dreamer! He was given a vision from God about the future. He knew, by the Spirit, what the future held! His brothers hated him because of these dreams.

Dreams can be powerful! If you can focus on a dream, you can accomplish things others haven't even thought about yet. Joseph had dreams that God gave him about being the ruler of a country. That dream got him into trouble with his brothers who tried to kill him. But years later, he became second in command to Pharaoh, King of Egypt. That position saved the lives of his brothers, the Children of Israel (Jacob), God's chosen people.

When my nephews were young, I used to tell them shamelessly that "you are one of my two favorite nephews." As they got a little older, they figured out that I only had two nephews and complained about my statement. I told them that fact did not change anything and they were still my two favorites. I was careful to spend time with both. I went on class trips and soccer games and Boy Scout events of all sort. It was worth every minute of my investment. Another thing to consider is your level of encouragement. Do you use your words to help forward their dreams? I encouraged them to do whatever their dreams lead them to do. If they believed in themselves, all things were possible.

Do these stories exist today? Are there young people who could go beyond conventional wisdom? There are! All around us are people who can do great things if we encourage them. Will you use your words to bless them? Young people encouraged in the right direction will do amazing things. Be an encourager. Support a dreamer and watch what they will do!

Lord, thank You that You plant seeds of dreams in our hearts. Help us to protect them from trouble. Guide us to nurture and cultivate them into the blessings You intended for us. By Your grace and through Your power, help us to grow people and opportunities today!

## APRIL 7    GOING THROUGH IT
Faith

Psalm 30:5b, 11-12 (NKJV)
Weeping may endure for a night, but joy *comes* in the morning.
*11 You have turned for me my mourning into dancing; You have put off my sackcloth and clothed me with gladness, 12 To the end that my glory may sing praise to You and not be silent. O LORD my God, I will give thanks to You forever.*

I had a difficult first quarter of 2015. It was a time of trials. I had skin cancer surgery. I got the flu. My best friend went to be with the Lord. We sold and emptied my parent's home and I had to watch things go out the door. I have gone through a time of sadness as almost everyone does in life. How do people make it without faith? I know that, when I face a challenge, I go to God for strength and support. What do others do? Have you faced some challenges so far this year? How have you handled them?

In life, there is no way around the challenges. You just have to face them. But people of faith are given strength to not only face them but to go through them. I have come to a place in my life where I ask what God is trying to teach me through this particular challenge. Trials refine us. They are there to make us better. If we go through life asking, "why do these things always happen to me?" rather than "what can I learn here", we are missing valuable lessons. Are you looking for those lessons? Do you try to figure out what God is trying to teach you? It may look bad right now but tomorrow will be better.

We all have lessons to learn. The question is will we learn them? He is the potter and will mold us into the shape He wants us to be but we need to stay on the Potter's wheel. Are you willing to be molded? Are you willing to trust the Potter? Will you remain in faith? He will teach you!

Thank You Father that You are willing to teach us things. That You are willing to refine us through our challenges. We know you have prepared a table for us past the valley. Help us to walk through that valley to the blessings you have prepared for us on the other side. Help turn our mourning into dancing. In your name we pray.

## APRIL 8   STAY THE COURSE
Faith

Luke 18:1-8 (NKJV) The Parable of the Persistent Widow
*¹Then He spoke a parable to them, that men always ought to pray and not lose heart, ² saying: "There was in a certain city a judge who did not fear God nor regard man. ³ Now there was a widow in that city; and she came to him, saying, 'Get justice for me from my adversary.' ⁴ And he would not for a while; but afterward he said within himself, 'Though I do not fear God nor regard man, ⁵ yet because this widow troubles me I will avenge her, lest by her continual coming she weary me.'"*
*⁶ Then the Lord said, "Hear what the unjust judge said. ⁷ And shall God not avenge His own elect who cry out day and night to Him, though He bears long with them? ⁸ I tell you that He will avenge them speedily. Nevertheless, when the Son of Man comes, will He really find faith on the earth?"*

We all have a tendency to doubt ourselves and want to give up at times. When others are persistent in their attacks and claims, we begin to wonder if we are right and if the fight is really worth it. We may be facing something that seems clear but a relentless foe tries to get their own way and it wearies us. Such was the case in the story of the persistent widow. She knew she was right but her adversary would not relent and the judge did not care about justice. We need to remember to stand up for justice and always do the right thing.

Are you facing a challenge where your adversary is trying to manipulate you into doing things their way? Does the judge seem to just want things settled as quick as possible and the easiest way for him? Have you lost heart and want to give in to just be done with the whole thing? Have you prayed about the situation? God is a righteous Judge and will bring about justice. He will vindicate you if you stay the course.

God asks you to come to Him in your difficulty. He will avenge you. But the key is that you cry out to Him. You must also believe He cares about you. You must remain in faith. When you go before the judge, pray first, that you be given the right words and that He will give you strength to endure. Matthew 24:13 (NIV) says *"¹³ but the one who stands firm to the end will be saved."*

Father, I thank You that You care enough about us to bring us justice. Thank You that we can always turn to You for help. We know You hear our cry and quickly come to our aid. Help us to remain in You and prevail. In Your name we pray. Amen!

## APRIL 9    I AM WITH YOU

Faith

Isaiah 41:10-11 (NIV)

*¹⁰ So do not fear, for I am with you; do not be dismayed, for I am your God. I will strengthen you and help you; I will uphold you with my righteous right hand. ¹¹ "All who rage against you will surely be ashamed and disgraced; those who oppose you will be as nothing and perish.*

Billy Graham says "fear causes us to doubt God's promises and disbelieve His love." I don't know about you but that is not where I want to be. God's word, through Isaiah, tells us not to fear for He is with us. What does it mean to have God with you? It means his favor goes before you making things go your way. King Jehoshaphat faced a huge army that was too powerful for Israel (2 Chronicles 20). Jehoshaphat appointed men to sing to the LORD and to praise him for the splendor of his holiness as they went out at the head of the army, saying: "Give thanks to the LORD, for his love endures forever." Israel triumphed over their enemy in spite of being outnumbered. God will bring His will to pass and protect His own.

Daily we face challenges that seem to overwhelm us. Did you realize it was a sin to be fearful of these challenges? It shows a lack of faith. God is our strength and shield. He will uphold us with His righteous right hand. What do you face today? Is there a project at work you are not sure how to complete? Is there tension in your family? Do you face a possible bad diagnosis? Whatever the issue, your God walks with you. In fact, He is within you. He will give you the strength to face and triumph over any challenge. He loves you! He has anointed you with all you need to accomplish the dream and rest assured, He has placed that dream in your heart. It would be a shame if you did not live your destiny because of fear, wouldn't it? Be bold! Go out and try new things. 2 Timothy 1:7 (NKJV) says *⁷ For God has not given us a spirit of fear, but of power and of love and of a sound mind.* God does not want you to be shy. You carry His image and likeness inside you. You are fearfully and wonderfully made. Live as a child of the Most High God today! Do great things in His name!

Father, we thank you that You go out before us paving the way for us to make a bold statement in Your name this day. Guide us into Your will for our lives and give us this day, what we will need to bring glory to You. In Jesus name we pray.

## APRIL 10 HE LOVES YOU
### Quality of Life

Romans 5:8 (NKJV)

*8 But God demonstrates His own love toward us, in that while we were still sinners, Christ died for us.*

He loves You! That's right! Even before you knew how to love, He loved you. In fact, it was Him who taught you how to love. So, what is love? Love is defined by Thomas Oord as "acting intentionally, in sympathetic response to others, including God, to promote well-being." God certainly does that. He always does things to promote well-being.

How do you love? Do you always look out for the good of others? In the case of Foster Children, the courts and the system are supposed to do what is in the best interest of the child. I am not always sure that is their objective. There are times, when children are returned to parents who do not always put the child's best interest first. It seems to be more about their pride (parents and system) than the welfare of the child. Pride gets in the way of too many things. Have you found instances where pride has clouded your judgment? Have you been overly concerned with what people would think?

The best tack to take is considering what God would think. The One who loves you and wants the best for each of His children should be the One setting the standards we follow. Do you follow God's standards? Do you know what His standards are? Do you love as He loved? That is a tall order. When our Pastor says "love as Jesus loved", I think I am not capable of that love. In my own power, I am not. But I am not in my own power if I let the Holy Spirit lead. The Spirit will show me and you how to love and give us the strength to accomplish that love. Will you ask for the Spirit to guide you? Will you love as Jesus loves? Ask for help and give it a try. His ear is tuned to the sound of your voice. He will answer. He, who loves you, will come through.

Lord, teach us how to love as You love. We know it is not easy but we know You will help us if we ask. Lord, we are asking for Your help to love our neighbors as ourselves. And Lord, please help us do a better job of loving ourselves too. We tend to fall short there. In your name we pray. Amen!

## APRIL 11 IF YOU WANT TO WALK ON WATER, YOU HAVE TO GET OUT OF THE BOAT

Faith

Matthew 14:25-33 (NKJV) Jesus Walks on the Sea

*25 Now in the fourth watch of the night [just before dawn] Jesus went to them, walking on the sea. 26 And when the disciples saw Him walking on the sea, they were troubled, saying, "It is a ghost!" And they cried out for fear. 27 But immediately Jesus spoke to them, saying, "Be of good cheer! It is I; do not be afraid." 28 And Peter answered Him and said, "Lord, if it is You, command me to come to You on the water." 29 So He said, "Come." And when Peter had come down out of the boat, he walked on the water to go to Jesus. 30 But when he saw that the wind was boisterous, he was afraid; and beginning to sink he cried out, saying, "Lord, save me!" 31 And immediately Jesus stretched out His hand and caught him, and said to him, "O you of little faith, why did you doubt?" 32 And when they got into the boat, the wind ceased. 33 Then those who were in the boat came and worshiped Him, saying, "Truly You are the Son of God."*

Are you a brave person? Can you accomplish great things for the Kingdom? The details of this story tell us that we need to take chances and be brave. In fact, it gets more specific and mentions the "F" word. You know, faith!

The disciples were in a boat crossing the Sea of Galilee as Jesus had instructed them. The wind and waves were against them so it was not easy going. All of a sudden, they thought they saw someone walking toward them on the water and they were terrified. They thought it was a ghost. Little did they know it was the Holy Ghost. Jesus told them not to be afraid. Peter, always the bold impetuous one, said "command me to come to You on the water" and then the crazy son of a gun got out of the boat! He was afraid of a ghost but stepped out on to the water? I don't get that. He actually walked on the water for a little while.

How about you? Are you willing to get out of the boat? Are you bold for the Lord? Most people are not. They are timid. Society teaches us we should not speak about religion or politics in polite company. In my opinion, if you don't speak about these things, the day will come when you will no longer have the chance. We notice, in the story, that Peter is OK for a while but then begins to sink. Why is that? As soon as he took his eyes off Jesus, he was distracted by the wind and began to sink. Isn't that a lot like us? Don't we start out great with a vision, walking on water but lose sight of the Creator of that vision and begin to sink? What lesson can we learn here that will help us achieve the destiny God has created for us? Simply said, keep your eye on the prize and that prize is Jesus. Hebrews 12:2 (ESV) says *"2 looking to Jesus, the founder and perfecter of our faith."* He will make all things possible. So, will you begin to be bold for the Lord? When you hear of someone's difficulties, will you ask if you can pray for them? Will you invite them to Church? What steps will you take to encourage them in their faith? 2 Timothy 1: (NKJV) says *"7 For God has not given us a spirit of fear, but of power and of love and of a sound mind."* Today, be bold. Be powerful, knowing whose power you wield.

Speak out with the sword of the Spirit. He will direct you in what to say. People are looking for a relationship with God. It may be through you that they find Him.

Father, give us the faith we need to trust You. We lose focus and turn our eyes away from you and begin to sink into the darkness. Reach out Your hand to us before we sink sending us a reminder of Your love and support. Be our Help and Shield today and every day. In Your name we pray.

# APRIL 12   W.O.W. – WITH OUT WORDS
Quality of Life

Titus 2:6-8 (NKJV)

*⁶ Likewise, exhort the young men to be sober-minded, ⁷ in all things showing yourself to be a pattern of good works; in doctrine showing integrity, reverence, incorruptibility, ⁸ sound speech that cannot be condemned, that one who is an opponent may be ashamed, having nothing evil to say of you. ⁹ Exhort bondservants to be obedient to their own masters, to be well pleasing in all things, not answering back, ¹⁰ not pilfering, but showing all good fidelity, that they may adorn the doctrine of God our Savior in all things.*

Is there someone in your place of business who people turn to when they are in need? What is it about that person that draws others to them? Do you want to be that kind of person? If you are kind and helpful to all people, what kind of reputation will you develop?

"Preach the Gospel of Jesus Christ every day and, if you have to, use words" was attributed to St. Francis of Assisi though there are questions about his authorship. The point is to walk the walk before talking the talk. When I started in Youth Ministry, the Church Pastor complained that Youth Group was not Christ-centered enough and we needed to do things differently. My response to him (looking back now, my *arrogant* response to him) was he was welcome to show up any Sunday evening and lead. Many organizations who want to evangelize come on too strong. They are like street evangelists preaching the end is near! Isn't it better to set an example of how to live and have people ask you questions about why you do what you do? There seems to be a strong argument that we need to "preach" the Gospel which involves speaking. I am suggesting we begin by living the Gospel which will get us an audience who will listen. As you know, I am not afraid to preach the Gospel if you have been reading the devotionals.

Our son Clayton came to us when he was 12 years old. As a Foster and now Adoptive parent, I thought he needed to hear that I love him and I am not shy about sharing that sentiment. It wasn't getting the desired results. In the beginning, there was no response. Later on, there was skepticism. I was bewildered. I came from a loving, affectionate home. It took years for things to come around but I learned valuable lessons from him. Many people had told him they loved him and then abused him. I was the first who said it and then set that example. I built on the promise of that "love" word. I had to earn his trust. I had to build and prove a good reputation. Jean and I have done that now but it took a long time.

Romans 10:17 (NIV) says *¹⁷ Consequently, faith comes from hearing the message, and the message is heard through the word about Christ.* I fully understand the Word of God must be preached but it is important to gather an audience and get them to believe you. To do that, it is best to set an example of the fruits of the Spirit which are love, joy, peace, patience, kindness, goodness, faithfulness, ²³ gentleness and self-control (Galatians 5:22). If you live your life in the Spirit, you will set an example that people will admire and want to follow. Then, you have earned the right to give an explanation of the faith you have in Christ. People don't care how much (or what) you know until they know how much you care.

Preach W.O.W. (without words) today! Show them you care. Be patient as our world is cynical and skeptical. Do it long enough and you will find the toughest curmudgeon will come around. I have done it! Ask God for patience because you will need it. Be bold for the Lord and He will be your shield! You will bring Him glory in this endeavor.

Lord, thank You that You have trusted us with the Gospel. You did not give it to us to hold for safe keeping. You gave it to us to share. Please, as You brought the animals to Noah, so bring us people who want to hear and learn about You. Thank you for the honor of preaching the Gospel even W.O.W! Amen!

# APRIL 13    CAN GOD TRUST YOU WITH MORE
## Attitude

Matthew 25:14-30 (NKJV) Selected Verses The Parable of the Talents
*14 "For the kingdom of heaven is like a man traveling to a far country, who called his own servants and delivered his goods to them. 15 And to one he gave five talents, to another two, and to another one, to each according to his own ability; and immediately he went on a journey. 16 Then he who had received the five talents went and traded with them, and made another five talents. 17 And likewise he who had received two gained two more also. 18 But he who had received one went and dug in the ground, and hid his lord's money. 19 After a long time the lord of those servants came and settled accounts with them.......20 "So he who had received five talents came and brought five other talents, saying, 'Lord, you delivered to me five talents; look, I have gained five more talents besides them.' 21 His lord said to him, 'Well done, good and faithful servant; you were faithful over a few things, I will make you ruler over many things........26 "But his lord answered and said to him, 'You wicked and lazy servant, you knew that I reap where I have not sown, and gather where I have not scattered seed. 27 So you ought to have deposited my money with the bankers, and at my coming I would have received back my own with interest. 28 Therefore take the talent from him, and give it to him who has ten talents. 29 'For to everyone who has, more will be given, and he will have abundance; but from him who does not have, even what he has will be taken away. 30 And cast the unprofitable servant into the outer darkness. There will be weeping and gnashing of teeth.'*

We are talking about the Kingdom of Heaven here and you are asked to be its Steward. A Steward is an awesome responsibility. You are in charge of and responsible for taking care of something that belongs to someone else. How will you invest what has been given to you? How will you advance the Kingdom?

Much, if not everything depends on attitude. There is a way of thinking that needs to be taught. Are you always preparing for the future or do you depend on others to support you? I know of a parent who was struggling financially and got back $1,500 of his child support payments from the court. Did he put that money in the bank for a rainy day? No, he bought a big screen TV. At that time, we did not have a big screen TV but we did have food on the table. Do you think he made a wise investment?

Do you hold a Stewardship position at home, work or Church? At home, all that you have belongs to God and you are its steward. At work, you are responsible for making profit for the company and stockholders. Almost everywhere you look, there are opportunities for you to steward something. How do you accept that challenge? God asks us to do everything as if unto the Lord. Do you take your responsibility seriously? Are you a good steward of that for which you are in charge? Ask the Lord and He will help you do it great!

Lord, thank You that You are always there to help us live our best lives. Guide us this day to the plan You have for us and help us to take care of that You have entrusted to us. In Your name we pray!

## APRIL 14    THERE IS WISDOM IN THE NAME
Relationships

2 Chronicles 1:1-12 (NKJV) Selected Verses    Solomon Requests Wisdom

[1] *Now Solomon the son of David was strengthened in his kingdom, and the LORD his God was with him and exalted him exceedingly....* [6] *And Solomon went up there to the bronze altar before the LORD, which was at the tabernacle of meeting, and offered a thousand burnt offerings on it.* [7] *On that night God appeared to Solomon, and said to him, "Ask! What shall I give you?"* [8] *And Solomon said to God: "You have shown great mercy to David my father, and have made me king in his place.* [9] *Now, O LORD God, let Your promise to David my father be established, for You have made me king over a people like the dust of the earth in multitude.* [10] *Now give me wisdom and knowledge, that I may go out and come in before this people; for who can judge this great people of Yours?"* [11] *Then God said to Solomon: "Because this was in your heart, and you have not asked riches or wealth or honor or the life of your enemies, nor have you asked long life—but have asked wisdom and knowledge for yourself, that you may judge My people over whom I have made you king—* [12] *wisdom and knowledge are granted to you; and I will give you riches and wealth and honor, such as none of the kings have had who were before you, nor shall any after you have the like."*

My Grandfather was named Solomon. There is something special in that name that brings wisdom. He was a wise man who knew when to speak and when not to speak. He had a way about him that brought people to him. He was respected. He was bold. He had business acumen. He came to the US in 1938 after fleeing Germany with his family leaving behind everything to take a janitor's job in a hotel where he scrubbed floors. A few years later, he was back running his own business. Solomon and my Uncle Marty ran Marty's Superette in New York City which was a local grocery store. I delivered groceries for them when I was a teenager. The point being, Solomon was not going to stay a janitor.

As much as he knew about business, he knew more about people. Solomon knew that how you got along with others was really the most important thing. Relationships are most important. Wisdom and knowledge in a vacuum don't amount to much. God gave us the Ten Commandments which are about our relationships to Him and each other. My Opah, Solomon, knew how to make each person feel special. He gave his full attention to you when you spoke.

What is wisdom? Is it knowing what to do, how to do it or *why* it should be done? I am of the opinion it is *why* you do it. Both Solomons knew that why mattered! The "why" is to glorify God and enjoy Him forever. We are taught to "seek first the Kingdom of God and all these things will be added unto you." Both Solomons were Godly men who drew closer to the Lord. When you follow the Lord, He will make your way blessed. Solomon, Son of David, was the wealthiest man who ever lived. He lived in splendor. Solomon, Son of Hertz, my Opah, was wealthy in relationships. Wherever he went, there were friends or soon to be friends. He was very funny too! Like I said, there is something special about the name.

Father, teach us the *why* of life. We know You give us the talents needed and provide the resources. Help us to live each day with goodness in our hearts to love those whom You love. Draw us closer to You. Help us to bring glory to You in thought, word and deed! In Your name we pray.

## APRIL 15   RENDER UNTO CAESAR
Quality of Life

Mark 12:17 (NKJV)

[17] *And Jesus answered and said to them, "Render to Caesar the things that are Caesar's, and to God the things that are God's."*

Render unto the IRS what is theirs. Why should we send them the money? They will just waste it anyway. Romans 13:1 (NIV) says *"*[13] *Let everyone be subject to the governing authorities, for there is no authority except that which God has established."* The authorities that exist have been established by God. If God establishes the authorities, shouldn't we obey them?

Today is the day we in the US have to file our taxes. It is time to render unto Caesar what is Caesar's. It is our duty to support the government that they may protect us and serve the least of these. Do you think they are the best choice for protecting the least of these? Instead of paying higher taxes, shouldn't the followers of Jesus be stepping up to the plate and taking care of others out of the overflow of blessing God has poured out upon us? When the Church runs a campaign to benefit people, there are no management expenses or waste. All the work is done by volunteers who raise the funding necessary to provide the benefit. Do you get personally involved in serving others? Is this your calling?

Today, you have the chance to make a difference! God has blessed you in many ways. It is not always financial blessing that is needed. Some people are the ones who can write a check. But God also calls us to lend a hand. He asks us to share time, talent and treasure. Where are you being called? What gifts and talents do you have to share? Don't sell yourself short. God values someone who is willing to take the time to listen to another and encourage them. Ephesians 4:11 (KJV) says- *"*[11] *And he gave some, apostles; and some, prophets; and some, evangelists; and some, pastors and teachers."* What are you called to do? Every gift is important. Will you use your gifts today?

Father, thank You for the gifts and talents You have given each of us. You have put a little of Yourself in every person. Help us to honor everyone as the child of God that they are. And in so honoring each person, help us to make sure they are cared for and valued. In Jesus name we pray.

## APRIL 16    ATTITUDE IS EVERYTHING
Attitude

Proverbs 15:13 (NKJV)
*13 A merry heart makes a cheerful countenance, But by sorrow of the heart the spirit is broken.*

Today, I went to lunch with my friend Steve and our discussion was about how many people will waste more effort telling you why they can't honor your request than it would take them to just do it! We went to our favorite diner and I have been going there more than 40 years. There was a new waitress. I ordered my usual chicken soup with a matzoh ball. She told me a matzoh ball would not fit in the cup with the chicken soup. I told her to just try it and see. I am sure it will work. I didn't tell her but I have ordered it that way for longer than she is old. And, as I suggested, it fit just fine.

There is an expression which says "people can brighten a room. Some by entering and some by leaving!" Which type of person are you? Are people happy to see you? When you call a business and they see the caller ID, do they draw straws to see who gets stuck taking the call? In our business, there are clients who are a real joy and others you wished were not your clients. Mike Michalowicz wrote a book called the *Pumpkin Plan* in which he maintains you should rid yourself of the bad clients because they ruin your whole demeanor and that ends up costing you money. They block the good clients from entering. I wear a hat that says Attitude is Everything! How you approach each situation really matters. Approach everything with joy, grace, peace and kindness and you will have a happy life. Speak with warmth and caring and others will want to help you. They will be happy when you arrive! There is evidence that suggests it takes more muscles to frown than smile. Let's go with the smile!

How do you want to be seen or remembered? What will people say about you after you are gone? I want people to think of me kindly. I want them to remember me as encouraging. I want to be known as the guy with the smile. And I want to make you smile! Today, know you are fearfully and wonderfully made in the image and likeness of God. You are His Masterpiece. You are awesome. With all that going for you, how can you help but smile?

Lord, thank You that You have created us in Your image. Remind us today of all the blessing You have given us and help us to live as blessed people shining Your glory in the world around us. Let us show the cheerful countenance that comes from knowing we are Yours. Amen!

# APRIL 17   FADING IN HEAVEN'S LIGHT

Encouragement

2 Corinthians 4:16-18 (NIV)

*16 Therefore we do not lose heart. Though outwardly we are wasting away, yet inwardly we are being renewed day by day. 17 For our light and momentary troubles are achieving for us an eternal glory that far outweighs them all. 18 So we fix our eyes not on what is seen, but on what is unseen, since what is seen is temporary, but what is unseen is eternal.*

Sometimes, you have to wonder if it is all worth it. This life is a struggle. We often face challenges that overwhelm us. The business world is always asking for 110% when we are having difficulty providing 100%. It makes you want to just give up and hide. Does it seem that way to you, too?

We are told not to lose heart; not to get discouraged! Why not? Because our hope is much larger than the current situation. We all face challenges. These difficulties are used to refine us; to build our character. Sometimes, I want to tell God I am already enough of a character and not to refine me so much. The issue for us is that we cannot see the benefit at the time. All we see is the pain. If we only look at this present moment, it overshadows everything. But, if we view it in light of eternity, this too shall pass. We are getting older and cannot do the things we used to do. We are slowing down. But our Spirit is drawing closer to Glory. You will endure through each challenge because of the One who upholds you. You will overcome each challenge if you remain in faith. Mandisa wrote a song called Overcomer. That is what you are!

> You're an overcomer
> Stay in the fight 'til the final round
> You're not going under
> 'Cause God is holding you right now
> You might be down for a moment
> Feeling like it's hopeless
> That's when He reminds You
> That you're an overcomer
> You're an overcomer

How do you remain in faith? By fixing your eyes on the One who will uphold you with His righteous right hand! He who promises is faithful. By focusing on Jesus, the true light of the world, you will not see the shadows and hear the voices that say you'll never accomplish this. Jesus will tell you that you can do all things through Him. Don't let the burden of the moment blind you to the glory that awaits those who stay in faith. You're not going under! You will prevail. Your future is sure in Him! Earth's troubles fade in light of Your glory!

Lord, thank You that You are always faithful and always there! Help us to remain focused on You. Carry us through the deep waters and bring us safely to the other side. The side where we will bask in Your presence. Uphold us in our struggles today. In Your name we pray!

# APRIL 18    BECOMING ONE OR REMAINING THAT WAY

Relationships

Genesis 2:22-24 (NKJV)

*22 Then the rib which the LORD God had taken from man He made into a woman, and He brought her to the man. 23 And Adam said: "This is now bone of my bones And flesh of my flesh; She shall be called Woman, Because she was taken out of Man." 24 Therefore a man shall leave his father and mother and be joined to his wife, and they shall become one flesh.*

I apologize! This one is very long but please read it. It is important.

What does it mean to become one flesh? Do the two people actually blend together? Are they not still separate people? The passage is very clear. A man shall leave his father and his mother and be joined to his wife. This becomes the primary relationship. Both people leave their parents to start a new family unit. This family unit is supposed to procreate and raise children who will also love and serve God. But to continue to serve God in this relationship, we must remain in the relationship. That will take commitment! Are you willing to hang in there?

The Bible tells us that man and woman are made of the same substance. It does not say so but, since we are both made in the image and likeness of God, we are also the same Spiritually. So why do we think so differently? It is good that we think differently because these differences develop new ideas and help us prove concepts. The world would be boring if we all thought exactly alike.

I have some friends who are getting married today. I am attending the wedding and I got them a gift. However, I wondered what I could give them that will last. I wanted to give them something that was not of this world. I asked God to lead me to find something. He suggested spiritual guidance.

Many people put more planning into the wedding than they do the marriage. How will you survive together? How will you resolve differences of opinion? Are you going to call it quits as soon as things get tough because they will get tough. Will you invite God into the marriage? Is He the foundation on which your marriage is built? When you both look to Jesus for direction, He will heal any disagreements.

In our forty years of marriage (Yes, just the sight of her still brings a smile to my face.), Jean and I have had seven foster children and adopted two. These children have taught me things. How does that apply here? One of the first things a foster child will do is something to get you angry to see if you will stick with them. They don't want to waste their time building a relationship if you are going to kick them to the curb as soon as they mess up. It is the same in a marriage. Does your spouse know you are willing to fight *for* them even more than you will fight with them? Are you committed to the relationship? Will you love them even when you don't like them? Can they trust you? Trust takes a long time to build and can be destroyed with one careless word. When you get angry, do not say bad things (Ephesians 4:26). But also, do not walk away as if they don't matter. Tell them you need a time out but *we will get back together to work things out!* Make sure they know they mean more to you than the difference you just had!

I have a critical nature which I am trying to overcome (I am asking God to remove my critical nature.). I am a master at finding fault. Are you a fault finder too? May I suggest you try being a good finder? Intentionally look for things you can praise in your spouse. If there is something that "bugs" you, discuss it at a calm time and put it into a praise sandwich. Praise them; tell them about how the item that "bugs" you makes you feel and praise them again. Think before you speak. How will my words make them feel? Is that the outcome I am looking for? How can I get the desired outcome? Just a little effort and thought here can produce huge dividends. Try praising each other today!

Lord, thank You for this wonderful person You have put in our lives; Your gift to us! Help us to cherish them as the gift they are. Help us to love them always and be kind. Teach us to be a good finder. As for me, remove my critical nature and give me a spirit of praise for them and You! In Jesus name I pray! Amen!

## APRIL 19   THINK BEFORE YOU SPEAK
Relationships

James 1:19-20 (NKJV) Qualities Needed in Trials
*¹⁹ So then, my beloved brethren, let every man be swift to hear, slow to speak, slow to wrath;*
*²⁰ for the wrath of man does not produce the righteousness of God.*

Relationships are the most important thing in this life and the next. It is our relationship with God through Christ that makes the next life possible. God thought relationships were so important that He gave us the Ten Commandments. The first four are about our relationship to him and the remaining six are about our relationships with each other. God put more emphasis on relationships to each other than to Him. It takes a lot of time to build a relationship and only seconds to destroy one with just a few harsh words. Wouldn't it be a good idea to be careful what we say? How can we do that?

James asks us to be slow to speak. How would our relationships benefit if we took the time to think about what we want to say and how we say it? Would there be fewer offenses? Would there be fewer hurt feelings? Would we all get along better? God has a plan for how we are to live and gentleness and kindness are just two of the things He wants us to follow. Taking time to think would be a great way to improve relationships. We would have the time to make sure we are encouraging others with our words. Hebrews 4:12 says *"For the word of God is living and powerful, and **sharper than any two- edged sword**, piercing even to the division of soul and spirit, and of joints and marrow, and is a discerner of the thoughts and intents of the heart."* All words are powerful! Be careful how you wield that sword. You don't want to cut anybody! Words can be sharp but they can also be soothing. Use your words to sooth and heal. Use them to build up! Use them to encourage!

As I have said, I have a critical nature. It is something I learned. I am asking God to change me but that takes time. I am pausing to think about how I want to respond to some of the things that happen with Jean. I know I want to use my words to bless her. I am thinking of ways to highlight her wonderful attributes and encouraging her to use the gifts she has been given. Many of us see only our faults and not our blessings. Wouldn't it be wonderful if you could be the one who shows your spouse or children all of their gifts and blessings and how much they mean to you? Why not try to be a good finder starting today? Ask God to help you get started blessing His creation!

Father, we thank you for all the gifts and talents you have given us. Help us to recognize them and use them to your glory. In Jesus name we pray!

## APRIL 20   YOU ARE CHOSEN
Faith

Isaiah 49:6-7 (NKJV)
*6 Indeed He says, 'It is too small a thing that You should be My Servant*
*To raise up the tribes of Jacob, And to restore the preserved ones of Israel;*
*I will also give You as a light to the Gentiles, That You should be My salvation to the ends of the*
*earth.'" 7 Thus says the LORD, The Redeemer of Israel, their Holy One, To Him whom man*
*despises, To Him whom the nation abhors, To the Servant of rulers: "Kings shall see and arise,*
*Princes also shall worship, Because of the LORD who is faithful, The Holy One of Israel; And He*
*has chosen You."*

Israel was called the Chosen People. But what were they chosen for? They were chosen to reveal God to the world. He chose to reveal Himself to Abraham and then to the Children of Israel (Jacob) who were Abraham's great grandchildren. They turned out not to be so great. In this passage, God is speaking to and through Isaiah. The Bible often speaks on several planes. God is speaking in past, present and future times. He often does this. Isaiah tells us God has chosen him (Isaiah) as a servant to restore Israel. Israel had fallen many times but God still loved them. But God also reveals His intention to restore the whole world, including creation. God tells Isaiah He will also give "You" as a light to the Gentiles. Who is the "You"? Since it is a capital letter, I believe it points forward to Christ. It also may be that it refers to Isaiah being God's voice to the people of his time who would listen. God's plan is to bring His Salvation to the ends of the earth. It seems as many are chosen here. It goes on to say He has chosen You.

How does it feel to be chosen? Were you aware that you have been chosen? Chosen for what? You are chosen to reveal God and His Salvation to the ends of the earth. Our Church asks us to make disciples who make disciples. How are you doing with that commission? Are you being a light to the Gentiles? Every day, you come in contact with new people. What impression are you leaving with them? Are they happier after meeting you? Are you shining God's light for those around you to see? When someone speaks with you, are they enriched for having had the conversation? You have been called. You have been anointed. You are empowered. You are blessed. What would you do today if you knew God paved the way for you and went with you? Well guess what! He did and He is with you now and always! Go ahead! Do something great today! You've got it in you.

Lord, thank You that You are always with us. You said You would go before us making the crooked places straight and paving the way. You said there is nothing we can't do with You on our side and we know You are always on our side. Please guide us in the way You would have us go.  And take us the best way, Your way. In Jesus name we pray!

# APRIL 21   THE BIBLE IS THE WORD OF GOD
Faith

2 Timothy 3:16-17 (NKJV)
*16 All Scripture is given by inspiration of God, and is profitable for doctrine, for reproof, for correction, for instruction in righteousness, 17 that the man of God may be complete, thoroughly equipped for every good work.*

These days, there is a lot of discussion about the authenticity and authorship of the Bible. There are those who say you can't take it literally. There are those who say it is irrelevant. Some say it was written by humankind. Where do you stand? Do you know the Bible well enough to know? If you don't know what it says, how can you have an opinion?

Paul wrote to Timothy to give him clarity about things concerning the Spirit and other things. Paul was speaking to Timothy about how a man of God is supposed to live. Paul was a mentor to Timothy as he is still a mentor to us today. In his charge to Timothy, Paul states all Scripture is "God breathed" or given by His inspiration to those who recorded them. After all, Moses is the author of the first five books of the Bible and he was not there at the creation of the world. How is it that he wrote all the details of something he did not witness? Could it be that God gave him the information? Could it be that "All Scripture is God breathed"? The Bible is God's Word, plain and simple! But here is the really good news. God's Word speaks very highly of you!

Psalm 139 says you are fearfully and wonderfully made. Jeremiah 29:11 says God has great plans for you. Ephesians 2:10 says *"For we are His workmanship, created in Christ Jesus for good works, which God prepared beforehand, that we should walk in them."* Genesis 1:27 says *"So God created man in His own image, in the image of God He created him; male and female he created them."* 1 Corinthians 3:16 says *"Do you not know that you are God's temple and that God's Spirit dwells in you?"* Ephesians 4:24 says *"And to put on the new self, created after the likeness of God in true righteousness and holiness."* Isaiah 43:25 *"I, I am he who blots out your transgressions for my own sake, and I will not remember your sins."* John 1:12 says *"But to all who did receive him, who believed in his name, he gave the right to become children of God..."* Deuteronomy 14:2 says *"For you are a people holy to the Lord your God, and the Lord has chosen you to be a people for his treasured possession, out of all the peoples who are on the face of the earth."*

Wow, you are awesome! You are thoroughly equipped for every good work! It is incredible all you have going for you. And these are all gifts from God. You did nothing to earn any of it. You are incredibly blessed by His grace alone. So how does someone with all those blessings live their life? Shouldn't you do awesome things? You have awesome talents. God thinks you are special. He gave you the right to be called His child. What will God's child do today? I am confident it will be something extraordinary! Go for it!

Father, You said we are fearfully and wonderfully made. You said You had great plans for us. You said we are Your children. Help us to live as such and do extraordinary things this day that bring glory to Your name. In Jesus name we pray!

## APRIL 22   LOOK TO THE PROMISES

Encouragement

Isaiah 55:11 (NKJV)

*¹¹ So shall My word be that goes forth from My mouth; It shall not return to Me void, But it shall accomplish what I please, And it shall prosper in the thing for which I sent it.*

What did God say in His Word? He made many promises to us. In Genesis 22:18, God promised Abraham the whole world would be blessed through Him. When God promises something, He comes through. God's Word is also the Bible. There are hundreds of promises in the Bible and God says His word will not return to Him empty. So, can we trust God's promises? Do you trust God?

When God speaks, things happen. He said "let there be light" and there was light. But how does that relate to us today. Since God made so many promises, He will fulfill them. According to one person's count, there are **3573 promises** in the Bible. A key to note is "it [God's word] shall prosper in the thing for which I sent it." God's promises are to prosper you. He wants good things for you. What does God want to accomplish in your life? Jesus said that He came that we might have life and have it abundantly.

What does an abundant life look like? Is it money? Is it fame? Or is it joy, peace, and relationships? That is a struggle I face daily. For what should we strive? The Bible says to "Seek first the Kingdom of God and His righteousness and all these things will be added unto you." Does that mean we should not look to earning a living first? It is unclear. It seems to me that God is saying if we seek Him and walk in His ways, He will provide for our needs. That doesn't mean we sit and wait. We do need to work at our chosen profession. But God wants to bless you. He has stored up blessings that He will release into your life if you remain in faith. You must believe these blessings are coming your way. There is a saying that says "you bring about what you think about." What are you thinking? Are you saying I am blessed? I am healthy? I am prosperous? Or does your life reflect another vision? What do you see in your mind's eye and speak out over your life? May I suggest you use your thoughts and words to change your life? Know that God loves you and wants to bless you. Give Him the chance! Speak out blessing today. I am blessed. I am prosperous. I am healthy. I am loved. I can do all things through Christ who gives me strength! Today, live as the child of God you were born to be. Live with abandon and shine His light in this dark world. Then, your life will have more meaning than you ever dreamed.

Lord, thank You for the abundant life You have brought to us. Help us live for You today with abandon, trusting You for all our needs. We know when we follow Your lead, all things work for our good, but the journey is scary. You stretch us to grow into Your dreams for us. Give us peace as we know You love us. Help us to remain in faith and grow into Your blessings! In Jesus name we pray.

## APRIL 23    I CAN DO IT MYSELF

Quality of Life

John 5:30 (NKJV)

³⁰ *I can of Myself do nothing. As I hear, I judge; and My judgment is righteous, because I do not seek My own will but the will of the Father who sent Me.*

I am a self-made man. At least, that is what our culture teaches us. We are the masters of our domain in the United States. People in our society think they have the power to do the things they want to do. I used to think that way too. If it's going to be, it's up to me! But, as I have said, with power (I am in charge) comes responsibility. I used to think I was in control. The down side for me was I felt personally responsible when things in the world around me went badly. So bad, in fact, I became depressed about the condition of our world.

Then I realized how powerless I really am. Things go on around me over which I have no control. Death comes to my dearest friend and I can do nothing to delay it. I am powerless except for one thing. I can turn to the One who is all powerful and do His will in this world. We know He wants the best for us. His will is perfect! When Jesus prayed in the Garden, he asked for the cup [of death] to pass from Him so he would not have to suffer. But then, the most significant part was His statement of "not my will but Thy will be done." Jesus knew following the Father's will is the right thing to do. Whose will do you follow? If it is your own, you will be limited to whatever you can accomplish in your own power. If you follow God's will, He will be the power behind you and "You can do all things through Christ who gives you strength!" Do you still want to do it on your own? Let me know how that works for you. But if you want all things to work for your good and the good of others, perhaps you want to follow the will of God. You have been given the gifts needed. Use them today!

Father, I thank You that You want the best for us! Help us to follow Your will to bring about Your plan. Lead us when we cannot see the path clearly. Guide us in Your ways so we can bring glory to you. Help us bring Your light into this dark world. Amen!

## APRIL 24    RAISE YOUR HANDS TO THE LORD

Attitude

Psalm 134:1-3 (NKJV) Praising the Lord in His House at Night

*1 Behold, bless the Lord, All you servants of the Lord,*
*Who by night stand in the house of the Lord! 2 Lift up your hands in the sanctuary, And bless*
*the Lord. 3 The Lord who made heaven and earth Bless you from Zion!*

Presbyterians (of which I am one) have sometimes been called the Frozen Chosen. They sit in the pews and listen to the message with little reaction most times. You would never hear an "Amen" from this crowd. In fact, they usually have to sit in the same place in Church each week. We usually sit in row 19 on the right. Do you know what you get when you cross a Presbyterian with a Jehovah's Witness; you get someone who stands on your front porch and doesn't know what to say! But seriously folks!

I attend the traditional Worship with my wife but I also love the contemporary Worship with all the music and activity. At our Church, we also serve Communion each week. This adds to my joy in coming to Worship. David has told us to lift our hands up to the Lord. When you are before God in a corporate worship situation, why not praise Him with everything you have? Sing, make music and lift your hands to the One who has given His very life for you! Psalm 103 says *Bless the Lord, O my soul, and all that is within me, bless his holy name!* When I hear the music, my hand goes up in the air by itself. I point to Him who blesses me! Go ahead! Don't be afraid. Really get into it. Bless the Lord with all that is within you. It's OK to even raise your hands to Him! Acknowledge Him as the object of your Worship. When you raise your hands to Him, He will bless you from Zion!

Lord, thank You that You give us the chance to praise and worship You for You are worthy. Let us experience the joy that true Worship can bring. Help us to know Your blessings which you have stored up for us in our hearts. Release them to us as we raise our hands in praise to You. In Jesus name we pray. Amen!

# APRIL 25    SEND US
Faith

Isaiah 6:8 (NKJV)
*8 Also I heard the voice of the Lord, saying: "Whom shall I send,
And who will go for Us?" Then I said, "Here am I! Send me."*

There are struggles everywhere in the world. The news report shows us all sorts of trouble wherever we look. What's worse is that, in the midst of tragedy, many people just walk by without giving notice. James 2:17 says faith without works is dead. Do your actions reflect your faith level?

There has long been the argument of faith vs. works. James is used by some to argue the need for works. I want to leave that debate to others. One thing I have always believed is that out of the overflow of blessings I am given, for which I am thankful, grows the desire to help others.

Fifteen plus years ago, Paty Villanueva met children who could not read and had little chance for an education. She had an education and her faith. She felt a calling from God to help others and God opened a door. As His plan unraveled, God brought a school to fruition that we now know as Hearts for Honduras School. There are about 200+ young people enrolled each year getting a good education. What if Paty had not heeded the call? What if she had just walked by someone in need? What level of faith would that demonstrate?

Today, it is your turn. Will you heed the call or will you walk on by and go about your business? Do you hear the call? Have you been blessed with gifts and talents that could benefit others? What will you do about it? Last year, I heard about Hearts for Honduras School from Dr. Cam Witt, a local Dentist. He told me about the rewards of serving the children at the school. I heard the call and it kept tugging at my heart. There were 10 other people on the team who also heard that call. God called us and we said "send us!" Send us He did and He does. We are on our way to La Entrada Honduras to answer the call. What are you called to do? Where are you called to go? Are you prepared to answer that call? It is nerve racking to leave your comfort zone.

I went outside the United States to a third-world country for the first time ever, I did not know any of the people with whom I traveled, I was 2,000 miles from home, I did not speak the language and I did not know how to do the job. Other than that, it was a piece of cake! When God calls, He takes you to someplace different. He called Abraham to leave his country and his family and go to a place I will show you. He took me to Honduras. I am on my way back. I was so blessed by the people of La Entrada last year; I want to do it again. I recommend you answer the call! Be bold! He will carry and protect you.

Father, thank You for Your call and Your blessings in that call. You have a way of taking us out of our comfort zone in order to grow our Spirit and refine our person. Protect us from evil and help us grow our relationships with the children and staff. By Your Spirit, bless everyone involved. Amen!

# APRIL 26   DON'T BE AFRAID

Relationships

Philippians 4:6-7 (NIV)

*6 Do not be anxious about anything, but in every situation, by prayer and petition, with thanksgiving, present your requests to God. 7 And the peace of God, which transcends all understanding, will guard your hearts and your minds in Christ Jesus.*

Are you ever anxious? Whenever I travel, I am always anxious about the trip. Did I remember everything? Will there be any issues? Will I arrive safely? My mind can develop a thousand things that could go wrong. As I am maturing in my faith journey, I am learning to let go and let God. I am dropping the worries and enjoying the journey more. When I worry, I cannot enjoy the people I meet. I am focused on what can go wrong.

Each time we approach another challenge of getting the job done, I ask you to think about relationships. There is a fine line between completing the task to which you are called and building the Kingdom. God is more concerned about relationships than task completion. I learned this year's lesson back when I went on a summer mission trip. The Site Leader told me he had plenty of contractors who could finish the job. It was our job to build relationships with the people we came to help.

I can be very task oriented. I focus in on what needs to be done and forget the people around me except those who can help complete the task. I lose opportunities to get to know people better and share the journey with them. I don't make memories. Do you find yourself in that boat? Are you so focused on the task and its completion that you don't build relationships?

Our team is here in La Entrada, Honduras for eight days to see 200-250 kids and staff for their yearly dental checkups. Our time is limited and the need is great! Upon what should we focus? If we are not careful, we can lose sight of the real mission which is to spread the love of Jesus to the ends of the earth. It just so happens that, at this time, the vehicle by which we get this opportunity is dental checkups at Hearts for Honduras School. Remember that the first graders have never seen a dentist before and are afraid. You see, we are all afraid of something. Let us go to God with our fears and He will give us the peace that passes all understanding.

Lord Jesus, please calm our fears. We are all afraid of something. Remind us, by Your Holy Spirit, that we have nothing to fear for You go before us preparing the way and walk with us to give us courage. Help us to focus on You and the people You love. Help us to be thankful for the time we have here in Honduras or anywhere else to build the Kingdom by spreading the Gospel of love. In Your name we pray. Amen!

## APRIL 27   IT'S ALL ABOUT YOU
Relationships

Philippians 2:3 (NKJV)
*3 Let nothing be done through selfish ambition or conceit, but in lowliness of mind let each esteem others better than himself.*

Why do you volunteer your time to help others? What do you get out of it? Do you do it to call attention to yourself, to get it on your resume or are you there to share the blessings God has given you? James 1:27 says *27 Religion that God our Father accepts as pure and faultless is this: to look after orphans and widows in their distress and to keep oneself from being polluted by the world.* Does it have to be limited to widows and orphans? Can't we look after all those whom God loves? Isn't that why we go? Is this about Religion? Some of us on the team did not hear about the trip through their Church so it may not be about religion at all. Then what is it about? There is something inside each human being that calls out to be connected to another human. God Himself said "it is not good for man to be alone." We were created to be in community. And it doesn't matter if the community is in your own town or 2,000 miles away. Something calls us to reach out to another person. In this case, it is kids. They are the easiest for us to embrace. They come to us in appreciation without prejudice. They don't care what kind of car you drive. They just love you in a simple manner. Perhaps it is because they came from God more recently and are closer to Him than we because of our cynicism. What if we could get back that childlike wonder and be like those kids again?

Luke 14 says *"10 But when you are invited, go and sit down in the lowest place, so that when he who invited you comes, he may say to you, 'Friend, go up higher.' Then you will have glory in the presence of those who sit at the table with you. 11 For whoever exalts himself will be humbled, and he who humbles himself will be exalted."* We are supposed to care for others and hold them in high esteem. We are to be humble. We are to consider other people's feelings and needs above our own. Does that mean I don't matter? Certainly not! You are God's masterpiece. You are made in His image and likeness. You are blessed. Of course, you matter. But we should not look only to our own interests. We should take care of others.

What brought you to the place where you decided to help others? Is it that calling from within that makes us want to be part of the community of God's people? Whatever the reason, when we approach others to "Help" we need to approach with humility. We know what we know and have what we have by the grace of God. It is all by God's grace that we are able to help. With that in mind, we must make our friends feel important. It is not about us and how we are in the position of strength where we can help them. It should be because we care about them and want to be in community with them. We are all one in God's eyes. How can you show the love of God to those you meet today?

Lord, Thank You for the gifts you have given us today and every day. Help us use those gifts to build the Kingdom by helping those You love. Help us to love them as

You love. Teach us your ways O Lord that we might know You better. And help us to know those You love better. Make our work here prosper in earthly and heavenly ways today. In Your name we pray. Amen!

# APRIL 28   WHY AM I HERE
Faith

Ephesians 2:8-10 (NKJV)
*⁸ For by grace you have been saved through faith, and that not of yourselves; it is the gift of God, ⁹ not of works, lest anyone should boast. ¹⁰ For we are His workmanship, created in Christ Jesus for good works, which God prepared beforehand that we should walk in them.*

Do you ever wonder why you were born in the time and place where you were born? How come you don't have to struggle to survive when many do? Did you do or say something special which gave you the great life and things you have and put you in the position to be of assistance to others? Ephesians tells us it is by God's grace alone. You did not choose the time and place of your birth. God did that for you. But He has a plan for your life to prosper you. It is your job to discover that plan and walk in God's ways wherever you are. You don't have what you have purely by your own hand and sweat of your brow. God gave you your life and good gifts. You have been blessed!

But here is consideration. God created us to do certain things according to His plan. You are His workmanship. More importantly, you were created to do good works. What does that mean? This verse tells us we were "created in Christ Jesus for good works." That means we are created in His image and likeness and designed to do good works in His name. Are you doing good works in His name or yours? Do you give glory to God for all He has done for and through you? It goes on to say these plans were "prepared beforehand that we should walk in them." What did God plan for you today? Was it to go on a mission trip? Is this about your desire to share or did God destine you to volunteer with the Hearts for Honduras Dental team or some other group? Do you even have a choice? It says these works were prepared "that we should walk in them". The key word is should. You do not *have* to walk in them but you *should*. You do have the choice. Which path will you walk? Are you going to bring glory to God through your walk?

When you decide to volunteer, what is it that makes you decide to help others? Is it that still small voice inside speaking to you? For me, God speaks through my subconscious. I don't have the answer (sometimes, I don't even know what question to ask.) or the idea and all of a sudden, the answer is clear. There is the whole plan with all the details. And the feeling is so strong that there is no doubt it came from Him. It is just knowing. It is walking by faith. Have you experienced anything like this? Where do you think these feelings come from? Better yet, what will you do about them? The next time you hear His voice or get "that" feeling, how will you respond? Will you agree with God's plan for your life and bring glory to Him? I hope so! Walking God's path is always the best route. Try it for yourself!

Father, we thank You that You are patient with us and give us many chances to listen and follow You. To whom do You wish to speak through our lives today? As we look back, we can see all the places and times when Your plan was the best way for your people to go. We are Your people. Be patient with us today. Give us the understanding and the strength to do Your will and walk in Your ways today; in Jesus name.

# APRIL 29    ANSWER TO A HIGHER AUTHORITY
## Attitude

1 Corinthians 10:31 (NKJV)

*31 Therefore, whether you eat or drink, or whatever you do, do all to the glory of God.*

Do you compare yourself to others? How do you measure up? What is the standard by which you determine the quality of your work? Are you trying to please yourself, others, your employer or your God?

Many people determine they are doing well by comparing themselves to others. I am a lot faster than Joe. I am smarter than Mary. What is the standard? Are Joe and Mary the standard? Should you compare your performance to theirs? Have you been given the same gifts? Will you be judged on a curve? God's standard is perfection. What if we compare ourselves to Him? Where does that leave us? Would you be feeling good about yourself if you were graded on His scale? Fortunately, God does not require perfection from us. He is patient with us asking us to be like Christ. He has set a good example for us in His Son! By His Spirit, He will *help* us to live according to His standard.

Today's verse tells us to do everything "all to the glory of God." It is all about attitude! The question is sometimes raised of how long have you been working for this company. The answer is "ever since they threatened to fire me!" Many people only work when the boss is watching. You work for a "higher authority." He is always watching! He never slumbers nor sleeps. If you work unto the Lord, will you do an outstanding job? You know the kind of work He wants. He wants you to bring glory to His name. Everything matters! Whatever kind of work you do, work to please God and not people! You will be assured of being far and away the best "you" that you can be! Don't be one of those people who says it is good enough. "Good Enough" is rarely good and seldom enough! Seek Ye first the Kingdom of God and all these things will be added unto you. Today, make God as proud of your work and your service to Him and others as He is of you. You are anointed, blessed, gifted and talented. Share those blessings with those you meet today! Do it now!

Lord, thank you for this day and every day. We have another chance to bring glory to Your name with the work of our hands and the words of our mouths. Direct our steps in Your ways. Give us the words we should say. Help us to speak, to be kind and loving to all Your children. In Jesus name we pray. Amen!

# APRIL 30   SING TO HIM WHO LISTENS
Faith

Psalm 68:4 (NIV)

*4 Sing to God, sing in praise of his name, extol him who rides on the clouds; rejoice before him—his name is the LORD.*

Do you thank God for all the little things you can do every day? Are you able to walk? Can you climb stairs? All these things are worth thanking God about. Let an attitude of gratitude flavor everything you do. Praise is a form of gratitude. It will make you happy. You don't sing because you are happy, you are happy because you sing! Sing to the Lord a new song,

When you sing praises to the Lord, He hears you and will turn His face toward you. Praise God in all things and He will bless you and care for you. When you praise Him, he commands His angels to go out with you and pave the way for you. He has them build His hedge of protection around you to keep you from harm.

King Jehoshaphat knew this principle and put people to sing praise God at the head of their armies as they marched out against their enemies. They praised God for all He had done for them in the past and what He would do in the future.  2 chronicles 20 says *"21 After consulting the people, Jehoshaphat appointed men to sing to the LORD and to praise him for the splendor of his holiness as they went out at the head of the army, saying: "Give thanks to the LORD, for his love endures forever."  22 As they began to sing and praise, the LORD set ambushes against the men of Ammon and Moab and Mount Seir who were invading Judah, and they were defeated."*

The battle was the Lord's alone and He defeated the enemies of Israel. God heard their praise and it reminded Him they were His people. It is good to remind God of His promises. As such, He defended His own! He did not choose this people for them to perish. He chose them to share His Word and reveal Him to the nations. In the same way, when you sing His praises, he will defend you. He is reminded you are His, made in His image and likeness. He turns His face toward you and blesses you whenever you praise Him! How will you praise Him today? Will you praise with word or deed or song? Any way will do. God longs to bless you. In fact, He has blessings stored up waiting for your praise to release them to you. Will you be blessed today? He desires to bless you. Help Him by praising Him in all things! We are asked to pray unceasingly. We can do that through songs of praise and thanksgiving. Will you pray with me?

Lord, Thank you for everything! Thank you that we are alive. Thank You that we can work and have jobs. Thank You for your patience and forgiveness. Thank You for every good gift You have given us. Help us to praise You at all times in thought, word and deed! In Jesus name we pray! Amen!

## MAY 1  DO THE IMPOSSIBLE WITH GOD
Faith

Romans 8:31-32 (NIV) More Than Conquerors!

*31 What, then, shall we say in response to these things? If God is for us, who can be against us? 32 He who did not spare his own Son, but gave him up for us all—how will he [God] not also, along with him [His Son], graciously give us all things?*

Have you ever approached a task that looked impossible? Perhaps, at work, you were assigned a project you had no idea how to complete. You are in way over your head, or are you? Sure, if you try it on your own, it may be more than you can handle. But here's the thing, you are never on your own! God is for you! Who dares to be against you? You and God are a majority!

God is for you! In Deuteronomy 28, God speaks about all the blessing He has for you if you will obey Him.

Here is a small list of those blessings:

*3 You will be blessed in the city and blessed in the country.*

*6 You will be blessed when you come in and blessed when you go out.*

*8 The LORD will send a blessing on your barns and on everything you put your hand to.*

*11 The LORD will grant you abundant prosperity......*

*12 The LORD will open the heavens, the storehouse of his bounty, to send rain on your land in season and to bless all the work of your hands. You will lend to many nations but will borrow from none.*

*13 The LORD will make you the head, not the tail.*

Sounds like a pretty good list to me. God wants to do all those things for us. In another place, it says "All these blessings will come on you and accompany you if you obey the LORD your God..." With all these things going for you, how can you not prosper and succeed in all the work of your hands? Even better, how about the work you do to the glory of God? Will He not bless that work? What should you do when you face a challenge that is more than you think you can handle? Why not turn to the One who has blessings stored up for you and desires to help you? In a conversation, a friend said he doesn't want to bother God with the small stuff. He figures he should handle some things on his own. But God wants you to come to Him with everything. He created us to be in fellowship with Him. He wants to hear all your thoughts and questions. He asks "so, how was your day beloved?" Do you go to God with everything or do you try to handle most of it on your own? What if you were on a first name basis with the best advisors available? Would you turn to them for advice on daily decisions? Why not turn to the One who created the whole universe for advice? Not only does He know everything but He is just waiting to share that knowledge with you! Ask Him! He will lead you in the right way.

Father, we thank You that You are always there for us when we have questions. Help up to turn to you at all times and not just when we are overwhelmed. Give us the confidence that You are always with us and you will always hear our voice and answer.

We might not like Your answer, but we know You always work things out for our best. Walk with us this day and lead us in the way we should go. In Jesus name we pray!

## MAY 2    LEAVING A LEGACY
Relationships

Matthew 6:19-21 (NIV) Treasures in Heaven

*¹⁹ "Do not store up for yourselves treasures on earth, where moths and vermin destroy, and where thieves break in and steal. ²⁰ But store up for yourselves treasures in heaven, where moths and vermin do not destroy, and where thieves do not break in and steal. ²¹ For where your treasure is, there your heart will be also.*

Each of wants to think we will build something that lasts. What if you could build something that lives on even after you are gone from this world? And on a smaller scale, what if you could be a part of something bigger than yourself, which could continue to serve even after you are no longer working at the project? Such is our chance each day. When we do our work as if unto the Lord, He will bless it in a way that will bring fruit that lasts. In fact, it will bear fruit again and again. What does it mean to store up treasures in heaven? How can we build treasures in heaven? By investing in people.

When you invest in people, you never fully know how far that fruit will blossom. Zig Ziglar tells a story about his high school coach named Jobe Harris who was a mentor to him. Jobe Harris was one of the young men who was mentored by the first Boy Scout official in the state of Mississippi, Thomas B. Abernathy. Mr. Abernathy was like a second father to Jobe teaching him all kinds of things that would benefit him and others for his entire life. These things would play a part in the lives of all the young men Jobe mentored. Jobe Harris taught Zig Ziglar many values that made him the man of God he became. But here is the twist. Mr. Abernathy never knew what he poured into Jobe Harris would later be poured into Zig Ziglar who would go on to marry Jean Abernathy, Thomas youngest daughter, after Thomas had passed away. Mr. Abernathy had a direct effect on his own future grandchildren. You never know how far your investment will travel and who it will benefit. How will you invest?

When we go on a short-term mission trip, do we go to change lives, or do we go to make ourselves feel better? I don't know about you but I am in the business of changing lives! Many times, we swoop in to a place and do a bunch of things "for the less fortunate" and then head back to our own lives without having made a lasting difference. Our thinking is earthly not considering why we want to help and what God wants us to do for others. If we paint a building, it is cleaner for a time. What if we paint God's love on a heart? What if we provide an education so people can better themselves? What if we tell them about God and how much He loves them and His gift of grace? Why we do things is always more important than what we do. Don't just give them a fish; teach them how to fish!

By participating in Hearts for Honduras school (or any worthwhile organization) in any way, you are building up treasures in heaven not only for yourselves but for others. I have heard the town of La Entrada, Honduras itself has improved its culture because of the school. People are being educated and are learning to do better. They are learning about God's love for them and who they are in Him. They are beginning to value themselves higher. As such, they are treating others better. The school is making a lasting difference on the whole community all because Paty Villanueva saw the opportunity to build treasures in heaven that will last. She invested in children and the cycle of improvement began. How can you be part of building the Kingdom? By building up people! Speak life into them. Give them hope! Of course, you have to solve the short-term problems. You can't teach kids about building their future when they are hungry now. Feed them! Then tell them about Jesus and His love for them. Tell them Jesus called you to come to them and that He wants the best for them. It is not about material things. It is about love. Don't go out to help people; go out to *love* them. There is a sign around the school that says "love wins." It is true. 1 Corinthians 13 says *"⁸Love never fails. ....¹³And now these three remain: faith, hope and love. But the greatest of these is love."* Leave a legacy of love! Love them and teach them God loves them, and you will build up treasures in heaven.

Father, Thank You that You love us and want to help us build treasures in heaven. Help us to leave a legacy that brings glory to You. Thank You for teaching us to love one another as You have loved us. Teach us Your ways that we might know you better. Write your story on our hearts. In Your name we pray. Amen!

# MAY 3   GREATEST IN THE KINGDOM
## Grace and Mercy

John 13:5-7 (NKJV) Jesus Washes the Disciples' Feet
*5 After that, He poured water into a basin and began to wash the disciples' feet, and to wipe them with the towel with which He was girded. 6 Then He came to Simon Peter. And Peter said to Him, "Lord, are You washing my feet?" 7 Jesus answered and said to him, "What I am doing you do not understand now, but you will know after this."*

Who does not want to be honored? Each of us wants recognition and sincere appreciation. It is a part of human nature. But it is the person who wants to serve others that is truly blessed. Luke 22:27 (NKJV) says *27 For who is greater, he who sits at the table, or he who serves? Is it not he who sits at the table? Yet I am among you as the One who serves.* Is it not the one who serves who will be honored by the Father because they are more like Christ? Did Paul not ask us to be imitators of Christ? How better to serve than to serve like Christ?

In April 2015, I was among a group of people who understood what it meant to serve. I was in La Entrada, Honduras at the Hearts for Honduras School with the Dental Team to do the yearly checkups for the 211 students, the teachers and the staff. I was one of 22 people who took vacation time to serve others. What an honor to be among these fine people. Their Christ-like example humbles me. It is not often you read a Scripture passage and then get to see it lived out in front of you. I did! Our group ranged in age from 22 to 70 all with the common goal of serving the people of HFH School. They were the hands and feet of Christ showing the love of Jesus in action and not just words. But why did this group choose to take time away from friends, family and business to help people they did not even know? Some of them are "repeat offenders" having served on the team 12+ times.

Why would someone give up their vacation for this? For me, it is such a blessing to be allowed to serve. My service was to the 15 people who were doing the dental checkups. I was the person sterilizing the instruments used to perform the service and they kept me busy. I got the honor of serving those who serve! Also, I got the chance to witness the enthusiasm with which they served. I got the chance to encourage team members when things were tough. The work was hard. We saw about 260 patients in four days. We worked from 8 am to 6 pm those four days. We spoke about the reasons for the service. We want to build the Kingdom and serve as Jesus asked us to serve; to take care of the widows and orphans.

We are also called to build relationships. It is only through a relationship that someone can be drawn to Christ. It must first be our relationship to a person that allows us to speak about a relationship to Christ. The most striking memory of this week for me was of Lizmarie; a six-year old girl who was terrified of the visit. She sat in Kathy's chair crying and would not let Kathy examine her teeth. Kathy was awesome and patiently showed her it was only a mirror and then demonstrated what the instruments would do but Lizmarie would have none of it! I worked right next to Kathy's chair and wondered what Jesus would have me do. I got the strong feeling (that's how God speaks to me) that Lizmarie needed a hand to hold so I took off my gloves and cleaned my hands. Then, I sat next to Lizmarie and held her hand. Her crying subsided and slowly, she allowed Kathy to do the cleaning and sealing of her teeth. God brought Lizmarie to Kathy because of her comforting way and called me to reassure Lizmarie. He used our gifts to bless one of His children. Lizmarie rose up victorious and with clean teeth! And what a blessing that was to us!

Have you ever been called to serve but hesitated because you are not sure what or how to do it? Don't worry! He will help and care for you. God does not call the equipped; He equips the called! Answer the call! There are many opportunities and many places. When you hear that still small voice saying "maybe I can do this" say YES! Jesus did not have to wash the disciple's feet. He chose to do it. He goes on to tell us that "What I am doing you do not understand now, but you will know after this." Well Lord, now, I understand!

Lord, thank You that you call us to serve! Thank you for allowing me to serve with such a wonderful group of selfless people. Thank you that we were able to change lives in Honduras in Your name and with Your provision. Thank you for all those who support Hearts for Honduras mission and bless each one of them. Bless all our sponsors. Bless all my team members and keep us safe until we meet again in Your name. All glory and honor are Yours. Thank You for the blessings of fellowship and safety You gave us by Your grace on this mission. In Jesus name we pray! Amen!

## MAY 4   BE AN ENCOURAGER
Encouragement

Proverbs 15:22 (NKJV)
22 *Without counsel, plans go awry, But in the multitude of counselors they are established.*

Why re-invent the wheel? Why not learn from the mistakes of others? You don't have time to make them all yourself. Everyone should be a mentor and have a mentor! Someone who can guide you through life's challenges and help you avoid the pitfalls. When you need someone with whom to discuss something, it would be great to have a listening ear of a person that cares about you. I had many such people. Of course, my Dad was the primary one but there were four men in particular that came along at times of transition in my life. It is said that when the student is ready, the teacher will appear. Wally Kowalenko, Ed Zinszer, Anthony Grausso and Brock Dutton were four men whom God placed in my life in His perfect timing. There are many more but one of these four told me to be brief. I am sorry this devotion is so long but what would you have me leave out? Each one of these men played a part in making me the man of God I am today.

Today is Wally's birthday. Here is a man who asked me to come live with him for the summer at a time when I was engaged in all-out war with my Mother. Wally was there to build my confidence at a time when I had none. He taught me many things about auto mechanics and about life. He taught me to believe in myself! Wally was always my champion ever since I was born which was when he came to live with our family. It is easy to accomplish things in life when someone believes in you. Wally was that someone at that time and now. He still encourages and believes in me today!

Edwin J. Zinszer came into my life through my girlfriend/fiancé/wife. Ed was the father of Jean's good friend Jimmy Zinszer from school. The families were very close. Ed was a most loveable and funny man. He had a lot of wisdom and was a great relationship builder. Ed had crippling arthritis which limited the things he could personally do. As such, he had to teach others (mostly his children and sometimes me) to do things he could not physically do any more. It taught him patience. He could explain to a novice how to repair an item. He taught his daughter Cyndi to change her own oil and service her own car. Ed was a strong man of God. It is said that you might be the only Bible some people ever get to read. I read the Zinszer Bible and learned about the Lord from Ed. He lived the Christian life! It took a few years but I came to know Jesus seven years after Ed went to be with the Lord. What can I say? I am a slow learner. But I did learn that lesson. Thank you Ed. Save me a seat please.

Next on the hit parade is Anthony J. Grausso. In 1973, my Dad and I rented our first service station. Dad was out of work and I was good at fixing cars. We decided we could make a living at this and we were right. One afternoon, Tony drove in to speak with us about joining the NJ Gasoline Retailers Association of which he was the Field Representative. There was something special about this man. He was humble and kind and always willing to share knowledge, if you would just ask. Two things stand out that I learned from Tony. First was to "play possum" as he called it. He taught me to always let the other guy think they are smarter than you and they will tell you all kinds of things that will be of benefit. Second, be careful about giving advice. You had to ask Tony for the advice. Someone once told me that unsolicited advice was criticism. Tony would never give advice but he would ask *"Now are you sure you want to do that?"* That always prompted me to ask why and he helped me avoid many costly blunders.

We come to Brock Dutton; a man fiercely devoted to God! I met Brock at a men's fellowship group at a local Church. I went there to enjoy fellowship with other Christian men who were more mature in their faith than I was. That was easy to find because I had just begun my walk with Christ. Brock is what I consider a Spiritual Giant in the faith. His main focus is building the Kingdom! He is going to be embarrassed about me talking this way about him because he is also humble. And he gets these devotions by e mail. We started out with Brock being my Spiritual Accountability Partner but that was more than 20 years ago. We meet for breakfast once a week whenever possible. Over the years, we have become advisors to each other and deep friends. As with the others, I love this guy! Brock has been an incredible advisor. If I had to narrow it down to one thing, it would be his best question, "What are you going to give up in order to take on that project?" I now hear that question in my head whenever I even begin to think of something I want to do. If I can't answer the question, I can't do the project.

I have heard that each person should have a Paul, a Barnabas and a Timothy in their life. You are supposed to be a Mentor, an encourager and a mentee. I have been blessed more than you can imagine. When you pour yourself into someone's life, you may never know how much it means to them. God has always blessed me in that He has always shown me the fruits of my labors and investments. I learned of one tonight. I never realized how much my investment of time meant to a young lady who was 8 at the time and a friend of our family. She revealed to me that she never forgot how I used to help her with her homework and the difference it made for her. I had long forgotten about doing that but she remembers it 40+ years later. You just never know how far those deeds will travel. What investment have you made in others? Do you even know what a difference it will make? God does! And He asks you to invest in people. I can tell you about the scores of people who have invested in me but I am not fully aware about those in whom I have invested. In whom can you invest? Also, ask God to reveal to you the fruits of those investments. You will be encouraged!

Father, I thank you for all the wonderful people You have brought into my life. Some were for a reason and some for a season. Thank You for revealing to me the fruits of those investments I have made. Your blessings are overwhelming! I ask that you bless all those who have blessed me and that I have blessed in Jesus name!

# MAY 5   NOS VEMOS ORTRA VEZ (UNTIL I SEE YOU AGAIN)
## Relationships

1 Corinthians 15:50-52 (NKJV) The Risen Christ, Our Hope

*50 Now this I say, brethren, that flesh and blood cannot inherit the kingdom of God; nor does corruption inherit incorruption. 51 Behold, I tell you a mystery: We shall not all sleep, but we shall all be changed— 52 in a moment, in the twinkling of an eye, at the last trumpet. For the trumpet will sound, and the dead will be raised incorruptible, and we shall be changed.*

We are told we shall not all sleep (die), but we will be changed. The Bible tells us the dead shall be raised and we shall be changed. Do you want to wait until the dead are raised to tell people how you feel about them? At the Resurrection, you might be speechless. Have you ever lost someone without getting to tell them something you really wanted them to know? Many of us leave things unsaid and live to regret our lack of expression. I have! There was a time when I would not tell those around me that I loved them. I left things unsaid. You never know if you will ever see them again. Although, if you accept Christ into your heart, you will see them again but it will be at the Resurrection. However, it is always better to speak what's in your heart now. Speak life! I don't want to wait. How about you?

When people know they are loved and appreciated, their life is usually more rewarding. I was in Honduras this week last year at Hearts for Honduras School. Honduras is a dangerous place. You never know what will happen. This was my second visit there and I had built relationships with the people of La Entrada. Particularly, Mauricio Erazo who is a vital part of that community and an important person to me. I had some time with him and he told me the story of how he came to know the Lord and why he runs the Youth for Christ camp. He is a hero in the Faith to me. There is something very special about Mauricio. At the end of our trip, Mauricio drove the big yellow school bus that took us to the airport. I have grown very fond of him and want to work with him to change our corners of the world. I am practicing my Spanish. A normal way of saying goodbye might be adios or hasta luego or chow. But that did not seem appropriate. I don't want to say goodbye anymore. I said "Nos Vemos Ortra Vez! Until I See You Again!" It may be next year when I return to Honduras. It may be the next time Mauricio comes to visit New Jersey. But it may be on the other side of Jordan in the next life. We never know. Here is what is important. I told Mauricio I am proud of him. I told him I admire his work. I told him he is my Brother in Christ. I used my words to build him up and encourage his work for the Lord! How do you use your words? Do you build up or tear down? May I suggest you build up? The tongue can build up or tear down. You choose how this will play out!

Father, help us to use our words to bless people and build them up in You. Give us the wisdom to know how to encourage and inspire. You said we should love one another as You loved us. Help us to claim Your promises. Guide us in Your ways that we may accomplish your will to spread Your grace to the ends of the earth. In Your name we pray!

## MAY 6    CELEBRATE THOSE WHO LOVE YOU
Encouragement

Proverbs 22:6 (NKJV)

*⁶ Train up a child in the way he should go, And when he is old he will not depart from it.*

Isn't it a parent's job to train their children in the right way to go? There is a book which is entitled "Everything I needed to know I learned in Kindergarten." We learn the basics on which we build in the very beginning. Do we tell the truth? Do we share? Do we speak kindly? Why? Because Mom taught us how when we were very young.

Today is my Mom's birthday. I was a miracle baby. Mom had a lot of difficulty delivering David, my older brother. Doctors told her she could never have another child. Surprise! She did not know she was pregnant but there I was. God called me to her for some reason and purpose and it is up to me to figure that out. It has taken a long time but encouraging people keeps coming to the forefront. Our world is discouraging. Everyone is telling you what's wrong and what you cannot do and it is taking its toll. My Mom had a very critical parent and it clouded her world vision. She was led to believe that she was limited. She also faced challenges that would have stopped others. She is a Holocaust survivor. Because of all the negative stuff in her life, she has a negative slant on her world view. Sometimes, she reverts back into negativity in our relationship. It is hard for her to be positive and hopeful. A person cannot give what they don't have to give. In spite of that, she taught us how to love and care for others and to love God. Trudy Springer raised two boys who are making a difference in the world in which they live. We were taught that we could! The expectation was set. Mom wanted David and me to make our world a better place; a place of justice and mercy. A place where people are told they are loved.

How does a person who has seen all that horror survive? By God's Spirit alone! No, my Mom is not perfect. No one is! But she is a reflection of our Heavenly Father. She has always loved us and taught us the way we should go. She does go negative on me from time to time but I call her out on it. I choose joy over sorrow and happiness over bitterness. I choose to look out the windshield of the future rather than the rear-view mirror of the past. Very bad things have happened in the past! I would be a fool to deny that fact. In light of those things, I choose to look toward God's grace and let His light shine in our lives. In the brightness of that light, you cannot see the shadows of all those bad things. Celebrate those who love you. I told Mom "as long as you keep having Birthdays, we will keep having parties." In her nineties, she is finally learning to celebrate! Happy Birthday Mom! I love ya!

Lord, thank You for teaching parents how to love us. We love because You first loved us. You are the source of all love. Thank You that you placed me in a loving and affectionate home where Your love was reflected and taught. Help us to all go out and love our neighbors as ourselves. Guide us in ways that will make our world a better place. In Your name we pray.

## MAY 7   HOME SWEET HOME
Relationships

Psalms 127:1-2 (NKJV)
*Unless the LORD builds the house, They labor in vain who build it; Unless the LORD guards the city, The watchman keeps awake in vain. It is vain for you to rise up early, To retire late, To eat the bread of painful labors; For He gives to His beloved even in his sleep.*

Is your home sweet? Are you at peace in your home? Do you get along with your family? Are things going the right way? Are you alone? It is a real blessing for a person to have a peaceful home life. But it is not always so. In many cases, there is strife in our homes. It is difficult to face the world when you have no sanctuary in your home!

Psalm 127 talks about the Lord building the house. What do you suppose that means? Is He actually the builder or the architect? As the architect, the Lord would be involved in the planning of how the house is to be built. By asking God into the planning stages, you are asking for His guidance in how to construct a relationship. The Creator of the universe also created us and knows how we are made. He would be the perfect One to consult when building a marriage. Most people spend more time planning the wedding than the marriage. If you invite the Lord in, He will bless your home and marriage "For He gives to His beloved even in his sleep." Isn't it a good idea to leave room for God's Holy Spirit in your home and marriage? Many of us follow our ego (easing God out). We think we know what is best. History has proven otherwise.

I know that God entering in has improved things in our home. I always believed in God but I did not understand that was supposed to mean He was in every part of my life. I thought He was there in case I needed Him but I had most things covered on my own! After all, He gave me these gifts and talents, didn't He? I should use them, right? It took a long time to understand that God wants to speak with us about everything; even the small stuff. If, by waiting for His guidance, I just hold back one wise guy comment, our lives will be better.

What if you are alone due to death or divorce? What if you have not yet found the one with whom you want to spend your life? Is home a sweet place for you? We were not designed to be alone so it probably is not to your liking. One thing to remember is you are never alone. God, by His Holy Spirit walks with you and within you! Psalm 121:4 says "indeed, he who watches over Israel will neither slumber nor sleep." He is always there to speak with you and comfort you. If you will let Him, He will lead you to the person He has ordained for you. In fact, that should be what we all do. We should let God find us our mate.

So, is your home sweet? If so, do you appreciate all that you have and thank and bless those there? If not, what part do you play in the discord? If you were more kind and patient, would it help? Are you trying to change the other person? All you can do is ask God to change you. Ask Him! Psalm 139:24 (NKJV) *24 And see if there is any wicked way in me, And lead me in the way everlasting.* God will lead you if you ask but you must listen carefully for His voice.

Hello Lord! Thank you for this and every day You grant us. Guide us in the ways we should go and teach us what relationships are supposed to be. Help us to think beyond the glitter of the wedding to the work and compromise of the marriage. Teach us to leave room for Your Presence in our homes and relationships. Give us the blessings You have stored up for us. In your name we pray! Amen!

## MAY 8   ARE YOU LOOKING FOR JESUS
Faith

Revelation 3:20 (NKJV)
<sup></sup>*20 Behold, I stand at the door and knock. If anyone hears My voice and opens the door, I will come in to him and dine with him, and he with Me.*

Are you looking for Jesus? He is here in my heart. How did He get here? In 1998, I heard Him knock and I opened the door. It is not really complicated you know! Jesus goes on to say He will come in if we open the door. To where? Actually, your body has been deemed the Temple of the Holy Spirit. Jesus wants to take up residence in your heart. In another translation, the word used is abide. He wants to live with you. He wants to be your companion. He wants to be right there just in case you want to talk.

Many people announce to others that they *found* God. He was never really lost. In fact, He was out looking for you. Jesus roams this world, by His Holy Spirit, seeking to save the lost. That's why He came. Are you lost? Do you ever wonder about your purpose? Do you have everything but still feel empty? Blaise Pascal said, "There is a God shaped vacuum in the heart of every man which cannot be filled by any created thing, but only by God, the Creator, made known through Jesus." With that in mind, why try to find satisfaction within ourselves. Jesus is knocking. Open the door! Let him in!

I have had several friends recently ask me how I can remain so calm and do the things I do in a relaxed manner. I point them to the source of my peace. Also, I share with them the same peace I have is available to them. Jesus stands at the door and knocks. Do you hear Him? Will you answer the door? He is waiting!

Thank you, Jesus, that You patiently wait for us to answer the door. Some of us are hard of hearing so could you knock a little louder? Some of us are cynical so could you send more testimony? By Your Spirit, call out to those who need You most and draw them to You. Only those You call will hear Your voice. I know You came for all people. Please be patient waiting for all to come to repentance and hear Your voice. In your name we pray!

# MAY 9   AM I OLD OR YOUNG
### Quality of Life

Joel 2:28 (NKJV) God's Spirit Poured Out
*28 "And it shall come to pass afterward That I will pour out My Spirit on all flesh; Your sons and your daughters shall prophesy, Your old men shall dream dreams, Your young men shall see visions.*

I have both dreams and visions. These writings are visions from the Spirit. Does that mean I am old or young? I choose young in the Lord. The Lord God has blessed me in many things. As a visual person, I see complete pictures of tasks to which God calls me. In fact, they flash up in my mind's eye so quickly I have trouble grasping the whole concept right away. And just as easily, I can lose them. I must record them as quickly as I can or risk loss.

God tells us, through the prophet Joel, He will pour out His Spirit on all flesh. God promised His Spirit to us almost 1000 years before Christ when the Holy Spirit came upon the Disciples at Pentecost. He who promises is faithful! What does it mean to have His Spirit poured out on all of us? In John 14, Jesus tells us *"26 But the Helper, the Holy Spirit, whom the Father will send in My name, He will teach you all things, and bring to your remembrance all things that I said to you."* We are told the Spirit will teach us all things. If you are like me, you will receive dreams and visions of the things you are to learn. Jesus goes on to tell us the Spirit will remind us of all He has taught us. Think about that. Do you realize how much information you already have? It is not lack of information that is the challenge; it is recall of that information. Jesus' Spirit will "bring to your remembrance" all things He has taught us. Is that good or bad? Sometimes, we do not want to be reminded of things we are supposed to do.

What dreams and visions has God already sent to you? Are they scary and overwhelming? Do you doubt you can accomplish them? Do you hope they will go away if you ignore them? God speaks to each of us in different ways. It is usually through that still small voice. You can choose to ignore it or you can be open to the Spirit's leading. I would ask you to be open to the calling. God can do great things through you! You are His masterpiece and He has already given you all the gifts and talents you need to accomplish the destiny He has ordained for you. *Please*, let nothing stand in the way of your destiny. God is for you! Who can stand against you? Nothing in all creation can keep you from your destiny except *you*! Which way will you decide today? Are you for or against "you"? God is for you! Why not side with Him and be who He called you to be?

Lord, help us to embrace the visions You have for us. You have great things planned for each of us. You said we are fearfully and wonderfully made. You said we are Your children. You said we can do all things through Christ who gives us strength. Help us to hear Your voice today, the Voice of Truth. By Your Spirit, help us today to be the victors You created us to be. In Jesus name we pray! Amen!

## MAY 10   WHO LOVES YA
### Quality of Life

Proverbs 1:8-9 (NIV)

*⁸ Listen, my son, to your father's instruction and do not forsake your mother's teaching. ⁹ They will be a garland to grace your head and a chain to adorn your neck.*

Mother's Day is a special time in our lives. It is a time to stop and consider all that Mom has done for us. Usually, a mother puts the needs of her children before her own needs and cares for them with everything she has to give. Such was the case in my life. I hope it was the same for you.

The Book of Proverbs is the Wisdom of Solomon. He was the king that asked God for wisdom above all else so God granted his request. Here, Solomon teaches us the value of our Mother's teaching. One simple example is I know how to tie my shoes and tell time. Mom taught me that. We are taught our Mom's teaching will be a blessing to us. Who could disagree with that? My Mom is in her nineties now. I am blessed to still have her. One thing about a ninety plus year old woman though. What comes into the mind comes out of the mouth uncensored. Sometimes it is even rude. Once an adult; twice a child. I am in the awkward position of having to correct my Mom's behavior. I do that by telling Mom "that my Mom taught me that was bad behavior and that she needs to correct the issue she has caused." She has a great deal of trouble arguing with her own teachings! She gives me this annoyed and bewildered look but has no rebuttal. It is comical at times. I never thought I would see my Mother speechless. By the way, I take after her in many ways.

Mothers are a blessing to us even though we may find them annoying at times. God ordained them to care for us and teach us things. A Mother's love is special. They have hopes, dreams and expectations for you. They want what is best for you. They will do anything to protect you! They give you the core values and the love you will need to build a life of distinction. Honor her. Love her. Cherish her. You never know how long you will have her in your life. In spite of everything, she loves you. Honoring your Mom will bring the blessings of God upon you. Be blessed today and show honor to Mom on her day and every day.

Lord, You said that honoring our Mothers would bless us so we would live long in the land You promised. Help us to understand our Mom's motive is to always help us do better. Lead us to Honor our Mom as she deserves. By Your Spirit, remind us of all she has taught us. Thank you for the blessing of our Moms. In Your name we pray! Amen!

## MAY 11   THE PAIN SEEMS MORE THAN I CAN BEAR
Grace and Mercy

2 Corinthians 1:3-5 (NKJV) Comfort in Suffering
*³ Blessed be the God and Father of our Lord Jesus Christ, the Father of mercies and God of all comfort, ⁴ who comforts us in all our tribulation, that we may be able to comfort those who are in any trouble, with the comfort with which we ourselves are comforted by God. ⁵ For as the sufferings of Christ abound in us, so our consolation also abounds through Christ.*

The Bible teaches us there is comfort in suffering. At first glance, that makes no sense. What comfort could there be in the loss of a friend? But after a closer look, it is revealed that suffering teaches us what we need to comfort others and that comforts us. Also, God does comfort us in our trouble. God never promised a trouble-free life if you accept Him. It is just the opposite. Our Lord told us "in this world you will have trouble." He warned us that it would not be easy. But He teaches that His consolation will abound in us also.

Recently, I lost a dear friend Carmen to ALS. This past week, I heard a friend of mine lost his friend to ALS. I don't think this is a coincidence. I spoke with my friend about this loss and told him I was available to speak with him any time if he needed me. I shared I was uniquely qualified to speak with him. You see, I had just been through the same loss. I am now able to comfort someone who is going through the same thing I went through only weeks ago. It is like God prepared me for just such a time as this. God does not waste anything. My loss prepared me to help someone else through their loss! Isn't that amazing?

I must admit I am still hurting from losing Carmen. He was such a part of my life that the pain is still there and will be for a long time. My former Pastor, Don Feuerbach, told me "The cost of loving much is grieving deeply!" That is very true. I am still grieving deeply. However, even in this grief, helping my friend would help us both. I am feeling better today than I did weeks ago. I can see I am walking through the Valley to the light on the other side. I now know there is "the other side". Like the Bible says, our consolation abounds in Christ. I can help my friend find his way.

Lord, thank you that Your consolation abounds. When we go through suffering, it is overwhelming. Please come to us in our suffering with Your grace, mercy and consolation. You are the God of all mercy. You are the God of all comfort. In Your mercy, walk with us through the valley and bring us to Your consolation. Prepare us to be a comfort to others who suffer as we do. Together, may we endure to Your rest. In Your name we pray. Amen!

## MAY 12   GIVE LOVE AWAY

Relationships

Matthew 14:17-21 (NKJV) Feeding the Five Thousand

*17 And they said to Him, "We have here only five loaves and two fish."*
*18 He said, "Bring them here to Me." 19 Then He commanded the multitudes to sit down on the grass. And He took the five loaves and the two fish, and looking up to heaven, He blessed and broke and gave the loaves to the disciples; and the disciples gave to the multitudes. 20 So they all ate and were filled, and they took up twelve baskets full of the fragments that remained. 21 Now those who had eaten were about five thousand men, besides women and children.*

Many are afraid there won't be enough to go around. The disciples were astounded that Jesus told them "you give them something to eat." Where would they be able to find enough food let alone pay for it? They were in the countryside with no stores around.

Jealousy comes from a feeling of lack. When a new child comes into a family, the existing siblings may feel they now have to share a smaller piece of the love pie. There might not be as much as there was or even enough for their needs. But love has a funny way of growing to be more than enough. Just like five loaves and two fish fed more than five thousand people with twelve baskets left over, a parent's love can do the same thing. That love is based on God's love which is infinite. We love because God first loved us. He taught us everything we need to know by giving Himself to and for us.

"Give Love Away" is the tag line at our Church. We are a church with many different missions and a lot of outreach. Our Pastor charges us to take God's love out into the world. But if we give it away, will we have enough for ourselves? Just like the feeding of the five thousand, not only will everyone be loved, there will be twelve baskets of left-overs. Come and get yours! We're open on Sundays.

Lord, just as You gave thanks to the Father in advance for what He would do in feeding the people, we thank You in advance that you will feed us with more than food. Thank You that You give us the food of Your love and the water of Your life. Just as You gave the food to the disciples so they could give it to the people, entrust us with Your Word that we can take it out to the world. In Your name we pray. Amen!

## MAY 13    YOU MEAN EVERYTHING TO ME
Love

### Isaiah 49:13-18 (NKJV) God Will Remember Zion

*13 Sing, O heavens! Be joyful, O earth! And break out in singing, O mountains! For the L*ORD *has comforted His people, And will have mercy on His afflicted. 14 But Zion said, "The L*ORD *has forsaken me, And my Lord has forgotten me." 15 "Can a woman forget her nursing child, And not have compassion on the son of her womb? Surely they may forget, Yet I will not forget you. 16 See, I have inscribed you on the palms of My hands; Your walls are continually before Me. 17 Your sons shall make haste; Your destroyers and those who laid you waste Shall go away from you. 18 Lift up your eyes, look around and see; All these gather together and come to you. As I live," says the L*ORD, *"You shall surely clothe yourselves with them all as an ornament, And bind them on you as a bride does.*

How many times have you wondered about what you should do in a situation? You wish you had someone with whom to talk. You would like to ask God but you can't bother Him with such trivial matters. He has a universe to run. He doesn't have time for your inconsequential problems. Reach out to God in all things. He wants a conversation.

Many times, we think God is too busy to worry about us when just the opposite is true. You are more important to Him than a nursing child is to its mother. He has inscribed you on the palms of His hands. This is true on more than one level. You can take a look at the palms of Jesus hands and see your inscription there. Thomas saw it 28 And Thomas answered and said to Him, "My Lord and my God!" Thomas recognized what Jesus did for him and still does for us today. God watches out for us always. He neither slumbers nor sleeps but watches over *you!* Are you aware of your Protector? Do you know how much He loves you? He adores you! God created the universe and all that is in it so He could have a relationship with you! The next time you think you don't want to bother Him with your problems, think again! If you are like me, you don't even understand how anyone could love that much let alone believe you are the object of His affection. You are His child. As such, He wants the best for you. Today, walk as if you understand you are a child of the King of Kings! Walk in your blessings!

Lord, we thank You that You care for us in more ways than we understand. We know You hold us ever before You and encircle us with Your protection as a shield. Help us to know You are there always. Grant us Your favor and Your peace. In Jesus name we pray!

## MAY 14   UNDEFEATED
Faith

1 Samuel 17:45-46 (NKJV)
*⁴⁵ Then David said to the Philistine, "You come to me with a sword, with a spear, and with a javelin. But I come to you in the name of the LORD of hosts, the God of the armies of Israel, whom you have defied. ⁴⁶ This day the LORD will deliver you into my hand, and I will strike you and take your head from you.*

Do you face challenges in your own power? We need to learn how to overcome challenges through the strength God provides. David did!

David was a shepherd boy of about 15 years of age. The armies of Israel were shaking in their boots because Goliath stood out there yelling taunts at them. The fact that he was nine feet tall may have been a contributing factor. No one wanted to face him for he was a fierce man of war. Yet David saw and heard Goliath and something came alive inside him. How was David able to be brave when others were terrified? In whose name did David step out?

David did not focus on the size of his opponent. David focused on the size of his God. He remembered that God had been with him before in protecting his father's livestock. David also used another principle. He remembered the times God had been with him and brought him success. Focus on your successes and not your failures! Focus on all God has done for you. Replay in your mind all the times God has brought you victory. Remember, God is for you. He is on your side. He loves you! The Lord will deliver your enemies into your hands. With God, all things are possible.

Father, we thank You That You go before us to pave the way and with us to give us Your strength. Be with us today in the battles we face and give us Your strength and wisdom. You said the waters would not overwhelm us. Give us courage to trust You and step forward in faith! In your name we pray! Amen!

# MAY 15   INTRINSIC VALUE
Attitude

Psalm 139 Selected Verses (NKJV)
*O LORD, You have searched me and known me. ......*
*¹³ For You formed my inward parts; You covered me in my mother's womb.*
*¹⁴ I will praise You, for I am fearfully and wonderfully made; Marvelous are Your works,*
*And that my soul knows very well. ¹⁵ My frame was not hidden from You,*
*When I was made in secret, And skillfully wrought in the lowest parts of the earth.*
*¹⁶ Your eyes saw my substance, being yet unformed. And in Your book they all were written,*
*The days fashioned for me, When as yet there were none of them.*

**Intrinsic** [in-trin-sik, -zik] adjective {Dictionary.com}

1. belonging to a thing by its very nature: It is the value that an object has "in itself" or "for its own sake" (i.e. the intrinsic value of a gold ring.)

Do you understand the value you have before you do or say anything? Do you realize you have worth even while at rest if only because God says you do? Many of us do not understand our intrinsic value which was placed in us by God at the time of our creation. Each human being was fearfully and wonderfully made. God's works are marvelous and you are one of those works. I have two stories to illustrate the importance of knowing who you are in Christ.

My wife Jean and I are foster parents. As such, we take care of other people's kids. Many times, these young people were not imbued with confidence and self-esteem. In fact, it is quite the opposite. Riding along in the car seems to be one of the best places for deep discussion. We were riding along when one of our sons said "My father told me I am a worthless piece of s—t." I was blessed with the ability to pause for thought at that point. After a few seconds, I began a response. I asked questions about all the accomplishments this young man had achieved one at a time. After 4 - 5 landmark accomplishments had been established, I asked "do you think your father could have been mistaken?" What if that had not been discussed? Would this young man go through life believing he was worthless?

Another son told me he was no good. During the time I was putting him to bed, he told me someone said he had the devil in him. Who would speak to a little boy that way? Another moment of clarity from the Holy Spirit yielded a great result. We drew an imaginary chart of the things people said about him and what God says in His Word about us. I asked him for all the bad things that people had said and pretended to list them on the left. Then, I listed all the good things God says on the right. God's list was much longer! After that, I asked him who he was going to believe; people or God? He chose to believe God! Who do you believe?

Please take another look at yourself as if through the eyes of the One who formed you! You are fearfully and wonderfully made! You are the image and likeness of God! You are one of His marvelous works! He loves you enough to give Himself up for you! That alone is reason to celebrate! Do you celebrate yourself? God does!

What have you accomplished? (He has given you gifts and talents.)

Whom have you helped?

Is your corner of the world a better place for you having been there?

Today is one of our son's birthdays. It is a time to celebrate the life of one of God's masterpieces. I would ask you to take another look at yourself today. You, too, are a masterpiece. It is time to celebrate you!

Lord, thank You that You created us all in Your image. We praise You because we are fearfully and wonderfully made. Open our eyes to Your truth about ourselves and others. Thank You that You gave us intrinsic value. Thank You that, before we do or say anything, we have value in Your eyes. Help us to live today as the wonderful creations You made us to be. In Your name we pray!

## MAY 16    IS JESUS AN ACCESSORY IN YOUR LIFE
Faith

John 14:12-14 (NKJV) The Answered Prayer
*12 "Most assuredly, I say to you, he who believes in Me, the works that I do he will do also; and greater works than these he will do, because I go to My Father. 13 And whatever you ask in My name, that I will do, that the Father may be glorified in the Son. 14 If you ask anything in My name, I will do it.*

Jesus is telling His disciples they would be able to do more things than Jesus Himself had done. Really? He tells them he is returning to His Father. And the most amazing thing He says is He will do whatever they ask in His name! Are you kidding me? Jesus will give me whatever I want? Well, not exactly.

You see, Jesus is not a cosmic vending machine. He is not there to give you whatever you want. There are some criteria. You have to ask something in His name. What does that mean? To be in His name means to be in His will. To do that, you must know His will and that takes being in His word and listening for His Holy Spirit.

Pastor Anne Havrilla said "If we only come to Jesus to fulfill a felt need, once we receive that need, we have no more need for God." I personally need God always. There is a place in my heart that only He can fill. What is the focus of your needs? Are you most concerned about the things you need or are you considering the needs of the community around you? The Bible says "Seek Ye first the Kingdom of God and all these things will be added unto you." Zig Ziglar said, "You can have everything you want in life by helping enough people get what they want!" Your focus is to be on others, especially God! When we decide for ourselves, we do it in our own power. We are easing God out (ego). When we open up to what God wants for us, He will lead us in the best way for us. Do you just want to talk with Him when you want something, or would it be best to have conversation about all the things that come up in your life? He loves you! He created the universe to support you. Remember to accessorize by wearing Christ! Be in Him. He has a great destiny for you. Ask Him to lead you there.

Thank You Lord that You are always there for us. Thank You that you will lead us in Your ways which will bless us more than we can ask or imagine. You said You would do whatever we ask in Your name. By Your Spirit, lead us to ask for the things You want for us. In Your name we pray!

## MAY 17   WHAT DO YOU SEE
Quality of Life

Proverbs 29:18 (KJV)
*18 Where there is no vision, the people perish: but he that keepeth the law, happy is he.*

Today, many people lack vision. They cannot see beyond what is right in front of them. Creativity is diminished. Problem solving has gone by the wayside. Taking the easy way out has become the norm. They only do what is required. At one time, our country was known for innovation. There are still a few bastions of hope in innovation mostly in the tech arena. But what about day-to-day living? Where are the people of vision who look at every situation and find a way to make it better? They are not as prevalent as they once were but they are still there. Have we stopped teaching critical thinking?

Every now and then, you come across someone with vision. And even more rare, you find a person with Spiritual Vision. That person sees things that God has revealed. I have met such a person in my friend Scott. He sees things others have not recognized, visions from God. Sometimes, he is too far ahead of the curve seeing things that others are not yet prepared to receive. Unfortunately, that happens. We must be patient and wait for the rest of the world to be ready. But the best part of this type of vision is that it is given for the good of others. Scott is always looking out for others. He is a connector. He is a person that tries to put people together for their benefit. This vision is a kind of love. It "is not puffed up; 5 does not behave rudely, does not seek its own" as it says in 1 Corinthians 13. This vision is given for the good of all. And the rare person who uses that gift to benefit others is an inspiration to many. That is what I have seen in Scott. He inspires me! He makes me want to do better and share more. I am blessed to know him. I want to be more like him.

A disappointment to me is that many parents take the easy way out and rather do things themselves instead of teaching the next generation how to accomplish things. Jean and I are teaching Clayton to solve problems. We have told him we want him to be able to, not only take care of himself, but others as well. We want him to improve his corner of the world! Instead of giving him all the answers or doing it for him, we ask leading questions trying to get him to draw his own conclusions. We are trying to raise a productive member of society; a person of vision! Many have sight but no vision. Will you expand your vision today and look toward improving your corner of the world? For without vision, the people perish!

Father, we thank You that You give us vision. Teach us to use the gifts You have given. Encourage us to take the steps to improve every situation with which we come in contact. Revive us to once again become the great nation of vision you created us to be. Help us to return to You and receive Your Spirit. For Your Spirit will reveal all we can become. In Your name we pray.

# MAY 18    SEEING IS BELIEVING OR IS IT
Faith

John 20:24-29 (NKJV) Seeing and Believing
²⁴ *Now Thomas, called the Twin, one of the twelve, was not with them when Jesus came.* ²⁵ *The other disciples therefore said to him, "We have seen the Lord." So he said to them, "Unless I see in His hands the print of the nails, and put my finger into the print of the nails, and put my hand into His side, I will not believe."* ²⁶ *And after eight days His disciples were again inside, and Thomas with them. Jesus came, the doors being shut, and stood in the midst, and said, "Peace to you!"* ²⁷ *Then He said to Thomas, "Reach your finger here, and look at My hands; and reach your hand here, and put it into My side. Do not be unbelieving, but believing."* ²⁸ *And Thomas answered and said to Him, "My Lord and my God!"* ²⁹ *Jesus said to him, "Thomas, because you have seen Me, you have believed. Blessed are those who have not seen and yet have believed."*

Have you ever seen a great illusionist? I saw Lance Burton in Las Vegas. He made cars disappear and people appear. It was amazing. Do you think these things actually evaporated? No, it was just an illusion.

In today's Scripture, we meet Thomas, the disciple a.k.a. Doubting Thomas. He was called doubting because he would not believe the Lord had risen unless he saw Jesus himself. Aren't we like that, too? You would think Jesus would be angry with Thomas for doubting, wouldn't you? Instead, Jesus showed such patience that He gave Thomas everything he needed to believe. And what happened? Thomas declared "My Lord and my God!" The doubter had now become an exuberant believer! Now Thomas would declare the raising of Jesus to everyone with whom he came in contact. He was on fire. Isn't that the way it is with most of us? We are skeptical at first and that is a good thing. We need to make sure things are what they are purported to be. But once we are sure, we excitedly take that information to anyone who will listen.

What about you? Are you excited? Are you willing to take the message out to anyone who will listen? That takes a special person. Sort of like the one God created when he created you. You see, Jesus told us we were to go and make disciples of all nations. And one thing I know about Him is He equips each of us with everything we need to accomplish our destiny. He asks you to tell others why you love Him and why He loves you. So why does He love you? Is there something special about you? Yes, there is! You are a child of the Most High God made in His image and likeness. You are fearfully and wonderfully made. You are His Masterpiece. But why do you love Him? He taught us how to love. I love Him because He is the only One who has never let me down. I love Him because He gave everything for me! I love Him because He taught me how to love. Scripture says we love because He first loved us. His love for us is perfect.

With that in mind, how shall we love others? Should we not share the love of Christ with them? That is what He calls us to do! You are probably afraid. What will you say? In Ephesians 6:19, Paul asks that you "¹⁹ Pray also for me, that whenever I speak, words may be given me so that I will fearlessly make known the mystery of the gospel". Don't worry! The Spirit will lead you. And you may get lucky and only have to set an example. Either way, He will be with you. So go, make disciples of all nations.

Lord, Thank You for loving us! You gave everything to show us all what we mean to You. Help us to show the world what you mean to us! Take away our fear of speaking about you. Strengthen our resolve. Start a revival and let it begin with each of us. In Your name we pray!

## MAY 19    P.U.S.H. - PRAY UNTIL SOMETHING HAPPENS

Prayer

Luke 18:1 (NIV)
*Then Jesus told his disciples a parable to show them that they should always pray and not give up.*

Prayer changes things. Not everyone believes that but for those who do, prayer changes things. It doesn't always change the things we want changed, nor the way we want them to be changed, but it changes things. Faith is an important factor. Jesus told people their faith had healed them.

Many times, we are not sure how to pray. We think we have to use just the right words in the proper format or it won't be heard. But prayer takes many forms. There are prayers of thanksgiving. There is intercessory prayer. And there are conversations with God. Those are my favorites. What if you don't know how to pray. Are you out of luck? Not at all! You see, we have help. Romans 8:26 says *"26 In the same way, the Spirit helps us in our weakness. We do not know what we ought to pray for, but the Spirit himself intercedes for us with groans that words cannot express."* When you can't even find the words, God's Holy Spirit will help you through your thoughts. Ask for help praying. Just talk to God. Jesus says you have not because you ask not! Ask and you shall receive the help you need. And keep praying until something happens.

Father, help us with our prayers. By Your Spirit, intercede on our behalf giving us the words we do not know how to express. And answer our prayers with Your best for us. We only know what we want. You know what we need. Lord, give us Your desires for us which is what we need! In Your name we pray!

## MAY 20   THE DAWN IS COMING
Grace and Mercy

Psalm 112:4 (NIV)

*⁴ Even in darkness light dawns for the upright, for those who are gracious and compassionate and righteous.*

This verse tells us how the light dawns for the upright. Who is upright? Romans 3:23 tells us all have sinned and fall short of the glory of God. Isaiah says we all, like sheep, have gone astray. None of us is righteous on our own. Are we gracious and compassionate? Not in our own power. You see, God is our light. He makes His face to shine upon us and be gracious to us. It is all Him. His grace alone makes us righteous. On our own, we cannot make it. From our point of view, it looks really dark!

No matter how dark it may appear, the light of God is coming. It is always darkest before the dawn. It may be Friday but Sunday is coming. Last night was the final session of GriefShare, a program I attended with my friend Christine. Her husband was my best friend as well as hers. It is a little over a year since Carmen passed and it has been a dark time. GriefShare has allowed us to see the light of the dawn of healing. While there is still the pain of our loss, there is hope. God is that hope. He returned from death and walked among us for 40 days to show us that there is life after death. From the Garden of Eden, God promised us good. Two thousand years ago, He showed us His plan. The offer still stands! Will you accept? The light of the dawn of Grace shines. Are you in its glow? Do you feel its warmth on your face? His grace surrounds you even at your darkest times. Although I felt I was walking through the darkness alone, His grace has dawned into my darkness. He offers the same to you. Will you take it?

Lord, thank You that You shine Your light into our darkness. Even as we walk through the darkness of this world, You shine the light of Your grace into our lives. Thank You for walking with us and lighting our way. In your name we pray! Amen!

# MAY 21  JOY IS COMING
## Quality of Life

Psalm 30:5 (NKJV)
*⁵ For His anger is but for a moment, His favor is for life;*
*Weeping may endure for a night, But joy comes in the morning.*

Our Heavenly Father does get angry with our bad behavior. I think it is more His disappointment. He knows we can do better but many times we take the easy way out. We sin! But He is the God of second chances. Although He is angry now, He will forgive. He will also help us if we ask.

We become afraid in the dark. Things look bad. We don't see how we can survive this trial. The evil one works under cover of darkness. He reminds you of all your shortcomings. With the dawn, bloom new possibilities. God has a plan to prosper you. If you will let Him, He will bring that plan about. We need to remain in faith and believe God will keep His promises. He is faithful. We worry about the issues we face because we try to control the situation ourselves. What is troubling you today? Will worrying make it any better? Have you done all you can to solve the situation? If so, why not leave the rest to the Lord? Joel Osteen said "Don't wait to thank God until you see the sunshine, dare to thank Him while it is still dark!". That is showing faith.

We tend to hang on to things we cannot change as if we can. Learning to let go is an important quality to a happy life. Yes, do the best you can to solve the challenge but know when it is beyond you. Continued anguish will not bring the solution. Give it your best. Work as if unto the Lord. But know when to let go and let God! Weeping may endure for the night but joy comes in the morning.

Lord I want to thank You now for Your blessings that You are sending our way. Thank You that You are working all things out for our good. Healing is coming. Blessing is coming. Promotion is coming. Thank You that Your plan for peace and blessing is on its way! Please give us Your peace while we patiently wait. In Your name we pray!

# MAY 22   YOUR DREAMS ARE NOT DEAD-RESURRECTION POWER

Faith

Numbers 17:7-8 (NKJV)

*7 And Moses placed the rods before the LORD in the tabernacle of witness.*
*8 Now it came to pass on the next day that Moses went into the tabernacle of witness, and behold, the rod of Aaron, of the house of Levi, had sprouted and put forth buds, had produced blossoms and yielded ripe almonds.*

Things in your life or business may seem dead. It may look like there is no chance of redemption but God may have other plans. Aaron's rod was a walking staff he had used for a while. It was a dead piece of wood. How could it come back to life?

The Israelites were questioning the authority of Aaron as High Priest and Moses as the Leader of Israel in Chapter 16 of Numbers. This rebellion was led by Korah and his followers who were rebelling against God's decision in leadership but they thought they were opposing Moses and Aaron. Moses was fully aware they were questioning God and he "fell facedown" because he feared God's wrath for the people. And God's wrath came in the form of fire which consumed the 250 men of the rebellion. Now that God showed them His decision, He wanted to show His power in choosing Aaron. His instructions were to place the walking staffs of the leaders of the twelve tribes of Israel in the Tent of Meeting in front of the ark of the covenant. God had caused Aaron's staff to bloom and bear fruit proving Aaron was His chosen High Priest. God took a dead piece of wood and brought it back to bearing fruit! What do you think He can do in *your* life?

Are there things in your life that appear dead? Are your dreams gone? Do you feel you cannot ever recover? God is a God of resurrection power. He can bring that which appears dead, like Aaron's staff, back to life! What seems impossible to you is simple for your God. He brought His son back to life for you. Won't He also resurrect what is dead in your life now? He's done it before!

If you want to witness a resurrection, you have to keep on going. You have to keep on believing. You may think your dreams will never come to pass. They may just come to stay. You may have just lost a job. God may have a better opportunity waiting. You may have lost a loved one. God may have ended their pain and suffering and taken them unto Himself. With that much power, why doesn't God return my loved one to me? Are you sure you want to take them away from God where there is no pain or suffering? God's power can bring the dead back to life. What is dead in your life? Is it your career? Is it your dreams? Genesis 18:4 asks "is there anything too hard for the Lord?" The answer is *no!* He can do all things. Will you believe and allow Him to bring things back to life for you?

Lord, we know all things are possible for You. You brought Aaron's rod back to fruition. Is there anything You cannot do? Please work in our lives to bring that which was dead back to life. You have done it before. We believe You can and will do it again! In Jesus name we pray.

## MAY 23    I STILL BELIEVE
### Grace and Mercy

Job 19:25-26 (NKJV)

*25 For I know that my Redeemer lives, And He shall stand at last on the earth;*
*26 And after my skin is destroyed, this I know, That in my flesh I shall see God,*

I know my redeemer lives. That is what Job said. He had just lost everything that was near and dear to him and he still praises God. His wife told him to curse God and die. After all he went through, he still praises his Creator. Job was able to stay in faith. Are you?

In this world you will have trouble! Jesus told us that. It is not how much trouble you have but how you handle it that matters. Many people ask why God allows bad things to happen to good people. That is an interesting question. In Job's case, the bad things were the work of Satan. Satan challenged God that Job would curse God if all his blessings were removed from him. God did allow this to happen probably because He knew how strong Job was in his faith. Job trusted God with everything! In the face of total calamity, Job said "The LORD gave and the LORD has taken away; may the name of the LORD be praised." His faith was unshakeable! How is your faith? Are you able to respond calmly when bad things happen? Do you look to find the lesson in the challenge? Do you remain in faith?

Job lost everything but remained in faith. Job came out with twice what he had before. Isaiah 61:7 says *"7 Instead of your shame you shall have double honor, And instead of confusion they shall rejoice in their portion. Therefore, in their land they shall possess double; Everlasting joy shall be theirs."* Do what you can and let God do what you can't. Stick with God. He's got your back!

I Know my Redeemer Lives - Nicole C. Mullen -

He lives to take away my shame And He lives forever I'll proclaim
That the payment for my sin Was the precious life He gave
But now He's alive and there's an empty grave

Lord, thank you that You always stick by us no matter what happens. Thank You that You take away our shame. Thank You that You love us so much that You came to redeem us from all our shortcomings. Please strengthen us to be like Job so that we can remain in faith to You!

## MAY 24   WHO IS YOUR ENEMY
Support

Ephesians 6:10-13 (NKJV) The Whole Armor of God
*10 Finally, my brethren, be strong in the Lord and in the power of His might. 11 Put on the whole armor of God, that you may be able to stand against the wiles of the devil. 12 For we do not wrestle against flesh and blood, but against principalities, against powers, against the rulers of the darkness of this age, against spiritual hosts of wickedness in the heavenly places.*
*13 Therefore take up the whole armor of God, that you may be able to withstand in the evil day, and having done all, to stand.*

We are fighting evil forces today. Paul wrote to the Church at Ephesus about many things that were causing them trouble giving advice on how to overcome the challenges. In this section of Chapter 6 of that letter, he advises them the only way they can stand against evil or the wiles of the devil is through God's power signified by His armor. He tells them they "do not wrestle against flesh...but against the rulers of darkness of this age." We are in the same battle daily.

Many people wonder why bad things happen to good people yet they never consider the "rulers of darkness" hand in the equation. Our world is a very dark place with more people being won over to that dark side daily. People are out for what's in it for them. And that is not just outside the Church. I have been in a Church where the status quo was more important to the members than the Word of God and His truth. The image of the Church mattered more than speaking the truth in love and following God's word. How do you see things? Do you call out the dark things looking for change or do you sweep it under the rug? Are you on the slippery slope where a little deviation from God's word is OK? The little things grow faster than you realize like yeast in dough. Before long, you are nowhere near what God wants for you. And it all happened gradually.

What does God's word say to you? I know it can be difficult to follow but do you read it? No one said it would be easy. In fact, Jesus said just the opposite. Do you want to follow God's will or would you like to go along with the world? Which choice yields better results in the (very) long run? Isn't it best to vote for and with God? Listen to your heart. You are fighting forces you cannot overcome without God's help. Put on His full armor and stand with Him. The battle is His and He will fight it if you let Him. It is only your job to *stand*. Don't you want to stand on His side? When you listen to God, He blesses you in more ways than you can imagine! Go with God and be blessed.

Lord, we face difficult times. Darkness prowls around like a roaring lion looking for someone to devour. Please help us not to become his next meal. Thank You for giving us Your armor which can protect us from the evil one. Please let us wear Your Spirit as the undergarment to that armor to give us the layer of protection needed to be able to stand for You! And once dressed, help us to *stand*! In Your name we pray! Amen!

## MAY 25   SPEAK LIFE
Encouragement

Proverbs 18:21 (NKJV)

*²¹ Death and life are in the power of the tongue, And those who love it will eat its fruit.*

There is power in your words. Words have the power to bless or curse. How will you use your words? Will you build up or tear down? What fruit will you eat?

All people need encouragement. As the verse says, life and death are in the power of the tongue. What you say can change someone's life. Do you encourage people? Do you encourage your spouse? Children need encouragement more than others. Too many of us are critical of their mistakes but don't offer enough encouragements when they are trying new things. In fact, you can become a "Good Finder". Look for the good in every situation and praise it when you find it. Sure, you need to discourage bad behavior. But why not put any correction in a praise sandwich?

Ephesians 4:29 says *"Do not let any unwholesome talk come out of your mouths, but only what is helpful for building others up according to their needs, that it may benefit those who listen."* Let us not love with words only. Let our deeds match our words. When you love someone, you do what is best for them. Building people up is the key phrase. This world seems to be focused on tearing people down. With just a few words and a smile, you can reverse that trend. Go out to be a Good Finder! How many people can you praise today? Be sincere! If you find someone without a smile, give them one of yours! Speak life into them!

"In every encounter, we either give life or we drain it; There is no neutral exchange." Brennan Manning

Father, we thank you for this day You have given us. Help us to use it to bless others with kindness. Help us to give life! Let our words encourage those we meet. Help us make encouragement a habit. In Your name we pray!

## MAY 26   HOW SHALL WE PRAY

Prayer

Romans 8:26 (NIV)

*In the same way, the Spirit helps us in our weakness. We do not know what we ought to pray for, but the Spirit himself intercedes for us through wordless groans.*

Sometimes, we face situations that are way beyond anything we have ever faced before. It is the elephant in the room. We are unprepared for it. It looks like our whole world may fall apart. This challenge is so overwhelming that we cannot see anything else. We have many things that need our attention but the elephant is all we can see. We can't take care of anything else.

What challenge do you face? Is it overwhelming? Does it take up all the staff's time and attention? And then there are things you can't say or do. You feel like your hands are tied. You don't know what to do first or at all. What do you do when you don't know what to do? Why not ask the One who can solve any challenge?

The Spirit can help us in our weakness. When we don't know what to do, the Spirit does. Why not turn to the Spirit? When we try to do things in our own power, we come against forces of evil that we cannot overcome. But with God, all things are possible! He can guide us down the correct path. His path! Yes, we face things that are beyond our capability. It is a good thing we are not going it alone. Pray! Use words or groans or whatever. Think, because God knows your thoughts. He loves you and wants what is best for you. He will protect you. By His Spirit, He will walk you through whatever you face. He is with you!

Father, thank You that You are always with us. We are in trying times. We need You now. Come to us and direct us in Your paths. Give us wisdom. Help us to remain together in You! In Jesus name we pray. Amen!

## MAY 27   WHOM SHALL WE FOLLOW
Faith

Acts 4:18-20 (NKJV)
*18 So they called them and commanded them not to speak at all nor teach in the name of Jesus. 19 But Peter and John answered and said to them, "Whether it is right in the sight of God to listen to you more than to God, you judge. 20 For we cannot but speak the things which we have seen and heard.*

In the passage above, Peter and John are in front of the Sanhedrin being grilled because of their teaching. The religious leaders don't want them speaking any more about Jesus. These are the leaders of the people. Shouldn't Peter and John listen to them? But what do they say? Those two rascals decide they should listen to God and not man! How about you? To whom do you think you should listen?

We come to many crossroads where we have to make tough decisions. The world asks us to do a lot of things that it wants us to do. We are offered fame and fortune. Luke 4 says 5 Then the devil, taking Him up on a high mountain, showed Him all the kingdoms of the world in a moment of time. ...... and I give it to whomever I wish. 7 Therefore, if You will worship before me, all will be Yours." He will offer you all kinds of things too. Yes, there are people who go the way of the world and culture. But you need to follow your God to be truly blessed.

When you stand at the crossroad of a big decision, how will you make the right decision? What is your motive? The world will plant fear, uncertainty and doubt (FUD). God has always revealed Himself as the One having a good plan for your life. He has always been faithful. For thousands of years, He has led His people to victory. Isn't that the way you want to go? How do you go down God's path? By digging deep into His Word and doing what it says. The Bible is an instruction manual for a blessed life. It has the answers, then and now! Your choice is to lean on your own wisdom or follow God's ways. When the world tells you that you can't, God says you can! Are you facing a big decision currently? What voice will you follow? You decide!

Lord, thank You for this day and every day. Thank You for Your Word which gives us the information to live a life pleasing to You. Help us to hear Your still small voice of Your Word. You have always offered us blessings for obedience. Show us Your way in the tough decisions we face today. Help us to make the right choice, Your choice. In Jesus name we pray! Amen!

# MAY 28   THE UNITY OF BELIEVERS
Relationships

Romans 15:5-6 (NKJV)
*"5 Now may the God of patience and comfort grant you to be like-minded toward one another, according to Christ Jesus, 6 that you may with one mind and one mouth glorify the God and Father of our Lord Jesus Christ."*

In this verse, Paul talks about being like-minded toward one another. Unity glorifies God. There are many places in the Bible that speak about the unity of believers and how important it is to God.

People have more similarities than differences but we seem to focus on the differences. At times, we are faced with differences of opinion that separate us. But God wants nothing to separate us. If we focus on Him, our similarities become more evident. Since we were created in the image and likeness of God, we have His seeds of greatness within us.

People can get hung up on issues. Are issues more important than relationships? Some are too liberal; some are too conservative. If a liberal and a conservative lock arms, they will be able to stand up straight. They can stand strong in the Lord. It is good for us to balance each other out. As in Paul's example of the body, not everyone can be an eye. Someone has to be a nose or the whole thing falls apart. What if you had two left legs? Wouldn't buying shoes become more difficult?

Are you going to let differences of opinion separate you from the people you love? It is all about relationships! The most important of these is our relationship with God. He wants to be in communion with us. And He wants us to be in relationship with each other. God does not want discord in His family. We need to approach the differences with humility and an open mind. We need to hear each other's side and respectfully consider how we can close the divide. Of course, we cannot compromise God's Word. His Word will not return to Him empty. Jesus said He did not come to change the Law but to fulfill it. We need to speak the truth in love. One part of the Law that we are called to fulfill is making disciples of all nations. On that, we should be able to agree and move forward together.

Father, thank You that You call us to unity into Your body, the Church. Help us to look for similarities rather than differences. Teach us Your ways that we might know you better. Bring out humility in us that will allow us to be open in mind and heart to the needs and concerns of others. Help us to understand the Spirit of the Law and live in such a way as to attract others into fellowship with us and You. Help us to praise You as one body. In Jesus name we pray! Amen!

## MAY 29    SET A GOOD EXAMPLE
Quality of Life

James 1:21-22 (NKJV)
*21 Therefore lay aside all filthiness and overflow of wickedness, and receive with meekness the implanted word, which is able to save your souls. 22 But be doers of the word, and not hearers only, deceiving yourselves.*

"The greatest single cause of atheism in the world today is Christians: who acknowledge Jesus with their lips, walk out the door, and deny Him by their lifestyle. That is what an unbelieving world simply finds unbelievable."    — Brennan Manning

James tells us to live our life doing what the Word teaches. Brennan Manning wrote something called the Ragamuffin Gospel. His quote tells us about why people are atheists. What example are you setting for those around you?

At our Church, we are charged with the responsibility of taking the Good News out into the world. I am not sure we always do that. What example do you set when you step outside the Church building? I heard a story of the man who always waves a friendly hello when he sees you at Church but gives a different kind of wave when you cut him off in traffic. And he is not telling you that you are number one either. Is that you?

People are watching to see how you live your life. What are they seeing? Are they learning about community? Do you care for others in a way that warms their hearts and builds a desire to join you? That is what we are supposed to do in Christ. We are commanded to love one another. We are to listen to those in need and try to help. The Church could easily solve the world's problems if they were willing to step outside themselves and love as Jesus loved. That is a lofty goal. When they look at your Church community, are they drawn in or repulsed? Do you greet a cynic with disdain or kindness? How do you welcome the stranger?

What do they see in us? Are we pulling together for the same cause or are we each looking to have our own way and grab glory for ourselves? God will not share His glory! I don't know about you but I am not willing to fight Him for it. I'd rather give Him the glory and enjoy the blessings of obedience. Each day, when we face the world, will we show unity and love to draw them to our Lord? Today is another opportunity for you to set a good example. Why not be the person others want to be around? Why not love others as you have been loved or would like to be loved? Go, therefore, and make disciples of all nations through your actions of kindness!

Lord, help us to be doers of Your Word. You gave us the Bible for our benefit "so that it will go well with us." You set an example of how to love. By Your Spirit, help us to draw others to You into the Good News. Help us to live Your Word! Keep us together as one so we can bring glory to Your Holy Name. In that name we pray!

# MAY 30 I STILL MISS THEM
### Grief

John 16:22 (NIV)
*22 So with you: Now is your time of grief, but I will see you again and you will rejoice, and no one will take away your joy.*

Losing someone is tough. But we all go through many losses. We lose people. We lose jobs. We lose pets. We lose opportunities. Every day, there are losses. But this is a time when we remember those who gave the ultimate sacrifice to secure our freedom. Many have sacrificed for the cause of freedom. But what about those they have left behind. There are many pictures of children and wives hugging a grave stone that remind us of a greater sacrifice. John 15:13 (NKJV) says *13 Greater love has no one than this, than to lay down one's life for his friends.* What about someone who would lay down their life for someone they don't even know? They secure the freedom of the yet unborn!

For people of faith, the loss is staggering. It was to me. But Jesus reminds us He will see us again. In fact, we are taught resurrection will come to all believers, so our loss is temporary. Eternal life means our joy will go on forever. Even so, the pain is overwhelming. What about those who do not share in the promise? Will their pain go on forever? Who do you remember today? Were they considered a war hero or are they just a hero to you? Time dulls the memory of the pain and the blessings of the person become more evident. It makes missing them harder. You do heal but you are never the same!

Believers have the promise of seeing their loved one again. How do you comfort someone who does not have that hope? Their loss is forever. Jesus tells us that, if we follow Him, we are His friends and we will bear fruit. And that the Father will give us what we ask in His name. Why not ask for the fruit of kindness? Ask the Father to send His Spirit to those who do not yet believe, that their hearts may be opened to the Good News. Ask Him to draw all people to Himself to share in the promise. Ask Him to deliver on His promise from Revelation 21:4 (NIV) when *"4 'He will wipe every tear from their eyes. There will be no more death' or mourning or crying or pain, for the old order of things has passed away."* That would be the world in which we all want to live. A world in which there were no longer pain to remember.

Lord, You promised us a world without pain or tears. Your offer is extended to all people. Today, we ask you to bring about that promise and extend the offer to people of every nation and tribe. Remove all hatred and bring about Your peace. Open all hearts to Your ways that each may ask You to enter in and abide. May Your peace which passes all understanding manifest itself in everyone bringing about the Kingdom of God here and now. We pray for peace in Your name! Amen!

## MAY 31    YOUR WILL BE DONE
Faith

Luke 22:42 (NKJV)

*⁴² saying, "Father, if it is Your will, take this cup away from Me; nevertheless, not My will, but Yours, be done."*

Jesus was the Son of God! He went to the Garden of Gethsemane to commune with His Father over upcoming events. Even He wondered if there was a way for Him to avoid the Cross and asked that the Cup of Death pass from Him. He asked the Father if it could pass but followed up with "Not my will Lord, but Your will be done!" You see, what was most important was that God's will (and His perfect plan) be done.

In our world, we want things our way. We want it now! What if we did things God's way? What if we followed His Laws and lived our lives as He leads? When we go our way, God lets us see how it will work out. My friend Mark says when you stand up and say I've got this; God sits down and lets you go on your own. But when you sit down and ask Him for help, He says "I've got your back." You decide. Who do you want in charge; you or God? Nevertheless, not my will but Thy will be done! For Your will always bring blessing.

Father, thank You that You always have a plan for our good. Help us to embrace that plan and live our lives for You which is really best for us. You know how we were made. You know how we should live. Lead us! Help us to sit down so You will stand up. And help us to stand up for You! Your will be done!

## JUNE 1    A NEW BEGINNING
Encouragement

Isaiah 43:19 (NKJV)
*19 Behold, I will do a new thing, Now it shall spring forth;*
*Shall you not know it? I will even make a road in the wilderness And rivers in the desert.*

Isaiah reveals God's plans to do a new thing. He revealed to Isaiah He was going to do a new thing. This new thing is to bring the Israelites back from captivity in Babylon. This is good news for them. But not everyone thinks something new is good. Many dislike change.

Many people are saddened when something comes to an end. In most cases, an end of one thing can be the beginning of another. Most times, God has to end the thing in which you are involved or you will never move to another thing. Most of us will not let go of what we have. Is it fear? I'm not sure.

About eight years ago, we were at another Church. Some awful things happened which caused our Pastor to leave. We were devastated! So much so that we ended up leaving that Church. Here is the thing. Nothing short of that disaster would have gotten us to leave that Church. There were many things there we knew were not right, but we were not hearing God's call telling us it was time to go. He had to do a new thing to get our attention. Only in this case, it wasn't a good thing. Or so we thought.

*But God* usually turns His new things into good things. It may take a while for the good to become evident. At first, it seems we miss what we had. But in time, we see why God has done this new thing. It took eight years for us to find the place to which we were called. How do you handle the new things God sends into your life? Do you pout because things have changed? Why not be patient to see what God is doing in your life? When we face new things, we don't always like the change. God has a plan for you, to prosper you, to give you hope and a future. We know God works all things for our good. Why not wait and see how His new thing will turn out?

Lord, thank You that You always work all things for our good. Please give us the patience to wait and see how your New Things will turn out. Help us overcome the fear of change. Help us to know that new can mean better. In Your name we pray!

## JUNE 2    NO MORE SHAME
Grace and Mercy

Joshua 5:9 (NKJV)
*9 Then the LORD said to Joshua, "This day I have rolled away the reproach of Egypt from you."
Therefore, the name of the place is called Gilgal to this day.*

What is reproach? Dr. David Cannistraci defines it this way. A reproach is a supernatural condition of shame or disgrace that settles into a person's spirit, coloring every aspect of their life. Reproaches are demonic devices that leave us feeling disgraced and unworthy. Like a heavy cloud, reproaches block out the light and warmth of the Father's love, leaving us in the chill of hopelessness.

For 430 years, the Egyptians had told the Israelites that they were of no value. Have you had someone criticize you? The Israelites were on the plains of Jericho after crossing the Jordan River. They were getting ready to conquer the Promised Land beginning with Jericho. But they were not mentally ready. They still carried feelings of unworthiness. They still carried the guilt of their former sin and the weight of their oppression. God commanded Joshua to circumcise all the men of Israel as a sign of His covenant with them since their fathers had perished in the desert. God was saying He was still willing to keep His promise to Israel. He is faithful!

Do you struggle with worthiness? Do you question yourself? Do you wonder how God can still care for you after all the bad things you have done? In your own power, you are not worthy because you are not perfect. But that is the mystery of the Gospel. You are worthy because God says you are worthy. Jesus righteousness is imputed to you by His will; not yours. You are fearfully and wonderfully made in His image. He wants to remove your sins from you and take them far away. He will blot out your transgressions. Today, He wants to roll away the reproach you have carried so long. 1 John 1:9 (NKJV) says *"9 If we confess our sins, He is faithful and just to forgive us our sins and to cleanse us from all unrighteousness."* He is willing to cover our sins with His love as if it never existed. What is it of which you are ashamed? What bad choices have you made that led you away from God? He calls out to you to return. He wants to be in relationship with you. He loves you! You are His masterpiece made in His image and likeness. Shame makes you run and hide. God wants you in His presence. It is the blood of the Lamb that makes you worthy! Wear the garment of righteousness provided for you by Jesus and come back into the presence of God. He misses you. He has been asking for you! He asked us to save you a seat. Here is one right next to me. Come worship the Lord our God with us. Sunday in coming!

Father, we are all sinners, for breaking one of Your laws is like breaking them all. Don't let our reproach block out the warmth of Your love from us. Remind us You love us with an everlasting love and want us with you. Remind us we are Yours and You are always willing to forgive if we would just ask. Today, reveal to us You have rolled away the reproach of our past and created in us clean hearts and new Spirits so we may return to You. Help us to accept Your invitation back into Your presence for which

Jesus prepared the way. Help us to accept Your gift of Grace. In Jesus name we pray! Amen!

## JUNE 3    WHO DO YOU SAY I AM
Faith

Matt 16:15-16 (NKJV)

*15 He said to them, "But who do you say that I am?" 16 Simon Peter answered and said, "You are the Christ, the Son of the living God."*

Jesus was spending time with his disciples speaking with them about who He is and what others think about his identity. When he asks Peter who he thinks Jesus is, Peter reveals Him as the Christ. Peter knew who Jesus was and is. But did Peter know who Peter was?

How about you? Do you know who you are? Who are you in Christ? What do people say about you? Who do *you* say you are? If you were at your own memorial service, what would people be saying? What kind of legacy will you leave?

What do you say when you talk to yourself? Remember, words take on meaning when they are spoken. You need to be careful what you say about yourself. The biggest obstacle to accomplishing a goal is yourself. The battle begins in your mind. It is about what you believe. And those beliefs will translate into the actions you take or do not take. If you don't believe you can do something, you can't. Whether you think you can or you think you can't, either way you are right! We have talked about what you say about yourself. But what does Jesus say about you? He says you are a masterpiece, the apple of His eye, holy, righteous and redeemed. You are beautiful. You are His friend and He is yours. You are made in His image. You are loved. With all that going for you, why do you sabotage yourself? Why not believe God and what He says about you and live accordingly? It is your choice. Why not choose to be who you were created to be? God is pulling for you. I am pulling for you. I ask you to pull for yourself. You are special. You are valuable. You are His!

Lord, please reveal to us who we are in you. We see the beauty of creation and ignore all the beauty you have put in us. Bring people into our lives who support and value us. Help us to see ourselves through Your eyes. In Your name we pray!

Write to me bob@calldrbob.com and request "Who I Am in Christ"

## JUNE 4 YOU CAN'T GIVE OUT OF AN EMPTY VESSEL
Grace and Mercy

Psalm 23:5 (NKJV)
*5 You prepare a table before me in the presence of my enemies;*
*You anoint my head with oil; My cup runs over.*

David praised the Lord for all the blessings He had poured out on David. We know David had more than he needed because he says his "cup runs over". When you have more than you need, you are in a position to help others. What about if you don't have enough?

My Cup is not running over. I am stressed, tired and run down. And now, people are all asking me for help. I feel I have nothing to give. "Put your mask on first." When you are on an airplane, they tell you to put on your mask first and then help others. Why? Because you cannot help others if you are not taking care of yourself. At the end of the Sabbath, Jewish people celebrate the Havdalah service of separation (from the Sabbath) to prepare for the week ahead. In that service, they have an overflowing cup of wine. Here are the instructions: "Fill a kiddush cup with either wine or grape juice, until the liquid overflows a bit onto the plate below. This is symbolic of our desire for blessings to overflow into the week." Those blessings that overflow can also be the source of blessings you can share with others. It is only out of the overflow that you can bless others. With that in mind, you need to take time to take care of yourself so you have the mental, physical and spiritual resources you need to take care of others. That is why God gave you the Sabbath! It is a time to rest, recharge and draw closer to Him. He will bless you through this time. Are you using it in that way?

Are you overwhelmed? Are you tired? Have you ever noticed when you are doing something for which you have passion, your strength is renewed? God is the source of that strength and passion. Isaiah 40:31 (NKJV) says *"31 But those who wait on the LORD Shall renew their strength; They shall mount up with wings like eagles, They shall run and not be weary, They shall walk and not faint."* Do you trust in the Lord? Do you wait on Him? Are you honoring the Sabbath rest? The Sabbath is God's gift to you. Will you accept it and be blessed by it? You decide!

Lord, thank You for the gift of the Sabbath rest. Help us to enjoy that time to be spent with You. Renew us by Your presence in our lives. Teach us to take time to be quiet and hear Your call. Give us our Sabbath rest and help us to accept it! In Your name we pray. Amen!

## JUNE 5  WHAT IS SUCCESS
### Quality of Life

2 Timothy 4:6-8 (NKJV)

*⁶ For I am already being poured out as a drink offering, and the time of my departure is at hand. ⁷ I have fought the good fight, I have finished the race, I have kept the faith. ⁸ Finally, there is laid up for me the crown of righteousness, which the Lord, the righteous Judge, will give to me on that Day, and not to me only but also to all who have loved His appearing.*

Paul finished well. But by whose standards? Was he wealthy? Was he famous? What did he have at the end of his life? He was pretty much alone and in prison. He requested someone bring him his cloak. Not very impressive by the world's standards indeed!

By what standards do you wish to be judged? The world will tell you that you need to drive this car, buy these clothes, shop here and live in this community. Really? Our culture has let Madison Avenue advertisers set the standards for our lives. Sorry, but that was done long ago by our Creator. I have come to a point where I care what He thinks. I want to live by God's standards because I know He set them for our good. If we live the way God desires, we will be rewarded in Heaven but also will reap benefits of peace and contentment here. We don't need so many things. We don't need such big houses. What if we decided to live well below our means? Would we have more resources available to help those in need?

What does success look like to you? Is it being happy? Is it being healthy? Is it good family relationships? Is it having good friends? Is it having peace of mind? If so, why not follow the One who offers you all of these and so much more? Blessing after blessing is there for you if you follow God's ways. All of this is within your reach. Read Deuteronomy 28. You will be blessed everywhere. You will lend and not borrow. Your enemies will be defeated. God will bless the work of your hands. He will grant you abundant prosperity. He will open the storehouses of heaven and pour out His bounty upon you. On top of all that, when you face the righteous Judge, He will hand you the Crown of Righteousness. That sounds like success to me! I want the things God has in store for me. Wouldn't that be good for you as well? Have you fought the good fight? Hopefully, you are not near the end of your race but you never know. Have you kept the faith? Be more concerned about how you look to God than to man. Work toward pleasing God. And you too are promised the Crown of Righteousness.

Father, guide us through the maze of decisions this world calls us to make. Help us to hear Your will for our lives. Teach us things that will bless us and turn our eyes away from the temptations that seduce us to evil. There are blessings in obedience. The evil one tries to distract us from Your plan. By Your Spirit, help us keep our eyes on You. In Your name we pray!

# JUNE 6    I'M NOT SURE I CAN DO THIS

### Faith

Philippians 4:12-13 (NKJV)

*12 I know how to be abased, and I know how to abound. Everywhere and in all things, I have learned both to be full and to be hungry, both to abound and to suffer need. 13 I can do all things through Christ who strengthens me.*

Paul knew both ends of the spectrum. Even in the worst of times, Paul still had faith that God would bring him through. As Job said, "I know my Redeemer lives." I am not as sure in my faith as Paul but I am working on it. I don't know if I can do all the things to which I am called. It is my human side which doubts. For we know God gives us everything we need.

Actually, I *know* I can't do it if I have to do it on my own! Last year was a tough year. I have lost my best friend and faced other challenges. I know that God uses challenges to refine us. He uses them to rub off our rough edges. I know I have a lot of rough edges but I could use a break.

We have a chance to take in another Foster Child who is seven years old. There is a chance we could adopt him but that is always uncertain. I am concerned we become attached and the adoption falls through for whatever reason. At that point, he would be removed and I am not sure I could handle the loss added to what has already happened. We have lost kids before and it is tough to handle. I know it is all part of God's plan and it will go according to His will. Even so, I am still stuck in my humanness and may not be ready for the loss. Jean, on the other hand, is all gung-ho! I am the conservative one who wants to throttle things back and take it slow. That is a reversal for me. But the point is God never gives us anything that is more than we can handle. 1 Corinthians 10:13 (NKJV) *says13 No temptation has overtaken you except such as is common to man; but God is faithful, who will not allow you to be tempted beyond what you are able, but with the temptation will also make the way of escape, that you may be able to bear it.* This basically tells us God will make a way for us to do whatever He calls us to do. It's a good thing too because I cannot do this in my own power. I will need to be in God's will and power.

How about you? Are you facing challenges that are above and beyond what you think you can handle? Are you trying to do it on your own? Know there are many things you can't do alone! You need His power which is readily available to you. All you need do is ask. He awaits your petition! Pray that you are in God's will and He will give you all you need to accomplish that to which He calls you. It is hard for us to remember. I struggle with that. Pray for me and I will pray for you. Together, we should be able to handle things with God's help.

Lord, help us to remember that You stand close by to aid us in whatever we need to do Your will. Your Spirit resides within us reminding us of all You have taught us and giving us the power to bear fruit in Your name. You will never leave nor forsake us! On that we can depend. Help us to be strong and courageous in Your name. Amen!

# JUNE 7   BECAUSE YOU SAID SO
Faith

Luke 5:3-5 (NKJV) Four Fishermen Called as Disciples
*³ Then He got into one of the boats, which was Simon's, and asked him to put out a little from the land. And He sat down and taught the multitudes from the boat. ⁴ When He had stopped speaking, He said to Simon, "Launch out into the deep and let down your nets for a catch." ⁵ But Simon answered and said to Him, "Master, we have toiled all night and caught nothing; nevertheless at Your word I will let down the net."*

Jesus is with His disciples and asks for Simon's help to be able to teach the people. He asks Simon (Peter) to bring the boat out a little from shore so He can teach without being crowded. Jesus needed a little space. After He is done teaching, He asks Peter to put out into the deep for a catch. He wants to bless Peter for the use of the boat. But Peter knows better. There are no fish to be caught at this time. Just to humor Jesus, Peter says, almost sarcastically, "at Your word I will let down the net." He was in for a big surprise. The catch was so great it almost sank the boats.

When you hear Jesus speak to you, do you try to ignore it and hope it will go away? I know I do. Do you always obey? Do you say we tried that once and it did not work? Have you done things in your own power and not succeeded? Are you willing to take Jesus at His word and work in His power?

I have been blessed to hear and see things others have missed. I try to ignore what God is trying to tell me or show me hoping it will go away and He will give up putting the idea in front of me. It doesn't work! He keeps reminding me of His will. He is patient with me. I cannot tell you how often I go to people with these ideas and they tell me "we tried that once and it did not work". Since these ideas are not mine but have been given me, I know where they are from and I know they are in His timing and part of His plan. Therefore, I know they will succeed. But others are not ready to listen. It used to frustrate me and I would argue with people. That is one of the rough edges God has rubbed off of me with circumstances. I have come to a place where I can be patient. I share these ideas with people and I am prepared for the "no". God has allowed me the patience to bring the idea up again and again just as He does to me when I resist. And it is working! What has happened is people are beginning to realize these are not my ideas but God's leading. Some of my "crazy ideas" are getting traction because God has built a reputation of giving me these and them working.

Are you hearing a call to do a "new thing"? Could these thoughts be coming from God? Does He want you to step out of your comfort zone and go a new way? Does He want you to launch out into the deep? What is holding you back? Many times, we don't believe it is God leading us. My experience is if the idea won't go away no matter how hard you try to ignore it, it is God speaking to you! A sure way to test ideas is compare the principles to Scripture. If this idea is consistent with what you have learned in Scripture, it is from God. God still speaks today. But remember, it is that still small voice. It is hard to hear over the roar of this world. Listen carefully and focus on God. He will guide you! Test Him in this and see if He will not throw open the floodgates of heaven and pour out so much blessing on you that you will not have places to store it all. (Malachi 3:10)

Thank you, Lord, for caring enough to remain close to us in our daily lives. Your Spirit lives within us and is ready to remind us of Your teachings and guide us if we will listen. Make Your presence known as we walk with You. Teach us Your ways O Lord that we may know you better and follow Your leading. Help us to let down out nets! In Your name we pray. Amen!

## JUNE 8   INNER BEAUTY
Relationships

*1 Peter 3:1-5 (NKJV)*
*¹ Wives, likewise, be submissive to your own husbands, that even if some do not obey the word, they, without a word, may be won by the conduct of their wives, ² when they observe your chaste conduct accompanied by fear. ³ Do not let your adornment be merely outward— arranging the hair, wearing gold, or putting on fine apparel— ⁴ rather let it be the hidden person of the heart, with the incorruptible beauty of a gentle and quiet spirit, which is very precious in the sight of God. ⁵ For in this manner, in former times, the holy women who trusted in God also adorned themselves, being submissive to their own husbands,*

Peter is talking about submission to begin with and that usually brings out negative thoughts. It speaks to the definition of meekness which is anything but weakness. If you can get past the first line, you will discover the discussion of inner beauty. God holds a gentle and quiet spirit very special. That is the real focus.

Win others over without words is what we should strive to do. It is our conduct that is supposed to set the example. We should exhibit a gentle and quiet spirit that will attract others to us. When they see the fruit of the Spirit displayed in your life, they will want to know more about what you have that gives you such peace. That will open the door to discussion of the Good News.  You see, that peace and gentleness are available to anyone who seeks the Lord. Who do you know that would benefit from a relationship with the Lord? How will you approach the subject? Wouldn't it be easier if they were to ask you about your relationship? So instead of focusing on making yourself outwardly attractive with clothes and jewels and material things, why not work on making yourself inwardly attractive with peace, kindness, gentleness, self-control and speech that glorifies God? Be inviting without words. Smile! Be friendly. And then conduct your life with love as you were shown by Him who loves you more than you can ask or imagine. The One who did give Himself up for you. Be beautiful inside and out and let His light shine forth from you!

Lord, let the beauty of Your glory shine its light into the dark places in our souls driving out any darkness. Then, let that light shine outwardly, attracting those to whom You wish to speak to us and give us the words You want to say to them. Today, let revival begin and let it begin with us. In Your name we pray. Amen!

## JUNE 9  THE LIES THAT BIND
### Quality of Life

John 8:31-32 (NKJV) The Truth Shall Make You Free
*31 Then Jesus said to those Jews who believed Him, "If you abide in My word, you are My disciples indeed. 32 And you shall know the truth, and the truth shall make you free."*

The Truth Will Set You Free. If the truth will set you free, then lies will bind you. Secrets are a type of lie as well and they will keep you from living the open and free life that God created for you. Whenever you try to keep a secret, there is a certain amount of guilt. And that guilt will hinder your life.

What lies have you inherited? Are there beliefs you have gotten from your environment? Lies about God? Lies about our origins? Lies about your abilities? Lies about other people? Has someone told you that you would never amount to anything? Has anyone told you that you cannot do a particular thing or that you are not good at something? Those are all lies and they can bind you in a way that will keep you from achieving your destiny.

When you were a baby, you did not know what could *not* be done. You had just come from God and were close to Him. As such, you were also close to your inspiration. As you spend more time in the world, people tell you more about what they think you cannot do and it begins to take its toll. These negative comments will set limits in your mind that will prevent you from accomplishing what blessings God has established for you. The battle goes on in your mind. How can you stop the damage negativity causes? By not letting it sink in to your mind. Compare what people say to what God says. If their comments don't line up with God's word, ignore them. Pretend they did not even speak. Pastor Joel Osteen says, "hit the delete key". People don't determine who you are. God already established that before you were born. Believe and live according to His plan. It is always a great life!

Father, thank You that Your plan for us is awesome. Help us to hear what You say about us and ignore the words of the naysayers. You made us in Your image and likeness. Let us hear Your voice; the Voice of truth. And let us live the truth that is found in Your Word. That we are fearfully and wonderfully made. That we are precious in Your sight. That we are Holy, Righteous and Redeemed by Your grace and in Your name. Let our accomplishments be in Your name and to Your glory. In Jesus name we pray! Amen!

Write to me at bob@calldrbob.com and ask for "Who are you going to believe?"

## JUNE 10    ARE YOU WHO YOU ARE CALLED TO BE
### Quality of Life

2 Corinthians 3:2-3 (NKJV)

[2] *You are our epistle written in our hearts, known and read by all men; [3] clearly you are an epistle of Christ, ministered by us, written not with ink but by the Spirit of the living God, not on tablets of stone but on tablets of flesh, that is, of the heart.*

He who trims himself to suit everyone will soon whittle himself away. - Raymond Hull

Who are you? Who were you called to be? Do you know? We are all put in this world for a purpose and our job is to figure out that purpose. 2 Corinthians 3 gives us some insight into what that might be. It tells us we are an epistle read by all men. An epistle is a poem or other literary work in the form of a letter or series of letters. But this epistle is not written on paper. It is written on people's hearts including yours. This literary work is a love story. It is the love of Christ poured out through His Apostles. Are you an Apostle? Be who God called you to be!

God calls you for a purpose. Ephesians 4:11-12 (NKJV) says [11] *And He Himself gave some to be apostles, some prophets, some evangelists, and some pastors and teachers, [12] for the equipping of the saints for the work of ministry, for the edifying of the body of Christ, God calls each of us to certain task for the equipping of the saints.* What is your task? Have you done a good job of listening and discerning what you were called to do? We are all called to share the good news. But are we supposed to do that as a full-time vocation? Probably, most of us are supposed to do what we are doing with an eye toward God and sharing His love as a part time job. We are always supposed to be prepared to give an answer as to the hope we have in the Lord even as lay people. As the Body of Christ, it is most important that we love God and love those who He loves. Are you sharing the love? What steps could you take to help others draw closer to God? It is our lives that people are reading. What does your life say? Is this the example you want to set to those who watch you? I hope so! If not, ask God to change you today.

Hello Lord! You asked us to come to you with our questions and concerns. Who is it You want us to be? Since we were made in Your image, help us to be more like You. Help us to see things through Your eyes. Help us to love as You love. Please write our stories on the hearts of the people with whom we come in contact that we may leave them better than we found them. Help us to be a blessing to others and glorify You in that process. In Your name we pray!

# JUNE 11    BETTER OR BITTER; YOU DECIDE
## Quality of Life

Hebrews 12:10-11 (NIV)
*¹⁰ They disciplined us for a little while as they thought best; but God disciplines us for our good, in order that we may share in his holiness.¹¹ No discipline seems pleasant at the time, but painful. Later on, however, it produces a harvest of righteousness and peace for those who have been trained by it.*

Does anyone like discipline? Why does a parent discipline their child? Is it just to be mean? Or could it be the discipline was for our good? Discipline teaches us which way we should go and removes our rough edges. Since God knows what is best for us, His discipline will ultimately lead to a more blessed life. There are many examples of discipline in the Bible which show us how it has helped many. Pastor Joel Osteen said "The pain of discipline is much less than the pain of regret. It is better to be uncomfortable for a little while than to make a poor choice and be uncomfortable for a very long time." Parents who do not discipline their children are setting them up for a life of pain.

How do respond to discipline? Are you angry or do you accept it as training you for a life of righteousness and peace? Without discipline, there is chaos. We need to know right from wrong. We need rules to guide our lives. Learning God's ways is an important part of living well. If you are a parent, do you want your children to live a blessed life? What things will you teach them to guide them on that path? Discipline does not have to be harsh. You can teach truths with stories in advance so your child will know what to do in a particular situation. Teaching them shows them you love them. You did teach them not to touch something hot, didn't you? Why? Because you care.

So, when you find yourself prevented from doing something you wanted to do, will you ask yourself "what am I supposed to learn here, or will you show frustration?" Life is full of lessons. Will you learn them? If God prevents what you perceive as an opportunity, you know it is for your good. Be still and observe. Try to learn the lesson. God loves you too much to answer certain prayers with a yes. Better or bitter. You decide!

Father, we all get angry and frustrated when we don't get our own way. Help us to see Your hand in things so we can understand why and learn to make better choices. Help us to see these things as lessons and not discipline. Help us to remember that discipline is showing love; that it is for our good. In Your name we pray!

## JUNE 12    I WANT TO LIVE LIKE THAT
Quality of Life

Ezekiel 33:10-11 (NKJV)

[10] *"Therefore you, O son of man, say to the house of Israel: 'Thus you say, "If our transgressions and our sins lie upon us, and we pine away in them, how can we then live?"' [11] Say to them: 'As I live,' says the Lord God, 'I have no pleasure in the death of the wicked, but that the wicked turn from his way and live. Turn, turn from your evil ways! For why should you die, O house of Israel?'*

How, then, shall we live? By caring for others as God cares for us. By being an awesome friend, which is something special. I have a friend for about 20 years who has become my spiritual accountability partner and much more. We met at a Church Men's Group when I was early in my faith walk. There was always something special about this man. It was obvious that he was strong in the Lord. I even took a course called Evangelism Explosion where he was my mentor. We visited the homes of people who had come to the Church and tried to answer their questions about their faith. Mostly, it was letting the Spirit speak. Anyway, he was like a Barnabas (Son of Encouragement) to me then and now. We became more than mentor/mentee pretty quickly. In fact, we meet for breakfast weekly to support and encourage each other and have for these 20+ years.

Today, at our breakfast, it occurred to me how awesome a friend he is to me and to so many others. He shared with me some of the tasks he has taken on to serve others where he now lives as an indicator of the challenges he faces and requests my prayers that God will give him the strength to continue to support others. He is an example of the person I want to be when I grow up. I would like to be that person now! I am working on it with God's help. The lyrics of the song "Live Like That" are below and there is a link to the YouTube video. I suggest you watch it yourself. There are questions about how you should live. If you belong to Christ, you should live the way Christ tells you through this song. I know my friend's heart has been changed and he is living with abandon. Pray for me that I may also live with abandon!

> What will people say of you?
> Does your action point to Jesus?
> Is your worship more than just a song?
> Are you proof that Jesus is who He said He is?
> When they see you, do they see Christ?

I want to live like Him. I want live with abandon never holding back. I want to live like my friend, like Barnabas. But I cannot do it on my own. I need Christ within me to make it happen. Ask Him!

Lord, please work within me to make me more like You. Thank You for putting my friend in my life as a living example of what it is like to walk with You. Thank You for these 20 years and please give us many more to fellowship in Your name. And most of all, help us to do and say things that point others to You. In Your name we pray!

Live Like That by Sidewalk Prophets:

Sometimes I think What will people say of me When I'm only just a memory When I'm home where my soul belongs

Was I love When no one else would show up, Was I Jesus to the least of us, Was my worship more than just a song?

I want to live like that, And give it all I have, So that everything I say and do Points to You

If love is who I am, Then this is where I'll stand, Recklessly abandoned Never holding back I want to live like that

Am I proof That You are who you say You are, That grace can really change our heart, Do I live like Your love is true?

People pass, And even if they don't know my name, Is there evidence that I've been changed, When they see me, do they see You

If love is who I am, Then this is where I'll stand, Recklessly abandoned Never holding back. I want to live like that.

## JUNE 13   PLAY FAVORITES
Relationships

Psalm 89:19-21 (NKJV)

*¹⁹ Then You spoke in a vision to Your holy one, And said: "I have given help to one who is mighty; I have exalted one chosen from the people. ²⁰ I have found My servant David; With My holy oil I have anointed him, ²¹ With whom My hand shall be established; Also My arm shall strengthen him.*

Who is your champion? Do you have someone who stands behind you to encourage and protect you? God was David's Champion and gave David the help, strength and skill for David to become Israel's champion. There is a need for such a champion in our world today. A champion is an upholder, an advocate, a defender, a supporter, and one who speaks up for a person or a cause.

*God is your Champion!* He is the one who speaks up for you. You are all highly favored. He wants the best for you and works His plan to provide just that. But you need to let Him work His plan. If God is your Champion, are you supposed to be someone else's champion? It seems as God sets the example for us on how we should live. Therefore, you need to be a champion for others. You need to make others feel special. Remember their names. Be courteous. Treat others with respect. Show them they are important to you even if you don't know them well.

When my nephews were little, I was very careful to show them both favor. One of the worst things we can do is compare people and circumstances. Comparison makes us bitter. What I did for one, I did for the other. I went on class trips. We babysat for a week while my brother was on a trip. I was involved. I always told them you are one of my two favorite nephews. As they got older, they figured out I only had two nephews. My answer was "that doesn't change a thing! You are still one of my two favorite nephews!" They were both my favorites and still are today. Favoritism causes jealousy in relationships. Cain killed Abel. Joseph was sold into slavery. Favoritism is not pretty. But here is the thing. I am asking you to play favorites! Treat everyone as if they are special because they are! Make them feel important because they are! Help them to like themselves because they were made in God's image and He does not make mistakes. Each person was formed as God wanted them to be. You are special! You are a Masterpiece! You are wanted! You are loved! The world will tell you different. But remember you are God's favorite *you!* Stand up tall, throw your shoulders back and live as the miracle you are!

Thank you, Lord, that we are highly favored by You. You designed us as we are for a purpose and gave us everything we need to live according to Your plan. Help us to be the Masterpiece you created us to be today. In Jesus name! Amen!

# JUNE 14   I AM MY BROTHER'S KEEPER
Relationships

Genesis 4:8-10 (NKJV)

*⁸ Now Cain talked with Abel his brother; and it came to pass, when they were in the field, that Cain rose up against Abel his brother and killed him. ⁹ Then the LORD said to Cain, "Where is Abel your brother?" He said, "I do not know. Am I my brother's keeper?" ¹⁰ And He said, "What have you done? The voice of your brother's blood cries out to Me from the ground.*

Are we our Brother's and Sister's keeper? Are we responsible for their welfare? When God asked Cain where Abel was, do you think He didn't already know? Why do you think Cain kill Abel? It was because of jealousy. If we are jealous, we will not seek to help. If our goal is to help and care for others, we will be happy when they succeed and not be jealous. James 1:27 (NIV) says *"²⁷ Religion that God our Father accepts as pure and faultless is this: to look after orphans and widows in their distress and to keep oneself from being polluted by the world."* It *is* our responsibility to care for our brothers and sisters.

As we live in this world, we are called to take care of those who cannot take care of themselves. That means many different things. If someone is in crisis, we can use our resources to "stop the bleeding". If they are in a generally bad situation, we can help them gain knowledge that will improve their situation. If they need a friend, we can just listen. Either way, whatever the challenge, it is always better when we work together to solve that challenge. What if we are the ones facing the challenge? Do we want others to come to our aid? What if that challenge is depression? Would it be good if someone who understood depression would come and stand by your side and walk with you to get you through the valley? What about when you have a joy in your life? Do you want others to celebrate with you? We are our brother's keeper in the good times and the bad! Who is your brother or sister? What about your waiter or waitress? Ask their names. How are they doing? Have you checked with them lately? When you speak with people, really listen so you can know how they are doing. We were created to live in community. Taking care of each other is part of that community. God has blessed you with love for others and skills to care for them. Will you use them in your next encounter?

Lord, you said it was not good for us to be alone. We know You are always with us but You designed us to relate to others as well. Help us live in community and love each other as You have loved us. Bring us to people we can help and people who can help us. Let us put down the electronics and talk to others. Give us the ability to really listen and get to know others. Teach us to share our joy and sorrow the way You designed us to live. In Your name we pray!

## JUNE 15    YOU WILL PREVAIL
Faith

Psalm 129 (NKJV) Selected Verses

*"Many a time they have afflicted me from my youth," Let Israel now say— ² "Many a time they have afflicted me from my youth; Yet they have not prevailed against me. "The blessing of the LORD be upon you; We bless you in the name of the LORD!"*

David knew there was an enemy against him but he knew God was with him. God's blessings are always on those who love Him.

There has always been an enemy against you. Long before you came into being, God's enemy, the devil, had set himself against you. Satan hates anyone who believes in God and will do whatever he can to separate us from God. Is the situation hopeless? Absolutely not! You and God are a majority and will always prevail. The only question is will you stay in faith?

In 2 Corinthians 4, Paul says *"⁷ But we have this treasure in earthen vessels, that the excellence of the power may be of God and not of us. ⁸ We are hard-pressed on every side, yet not crushed; we are perplexed, but not in despair; ⁹ persecuted, but not forsaken; struck down, but not destroyed...".* How does someone remain optimistic in the center of all these trials? It takes faith in God to stay on the path. We have hope in Him that He will work all things out for our good. Through the trials of the Bible, we see God's faithfulness to His people. No matter what obstacle they face, God delivers them from harm. There is no reason for despair. We are victors against the enemy by God's power. God is always with us no matter what. He will be your strength and shield. He is an ever-present help in times of trouble. There is nothing to fear for God will uphold you with His righteous right hand! He is with you! Fear not! Walk forward in Faith.

Thank You Father that you have been with us from before our birth. Thank You that You will never leave nor forsake us. With You is victory! Give us courage to stand in Your grace and face the enemy in victory. With You, all things are possible. May Your Holy Spirit remind us of Your protection and love at all times. In Jesus name we pray!

# JUNE 16   I'M STILL GOING
Support

Daniel 3:23-25 (NKJV)

23 *And these three men, Shadrach, Meshach, and Abed-Nego, fell down bound into the midst of the burning fiery furnace.* 24 *Then King Nebuchadnezzar was astonished; and he rose in haste and spoke, saying to his counselors, "Did we not cast three men bound into the midst of the fire?" They answered and said to the king, "True, O king."*

25 *"Look!" he answered, "I see four men loose, walking in the midst of the fire; and they are not hurt, and the form of the fourth is like the Son of God."*

In this story from Daniel, Shadrach, Meshach, and Abed-Nego are facing a terrible consequence for not bowing down to the king's idol. They have been thrown into a fiery furnace to be burned alive for their crime. King Nebuchadnezzar's plan was to destroy those who did not follow his command. But God had a different plan. This time, God decided to enter the furnace with them.

God's plan can be anything. He can decide to prevent the issue entirely or carry you through it. King Nebuchadnezzar was astonished! The only thing the fiery furnace did was burn off the cords that bound the three men. But the best part of the story is the fourth "man" walking in the midst of the fire. The Son of God was in the fire with them. Your Lord will never leave nor forsake you. You matter that much to Him! The Son of God loves you and will do anything for you. He would enter the fiery furnace for you and with you and bring you out the other side. Even though you go through the valley of the shadow of death there is nothing to fear. He is with you. Whether it is around or through the trial, I am still going where He leads! How about you?

Lord, thank You that You are always with us in the trials and the joys. If it be Your will, bring us more joys that trials but Your will be done. Refine us to be who You want us to be that we may bring glory to Your Holy Name. Amen!

## JUNE 17   WILL YOU GO        BEARERS OF THE GOOD NEWS
### Grace and Mercy

Matthew 28:18-20 (NKJV)

*18 And Jesus came and spoke to them, saying, "All authority has been given to Me in heaven and on earth. 19 Go therefore and make disciples of all the nations, baptizing them in the name of the Father and of the Son and of the Holy Spirit, 20 teaching them to observe all things that I have commanded you; and lo, I am with you always, even to the end of the age." Amen.*

Jesus spoke to His eleven remaining disciples and charged them with the task of spreading the Good News (Gospel). He told them to go to all nations. No one was to be excluded. This was not meant to be a club where only the members enjoy the benefits. Jesus was talking about outreach here.

Too many people today try to keep the benefits for themselves. Maybe they think they were lucky enough to discover the Good News so it must be rationed because there may not be enough to go around. Our Lord specifically told us to take it to all nations. It is love. There is always enough love to go around. Like the feeding of the five thousand, there is always more left over. Our Church has a motto which is "make disciples who make disciples". It is the concept of multiplying. As in other miracles, there is always enough. Are you making disciples? Many tell me they are not ones to share their faith. They tell me faith is a private thing. They tell me they don't know how. Something as good as Grace should not be hoarded! It is so valuable that it should be offered to all. That is what Jesus asks us to do! He will equip you for the mission. And you are not asked to do this alone. Jesus promises to *be with you always*. That's *always*! He will never leave nor forsake you. He loves you that much!

So why not step out in faith? You have been given an incredible gift and asked to share it with others. Don't worry about what to say or how to say it. Just love others as yourself and they will figure it out. Love with deeds! Treat others well. They will come to understand why. Sooner or later, they will ask you why you are so nice and calm. Then you can tell them about your Lord and how He is always with you. Live in such a way as to make people notice you are different which will cause them to ask why. Go, make disciples! Here is the charge our former Pastor Don Feuerbach gave us. See if this will work for you as well as it works for us.

> "Liberty Corner, you are the bearers of the good news to the world. It matters how you live your life. It matters what you say and how you say it. It matters what you do and how you do it because someone is watching you wanting to know what it means to follow a risen Lord. So, go out and love your neighbors and serve the Lord. "

Lord, help us today to follow You! Let our lives bring glory to You and blessing to those we meet. Let us be the bearers of Good News to all nations. Remain with us and give us the strength to carry out the mission of making disciples in Your name! Amen!

## JUNE 18    BUILT UP BY LOVE

Encouragement

*1 Thessalonians 5:8-11 (NKJV)*

*8 But let us who are of the day be sober, putting on the breastplate of faith and love, and as a helmet the hope of salvation. 9 For God did not appoint us to wrath, but to obtain salvation through our Lord Jesus Christ, 10 who died for us, that whether we wake or sleep, we should live together with Him. 11 Therefore comfort each other and edify one another, just as you also are doing.*

Do you build others up or tear them down? Our culture thinks it is cool to denigrate one another. It is funny to be sarcastic. Many of us have this passive aggressive thing going on. It is not good. Many people walk around barely getting by feeling poorly about themselves. Each negative comment is another jolt. Why don't we build each other up instead?

This passage speaks about putting on faith and love. We could all use a little more love. Shouldn't our speech be glorifying to God and edifying to all those who hear it? I know many people who still struggle with the after effects of being told they are worthless and would never amount to anything. What if you told a child you are a winner? You can do anything to which you put your mind. There is nothing that can stop you! Would that child attempt great things?

We had a foster child who would say they could not do things and then get frustrated and angry. I was aware of this issue before they came to visit. When we got to a point of frustration, I asked if he had assembled a similar toy. He said he had done it with my help. With that in mind, I asked if he thought I would help him again and he said yes. My conclusion was that you can do this then with my help and I am willing to help. I asked him to stop saying "I cannot do this". Instead, ask for help and I will be there. That is the model our Heavenly Father wants us to follow.

Your heavenly Father is the same only better. In fact, He is the best at helping because His help teaches us His ways which are always a blessing to all. He is always willing to help if you will just ask. It doesn't need to be a fancy prayer. "Help me Jesus" will do. God loves you so much, He longs to come by your side. Ask Him! He won't disappoint. He will send someone to your aid.

Just a few kind words can change everything. Many people have done amazing things because someone encouraged them. They have moved forward because someone said "I know you can do this"! Be that person. Speak words of encouragement! Speak words of praise! Speak blessings into the lives of the people around you and watch them blossom into the destiny God created for them. It will bless you as well.

Lord, help us to build up rather than tear down! Help us to use our words to bless people and encourage them to do great things in Your Name.

# JUNE 19   WHAT DEFINES YOU; SUCCESS OR FAILURE
Encouragement

John 18:15-27 (NKJV) Selected Verses
*15 And Simon Peter followed Jesus, and so did another disciple. Now that disciple was known to the high priest, and went with Jesus into the courtyard of the high priest. 16 But Peter stood at the door outside. Then the other disciple, who was known to the high priest, went out and spoke to her who kept the door, and brought Peter in. 17 Then the servant girl who kept the door said to Peter, "You are not also one of this Man's disciples, are you?" He said, "I am not.". 25 Now Simon Peter stood and warmed himself. Therefore they said to him, "You are not also one of His disciples, are you?" He denied it and said, "I am not!" 26 One of the servants of the high priest, a relative of him whose ear Peter cut off, said, "Did I not see you in the garden with Him?" 27 Peter then denied again; and immediately a rooster crowed.*

Are you going to let past failures hamper your future? What defines you? Do you focus on your failures or on your successes? One of the biggest epic failures ever was Peter denying Christ. He didn't do it once; he did it three times *the same night!* **Epic failure!** And it was recorded so we read of it two thousand plus years later.

God seems to talk in threes. "You will deny me three times." "Feed my sheep." "I am the Lord your God." When it is important, the Lord tells us repeatedly. Jesus told Peter that Peter would deny Him three times. Jesus knows the future and knew of the denials. And yet, Jesus also knew the He would build His Church on the Rock called Peter. Peter knew as soon as he heard the rooster he had failed miserably, and he focused on that failure. But Christ looked into the future to see the fire and passion that would emanate from Cephas as soon as he sorted it all out. We have the Bible and hindsight to show us that Jesus was the Christ and that the prophecies were true. Peter did not. And the claims of the prophecies were way beyond possible as Peter saw them. Jesus knew that, given time to understand, Peter would take the good news of God's grace to the world. Jesus believed in Peter! Too bad Peter didn't believe in himself.

What about you? We all struggle with belief in ourselves. We don't always understand the gifts that God has placed within us. Are you a winner or a loser? Who determines that? Do you focus on your successes or do you dwell on your failures? God has a great destiny for you and has equipped you with everything you need to achieve that destiny. If you focus on your failures, you won't reach your destiny. What will you do? Will you use the gifts He has given you or will you focus on all the reasons why not? You are equipped, empowered, anointed, gifted, capable, favored, and destined for greatness. The battle is in your mind. Why not allow God to be your encourager and believe what He says? Then, you will be the success that He destines.

Father, You have equipped us for great things but we focus on what we cannot do. You have given us gifts and talents for our destiny and we ignore them. By Your Spirit, break the chains that bind us in disbelief and carry us to where You planned us to go. Let our success in Your eyes be great and bring glory to Your Holy Name. In Jesus name we pray!

## JUNE 20    ALL THINGS ARE POSSIBLE WITH GOD
Encouragement

Matthew 16:18 (NKJV)
*¹⁸ And I also say to you that you are Peter, and on this rock I will build My church, and the gates of Hades shall not prevail against it.*

Peter just experienced epic failure. He had denied Christ three times. Peter was very sad over his failure but that did not stop his destiny. God's plan would not be thwarted by the mistakes of one man. No, God can bring something good out of something bad. He told Peter He would build His Church on Peter as the foundation. No matter how bad it looks, God can make a way. He will work things to your benefit. What challenges do you face? Is it the loss of a job? Is it the loss or betrayal of someone close? Is it the loss of health? Jesus understands.

In 2000, I was fired from my job as National Account Manager for a software company. I won the Vice President's award for Outstanding Service in January and was fired in July. From champ to chump in six months. I had a new boss who saw things differently and we did not get along. The loss of this job hurt! In fact, I went into a time of depression that would last several years. I could not see any good that might come out of this.

God has a funny way of working things out for our good. When I left the company, they agreed to give me back my reseller status to sell the software on my own. Our largest client agreed to buy through me resulting in large commissions. I also learned I was not designed to work in the corporate environment. But this might be the best part of it all. I learned what it means to face depression and the darkness and hopelessness that follow. I also learned my Lord walks with me through the darkness and leads me back to His glorious light! I learned empathy. When someone else speaks about a hopeless situation, I can say *with certainty* that it is not hopeless. Been there! Done that! Got the tee shirt! And, by the Grace of God, I'm still standing. Jesus is my anti-depressant!

What do you face today? You are not alone. Others have walked that path. Firstly, your Lord walks with you even if you don't see Him. He will never leave nor forsake you. Secondly, God "works all things for the good" of all people. It does not appear that way at the time. The evil one is in the world looking for whom he can devour. That is why so many bad things happen. God can be your Shield if you trust in Him. Psalm 46:1 (NKJV) says *"God is our refuge and strength, A very present help in trouble."* Do you seek Him or do you try it on your own?

I was at coffee hour one morning after Church speaking with someone I did not know well. He spoke about the weather at first but I had a *sense* there was something deeper he wanted to discuss. I asked how he was since he seemed sad. At that point, he told me he suffered from depression and was struggling at the current time. I *knew* how he felt and told him I had been through that valley but managed to get through with God's help. You see, even though you are in the valley, God has prepared a table of blessing for you, in the presence of your enemies (Psalm 23), on the other side. And

He will guide you through that valley. Do not give up. Keep walking! Epic failure (in your mind) can turn out to be the springboard to launch a new success. Weeping may last for the night but joy comes in the morning. Weep if you must. It cleanses you. But remember, joy comes in the morning. Look to the Lord, the source of all blessing, and He will work all things out according to His gracious plan. He loves you!

Lord, thank You that You always work out things for our good. Even when we mess up, You can turn it around! Thank You for always walking with us and helping us through the struggles. It is comforting to know You are there and will answer us when we call. In Your name we pray!

## JUNE 21    PRAY HOW
Prayer

1 Thessalonians 5:16-22 (NKJV)

*16 Rejoice always, 17 pray without ceasing, 18 in everything give thanks; for this is the will of God in Christ Jesus for you. 19 Do not quench the Spirit. 20 Do not despise prophecies. 21 Test all things; hold fast what is good. 22 Abstain from every form of evil.*

You want me to what? Pray without ceasing? How can I do that? I have to work. I have a lot on my plate. How can I pray without ceasing? I don't really even know how to pray! What do I say? It is difficult for some people to pray let alone pray without ceasing. Are you one of those people?

Prayer is not that difficult. It is supposed to be a conversation with God. In Adam and Eve's time, they were face to face with God in the garden so they were able to just talk. Why can't it be the same now? It can! All God ever wanted was a relationship with His creation which is *you*. He does not need fancy words or even many words. "God help me" is a prayer. "Jesus" is a prayer. "Thank You Lord" is a prayer! It is not so difficult. I talk to myself; I answer myself and sometimes I find myself saying *huh*. But I have found a better conversation. I talk to the Lord instead. It is a much better conversation. I do most of the talking but that doesn't surprise any of you who know me personally. And He does answer me. But God is a doer, not a talker. His answers come quietly but I know they are from Him. No one else could give me these miracles or the peace that goes with them. You should try it! You can do it all day.

Another thing you can do is listen to Christian radio. I listen to my local Christian radio station that plays praise and worship music all day long. I drive with my hand in the air in praise of my God. I admit I do take some time during the day to work but I don't let that interfere with my praise and prayer. After all, I try to do everything as if unto the Lord. The work I do is a form of worship. I employ the gifts and talents given me to the glory of the Giver.

So, it is possible to pray and worship without ceasing. I didn't think so either but I was wrong. Prayer comes in many forms. I sing many of my prayers. You can too. You will please the Holy Spirit and create joy and peace in yourself. It all sounds good to me. See if it works for you.

Help us to pray Lord. You promised that Your Holy Spirit would teach us how to pray and would give us the words we need to speak or even no words at all. We need you! With You, all things are possible. Even praying without ceasing becomes possible. Thanks be to God!

## JUNE 22   A UNION TO LAST
Relationships

Genesis 2:18-24 (NKJV) Selected Verses

*[18] And the LORD God said, "It is not good that man should be alone; I will make him a helper comparable to him." ......[23] And Adam said: "This is now bone of my bones And flesh of my flesh; She shall be called Woman, Because she was taken out of Man." [24] Therefore a man shall leave his father and mother and be joined to his wife, and they shall become one flesh.*

God created Adam (man) and placed him in the garden. Immediately, it became clear that it was not good for Adam to be alone. (God must have known he would do something stupid.) We were not designed to be alone. Fellowship with God is our primary purpose but God knew we needed fellowship with someone comparable to us. He decided to make woman and Adam called her Eve. This was the first marriage and the design for the future. This was a union of two people that would become one. They were joined on the physical and spiritual levels. We too were joined together on this day!

Marriage has always been something special. It is a friendship and so much more. The bonds created are what make the two one flesh. Too many people put more planning into the wedding and not enough into the marriage. It is difficult, in the beginning, to realize that all other relationships have to take a back seat to this new relationship. Many times, when this dynamic changes, relationships are strained. Everyone is trying to figure out their status and noses get out of joint. My wife and I fought our first Christmas and ended up being apart. That was a mistake on my part but I learned that we need to stick together. After 40 years of marriage, she is my best friend. We still disagree but my hearing is not as good so I don't realize she is disagreeing with me. She smiles when she says no! We have become one flesh. There is no one else in the world with whom I would rather spend time. Sure, I would like to meet Joseph Prince as long as I can take Jean with me. I have left my father and mother and Jean's mother. It is just us now and it is a powerful us! We are strong in the Lord. He equips us for things that scare me. We are considering accepting a seven-year-old foster son. What were we thinking? Well, with my life partner by my side and the Lord our God with us, we can do all things! Invite God into your marriage and see how He will bless your lives too.

Father, bless our marriage and all marriages in Your name. Help us to live for You bringing glory to You in all that we say or do. Lead us in Your ways. Let Your love shine through us and around us and from us to those You put in our lives. Thank You for my bride, partner and friend! Hold her in the palm of Your hand as she is a blessing to me. Bless us that we may be a blessing to those we meet. In Your name we pray.

# JUNE 23   WHAT SHALL WE DO
## Grace and Mercy

Micah 6:6-8 (NKJV)
[6] *With what shall I come before the LORD, And bow myself before the High God? Shall I come before Him with burnt offerings, With calves a year old?*
[7] *Will the LORD be pleased with thousands of rams, Ten thousand rivers of oil? Shall I give my firstborn for my transgression, The fruit of my body for the sin of my soul?* [8] *He has shown you, O man, what is good; And what does the LORD require of you But to do justly, To love mercy, And to walk humbly with your God?*

Our sin is great! For all have sinned and fall short of the glory of God (Romans 3:23). But does that mean we are beyond redemption? Not at all! God worked out a plan of redemption before the beginning of the world. And His plan will not be thwarted. His love for you is beyond your comprehension. Even you can't mess it up.

So how can you pay for your sin? In the times of Moses, God established a sacrificial system where animals could be sacrificed to atone for the sins of the people. Hebrews 9:22 (NKJV) says *"And according to the law almost all things are purified with blood, and without shedding of blood there is no remission [of sin]."* Something has to die to atone for sin. Since all of us sin, a lot of animals have to die. But God did not want for all these animals to have to be sacrificed. It is His will that we live better lives. He has given us an example to follow in Jesus. The example is to do justly and to love mercy and to walk humbly with our God. To be courageous men and women of God. Do you think you are capable of this on your own? I know I am not. That is why God provided a way for us to be redeemed through the sacrifice of His Son. Jesus, the perfect sacrifice, bought our redemption at a very high price. He gave it all so you can walk with your God. Do you walk with Him? Do you show mercy to those God loves? Do you seek justice for God's creation? It is not sacrifice that God wants but love! He wants you to love Him and love who He loves. He has placed His love inside you. He has written His word on your heart. If you love, will you be just? Will you be merciful? Will you share the love He has given you? If so, you will be able to walk humbly with your God. Will you start today? Be courageous for Him!

Father, we thank You that You have given us all things and have made the way clear for our redemption. Let Your Spirit remind us daily of Your love that we are supposed to share with others. Help us to do justly, love mercy and walk humbly with You. In Your name we pray.

## JUNE 24   HOW SHALL WE LIVE
### Quality of Life

Joshua 1:8 (NIV)

*8 Keep this Book of the Law always on your lips; meditate on it day and night, so that you may be careful to do everything written in it. Then you will be prosperous and successful.*

How are we supposed to live? Is there some way for us to know what to do? Why I'm glad you asked. God gave us a book He called the Bible.  Some have said it is an acronym for Basic Instructions Before Leaving Earth. It does tell us how we are supposed to live.

As you go through life, there are so many distractions. It is easy to get sidetracked. So how can we keep our focus on what really matters? We can remain focused on God's Word, the Bible. Joshua told the Israelites to always be reciting the contents of the Book of the Law. He was speaking of the Five Books of Moses. We have 66 Books of the Bible now and they contain much wisdom. The best way to live is to know God's wisdom through His Word and to follow what you know. James 1:22 (NKJV) says *"But be doers of the word, and not hearers only, deceiving yourselves."* We are created to follow His plan. He gave us the instruction manual. He also promised we would be prosperous and successful if we followed it. Do you want to be prosperous and successful? OK! Read the Book and do what it says! You don't have to do it alone. John 14:26 (NIV) tells us *"26 But the Advocate, the Holy Spirit, whom the Father will send in my name, will teach you all things and will remind you of everything I have said to you."* We have help that will remind us of what we need to know and guide us in God's ways. He will help keep the Book of the Law on your lips. Speak it too!

Thank You Lord for Your Book of the Law. Thank You for Your Holy Spirit who will keep that Book on our lips. May it lead us to be prosperous and successful and bring glory to You.  In Your name we pray!

## JUNE 25    SPEAK BLESSINGS
Encouragement

Ephesians 4:29 (NKJV)

*29 Let no corrupt word proceed out of your mouth, but what is good for necessary edification, that it may impart grace to the hearers.*

No unwholesome talk should come out of your mouth. Instead, we are supposed to use our words to build people up. Words are powerful. God spoke all of creation into being with words. Use your words to bless someone today!

Do you listen to the news? Are you enjoying the stories they offer? Everywhere you turn, there is more hate, cruelty and denigration. Our world is a dark place. What if you could change that? What if you could be the source of encouragement in your part of this world? You have the power and that power is the power of your tongue. James Chapter 3 talks about all the bad things that the tongue can do. What about the good things? You can speak blessing into someone's life. You could tell them you are proud of them. You could say theirs was a great idea. You could say you appreciate them. You could say thanks for being there for me. So why don't you? Also, what do you say to yourself? Do you celebrate your wins?

It is time for a change. We spend too much time on the bad news. Let us turn our eyes in a different direction. Let us look to the author and perfecter of our faith and ask Him what He sees in us and others. My Mom told me "if you can't say something nice, don't say anything at all." I think there is a better way. Practice saying nice things. Look for the good in all situations and people. Speak blessings into the lives of others and yourself.

Lord, change the lens through which we look at the world. Give us Your eyes to see things as You see them. You see what we can be rather than what we are. You see the great creation You have made. Help us to see ourselves and others as You see us. In Your name we pray.

## JUNE 26 BRING FORTH GOOD THINGS
Attitude

Matthew 12:33-37 (NKJV) Selected Verses

[33] *"...for a tree is known by its fruit.* [34] *Brood of vipers! How can you, being evil, speak good things? For out of the abundance of the heart the mouth speaks.* [35] *A good man out of the good treasure of his heart brings forth good things, and an evil man out of the evil treasure brings forth evil things.......* [37] *For by your words you will be justified, and by your words you will be condemned."*

Be careful what you say and how you say it. Your words are powerful. Also, many are watching you to see how you live. They want to see how followers of Almighty God live and behave. You have a chance to speak blessings into the lives of others. Will you do it? Where will those blessings come from? They must come from your heart.

Today's verses (which include one of my life verses) speak about your speech and its source. It tells us that that source is what is in our hearts. What type of speech do you want coming out of your mouth? If you want it to be wholesome and edifying, what would need to be in your heart? Would good thoughts need to be in your heart? Would you have to get rid of all rage and bitterness? When the stresses of life press in on you, that which is in your heart will come out. You cannot hide your true feelings. What is inside of you will come out. You can be the encouraging person God made you to be. The Holy Spirit will help you. I have an anger problem. I get angry about the silliest things like the drawers not being closed. I am asking God to remove this from me so I can be more of a blessing to my family. He is helping me to put less emphasis on things that don't really matter. What do you want to lose? If there are things within that scare you, ask God to take them away or give you the tools to lessen them. The Potter will remake you if you are willing to get back on His wheel! What is in your heart? Do you like what you see? You are not stuck with who you are. You can change or, more accurately, God can change you. Ask for help and He will answer.

Lord, you made us in Your image but sometimes that image gets tarnished. Please polish us so we can be more like You. Help us to get back on Your Potter's wheel so You can remold us to be the blessings You intended for us. We cannot change on our own but You can change us. Change us Lord! Make us more like You! In Your name we pray. Amen!

## JUNE 27    JUST AS I AM
Faith

Romans 8:1 (NKJV)
*There is therefore now no condemnation to those who are in Christ Jesus, who do not walk according to the flesh, but according to the Spirit.*

What do you need to do to be accepted by God? Are there steps you need to take to cleanse yourself from the sin that permeates all of our lives? Are you worthy of forgiveness? Peter denied Christ three times and still received grace. Who decides one way or the other? What does it mean to be in Christ Jesus and how do you know if you are? This verse tells us that there is no condemnation for those in Christ. How can I be in Christ?

Just As I Am, the Song, was written in 1835 by Charlotte Elliott and became the official 'altar call' song of the Billy Graham Crusades. Many souls have found Jesus as Savior in response to the simple beauty of this song. It warms my heart every time I hear it. It reminds me of the incredible gift offered to all of us. The gift I have accepted.

Have you accepted the gift? You see, there is nothing you could do to earn grace. It is a free gift. All you need do is ask. To be in Christ is to invite Him into your heart to abide with you. Open the door and let Him in. He will do the cleansing and preparation and will remake you in His image from the inside out. You don't deserve it. You can never earn it. You can never pay Him back. But you can enjoy grace because of what Jesus has done and because He *says* you are worthy. He says you are holy, righteous and redeemed! You are His and He wants you to be with Him where He is and to remain with Him always. He accepts you just as you are! He invites you into His presence. He wishes that none should perish. Will you accept the gift? Invite Him in to abide with you! He is calling. *Answer the door!*

Jesus, we hear Your call. You offer us grace in our wretched states. You invite us to come to You just as we are. Please help us to overcome the unworthiness of our souls and bid us come to Thee.  Give us strength so we can say Lamb of God, I come and take those steps! In Your name we pray. Amen!

Just as I am, without one plea, But that Thy blood was shed for me,
And that Thou bidst me come to Thee, O Lamb of God, I come, I come.

## JUNE 28    HOW DO YOU ACCEPT COMPLIMENTS
Support

Luke 18:18-19 (NKJV)

*18 Now a certain ruler asked Him, saying, "Good Teacher, what shall I do to inherit eternal life?" 19 So Jesus said to him, "Why do you call Me good? No one is good but One, that is, God.*

Jesus just met the rich young ruler who wants to learn about eternal life and how to earn it. Jesus does not focus on the question asked but, on the compliment, given him. Jesus rebukes him for the compliment telling him only God is good. Is this setting a precedent? Are we supposed to reject compliments? Are compliments only for God? I don't think so. I believe it all depends on how you handle them.

If you take the compliment as boasting about your gifts and talents, that is pride. But if you take them as praise of the gifts God has given you, you are giving Him the glory. Do you think God is glorified when you use the gifts He has given you?

Do you have children? What if your son or daughter came to you and said "I am a loser, I am a nothing, I am a nobody. Nothing good ever happens to me." How would that make you feel? Would it make you feel proud? Would you tell them you are glad they finally figured it out? Or would it break your heart? It would break mine! How do you think your Heavenly Father feels when you reject a compliment that highlights the gifts he has given you? That's right. The gifts He has given you! Are you worthy? Probably not. But God, by His grace, says you are. He says you are fearfully and wonderfully made. If He says so, I believe Him. Why don't you? When given a compliment, do you say thank you or do you give some sort of excuse? Are you going to argue with God? Are you going to disrespect your Creator by not acknowledging the gifts He has given you? That *is* what you are doing. When you refuse a compliment on a gift God has given you, you are disrespecting the Giver of those gifts.

When someone says you did a good job, say *thank you*. Don't be arrogant about it but acknowledge the gifts you have been given and use them to the glory of the Giver. Don't be ashamed of doing a good job. God is the one who created the work of your hands and gave you the talents to do them. Please practice the words "thank you"! Acknowledge the Giver and accept the compliment. Make Him proud of you. He loves you. *Let Him enjoy your success.* It was Him who gave you the tools.

Father, we thank You for establishing the works of our hands and giving us the talent and opportunity to use them. Help us to bring glory to You through our good works. Help us to remain humble in our acceptance. In Jesus name we pray!

## JUNE 29    SPREAD YOUR WINGS
Faith

Isaiah 40:30-31 (NKJV)
*Even the youths shall faint and be weary, And the young men shall utterly fall,  ³¹ But those who wait on the LORD Shall renew their strength; They shall mount up with wings like eagles, They shall run and not be weary, They shall walk and not faint.*

Have you ever wanted to do something but did not because of what others would think? Do you lack the confidence to try? Have you been told you are too young? Without trying, there would be no innovation! As it says in the movie, South Pacific, "You've got to have a dream if you are going to have a dream come true."

Do you have dreams? Are you taking steps on a daily basis to move closer to those dreams? If not, why not? There are always setbacks and disappointments. Remain focused on the gifts and talents and dreams given you by your Creator. He has given you those dreams and all that you need to accomplish your destiny. Pastor Joel Osteen says a setback is just a setup for a comeback. If you focus on the dream and not the setbacks, the Dream Giver will help you try again and succeed. "Even the young men shall utterly fail! But those who *wait* on the Lord shall renew their strength."

What does it mean to *wait* on the Lord? Here are the meanings I want you to consider now:

- to remain inactive until something expected happens
- to perform the duties of an attendant or servant
- to halt and wait for another to join one or catch up

With these possible definitions in mind, we have several ways to interpret "*waiting* on the Lord". You can wait for the Lord to make a way. You can be patient knowing the He will bring you everything you need. You can serve the Lord while you are *waiting* for your dream. Many an actor has waited tables while waiting for their big break. You can halt and wait for God to join you which would be His timing. None of these seem like bad options.

What do you do while you are "*waiting*"? This is not passive but active *waiting*. Love and serve others while waiting. Keep the dream alive in your mind. Always be thinking about steps you can take. Pray and *listen*. God speaks in a "still small voice." The world will tell you that you can't. God will reveal the way! Listen for clues as to how others fit into the dream. Many times, you were not meant to do it alone. Someone else might have the piece of the puzzle you have been missing. Are you familiar with the names Bill Hewlett and Dave Packard? Is this the right time for the dream? Is God closing doors to slow you down? Is there another invention that will make your dream possible? Is there a need? All these things have to be considered. Are you in His timing or your own? You either have everything you need or something is on the way. Most of all do not become weary. Your renewed strength is coming as you *wait* on the Lord!

Thank You Lord that you give us dreams and all we need to live them. Help us today to live the dream! Give us patience to wait on Your timing and serve You while waiting. Remind us You have given us a destiny, but it is on Your schedule. In Your name we pray! Amen!

## JUNE 30   THE PRESENCE OF GOD WITHIN US
Quality of Life

Revelation 21:3 (NKJV)

*3 And I heard a loud voice from heaven saying, "Behold, the tabernacle of God is with men, and He will dwell with them, and they shall be His people. God Himself will be with them and be their God.*

Do you want to experience the Presence of God in your life? Revelation speaks of God dwelling with us. The Bible goes even further saying your body is the Temple of the Holy Spirit which means God dwells *within* you. So how come we have trouble feeling His presence and hearing His voice? Could it be we are not tuned in correctly?

In the old days (when I was a kid), we had transistor radios that had a tuning dial for selecting stations. When you tuned to a station, you had to make fine adjustments to get it just right or you would get static and distortion. It was hard to hear if it was not set right. The same may be true in your life. You may not be tuned in just right. The static is keeping you from hearing clearly the call and feeling the Presence. What can we do about this issue? We can do a better job of tuning in to God. By focusing in on God, through His Word, we will be better equipped to observe His hand in our lives. We are asked to pray unceasingly. We can listen to Christian Radio praise and worship music. This will give us a better focus but how can we manage this. In the 1990s, people wore WWJD bracelets to remind them of Jesus and ask "What Would Jesus Do?" We all need reminders. What can you use as a reminder to help you focus on Jesus? Is it a bracelet? Is there something in your life that you can use as an "anchor" to tie you to thoughts of Christ? Below is St. Patrick's prayer. It is a bit long. I have my own version that helps. It goes like this: Christ before me; Christ behind me; Christ beside me; Christ within me. Let Christ within you, by His Holy Spirit, burst out like radiant diamonds you cannot contain. And let the world see what following a Risen Lord looks like played out in you! To God be the glory!

Father, thank You that You have come to live within us! Send Your Holy Spirit to show us Your Presence and remind us of You in our daily lives. Thank You that You are our God. Help us to be your people. Write Your story on our hearts. Make us Your people. In Your name we pray!

"Christ with me, Christ before me, Christ behind me, Christ in me,
Christ beneath me, Christ above me, Christ on my right, Christ on my left,
Christ when I lie down, Christ when I sit down, Christ when I arise,
Christ in the heart of every man who thinks of me, Christ in the mouth of everyone who speaks of me,
Christ in every eye that sees me, Christ in every ear that hears me."   — St. Patrick

## JULY 1    SPEAK THE TRUTH
### Quality of Life

Isaiah 40:8 (NIV)

*⁸ The grass withers and the flowers fall, but the word of our God endures forever."*

Isaiah tells us *the only constant truth is the Word of God.* All else fades away. But these days, people are trying to change the Bible only reading the parts they like. The Bible talks about things we are to do and a way of life that pleases God. It is discipline and most of us don't like discipline. But are we to only follow the parts we like? Will we have a fruitful life if we do what we think is best? The Old Testament calls that "doing what's right in our own eyes." Whom do you want to please, man or God?

Ephesians 4:15 (NKJV) says *"¹⁵ but, speaking the truth in love, may grow up in all things into Him who is the head—Christ..."* If we know that someone is not following God's word and is headed for trouble, should we tell them or mind our own business? We always run the risk of offending someone when we point out their departure from God's will. But should we just let them go? Isn't it our duty to speak the truth in love? Many churches water down the Gospel to make it more palatable to people. The Gospel is offensive to those who are perishing. God wishes that none should perish. With that in mind, I am supposed to speak the truth as kindly as I can but it needs to be the truth. Know this! God loves you enough to give Himself up for you. But you still need to follow His ways for your own good. His Spirit will guide you in His ways.

Lord, thank You for Your truth. Your Word is truth. Help us to know Your Word and speak its truth in love to those who need to hear that truth. In Your name we pray! Amen!

## JULY 2    I DON'T BELIEVE IN GOD
Relationships

James 2:19 (NKJV)

*¹⁹ You believe that there is one God. You do well. Even the demons believe—and tremble!*

So, you don't believe in God. That's OK! He believes in you. But what about the fact that Satan's demons believe in God? The heavens declare the glory of God. Why don't you believe? Did you have some sort of bad experiences? Sometimes, the same person who waves to you real friendly in Church on Sunday gives you a different kind of wave when you cut him off in traffic on Monday and he is not telling you that you are number one. That is not setting the right example. I read the following quote from Brennan Manning and it really struck me. "The greatest single cause of atheism in the world today is Christians: who acknowledge Jesus with their lips, walk out the door, and deny Him by their lifestyle. That is what an unbelieving world simply finds unbelievable." — Brennan Manning

How do you show the world what it means to follow a Risen Lord? How do you live? Is your life setting the example you want to set? Many of us are short-tempered and can be downright nasty to others. A friend once said that some of the nastiest people he ever me were those who had attended many Bible studies. Do you think they learned what God really wanted them to know? In the Old Testament, God gave us the Law hoping we would follow it. That did not work out well. Then, God sent Jesus to show us how to live the Spirit of the Law since we failed at the letter of the Law. Do you understand the Spirit of the Law? Love the Lord your God...and love your neighbor as yourself. It is all about love and relationships. That is what God expects of you. He wants you to do justly and love mercy and walk humbly with Him (Micah 6:8). Can you do that? If you do, people will notice. They will want to see what these "Christians" are about. They will want to know more about relationships and how they can develop one with the Lord. Isn't that the example we are supposed to set? Wouldn't that be loving your neighbor as yourself? So today, wave to people with your Church wave with all the fingers together in the air. Oh yes, and smile too! Show them what it means to follow a Risen Lord!

Father, help us to follow You in a way others will notice and admire. May we be examples of Your Son and show the Spirit of the Law. May we share the Good News with all those with whom we come in contact. Help us to shine Your light into all the dark places we encounter. In Your name we pray!

## JULY 3    I'M NOT SURE I CAN GO ON – SUCCESS TO PANIC!
Failure

1 Kings 19:4 (NKJV)

⁴ *But he himself went a day's journey into the wilderness, and came and sat down under a broom tree. And he prayed that he might die, and said, "It is enough! Now, LORD, take my life, for I am no better than my fathers!"*

Elijah had just come off one of the biggest victories of his career. He had just asked the Lord to send down fire to consume his sacrifice. He prayed in 1 Kings 18: "³⁷ Hear me, O LORD, hear me, that this people may know that You *are* the LORD God...." And the Lord did just that; He consumed every trace of the sacrifice. The people saw this, believed and executed the 450 prophets of Baal, the false god and turned back to the God of Israel. Elijah was a hero because of this. This was his mountaintop experience.

But we often go from success to panic. What if I can't do that again? What if this was a freak accident? What if I just got lucky? What if...What if? Shortly after his huge success (which was God's hand), Queen Jezebel threatens to kill him and Elijah runs for his life into the wilderness. Now he is feeling sorry for himself. He asks the Lord to take his life. Why? Didn't he just prove the Lord was the only true God through his prayers? Had God not established Elijah as His Prophet? It looks like complete success to me! What is it about human nature that there is such a big letdown after a tremendous success?

I think there is a clue in the text. Isaiah says "...for I am no better than my fathers!" Isaiah is assuming he made these things happen. Yes, he did pray and his prayers were answered because God loved him and the prayers were in God's will. But Isaiah makes the mistake of comparing himself to his ancestors as if any of them could have accomplished this feat alone. It was God who consumed the sacrifice, not Isaiah. Isaiah lost sight of that. When we take our eyes off of the One who controls the universe, we take things out of context. With great power comes great responsibility. If Isaiah had the power to affect this miracle, he would be responsible for the outcomes. I have made that mistake.

I used to be terribly depressed around Christmas time. I thought I had the power to improve my corner of the world. As I looked around, there were people stealing other people's Christmas gifts and a host of other nasty things. I could not bear to face the anniversary of my Lord's birth. I was embarrassed I had not cleaned up things as if I could. I forgot that God is the One with the power and all I was responsible for was what He asked me to do. I cannot change the actions of others but I can change my heart to be obedient to my Lord. I had to let go and let God! A friend gave me a button that says, "It's not my fault!" I learned to do what I could and let God do what I cannot. Once I learned this lesson, I was able to enjoy the holidays and do what I can; not what I can't! I learned to acknowledge the power Source.

Do you ever feel it is enough? Most of us do at times. I ask you to step back and look to the Source of the power. Focus on Him and you can relax and do only what He asks. He never gives you more than you can handle. And if you are overwhelmed, write to me. ([bob@calldrbob.com](mailto:bob@calldrbob.com)) *Let me remind you how much God loves you.* For, just as He did for Elijah, He will come to you. Listen for His still small voice and watch for His provision. You are His child and loved!

Lord, You know how fragile we are. Remain with us in the failures and the successes. When we succeed, we lose sight of the source of the power that created the success. We think we caused the success and become unsure we can repeat or continue that success. Please have Your Spirit remind us of all we are and what we are not. Help us to let go and let You. In Your name we pray.

## JULY 4   I'M INDEPENDENT
### Quality of Life

John 6:68-69 (NKJV)

*68 But Simon Peter answered Him, "Lord, to whom shall we go? You have the words of eternal life. 69 Also we have come to believe and know that You are the Christ, the Son of the living God."*

You think you can do all things on your own. You don't need anyone. You can do it yourself. Have you ever faced a challenge that was so large you couldn't see your way around it let alone find a solution? Have you ever faced cancer? I have heard the "C" word from my doctor. Fortunately, it was skin cancer and it was caught early. But my friend had breast cancer and it rocked her whole world. She was so distraught that she and her husband were paralyzed with fear. They could not think about a solution. Do you run toward God or away from Him at times of trouble? I wonder what people without faith do in a crisis? I run toward God. As Peter says, He is the One with the answers.

Jesus had just fed the five thousand. After that, He walked on water to reach the boat with the disciples. It was becoming clear He was not of this world. He asked people to believe and follow Him. What He was asking seemed too difficult to understand or too costly to some and they turned away. But there were those to whom it became clear Jesus was the Messiah. Jesus asked the twelve if they were going to turn away also. Peter said "Lord, to whom shall we go?" The twelve were beginning to understand that Jesus was the Creator God. There is nowhere else you can go. He is the beginning and the end and everything in between. When there is nowhere else to go, what do you do? Do you rely on your own intellect? Are you the Captain of your own ship? Is it all up to you? I hope not! Jeremiah 17:9 (KJV) says *"9 The heart is deceitful above all things, and desperately wicked: who can know it?"* Is that the desired source for your future? Do you really want to live in a world ruled by mankind's heart and not God's truth? Do you want to do it yourself? If following God and His ways seems right to you, how will you do that? Is He in your life? He is willing. Invite Him in. He will bring you comfort. He loves you!

Lord, thank You for being there whenever we need a place to turn. We can always count on You. Help us to know and trust You when things get tough. Also, be there in our joy that we might know every good gift is from You. In Your name we pray. Amen!

## JULY 5    WHAT IS IT YOU SEEK
Relationship

### John 6:26-27 (NKJV)

*26 Jesus answered them and said, "Most assuredly, I say to you, you seek Me, not because you saw the signs, but because you ate of the loaves and were filled. 27 Do not labor for the food which perishes, but for the food which endures to everlasting life, which the Son of Man will give you, because God the Father has set His [God's] seal on Him [Jesus]."*

When you look to Jesus, what do you look to Him for? Is He some sort of cosmic vending machine to give you what you want? Do you look to Him to provide for your needs; the needs of this world or for what He wants for you? Yes, Jesus wants to provide for your current needs but He really wants to have a relationship that can provide for your eternal needs. He is the way and the truth and the life now and forever. How can you have that relationship?

For more than two thousand years, people have been trying to figure out that relationship. Many religions have been formed in an attempt to answer the relationship question. Just who is this Jesus and what does He want from us? Does He seek certain tasks from us? How do we know if we are good enough? What is it He requires? Is it religion or relationship that Jesus wants? It is relationship! Pure and undefiled religion before God and the Father is this: to visit orphans and widows in their trouble, *and* to keep oneself unspotted from the world. (James 1:27). It is also a right relationship with Jesus. Once you build that relationship, Jesus will give you everlasting life. This is the food which endures.

There is nothing you can do to be good enough! Works of kindness on your part are out of the overflow of the blessings God gives you freely through Christ. These blessings are because God loves you and not because of anything you can do. He wants to be in relationship with you. All you need do is invite Him into your heart and your life. You will never be the same. Jesus changes everything! His love is so overwhelming that you cannot remain the same. You will become a better person for just the knowledge of Him. And all it takes to receive this food that endures to everlasting life is to open the door and invite Him in. Will you open the door? You know He is there. You might be afraid of the changes He will make. So was I! I opened the door May 31, 1998 after months of trepidation. It is quite a story. But what would people think? Would I be betraying my roots? What would my family say? Now, nothing else matters! Christ alone is my cornerstone. Sure, I still have my faults. Ask Jean. I get grumpy when I don't get my way. But I recognize my faults and I ask Jesus to remove them. Rub off the rough edges please Lord. And that rubbing hurts. I fall down but I get up again. He dusts me off and says "you'll do better next time." And He gives me a next time. Thank You Lord!

Why do you seek Him? I seek Him because I want to become all He has designed me to be. I know I cannot be my best me unless Jesus remakes me in His image. I am willing Lord. Come Lord Jesus.

Come Lord Jesus! Feed us with food that lasts. By Your Spirit, guide us in Your ways. Your ways are truth and love. Help us to love one another as You have loved us. Give us this abundant everlasting life. In Your name we pray! Amen!

## JULY 6    SINGING THE BLUES

Faith

Psalm 30:11–12 (NKJV)

*11 You have turned for me my mourning into dancing; You have put off my sackcloth and clothed me with gladness, 12 To the end that my glory may sing praise to You and not be silent. O LORD my God, I will give thanks to You forever.*

For those of us who have faith in God, weeping may last for the night, but joy comes in the morning. Our God works out all things for our good. Even though we go through trials, we have the strength to face those trials and be transformed by them. The Lord our God will walk with us through the trouble and bring us out on the other side. And when we come through the trial, we will rejoice and praise Him who gave us strength.

Are you going through a difficult time? When things seem their darkest, we tend to think we are alone and will not make it through. But faith can strengthen us. It can help us to endure knowing this test can become our testimony. Our God will use what we face to refine and transform us into the people He designed us to be. He will never leave nor forsake us! No matter what, God is there for you. Reach out to Him when you are afraid. He will be your strength and shield. You do not have to go it alone. He walks with you and will carry you when need be.

Lord, we thank You that You are always there for us no matter how dark the night appears. Help us to remember the dawn always follows the dark of night. After all, You are the light of the world and You come to each of us to calm our fears and bring us through whatever challenge we face. Be with us today Lord. We need You. Turn our mourning into dancing. In Your name we pray.

## JULY 7   BE STILL AND KNOW
Quality of Life

Psalm 46:10 (NKJV) ¹⁰ *Be still, and know that I am God; I will be exalted among the nations, I will be exalted in the earth!*

How still are you during your waking hours? I heard a sermon by my former Pastor Don Feuerbach about being still. Are you good at that? I'm not! My mind is always racing to the next thought. In fact, I tell people my mind is a scary place. It can be overwhelming. I am a visual person. My ideas (or the ideas God gives me) appear all at once in a flash. It happens so fast I have to record it or lose it. I see things quickly and sometimes things others don't see. I have come to appreciate the gifts God has given me. That doesn't mean they don't scare me. But being still is difficult for me. I keep saying I want to take a day off but when I try to be idle, my mind races about things I could or should do. It is frustrating. When I'm busy, I want to relax. When I try to relax, I want to get busy.

How can we learn to be still? The *Wall Street Journal* has an article on Hurry Sickness. Why are we in such a hurry? Where are we going? Have you ever had someone race around you on the road only to have you pull up right behind them at the next traffic light? Albert Einstein said "There are only two ways to live life. One is as though nothing is a miracle. The other is as though everything is." If you go too fast, you won't be able to see the miracles. Sometimes, when I wake up, I just watch my wife sleep and notice all the special things about her that God created. Have you ever taken the time to really look at a baby and see that miracle? Why wouldn't you want to take time to smell the roses?

But how do we slow down? I have a wild and crazy idea. It came from some book called Exodus and it says "Remember the Sabbath Day and keep it Holy." What a crazy thought. Pastor Don said busyness kills the soul. He also said love and hurry are incompatible. Do you think this Exodus story has some merit? What does it mean to remember the Sabbath day? Could you actually schedule time to be unscheduled? Do you have a category in Outlook named "Nothing"? Maybe you should create one. What if you put open time placeholders into your Outlook calendar called "Nothing" and set them to "Busy"? Would that fool you or others? Do you really need to fool yourself or would listening to God's plan for us just be a good thing to do? I am sure there are other suggestions counselors and therapists may have but God's word gave us the plan thousands of years ago. If we would just listen, we would be so much better off. Below is a little exercise that comes from Psalm 46. Read it *slooooooowlyyyyy* and see if it works for you.

Be still, and know that I *am* God;
Be still, and know that I *am*
Be still, and know that I
Be still, and know
Be still,
Be

Lord, we thank You for Your Sabbath Day which was Your gift to us. Help us to bask in Your Peace and Grace one day a week as You planned. Let Your Spirit quiet the voices inside that scream hurry. Help us to just be! In Your name we pray. Amen!

## JULY 8    WHICH ARE YOU
### Quality of Life

Psalm 118:24 (NKJV)

*24 This is the day the LORD has made; We will rejoice and be glad in it.*

Some people say Good morning Lord; others say Good Lord it's morning. Which are you? Abraham Lincoln said "Folks are usually about as happy as they make their minds up to be." It seems that it is a choice. What choice will you make? It is my contention that attitude is everything. The attitude with which you start the day makes all the difference. How will you start your day?

The Lord made all our days. It was His intention that we be blessed in all our days. He made them so we could rejoice and be glad. Are you glad in the morning? Shouldn't you be? If you focus on the blessings God has given you, you will be able to enjoy each day as it comes. What will today bring? Will it bring happiness? Will it bring joy? It can if you decide that is what you want! You can be as happy as you make up your mind to be. The battle begins in your mind. Make the decision to be positive. It is your choice. Make the choice to rejoice!

Good morning Lord! Thank you for this day and every day. Help us to rejoice in the day You have given us. In Your name we pray!

## JULY 9    ARE YOU HUNGRY FOR MORE
Relationships

Matthew 5:6-16 (NKJV)

⁶ Blessed are those who hunger and thirst for righteousness, For they shall be filled.

⁷ Blessed are the merciful, For they shall obtain mercy.

⁸ Blessed are the pure in heart, For they shall see God.

⁹ Blessed are the peacemakers, For they shall be called sons of God.

¹⁰ Blessed are those who are persecuted for righteousness' sake, For theirs is the kingdom of heaven.

Where are you in your walk with Christ? Is it good enough? Are you satisfied to attend Church on Sundays? Is the Kingdom of Heaven yours? How about your walk of faith? If you seek a deeper relationship, the Lord is available and wants to meet you where you are.

I have come to a place in my spiritual walk where I desire a more intimate relationship with my Lord. I seek Him in my life through His word. I hunger for a better world knowing that He can make that happen. I am unhappy the world is such a dark place where people just do what is good for themselves. It is very frustrating. But every now and then, I am pleasantly surprised by something. In late June, I met a Brother in Christ. I was at a seminar and heard a man speak about his ministry and how it was impacting lives and benefiting his community and I had to know more. During the break, I approached Rev. Clarence asking him if he would share details of how this ministry worked. Clarence invited me and my Pastor to visit with him to learn about what they do and how they do it. The visit was extremely helpful. When I arrived, Clarence greeted me like we were long lost brothers. This was not of my doing. The Holy Spirit arranged that meeting and the relationship and I am blessed by both.

I have sought revival in our community. It is my feeling we need to draw closer to God to rebuild our morals and values to live the good life God intended. I believe it will take outreach to the community around us. All the things that have been revealed in my heart are things Clarence has done and he is willing to share them with us. I think it is time for Disciples who become Apostles; to be sent out. Clarence told us of their training programs that help make that possible. Now, we have a plan to reach every man in our Church for Christ leading them closer to spiritual maturity. Once there, we can go out to the surrounding community. When we hunger and thirst for God's righteousness, that righteousness will bring incredible blessing to us and those who walk with us. For ours is the Kingdom of heaven!

Father thank You that You bless us in our efforts to draw closer to You. Thank You that You have given us the calling to share Your Good News with those around us. We seek revival Lord. By Your Spirit, draw people closer to You through our words and deeds. Let Your love be evident to others in our actions. In Jesus name we pray. Amen!

## JULY 10   FLAWLESS
### Grace and Mercy

2 Corinthians 5:17 (NKJV)

*17 Therefore, if anyone is in Christ, he is a new creation; old things have passed away; behold, all things have become new.*

Sometimes we sit and look at ourselves as if we are completely lost and worthless. We have had an awful day and everything we touch has turned out badly. We feel as if nothing is going to go our way. We think everyone is against us; that we can do nothing right. Momma said there would be days like this and here they are. But all is not lost. There is a God and He is still on His throne. And best of all, you are His heir; made in His image and likeness!

It all happens when you invite Christ into your heart. At that moment, you become a new creation. The light of Christ is so overwhelming that it overshadows any faults that you may have. They are hidden by the glory of amazing Grace. Your flaws have passed away and you become flawless in the sight and light of Christ. Behold, all things, including you, have become new. So whatever faults you have, they will be erased. Those shortcomings, gone! Anger, doubt, pain, unworthiness all washed away by the flood of grace. You are flawless in the eyes of your Creator. That is quite an inheritance to live up to, isn't it? With that in mind, how will you show your new status to those you meet? Will you have a renewed confidence? Will you be kinder? Will you be more gracious toward others? Shouldn't you be passing on what you have received? Then go out and praise the works of others! Become a good finder. They already know what they are doing wrong! You tell them what they are doing right and praise them for it. People will repeat activity for which they are praised. What would you like to see from others? How can you praise them in a way that will lead them to repeat that good behavior?

Below are the lyrics to Flawless by Mercyme and the link to the video. Learn the chorus and sing it to those you love. They will become so much better in your eyes. And your positive expectancy will lead them to go up higher and accomplish much more. Love them into their destiny by extending the grace you have received. Remember, the Cross has made you flawless.

Father, thank You for Christ and Your Grace which makes us flawless. You have wrapped us in the righteousness of Christ so that our faults are no longer visible to You. While You are in the process of making us new creations, take away all the old faults and make us more like You. Give us Your eyes to see our brothers and sisters through the lens of love; Your love! For in You, we are new creations. In Jesus name we pray. Amen!

Mercy Me - Flawless

No matter the bumps No matter the bruises No matter the scars Still the truth is The cross has made The cross has made you flawless No matter the hurt Or how deep the wound is No matter the pain Still the truth is The cross has made The cross has made you flawless

## JULY 11  ARE YOU A GOOD READ
Encouragement

1 Timothy 4:12 (NKJV)

*¹²Let no one despise your youth, but be an example to the believers in word, in conduct, in love, in spirit, in faith, in purity.*

When a book is really enjoyable, people say it is a "good read." People say your life may be the only Bible a person ever reads. If they read your life, would you like the review? Would it be encouraging? Paul tells Timothy to be an example in word, deed and spirit. What does it mean in "spirit"? I think it means we are to have a right attitude toward whatever we do. With a poor attitude, you will set the wrong example. What example do you want to set?

I came to Christ later in life. I was 46. I had always known of Him but never taken it any further than knowing (head knowledge). One of the blessings I have had is friends of all ages. One such friend was Ed. I met him through my wife's family. Jean had become friends with Jim and Ed was his dad. Ed had physical challenges that limited his ability to do many things but he had a strong spirit. I later learned that was the Spirit of the Lord that burned within him. Ed was a doer even if he could not physically do it himself. He had five kids and he taught them (probably) more than they wanted to know at the time about how things are done. Ed set an example. It was his book I was reading because I had not yet come to reading the Bible. I watched how Ed conducted his life. How he faced difficulties and challenges and navigated through them. He had a confidence. He knew where he was going. No, he wasn't perfect. None of us are. But there was a confidence and determination that was unmistakable. He knew who he was and whose he was. And, slowly, patiently, Ed planted seeds of how life should be lived even though he never mentioned the Gospel. He lived it! He was an awesome friend and mentor to me. I loved him. I'd say he was a good read. He went to be with the Lord in 1989 before he got the chance to see those seeds take root and grow. But he knew what he was doing. Ed followed what his Lord requested. He planted seeds. He watered and he waited. But God gave the increase. Those seeds led me to the Lord.

What seeds are you planting? Do you share the Good News with others in word and deed? Are you leading people closer to or further from the Lord? Are you a good read? Go out and show the world what it means to serve a Risen Lord! Plant seeds!

Lord, help us to *be* the good news to others. Give us opportunities to share You with a hurting world. Let our actions speak louder than our words and our story draw people closer to You. May we live in such a way that others want to learn why. Let us *be* the example and conduct ourselves in love, in spirit, in faith, in purity. In Jesus name we pray! Amen

## JULY 12 PEOPLE OF VISION
### Attitude

Prov 29:18 (KJV)
*Where there is no vision the people perish....*

Are you a person of vision? Do you see things others do not see? God has blessed me with a different kind of vision. He allows me to see things His way and gives me insights that I don't have on my own. Without vision, what would the world be like? New things would not be developed. There would not be new ideas. Our verse tells us the people perish. They might even die of boredom.

There are people out there who have no vision. They can just suck the life right out of you. No matter how nice a day it may be, they can come up with a list a mile long why things will be bad. Those are not the people you want around. You were made for great things. You won't soar to new heights surrounded by negative people. Look for people of vision; people like yourself! When He created you, God put vision within you. That vision works when it is linked to others with vision. You encourage one another. Positive people create an atmosphere of creativity that can produce incredible things when we are able to follow God's lead. In fact, this atmosphere draws in God's power. He wants to shower you with blessings and all things good. Test Him in this and see if He will not throw open the floodgates of Heaven and pour out His blessings upon you. So much so that you will not have storage enough to hold them.

Thank You Lord that you bless us with vision. Help us to use that vision to Your glory. Help us to see what You see and lead us to what You would have us do. Bring others with vision to us so that, together, we can help bring about the kingdom of heaven with Your help and in Your name.

## JULY 13   WHY DO YOU COMPARE YOURSELF TO OTHERS
Attitude

Galatians 6:4-5 (NKJV)

*4 But let each one examine his own work, and then he will have rejoicing in himself alone, and not in another. 5 For each one shall bear his own load.*

I am not as good as Joe. I wish I had his voice. I wish I had her creativity. My question is what would you do with someone else's talents if you are not doing all you can with your own? Theodore Roosevelt said "Comparison is the thief of joy." Wishing for something someone else has will steal your joy. You were not made to use talents given to others. You were designed to run your own race. You were born in this place and time for a reason. It is your job to discover that reason and purpose. You will not figure that out if you keep trying to live someone else's life.

Are you a parent? Have you ever compared one of your kids to another? Have you ever said "why can't you be more like your brother?" Is that a question that will bring out the best in each child? Children who are compared grow up to compare and question themselves. Don't let the "comparison thief" in to your lives.

Galatians tells us we can be proud of our accomplishments. God designed us to bloom where we are planted and to live with the gifts He has given us. When you try to use gifts given to others, it is like trying to put on size ten shoes when you have size twelve feet. It just isn't going to work out well. Zig Ziglar says *"you were designed for accomplishment, engineered for success and endowed with the seeds of greatness."* You are God's masterpiece. Be who you were called to be. The Caller designed you to be great in the place He put you. Be wonderful! Be yourself! Be Happy! Be His!

Lord, thank You for creating each of us just as You designed us to be. Thank You for the gifts You have given us. Help us to use them to Your glory. Thank You that Your plan for us is for our good. Thank You that You call each of us by name and love us just the way we are. Help us to be who You call us to be. In Your name we pray!

# JULY 14   JUSTICE OR MERCY – YOU DECIDE
### Grace and Mercy

James 2:8-13 (NKJV) Selected Verses

*⁸ If you really fulfill the royal law according to the Scripture, "You shall love your neighbor as yourself," you do well; ⁹ but if you show partiality, you commit sin, and are convicted by the law as transgressors. ¹⁰ For whoever shall keep the whole law, and yet stumble in one point, he is guilty of all...... ¹² So speak and so do as those who will be judged by the law of liberty. ¹³ For judgment is without mercy to the one who has shown no mercy. Mercy triumphs over judgment.*

Do you want to be shown justice or mercy? Many people complain things are not fair. To be truly fair, we would have to invoke full justice. Justice requires judgment and I am not sure anyone wants to face judgment. We all want justice but most would not want to be held accountable for their actions. Do you offer fairness to everyone else? Scripture tells us that, if we break one point of the law, it is as if we are guilty of all. That is a very high standard which we cannot meet. But, thank God, there is Grace!

Our Creator knows how we were formed and what we can do. He knows we cannot keep the whole Law. The standard is too high for us. With that in mind, He made a way for us to give it our best and, when we don't measure up, to try again. Our Lord is a Lord of mercy. He loves us! He asks us to love our neighbors as ourselves. That includes offering them grace when they fall short of the mark. Are you gracious? Do you allow others to recover from mistakes? Do you hold them to standards you know you cannot meet? This passage tells us we will be judged without mercy if we show no mercy. Matthew 7 (NKJV) *"Judge not, that you be not judged. ² For with what judgment you judge, you will be judged; and with the measure you use, it will be measured back to you."* Are you generous?

How do you want to be judged? Do you want mercy? If so, you are asked to offer mercy to others. It is not our job to judge; it is our job to love. Part of that job is speaking the truth in love. That means you will share with people that what they are doing is contrary to God's Law, but you will leave open a path of restoration. You might ask "are you sure you want to do that?" Showing mercy does include telling the truth. But it is to be done with a gentle spirit and with restoration as the intention. Be loving and kind to those who have strayed because you will be among them sooner or later. Remember, mercy triumphs over justice. Be merciful today!

Father, we thank You that Your mercy triumphs over Your justice. It is only by Your Grace that we live! Help us to speak the truth in love when others stray. Help them to be gentle to us when we stray. May we offer mercy over judgment by the example You have set for us through Jesus. Your grace is incomprehensible! In Jesus name we thank You and pray. Amen!

# JULY 15    ALL THINGS ARE POSSIBLE–DRY BONES LIVE
Faith

Ezekiel 37:1-6 (NKJV)

*The hand of the LORD came upon me and brought me out in the Spirit of the LORD, and set me down in the midst of the valley; and it was full of bones. ² Then He caused me to pass by them all around, and behold, there were very many in the open valley; and indeed they were very dry. ³ And He said to me, "Son of man, can these bones live?" So I answered, "O Lord GOD, You know." ⁴ Again He said to me, "Prophesy to these bones, and say to them, 'O dry bones, hear the word of the LORD! ⁵ Thus says the Lord GOD to these bones: "Surely I will cause breath to enter into you, and you shall live. ⁶ I will put sinews on you and bring flesh upon you, cover you with skin and put breath in you; and you shall live. Then you shall know that I am the LORD."'"*

My friend David wrote me with this verse. Thank you, David, for reminding me what our God can do! Many times, we face situations that seem hopeless. Our dreams have died. It doesn't look like there is any way to revive the situation. But then again, we do not know what God knows nor can we do what God can do.

The book of Ezekiel is full of prophecy from beginning to end. God speaks through Ezekiel to the people of Judah in exile in Babylon after ignoring God's word to them. They were in exile about 70 years so things looked hopeless. But with God, all things are possible. God speaks to Ezekiel and tells him to speak to a valley of dried bones and these bones came back to life as the whole House of Israel. Is there anything more hopeless than dried bones? And yet, the Lord God Almighty can bring them back to life.

What are you facing today? The end of a dream? The loss of a loved one? The loss of a job? Are you in a valley surrounded by dry bones? Well take heart. One word from the Lord can bring dead dry bones back to life. Considering that, what do you think God can do with your hopes and dreams? But you must believe in Him for it to take place. Lack of faith will bring lack of results. Now faith is being sure of what we hope for and certain of what we do not see! (Hebrews 11:1) Do you believe? I mean, really believe that God can do these things? Without faith, these things are not possible. But when you believe, when you trust God, He will bring dead things back to life. He did it for Lazarus! He did it for Jesus! Why wouldn't He do it for you? He who promises is faithful. And He loves you enough to give Himself up for you. That is how much He cares. He raised Israel from the dead and returned them to their own land. What do you need Him to do for you? Ask!

Father, Your power is beyond our comprehension. Show Yourself as the Lord God Almighty of Israel. Teach us Your ways and strengthen our faith in You. With You, all things are possible. May our prayers be bolder as our faith and trust in You grow. In Jesus name we pray. Amen!

## JULY 16   COME BOLDLY BEFORE THE THRONE
Grace and Mercy

Hebrews 4:16 (NKJV)

*16 Let us therefore come boldly to the throne of grace, that we may obtain mercy and find grace to help in time of need.*

We have learned all things are possible with God. We know He can do all things. After all, He created the universe and all that is in it. Yet we do not go to Him with our requests. He might be busy running the universe or something. We wouldn't want to bother Him. We go through life trying to do things in our own power. But didn't Jesus say He came that we might have life and have it more abundantly? Yes, He did! It is clear that God wants to bless you. But He wants you to ask for His blessings. James 4:3 says *"You have not because you ask not."* Why not ask?

God tells us that if we tithe, He will open the floodgates of heaven. Jesus tells us He came that we may have an abundant life. Blessing after blessing is stated yet we do not accept them. Is it a question of worthiness? Are we afraid that we don't deserve the blessings? Why not? Your Creator says you do and offers them. The writer of Hebrews suggests we come boldly before the throne of grace. God's throne is a throne of grace. He desires to bless you! He wants to give you gifts. But a gift that is not accepted is not a gift at all. You see, the giver receives their blessing when you accept the gift. If you don't accept, they are slighted and do not receive the blessing of giving. The giver and receiver are blessed by the process. What if you don't accept the gift? Do either receive a blessing? Your Father in Heaven wants to give you a gift. Take it so that you and He can be blessed by it. He loves you and wants what is best for you. He will send good things to you if you will let Him. Will you?

James 1:17 (NKJV) says *17 Every good gift and every perfect gift is from above, and comes down from the Father of lights, with whom there is no variation or shadow of turning.* We know all things are from You Father. Help us to accept these blessings in the spirit of love in which they were given. Help us to share with others that which You give us. May we accept these blessings and become a blessing to everyone we meet. In Your name we pray!

# JULY 17   WORK IS AN ACT OF WORSHIP
Relationships

Psalm 90:16-17 (NKJV)
*16 Let Your work appear to Your servants, And Your glory to their children. 17 And let the beauty of the Lord our God be upon us,*
*And establish the work of our hands for us; Yes, establish the work of our hands.*

This Psalm was written by Moses. Moses is asking God to reveal His work to His children. Also, God has plans for us. Moses is asking God to lead us to the work He has for us. When we do the things God ordains for us, they go well. It is always best to be in God's will.

Last week, I worked with our youth group on a stay-cation kind of work trip. Our Church participates in a local endeavor where we stay at the Church and travel locally to do repairs to homes damaged by Hurricane Sandy. It was amazing to watch 40+ teenagers really pitch in and make things happen. I was struck by the fact that these 14-18-year olds really stepped up and did the work. They did not need to be told what to do. They were there to serve others and serve they did!

Sometimes, we sign up to do something because it will look good on our resume'. There were a few kids there who needed community service hours. I got the feeling they were there to check something off their list. But the majority were there to build relationships. They worked hard because they wanted to make life better for someone they don't even know. On the site where I worked, we did not get to meet the homeowners. That was a little sad. I like to meet the people I serve. I want the chance to tell them why I serve. I serve because of all God has done for me. And our Student Life Pastor has taught our youth the same thing. They are awesome young people. James 2:17 (NKJV) says *"17 Thus also faith by itself, if it does not have works, is dead."* Our youth have faith. And that faith in evidenced by the works they do in the name of Christ. Out of the overflow of blessings God has given them, they are blessing others including me. It is pure joy to watch them work. One of the funny parts to watch is them all fall asleep as soon as the van starts moving on the way to and from the worksite. That is my quiet time. But it was a real blessing to work side by side with these awesome young people. I am discouraged when I look at the world at large. But I am revitalized when I get to see our youth step out in faith!

They are who they are because we have invested our time in them to share our faith. We planted seeds and God has given increase. His Holy Spirit has dwelled richly in their hearts and brought about spiritual growth. There is a fire in these kids. Now let us continue to fan the flames and encourage them in their walk with God. May it help grow us all!

Lord, thank You for establishing the work of our hands. You give us meaning and purpose through that which You ordain for us. Give us the talents and the strength we need to produce the fruits of our labors to Your glory. In Jesus name we pray!

## JULY 18    START WHERE YOU ARE
Relationships

2 Timothy 2:2 (NKJV)

*² And the things that you have heard from me among many witnesses, commit these to faithful men who will be able to teach others also.*

Paul was writing to Timothy who was his disciple. Paul poured his teaching into Timothy because he wanted the legacy of the Gospel to live on. Paul wanted to multiply his teaching through others so that the Gospel would be taught throughout the world as Jesus commanded. He expected Timothy to teach others.

The Church to which I belong says we are to make disciples who make disciples. We are to multiply our efforts in sharing the good news with everyone who will listen. Many are hesitant to teach because they say they don't yet know enough. My former Pastor Don said "Discipleship is just teaching people what you do know. Start where you are." Whatever you know, you are in a position to teach. There is also no shame in saying I don't know but I will find out for you. The note in my study Bible says, "If the church were to consistently follow Paul's advice, it would expand geometrically as well taught believers would teach others...." Are you teaching what you know to others or will you go to your grave with your music still in you? When would be a good time to start teaching? Are there things that you know and do that would be valuable for others to continue? Teach them those things.

We are called to make disciples. I was in a men's group about 15 years ago and the question came up of "What would you do if someone asked you about how to establish a relationship with Christ?" The men said they would get the Pastor. In Matthew 28:19-20 (NKJV) Jesus tells us all *"¹⁹ Go therefore and make disciples of all the nations, baptizing them in the name of the Father and of the Son and of the Holy Spirit, ²⁰ teaching them to observe all things that I have commanded you; and lo, I am with you always, even to the end of the age."* Each one of us is to be prepared to tell the story. Just tell them your own story about how you came to know Him. It does not have to be well-scripted or contain certain words. What were you like before? What led you to accept Christ? What difference has it made in your life? That is all you need do. This link takes you to the process which is simple.

Don't be selfish and keep your knowledge hidden. Share with others. There is synergy when we work with others. Teaching someone what you know creates that synergy and blesses you both in the process. Be a blessing to someone else today and share what you know about things you do and about your Lord.

Father, thank You for Your blessings and grace. Help us to multiply that blessing by giving it away to others in Your name. When we share You with others, all are blessed. Teach us Your ways and send us out as a blessing that we may glorify You. In Jesus name we pray. Amen!

## JULY 19    BE A BLESSING
Attitude

Genesis 27 (NKJV) Selected Verses

[4] *And make me savory food, such as I love, and bring it to me that I may eat, that my soul may bless you before I die.". [27] And he came near and kissed him; and he smelled the smell of his clothing, and blessed him and said:*

*"Surely, the smell of my son Is like the smell of a field Which the LORD has blessed. [28] Therefore may God give you Of the dew of heaven, Of the fatness of the earth,*

*And plenty of grain and wine. [29] Let peoples serve you, And nations bow down to you. Be master over your brethren, And let your mother's sons bow down to you. Cursed be everyone who curses you, And blessed be those who bless you!" ... [33] Then Isaac trembled exceedingly, and said, "Who? Where is the one who hunted game and brought it to me? I ate all of it before you came, and I have blessed him—and indeed he shall be blessed."*

This is the story of Isaac blessing Jacob. Jacob stole the blessing from Esau as Rebecca, his mother, arranged. Both Jacob and Rebecca knew how powerful the father's blessing was and is. Jacob's whole future depended on receiving that blessing. Words are powerful. God created the universe, light, plants and animals and started time with His words. You bet they knew how powerful words are!

What words will you speak and to whom? Each day, you come in contact with so many people. Family, friends and coworkers plus all the people in between your destinations. Do you speak words of encouragement? How many of the people with whom you come in contact are hurting in one way or another? Which one lacks confidence? Which one has been verbally abused? Which one is afraid? What will you do to improve their situation? Speak words of blessing into the lives of those around you. Tell them they are loved. Tell them they matter. Speak to each person you meet and really listen. Ask your waiter or waitress their name. People like to hear the sound of their own name. You can be a one person encouraging machine. Do random acts of kindness! Put a smile on God's face. He likes it when you bless others. Bless someone with your words today! You cannot be a blessing without being blessed by that act. Just as Isaac's blessing indeed blessed Jacob, so your words can bless family, friends and even strangers.

Lord, You have blessed us in so many ways! You came to us to give us the blessing of Your presence and spoke blessing into our lives. You offer us Your grace. Part of that grace is Your love and compassion. Help us to notice others and share Your grace with them. Lord, help us to be a blessing to those whom You love. In Your name we pray. Amen!

## JULY 20   SPONGE BOB
### Grace and Mercy

Colossians 3:16 (KJV)

*16 Let the word of Christ dwell in you richly in all wisdom; teaching and admonishing one another in psalms and hymns and spiritual songs, singing with grace in your hearts to the Lord.*

What does it mean to let the word of Christ dwell in you richly? How do you know if it is even in you at all? If Christ's work is in me, how can I enjoy it richly? What if I am new in my faith? How will I be able to grow? Paul speaks about wisdom, teaching and admonishing one another. He also mentions psalms and hymns. Could these be ways for us to grow spiritually?

I soak in God's goodness and teaching. That has two meanings. Firstly, I absorb all I can get from God like a sponge absorbs water. I want to get to know Him better and I ask Him to teach me His ways. Secondly, I soak in God's word as one would soak in a tub. I marinade in the juices of God's spirit to have His teachings penetrate to the deep places in my mind, heart and soul. You might say I meditate on His word and His grace. That is how I let His word dwell in me richly! Allowing God to penetrate my ego and pride has helped to lessen them and lead me into a closer walk with Him. I find myself saying things to comfort people that are much wiser than I am, knowing that God is speaking through me. The word of Christ is coming out. It is the grace of the Lord entering my heart and giving me what is needed to be a comfort to me and others. By His word, He offers us all wisdom. All we need do is accept the gifts He provides. How about you? Do you allow God to speak to and through you? Will you ask Him for wisdom and discernment? Will you accept what He provides? If you do, you can have the Lord's grace in your heart singing and teaching others what He has given you!

Lord, thank You for the word of Christ! May it dwell in us richly so that we can share You with others. Help us show what it is like to be a follower of Jesus. May the joy You provide cause us to sing. May the Grace You give us cause us to reach out to a hurting world in love and compassion sharing the good news. In Your name we pray. Amen!

## JULY 21    SPEAK THE TRUTH IN LOVE

Love

Ephesians 4:14-24 (NKJV) Selected Verses

*14 that we should no longer be children, tossed to and fro and carried about with every wind of doctrine, by the trickery of men, in the cunning craftiness of deceitful plotting, 15 but, speaking the truth in love, may grow up in all things into Him who is the head—Christ— ........17 This I say, therefore, and testify in the Lord, that you should no longer walk as the rest of the Gentiles walk, in the futility of their mind,......20 But you have not so learned Christ, 21 if indeed you have heard Him and have been taught by Him, as the truth is in Jesus: 22 that you put off, concerning your former conduct, the old man which grows corrupt according to the deceitful lusts, 23 and be renewed in the spirit of your mind, 24 and that you put on the new man which was created according to God, in true righteousness and holiness.*

You have heard it said that we should speak the truth in love. What does that mean exactly? Some people have the opinion the truth will offend someone and so we should not be offensive but politically correct. What does that mean? Should I be politically correct or right with God? Others question truth. They say there is no absolute truth. They say it is all relative. Does that mean it pertains to family? If it is all relative, there is no right and wrong. There is only opinion. And, of course, my own opinion is the most important, isn't it? It reminds me of the phrase in the Old Testament where "each person did what was right in his own eyes." That sounds like chaos to me. Should we abandon all law and just do what we think is right? In the Bible, the foolishness of this concept was proven time and time again. When Israel strayed from God's truth, He gave them over to their foolish desires and they suffered as a consequence. So why do people want to try that again? Learn from the mistakes of others. You don't have time to make them all yourself!

Speaking the truth in love is a difficult process. It is hard to figure out whether to be truthful or loving. Is it really the only choice? Do we have to be truthful or loving? Why can't it be both? Actually, it should be both. It is not loving to *not* tell someone the truth. A while back, a school district told an ethnic group they were doing well in their education. Each year, they were promoted to the next grade. When they graduated, they were unprepared for higher education. The school system lied to them. They were not really doing well at all. Was it loving to lie about the education? Would it not have been more loving to tell them the truth and give them more help? Had they been told the truth about needing more help, that would have been truth and love. You can and should have both! Speak the truth in love keeping their best interest in mind!

Thank You Father for Your truth. You word is truth. You bless us through Your word which takes us down the right path. Thank You that Your plans are always for our good. You know what is best for us and lead us in that direction. Help us to be truthful with kindness, grace and compassion. In Your name we pray! Amen!

## JULY 22  EVERYONE NEEDS A FRIEND
Relationships

1 Samuel 18:1-3 (NKJV)
*Now when he had finished speaking to Saul, the soul of Jonathan was knit to the soul of David, and Jonathan loved him as his own soul. ² Saul took him that day, and would not let him go home to his father's house anymore. ³ Then Jonathan and David made a covenant, because he loved him as his own soul.*

Jonathan and David were more like brothers than friends. In 1 Samuel 18, it tells us their souls were knit together, and Jonathan loved David as himself. Jesus told us to love your neighbor as yourself. David and Jonathan had that kind of love. Everyone wants to have a real friend like that, don't they? I know I do. In fact, I had such a friend in Carmen for many years until his passing.

Have you ever gone to camp with kids you don't know? There you were in a place with all new kids wondering if anyone will like you? When you are little, it is very scary. But it is even a factor when you grow up. We all still wonder if people will like us. But what if they don't? Not everyone will like us. I heard an interesting statistic. 25% of people will never like you. 25% of people will not like you but can be convinced to like you. 25% of people will like you but can be convinced not to like you. 25% of people will like you no matter what and all that is OK. Not everyone was destined to like you. What is important is that God loves you and you need to love yourself. Bernice Lopez (a friend I met with today) says "That's OK. I love myself enough for the both of us." You certainly should feel that way even if you are not willing to tell them. Love you! God already does! You are His masterpiece! All the rest comes later.

Zig Ziglar said "When you go out looking for friends, they are hard to find; When you go out to be a friend, you will find friends everywhere!" If you are concerned about being liked or finding friends, go out looking for others who may feel the same way and be a friend to them instead. When you focus outside yourself, God will send you all you need. He will bring others to you. I saw that happen today during Vacation Bible School. One young man was anxious about finding a friend. Another decided to be that friend. It was awesome! Thank You Lord!

Father, help us to let Your Spirit shine out from us so that others will be drawn to us. Let us share Your love with those we meet. Help us to become a friend to those who need a friend. And in that process, let us find friends with whom we can be a comfort to each other. Let Your light in us and Your light in them shine together to brighten our corners of the world. In Your name we pray! Amen!

# JULY 23   TO WHAT WERE YOU CALLED
Encouragement

Ephesians 4:11-13 (NKJV)

*11 And He Himself gave some to be apostles, some prophets, some evangelists, and some pastors and teachers, 12 for the equipping of the saints for the work of ministry, for the edifying of the body of Christ, 13 till we all come to the unity of the faith and of the knowledge of the Son of God, to a perfect man, to the measure of the stature of the fullness of Christ;*

Paul tells us about the callings Jesus gave His disciples. Each of these callings are for building up the Body of Christ. To do that, the saints need to be equipped. Part of the shortcoming of the Church as a whole today is the lack of training. We ask people to share the Good News but we don't teach them how.

What were you called to be? There are a lot of different things out there but glorifying God through the talents he has given you is where to begin. I was called to be an apostle and a teacher. Our Church asks us to make disciples who make disciples. I feel drawn to that. In order for that to work, we must first reach out to new people in Jesus name. I guess I also see myself as an evangelist because I have a heart for leading people to Jesus.

Once we enter into a relationship with Christ, He will transform us into who He wants us to be. But for us to be able to reach out to others, we will need training. That is where the gift of teaching becomes important. God has given me the ability to teach others His ways and how to share the Gospel. We need to equip the saints for the work of ministry. God always gives you what you need to do whatever He asks you to do. He will never leave nor forsake you. He sent His Son to walk with you!

What about you? What blessings has God given you? Are you an apostle, prophet, evangelist, pastor or teacher or something else? God has many blessings that He pours out on His people. Are you one of His children? Have you accepted His offer and His gifts? If not, will you come into a relationship with Him today? He stands at the door and knocks. It is a simple process of four steps. Why not take those steps now and join the family of faith? Go to http://www.4stepstogod.com/ and take the steps. When you do, you will be transformed into what He calls you to be slowly, day by day until you come to the unity of the faith and of the knowledge of the Son of God. Then, you will know and be prepared for your calling! You will be holy, righteous and redeemed in His name and by His grace!

Lord, thank You for Your gift of grace! Thank You that You call us into relationship with You. Entering into that relationship transforms us into who You want us to be. We become equipped, empowered and anointed with the special gifts You have for each of us. Thank You for Your love that sent Your Son to give Himself for us even before we knew You. Let Your transformation take place in us to share that love and become all You call us to be. Above all, may we bring glory to You and build the Body of Christ! In Jesus name we pray!

## JULY 24   WHO IS IN YOUR HEART
Faith

Ephesians 3:14-19 (NKJV)

*[14] For this reason I bow my knees to the Father of our Lord Jesus Christ, [15] from whom the whole family in heaven and earth is named, [16] that He would grant you, according to the riches of His glory, to be strengthened with might through His Spirit in the inner man, [17] that Christ may dwell in your hearts through faith; that you, being rooted and grounded in love, [18] may be able to comprehend with all the saints what is the width and length and depth and height— [19] to know the love of Christ which passes knowledge; that you may be filled with all the fullness of God.*

Paul, in his letter to the Ephesians, speaks about Christ dwelling in our hearts through faith. When He dwells in us, we will be grounded in love because God is love. It is beyond our comprehension the magnitude of that love. We just have to try to understand. Jesus said in John 15, *"Greater love has no one that this, than to lay down one's life for one's friends."* We are His friends if we put our faith and trust in Him.

This week, I was at Vacation Bible School Sports Camp. I spent the week with young people from four to twenty-four. The campers were four to ten with older youth as leaders and volunteers. It was awesome to watch the growth in all the age groups. The kids are learning new things and growing in the Lord. The leaders are gaining confidence as they help build the younger ones. The adults are gaining love and respect for the youth while helping them guide the younger ones. And the organizers are seeing the fruits of their labors come to fruition remembering why we do this in the first place. It is a wonderful time all around.

Thursday is the day we invite the kids into a personal relationship with Jesus Christ. Things all week have been leading up to this moment. The Lord has helped us prepare for a time when He will knock at the door of their hearts and ask to be let in. This will be the beginning of a loving friendship that will last for eternity. He will never leave nor forsake any of us if we invite Him in. The Sports Ministry Team did a great job of setting the stage and explaining what it means to follow a Risen Lord. Now the time has come for us to ask the question. "Do you want to start an eternal friendship with Jesus?"

What about you? Do you have such a friendship? Times look dark. Your adversary the devil walks about like a roaring lion, seeking whom he may devour. But God is still on the throne. When the outlook isn't so good, try the up-look. It is always better. Put your faith and trust in the One who will always be your friend and always love and protect you!

At the moment after the introduction and invitation, the kids are invited to join us in another room to answer any questions and to go through the 4 steps to God. We tell them that God loves them (and you), that we are all sinners, that Jesus paid the price for those sins and that, now, we can receive the gift of His grace and forgiveness by inviting Him into our hearts. He will be our Lord, Savior and Friend forever. I got the chance, with God's help, to explain that to sixteen second and third graders who said they wanted to begin a friendship with Jesus. It was awesome. At a time when the world spews hatred, sixteen young ones in my group entered into a loving relationship which will change them forever. They became children of God. There were others in the rest of the grades as well. God showed us again the height and width and depth of His love and continues to offer it daily. I know how dark things look at times. I ask you today to look toward the Light. The Light of the world loves you. Shine today letting that Light which is inside you burst out!

Father, thank You that You wait patiently for each one of Your children to come to You. You do not force Your way in but gently knock at the door of our hearts hoping that we will open the door and invite You in. Thank You that many kids threw open the door yesterday. We pray that many more children of all ages will open the door today, that You may abide with them too! In Your name we pray! Amen!

## JULY 25　THANKS FOR BEING A DOUBTING THOMAS
Faith

John 20:26-29 (NKJV)

*²⁶ And after eight days His disciples were again inside, and Thomas with them. Jesus came, the doors being shut, and stood in the midst, and said, "Peace to you!" ²⁷ Then He said to Thomas, "Reach your finger here, and look at My hands; and reach your hand here, and put it into My side. Do not be unbelieving, but believing." ²⁸ And Thomas answered and said to Him,* **"My Lord and my God!"** *²⁹ Jesus said to him, "Thomas, because you have seen Me, you have believed. Blessed are those who have not seen and yet have believed."*

What causes people to doubt? Is doubt always a bad thing? The most famous doubter in history was the disciple Thomas. He was not with the others when Jesus appeared to them the first time. The disciples told him they had seen the Lord but Thomas would not believe unless he saw Jesus for himself. The Lord gave him that chance and gave him the proof he needed eight days later. Thomas got to see and touch Jesus. Jesus did not chastise Thomas for doubting but answered his questions. Could it be that Jesus wanted to build up Thomas as an unimpeachable witness?

So, Thomas became an eyewitness to Jesus' resurrection. In a court, much credibility is given to an eyewitness to a crime. Therefore, much credibility goes to Thomas because he has now "seen" Jesus. Thomas did not want to be fooled. Once he had the proof he needed, he came to a dramatic conclusion. Thomas said "My Lord and my God!" Thank you, Thomas!

Seeing is believing isn't it? We believe that to which we are eyewitnesses more so than what we hear. But Jesus was going to return to His Father soon and needed to establish His witnesses here on earth. These witnesses were to be Jesus witnesses to "the ends of the earth." They better be really sure in their belief, hadn't they? Jesus went to people who had a reputation for researching things to be sure. People who were known to share only the truth they had proven. Such was Thomas. He wasn't taking anybody's word for it. He would investigate for himself. He would get to the bottom of the story. If Thomas said so, you could take it to the bank. Now that Thomas had done his research, what conclusion had he reached? Thomas was certain Jesus was who He said. Thomas declared Jesus his Lord and God. Thank you, Thomas. Now, I have no questions. I can trust your observations.

Have you seen Jesus? I hope to see Him someday but as yet, I have not. And yet, I believe He is my Lord, my Savior and my Friend. How can I make that observation? I believe because of the writing of trustworthy people who themselves cared enough to make sure the story was true. They sought the proof I would need so I can just believe. Romans 10:17 says *So then faith comes by hearing, and hearing by the word of God.* We get to hear the story and know it is true because we cannot touch His hands and His side. Thomas has done that for us! Blessed be the ones who doubt for they will be seekers of the truth and that truth will be, for us, a blessing!

Lord, thank You for the doubters of this world who will become seekers of the truth. You are that Truth. We are blessed to know You through the work of those who got to see and touch You and wrote down Your Word. As they wrote it down for us to read, I ask You to write Your story on our hearts. In Jesus name we pray!

# JULY 26   ARE YOU LISTENING
## Attitude

1 Samuel 3:7-11 (NKJV)

*⁷ (Now Samuel did not yet know the LORD, nor was the word of the LORD yet revealed to him.) ⁸ And the LORD called Samuel again the third time. So he arose and went to Eli, and said, "Here I am, for you did call me."*
*Then Eli perceived that the LORD had called the boy. ⁹ Therefore Eli said to Samuel, "Go, lie down; and it shall be, if He calls you, that you must say, 'Speak, LORD, for Your servant hears.'"*
*So, Samuel went and lay down in his place. ¹⁰ Now the LORD came and stood and called as at other times, "Samuel! Samuel!" And Samuel answered, "Speak, for Your servant hears [listens]." ¹¹ Then the LORD said to Samuel: "Behold, I will do something in Israel at which both ears of everyone who hears it will tingle.*

Speak Lord, for Your servant listens. Is that your attitude? Are you listening for the will of the Lord? Samuel was the son of Hannah, a woman who prayed to God for the blessing of a son as she was barren. She promised that, if God gave her a son, she would dedicate him to the Lord. Samuel was a disciple of Eli, the High Priest at the Temple, at this time because Hannah kept her promise. And God spoke to Samuel. The important part was that Samuel heard God! God speaks to many but few hear His words. Do you hear God's words? If you hear Him, how do you answer? If you are like me, you probably ignore what you hear hoping it will go away. Here is a news flash. It will not go away. God will continue to call and He will become progressively more persistent. His word will not be thwarted!

It was Eli who understood that the Lord was calling. Eli had probably never heard the call himself. Eli was not the best person because he had ignored the corruption of his sons and had fallen away from the Lord. And yet, Eli was the one who recognized the Lord's call to Samuel. Samuel was to be a Prophet of the Lord God of Israel. Samuel did not yet "know" the Lord but that was about to change. God decided to reveal Himself to Samuel because He wanted to do a new thing in Israel. One of those things was to overthrow the leadership of the corrupt Eli and family. But there were other things to which He would call Samuel. Samuel was the Prophet who would anoint David as King and be a powerful voice to Israel. It would be good for you to read 1 & 2 Samuel and see how the Lord worked in the lives of His people. God always blesses the obedient.

Do you hear God's calls in quiet little ways but try to ignore them? Are there things you know God wants you to do but you are afraid of what others will think? Do you think you should listen to God or man? I have come to a place in my Spiritual Life where I care about what God thinks. It is more important to do what God asks because it always works out best. When you follow God's plan for your life, it will yield blessing upon blessing. 1 Corinthians 2:9 (NKJV) *⁹ But as it is written:*

*"Eye has not seen, nor ear heard, Nor have entered into the heart of man the things which God has prepared for those who love Him."* Listening to God and following His lead makes all things possible. It is the blessed life we all want. The Lord longs to bless us in ways

we cannot even imagine. Following His Word will give us the opportunity to live in those blessings. Do you live in the fruit of the Spirit? Galatians 5:22-23 (NIV) says *²² But the fruit of the Spirit is love, joy, peace, forbearance, kindness, goodness, faithfulness, ²³ gentleness and self-control. Against such things there is no law.* How would you like to have all these things? I would be happy with self-control. You can if you will follow the Lord. When He calls, say "speak Lord, for Your servant listens!"

Lord, help us to hear and obey Your call. The world drowns out Your call these days. Teach us to cut through the noise and hear the clarion call to Your ways. Strengthen us to be able to follow You rather than the world. Bless us with Your leading so we might do what is right in Your eyes rather than our own. Help us to please You rather than ourselves. In Your name we pray! Amen!

## JULY 27    WHY ARE THINGS SO TOUGH
Support

1 Peter 5:8 (NKJV)

*8 Be sober, be vigilant; because your adversary the devil prowls about like a roaring lion, seeking whom he may devour.*

Life is tough! There is no doubt about that. Many are struggling asking where God is in the midst of all this trouble. Have you ever wondered why God allows things to happen? What if it is not God that is letting all these bad things happen? What if there was someone else causing all these challenges? What if we had an adversary who was doing things to harm us? There is! And his name is Satan, Lucifer, the accuser, the serpent, the evil one and many other terms. I have been told by a Pastor that she did not believe in Satan. I find there are more and more people who feel the same way. They totally discount that someone could be sabotaging their life. In fact, when I mention the adversary, I can see people sort of back away and question my sanity. Do you believe Jesus and what he says? Well Jesus said in Luke 10:18 (NIV) *18 He replied, "I saw Satan fall like lightning from heaven."* If Jesus said it, I believe it. We are fighting in the Spiritual realm. Let us make sure we have on the full armor of God and use the tools he has given us.

Peter warns about the activity of our adversary. He tells us Satan prowls around like a roaring lion looking for whom he can devour. You are prey for him. He works as hard as he can to disrupt your life hoping to make you angry with God and drive a wedge into your relationship. If things are going badly, you will be upset with God because you think He allowed the difficulty. Just as the serpent deceived Eve, he works today to deceive you. In many cases, it is working. Ephesians 6:12 (NKJV) warns *12 For we do not wrestle against flesh and blood, but against principalities, against powers, against the rulers of the darkness of this age, against spiritual hosts of wickedness in the heavenly places.* This is not an ordinary battle. You cannot fight this one on your own!

What is encouraging about fighting in a spiritual battle against a fierce enemy? Just the fact we are given everything we need to stand in the battle. We are given the armor to protect us. We are never subjected to a temptation beyond what we can handle. God allowed Job to go through all he faced because it would refine him and Job glorified God in the process. Job said "I know my Redeemer lives." God gave him double what he had before. God loves you and will always work things for your good. The trials are there to refine you, not to harm you. A kite only rises against the wind. Be thankful you are being tested. It means you are on the path to the destiny God has ordained for you. You are closing in on victory.

We thank You Father that You are always there for us even when we don't see You at work. We know the end is victory. You prevail and You have a place for each of us in Your plan. Draw us to You and place Your hedge of protection around us this day and every day. We know we need to be refined but be gentle with us in that process. But most of all Your will be done! In Jesus name we pray. Amen!

# JULY 28   IT IS YOU
## Grace and Mercy

2 Samuel 12:4-9 (NKJV) Selected Verses

*⁴And a traveler came to the rich man, who refused to take from his own flock and from his own herd to prepare one for the wayfaring man who had come to him; but he took the poor man's lamb and prepared it for the man who had come to him." ⁵So David's anger was greatly aroused against the man, and he said to Nathan, "As the LORD lives, the man who has done this shall surely die! ⁶And he shall restore fourfold for the lamb, because he did this thing and because he had no pity." ⁷Then Nathan said to David, "You are the man! Thus says the LORD God of Israel: 'I anointed you king over Israel, and I delivered you from the hand of Saul......⁹Why did you despise the word of the LORD by doing what is evil in his eyes?*

Do you do the right thing? When someone comes to you to speak about an issue they have with something you have done, what is your position? Are you defensive? Do you try to cover up your faults? This is a story about King David and one of his failures. And David was considered a man after God's own heart. The Bible does not show us perfect people.

In this story, the Prophet Nathan went to King David to confront him about Bathsheba and Uriah. Nathan tells David a story about a rich man who steals a lamb from a poor man's flock rather than use his own. When the story is told to him, David is incensed by the arrogance of the man who would take something that belonged to another use it as his own. He vows punishment for this misdeed. Then, Nathan reveals that David himself it the culprit. He stole another man's wife. As great as David was, he still had faults. Even though God would punish David for this wrongful act, He would still redeem David.

What about us? Do we have faults? Why would a perfect God want anything to do with imperfect people? Because His grace, mercy, love and compassion overshadow His judgment! While He wants us to strive to be more like Jesus, He still knows how we were made. He knows our hearts are deceitful. He knows we cannot meet the standards He set which are perfection. Throughout the Bible, we see examples of people who fall short of the mark and sin. Yet God redeems them! He offers the same redemption to us today. His grace, mercy, love and compassion eclipse any judgment we deserve. We are His children, made in His image, and He is our loving Heavenly Father. Today, walk in the grace He offers. Be bold. Be loved. Be redeemed!

Father, thank You that Your love for us overshadows all else. Thank You that You made a way for us to return to You if we make a mistake. We know that perfection is the goal but compassion is Your practice. Help us to strive to be more like Your Son but catch us when we fall as You know we will. Remind us of Your ways and let Your Spirit guide us in them. In Your name we pray.

## JULY 29   WHAT DO I SAY

Relationships

1 Peter 3:15 (NIV)

*15 But in your hearts revere Christ as Lord. Always be prepared to give an answer to everyone who asks you to give the reason for the hope that you have. But do this with gentleness and respect,*

What if someone asked you about your relationship with Christ? What would you say? Many people I know are not prepared to share their faith with others. Peter tells us we are to always be prepared to speak with people about the hope we have in Christ. Most are not! Are you?

Do you have a relationship with Jesus? When you wake up in the morning, is there music in your heart? Is there a spring in your step? Do people wonder why you are always so happy? If not, why not? In the song Multiply by NeedtoBreath, it says God's love is like radiant diamonds bursting inside us, we cannot contain. Is God's love bursting inside you? Do you have trouble keeping it inside? That is a good thing. It will let you live the life God intended for you. He wants you to be excited and happy. He came that you may have life and have it abundantly. Would you like to live an abundant life on every level? That is what He wants for you. If you live that kind of life, do you think people will notice? When they ask you why you are so happy, what will you tell them? Since I know you want to live the abundant life and I know people are going to ask about why, shouldn't you prepare now to give them an answer? After all, the abundant life is coming.

How can you learn what to say? Firstly, it is just a conversation. What is your story? Your personal story of who God is in your life and how you feel about Him is what to share. It does not have to be complicated. Just tell people about how you felt before and how you feel now. Second, there are courses and resources to help you frame that story.

In my life, I have developed a patience that astounds me. I have learned to speak with love. I have learned to see things I could not see before. I hear what is behind what people are saying. God now reveals things to me I would have never noticed before. I have an attitude of gratitude that flavors my whole life. How about you? What's your story? Can you share the story? That is all you need do. Be real! Be honest! Be who God made you to be! Be you! You are awesome!

Lord, thank You that you offer us an abundant life. Help us to share with others all the blessings You have given us. Make us bold to tell others what You have done for us. Give us the words and the opportunity to speak them. In Your name we pray. Amen!

## JULY 30    NO ONE CAN MAKE YOU FEEL INFERIOR WITHOUT YOUR PERMISSION

Support

Jeremiah 1:4-10 (ESV)
*Now the word of the Lord came to me, saying, "Before I formed you in the womb, I knew you, and before you were born I consecrated you; I appointed you a prophet to the nations." Then I said, "Ah, Lord God! Behold, I do not know how to speak, for I am only a youth." But the Lord said to me, "Do not say, 'I am only a youth'; for to all to whom I send you, you shall go, and whatever I command you, you shall speak. Do not be afraid of them, for I am with you to deliver you, declares the Lord." ...*

Eleanor Roosevelt said No one can make you feel inferior without your consent. That means you are the one who determines how you feel. Jeremiah tells us what God says about us and it is all good. Knowing how God feels about you should make you confident in yourself. Does it?

The Lord spoke to Jeremiah telling him that He appointed him to be a prophet to the nations and anointed him to do great things. All of God's promises are promises to all His children. He went further to say that He will go with us and deliver us and we should not be afraid. If the Lord God be for us, who can stand against us? We have the promise of God's support. With that support, we can do what He calls us to do.

Are you afraid to do certain things because of what people might think of you? Do you think that you do not have what it takes to accomplish the goal? Do people tell you that you are too young to do something? Do you believe them? I believe that God put dreams in every heart. In addition, He equips us for the tasks necessitated by the dreams. If He calls you to be a Prophet, He will give you the words! With that in mind, why should you feel unqualified? Is it because you are not acknowledging your gifts? In some instances, I don't know how I know something but I just know! That wisdom is a gift from God. Should I just ignore it? If I do, He will just bring it around again and again until I accept it and act. There is no way around what God destines for you. If He has destined you for great things, and He has, why not act on the dreams? Be the Prophet if so called. Go to whom you are sent. Speak to those to whom you are commanded. And do not be afraid! The Lord your God goes with you and will give you whatever you need. You are His and you are equal or greater than the task to which He calls you. Step out in faith and assurance today!

Lord, thank You that You call us to great and small things in Your name. Equip us for the tasks and give us the boldness to carry out what You ordain. Let us bring glory to You and comfort to those to whom You send us. In Your name we pray! Amen!

# JULY 31   WORDS ARE POWERFUL
## Encouragement

Romans 10 (NKJV) Selected Verses

[13] For "whoever calls on the name of the LORD shall be saved." [14] How then shall they call on Him in whom they have not believed? And how shall they believe in Him of whom they have not heard? And how shall they hear without a preacher? [15] And how shall they preach unless they are sent? As it is written: "How beautiful are the feet of those who preach the gospel of peace, Who bring glad tidings of good things!" ...[17] So then faith comes by hearing, and hearing by the word of God.

Words are powerful. What you hear or listen to can make a big difference in your life. You can speak things into or out of existence. In Genesis 1, God spoke the universe into being with His words. Words are powerful! Even faith comes by hearing. Be careful what you allow into your mind through your hearing.

Paul spoke about people calling on the name of the Lord. This indicates a person *must speak* the Lords name indicating the power of the spoken word. Romans 10:9 says [9] that if you confess with your mouth the Lord Jesus and believe in your heart that God has raised Him from the dead, you will be saved. So speaking is the important part. People need to speak truth and love to themselves and others. Calling is speaking. In Spanish, what's your name is actually "how do you call yourself?" So, how do you call yourself? Do you call yourself names? Why?

What do you speak on a daily basis? Are you speaking good things? Do your words reflect the fruit of the Spirit? We have learned that our words matter. What do you say when you talk to yourself? Are you encouraging and kind? Life can be rewarding. The words you choose can make a positive or negative difference. What would your life be like if you would use your words to change things for the better? You can you know? Speak blessings to everyone you meet. Look for something on which you can complement someone. You can find something good to say. Even a "good morning" and a smile can make an awesome difference. Positive words improve the atmosphere wherever you are. Did you know you can control the atmosphere around you? Why not try complimenting your family, friends, co-workers and even strangers? It will make the day go better! Yes, there is power in your words.

In the same way, there is also power in my words. Today, **let me speak these words over you.** You are accepted, approved, anointed, blessed, chosen, empowered, enabled, favored, gifted, guided, holy, intelligent, joyful, kept, loved, a masterpiece, righteous, redeemed, strong in the Lord, talented, unsinkable and worthy! Copy this list and put it on your refrigerator. Read it daily. Add to it as you think of things. You are an awesome creation of our awesome Lord. No one has your unique gifts and talents. You were designed to bring glory to God through the work of your hands. Go out and be spectacular today and give God the glory for who He made you to be.

Lord, we thank You for all the blessings You have put into each of us. Your design is perfect. We have the right gifts and talents for the race You call us to run. Please lay out that race before us and lead us safely through the course. Let our choices along the way and our crossing the finish line bring glory to You with each step. May the words of our mouths and the meditation of our hearts be pleasing in Your ears and may our lives be a blessing to others. In Your name we pray!

# AUGUST 1    I BLEW IT
Failure

Jonah 1, 3 (NIV) Selected Verses    Jonah Flees From the LORD

*[1] The word of the LORD came to Jonah son of Amittai: [2] "Go to the great city of Nineveh and preach against it, because its wickedness has come up before me." [3] But Jonah ran away from the LORD and headed for Tarshish. ...... to flee from the LORD. [4] Then the LORD sent a great wind on the sea, and such a violent storm arose that the ship threatened to break up......[15] Then they took Jonah and threw him overboard, and the raging sea grew calm.... [17] Now the LORD provided a huge fish to swallow Jonah, and Jonah was in the belly of the fish three days and three nights.......Jonah 3  Then the word of the LORD came to Jonah a second time: [2] "Go to the great city of Nineveh and proclaim to it the message I give you." [3] Jonah obeyed the word of the LORD and went to Nineveh.........[10] When God saw what they did and how they turned from their evil ways, he relented and did not bring on them the destruction he had threatened.... But to Jonah this seemed very wrong [the death of the plant and the forgiving of Nineveh], and he became angry.... [10] But the LORD said, "You have been concerned about this plant, though you did not tend it or make it grow....... [11] And should I not have concern for the great city of Nineveh, in which there are more than a hundred and twenty thousand people............?"*

Jonah did not listen to the Lord but decided to go his own way. Jonah did not want to preach to the Ninevites because he did not want to offer them God's forgiveness. After all, anytime God sends His Prophet to a people, it is for them to repent and be forgiven. Jonah did not feel the Ninevites deserved forgiveness. Nevertheless, God will be obeyed. He saved Jonah with a huge fish who would deliver him on to the shore where he would be asked again to go to Nineveh. Our God is a God of second and many chances.

You blew it! You made a big mistake and now you look really bad. You are embarrassed to face God. After all, you don't deserve another chance, do you? Do you think God has enough compassion to redeem you? When Peter asked Jesus how many times a person should forgive another, Jesus said "seventy times seven." That is 490 times and I think that means for the same issue. In other words, keep forgiving them. If the standard is for man to forgive 490 times, how many times will God forgive you? With God, there is always forgiveness. But even better, there is redemption. It is like it never happened. Jonah disobeyed God, was redeemed and then became angry with God for forgiving the Ninevites. Can you imagine that? Can you imagine being angry with God for forgiving someone else? I guess Jonah did not think they deserved forgiveness. What about you? Do you deserve forgiveness? The truth is none of us deserve forgiveness. It is God's gift He freely gives to those with a contrite heart. *If we confess our sins, He is faithful and just and will forgive us our sins and cleanse us from all unrighteousness.* (1 John 1:9)

God has compassion for all of His creation. Sin caused a curse on mankind and all of creation with them. But the good news is redemption is available for all of creation as well. God is willing to forgive us today. All we need do is confess, repent and ask. The confession and repentance part is the tough part. But go ahead and give it a try.

But by the blood of Christ (the Cross), you are holy, righteous and redeemed. Turn away from your mistakes and toward the destiny and blessing God has stored up for you. You may have blown it but God can repair the damage and turn your scars into stars. The Cross already won the war! Turn to Him and let Him help. In Jesus name we pray!

Greater by Mercyme

There'll be days I lose the battle Grace says that it doesn't matter Cause the cross already won the war

I am learning to run freely Understanding just how he sees me And it makes me love him more and more

## AUGUST 2   PICTURE THIS
Encouragement

Isaiah 41:13 (NKJV)

*13 For I, the LORD your God, will hold your right hand, Saying to you, 'Fear not, I will help you.'*

You are special! If God had a refrigerator, your picture would be on it. On our refrigerator are a multitude of pictures of things important to us from family and friends. There are wedding invitations. There are cards we received and other things important to us in life. What do you think God's refrigerator would look like? Would He have all the things important to Him? It would be a mighty big refrigerator then because you are important to Him.

Sometimes, I don't feel as if I matter to anyone. I get in those moods where everything seems tough and I feel I am working alone. Do you have those times? Days where everything seems to be more difficult than it should be. Multiple issues come up at what seems the worst possible time. The whole world seems to be against you. It is one of *those* days. You could become discouraged. But God has another plan.

Remember when you were a kid and things did not go well? If you had a bad day at school, you would come home and tell your parent. You did not even have to tell them; they already knew by your sagging shoulders. What did they do? They sat with you, listened to your story and made you something special to eat. Most likely, they held your hand. Isaiah tells us God will hold our hand. Our Heavenly Father will not only hold our hand but He will help us! The Creator of the universe will come to your aid! What could be better than that? Is there anything He cannot do? Whatever challenge you face, He has the answer. And He tells you that He *will* help you! There is no reason to worry. You can do all things through Him who gives you strength. He has already offered the help so asking should be easy. Are you asking Him for help? Do you have conversations with God letting Him know what you face? He will give you what you need to face what He asks you to face. You are never alone. For the Lord your God will hold your right hand and quell all your fears if you let Him. Take His hand and let Him!

Father, Your promises are sure and You are faithful. Thank You that You care enough to hold our hand and help us through life's challenges. We couldn't do it without You. Help us to realize we never walk alone. Answer us when we call. Help us to call often and to dwell in the center of Your love. In Your name we pray. Amen!

## AUGUST 3    ARE YOU REALLY EVER ALONE

Encouragement

Deuteronomy 31:6 (NKJV)

*⁶ Be strong and of good courage, do not fear nor be afraid of them; for the L*ORD *your God, He is the One who goes with you. He will not leave you nor forsake you."*

Variants of courage appear 23 times in the Bible. Strong appears 36 times. Apparently, God wants us to be strong and courageous. But that is not always easy to do. We get scared we cannot handle the situation. We worry. Worry is a tool of the accuser. God tells us in this verse the He is always with us. He is our Helper. Romans 8:31 says *"if God be for you, who can be against you?"* God is for you.

Are you lonely today? The Lord will never leave nor forsake you. The Lord will walk with you wherever you go. Even knowing that, we still sometimes need human companionship. We cannot see God so we think He is not there. What about having another person walking by our side? It makes things easier. I have always said two people working together can accomplish as much as five people working alone. Today, my Pastor Don stated he was working alone as the other Pastors were out of town for various reasons. I reminded him of my offer to help with the services any time he needed with the caveat that anything he wanted me to read be at least 18-point font. He worked alone because he did not ask. Do you ask for help? You have not because you ask not (James 4:3). Why don't you ask? What would you attempt if you knew you could not fail? If you ask others to work with you, between you all (or y'all), you will have all the talents and experience you need to succeed. You will not fail!

In the Footprints Poem, the person asks God why he was alone at the most trying times of his life since there were only one set of footprints. God replies "It was then that I carried you." God is always there to carry you when things get tough. God goes before you and with you always. He is your Helper, your Friend, your Provider, and your loving Heavenly Father. He wants the best for you and will lead you to it if you let Him. Are you alone? Maybe physically but not Spiritually. The Lord Your God goes with you and holds you fast with His righteous right hand. Rest secure knowing you are loved and never alone!

Lord God, thank You that You are always with us. Help us to be strong and courageous in the face of the opposition we face each day. Remind us that You are for us and we can stand by Your power. Use Your love to drive out our fear. Let Your Spirit remind us of that love always. In Your name we pray! Amen!

# AUGUST 4   CREATE YOUR OWN TEAM
## Encouragement

Ecclesiastes 4:9-12 (NKJV) A cord of three strands is not easily broken...
*9 Two are better than one, Because they have a good reward for their labor.*
*10 For if they fall, one will lift up his companion. But woe to him who is alone when he falls, For he has no one to help him up. 11 Again, if two lie down together, they will keep warm; But how can one be warm alone? 12 Though one may be overpowered by another, two can withstand him. And a threefold cord is not quickly broken.*

Our culture boasts about being a loner. I can do it myself! You hear about the self-made man so often. People work from home during the day so they don't see anyone. We text rather than talk. Our society is going in that direction. Is that a good thing? Are we meant to be alone? God didn't think so! In Genesis 2:18, it says *"18 And the LORD God said, "It is not good that man should be alone; I will make him a helper comparable to him."* We were designed to have a comparable helper. Things always go better with help.

Today's verse teaches us it is better to work with another because there will be a good reward for their labor. My expression is two people working together will accomplish as much as five people working alone. There is synergy in teamwork. There is also safety in numbers. Two can stand back to back and protect themselves. But teamwork also makes me think of marriage. This is the ultimate partnership. The two shall become one flesh. That was the Lord's design. He knew two are better than one. How about you? Are you aware it is better not to be alone? Aside from the human companionship, God is always with you. You are the apple of His eye and He always keeps you in His view. What position will you take? Are you better being a loner or do you want to share your life with someone? Do you have really close friends? Is there someone special in your life? Do you know your Lord well? If not, He is ready and waiting to meet you. You, your spouse and your Lord are a cord of three strands that is not quickly broken. In fact, the bond with your Lord will never be broken. He will love you forever. Give Him that chance, will you?

Lord, thank You that You created a helper for us and that You are always with us. With You, all things are possible. Help us to be in fellowship with others and to live our lives according to your design. Thank You that we have You to help us. Thank You that You have a special someone ordained for us so we will not be alone. In Your name we pray!

## AUGUST 5 ARE YOUR REQUESTS BOLD ENOUGH
### Quality of Life

Acts 3:6 (NKJV)

*⁶ Then Peter said, "Silver and gold I do not have, but what I do have I give you: In the name of Jesus Christ of Nazareth, rise up and walk."*

This man asked for alms but received a miracle instead. Peter and John were on their way to the Temple at the ninth hour which was the hour of prayer. They encountered a beggar at the gate looking for a handout. He looked at Peter and John hoping they would give him something. They saw him and asked him to look at them. Then Peter said, "Silver and gold I do not have, but what I do have I give you: In the name of Jesus Christ of Nazareth, rise up and walk." For what do you ask? Is it enough?

God wants to bless you with more than you can ask or imagine. He has blessings stored up with your name on them and longs to give them to you. He created a universe to support you. He has written your name on the palms of His hands. And yet, you ask for a few coins or a crust of bread. You are an heir with Christ to the Kingdom of God! You ask for *alms*. You have not because you ask not! All these blessing of which I speak; they are yours for the asking. But the key is you need to ask. For what do you ask? Are your requests bold? John 14:13-14 (NKJV) says *¹³ And whatever you ask in My name, that I will do, that the Father may be glorified in the Son. ¹⁴ If you ask anything in My name, I will do it.* And you ask for alms. I want to point out the "whatever you ask in My name" part. This addresses your motive. Why are you asking? Is it selfish desire or are you wanting to help others? Yes, there are things that you need for yourself. God wants you to be blessed. When you ask for things that will benefit others as well, God desires to open the floodgates of heaven and pour out more blessings than you have room to handle. Boldly come before the Throne of grace and ask your Heavenly Father for the things He wants you to have. Live in the center of His will and be blessed through His grace. You are His beloved child. You are the Prince or Princess. Walk boldly before your Father and ask for His blessing. In Jesus name!

Thank you, Father, that You bless us daily with much more than we deserve. It is by Your grace that we live. Show us Your grace and compassion and help us to pass them on to others so they will know we are Your followers. Let our light, the light You gave us, shine into the lives of others and may we be a blessing to many. All this to bring glory to You. Amen!

## AUGUST 6   WHAT IF I TRY AND FAIL
Failure

Galatians 6:9-10 (NKJV)

*⁹ And let us not grow weary while doing good, for in due season we shall reap if we do not lose heart. ¹⁰ Therefore, as we have opportunity, let us do good to all, especially to those who are of the household of faith.*

Have you ever not tried something because you were afraid you would fail and it would not come out right? Failure is not such a bad thing. Failure is the stepping stone to success. Thomas Edison had 10,000 failures in the incandescent lamp but you remember attempt 10,001. What if he had said *enough* and quit! We might be in the dark. When interviewed, he said he had not failed, he had just discovered 10,000 ways it would not work. Now that is the right attitude.

Are you surrounded by people who say things like "we tried that once and it didn't work?" How about the ones with "we've always done it this way." There are those who would stifle creativity and progress. Try to avoid them if you can although that may be hard especially if you work with them or they are your family. But you do have the right to ignore negative comments and continue on the path to your destiny. God has a great plan for your life. He has given you all you need to reach that destiny. All you have to do is keep trying.

When I was a kid, I failed a few times. Alright, I failed a lot. My Mom was frustrated by my out-of-the-box ideas. I am of the "wait 'til your father gets home" generation. I had to suffer the anguish of waiting. Dad was home for breakfast since he worked late. My Dad was an encouraging guy of few words. You know what he said? "You'll do better next time!" That was it. He knew I would fail at things but he wanted me to go on to success. Don't stop at failure. Do not grow weary while doing good! Success can be just around the corner. Don't Give UP!

Father, thank You that You have a great plan for our life. Lead us through the hard times on our way to the blessings You have stored up for us. Remind us good awaits and give us the passion and the stamina to keep going. Thank You for all You have done for us. Help us to do good for others in Your name.

## AUGUST 7    UNIMPEACHABLE
Faith

### Acts 1:8 (NKJV)

*⁸ But you shall receive power when the Holy Spirit has come upon you; and you shall be witnesses to Me in Jerusalem, and in all Judea and Samaria, and to the ends of the earth."*

What kind of witness are you? If you saw an event take place, would you be able to accurately describe what you saw? Are you a witness for Jesus? If you are going to be a witness for Jesus, what type of witness should you be? Thomas, the apostle, had his doubts about Jesus. He had to be convinced and Jesus knew it. But once he had the facts, he became the ultimate witness. Thomas had seen for himself the proof with his own eyes. He saw the wounds himself. And he declared "My Lord and my God." There was no more doubt! He became unimpeachable.

Jesus asked us to be his witnesses to the ends of the earth. You and I have not seen the wounds in His hands and side. How will we witness to His identity? We have His Word, the Bible. Many say it is just an old book but science is discovering and proving the things it contains. Lee Strobel set out to disprove the Bible and found himself a believer in the process. What about you? Do you believe? *Faith is being sure of what we hope for and certain of what we do not see.* (Hebrews 11:1) We were not eyewitnesses to the miracles but we have the testimony [the Bible] of those who were. Are you convinced? If not, study the information. I did and found it compelling. Seek answers to those nagging questions. All who seek shall find. And when you find your answers, share the good news with the world. The Bible has stood the test of time because it is the truth; God's truth! Know for sure that He loved you! *For God so loved the world that He gave His only begotten Son, that whoever believes in Him should not perish but have everlasting life.* (John 3:16) Know in your heart that He is your Savior, Friend and Lord. And be unimpeachable! Know the truth and that truth shall set you free.

Lord, we thank You for Your truth. It remains the same no matter how many times we tell it because it is the truth. Open hearts and minds to Your message and help us by giving us the words people need to hear. Help us to speak Your truth in love. And may our message be accepted bringing glory to Your precious name. Amen!

## AUGUST 8   DO ALL GOOD DOGS GO TO HEAVEN
### Grief

Job 12:7 and 10 (NIV)
*"Ask the animals, and they will teach you...In God's hand is the life of every creature, and the breath of all mankind."*

Job tells us animals will teach us about God and His love. For each and every creature, us included, are in the palm of His hand. We all matter.

Have you ever wondered if your pet will be with you in Heaven? You are not alone. Many people think animals do not have a soul and do not go to Heaven. Solomon said in Ecclesiastes 3:19: *"After all, the same fate awaits human beings and animals alike."* One dies just like the other. They are the same kind of creature...The God who created us created each animal as He wanted them to be. And all of creation is under the curse of sin. Romans 8 tells us *[20] For the creation was subjected to frustration, not by its own choice, but by the will of the one who subjected it, in hope [21] that the creation itself will be liberated from its bondage to decay and brought into the freedom and glory of the children of God.* All of creation can also be redeemed and Christ came to accomplish that redemption.

God loves all His creation. Matthew 6:26 says *[26] Look at the birds of the air, for they neither sow nor reap nor gather into barns; yet your heavenly Father feeds them."* He loves the birds of the air and the puppies of the ground as much as He loves you. We all matter to Him. He puts these beautiful creatures into our lives at just the right time. A time when we need them. Milo came to us just after we lost Taco. I didn't want another dog but God had other plans.

Our Lord wants us all to be with Him where He is. He is at the right hand of God the Father. And we get to go there to with Duchess and Becky and Danny and Rocky and Benjamin and Teddy and Taco and Rufus and all of our beloved friends. To err is human; to forgive is canine!

Thank You Lord for all our four-footed friends! They are awesome. They come into our lives to rescue us rather than be rescued. And each one is perfect for our needs. Thank you that dogs got to be our best friends by wagging their tails and not their tongues. Help us to appreciate the incredible gift You have given us with each one of our pets. In Jesus name we pray.

# AUGUST 9    GOD'S TIMING IS PERFECT

Faith

Galatians 4:4 (NKJV)

⁴ *But when the fullness of the time had come, God sent forth His Son, born of a woman, born under the law,*

God has a plan. Most of the time, we don't understand. He could have sent Jesus at any time but He chose the right time and place. But when the fullness of time has come, God will initiate that plan. Things seem to just happen out of nowhere. To us, it seems strange but as we look back, we see how things fit together perfectly. Habakkuk 2:3 ESV says "For still the vision awaits its appointed time; it hastens to the end—it will not lie. If it seems slow, wait for it; it will surely come; it will not delay." God has a plan!

God sends what you need when you need it even though you may not even know the need yet. Dogs appearing, working late, traffic and other things are all God's timing. He needs to get you where you need to be in His plan at the precise time He wants you there for His reasons. Maybe it is to meet the love of your life. Perhaps he knows you need a faithful companion to cheer you up. He might want you to meet someone who will benefit your future. Or, you might be the answer to someone's miracle and your gifts and talents are just what they need. Whatever the reason, God has a plan.

Taco appeared at a time that we needed a dog. Our first foster son found him in a park just before coming to visit us for the weekend. I did not want him to bring the dog because I know I would be "stuck" with him if I allowed the visit. I never want another dog because of the pain of losing them. I am always the one who takes them to be put down when needed and it hurts. You know the rest of the story. Taco, a 4-pound Chihuahua, came to live with us for the next two years. He needed a home and we (according to God) needed a dog. Who rescued who? What a sap I am for a cute puppy face.

We lost Taco two years later but he passed peacefully with a smile on his face. Our friends lost their dog and were devastated. I know how they feel. Been there; done that; got the t-shirt! I wrote an Encouragement Daily about the loss of a pet and a funny thing happened. Another friend wrote and shared her story about a dog appearing in her life at a time she needed comfort and remained with her for years to be her faithful friend. She wrote me this long story which brought tears to my eyes which salted my breakfast. She is smart enough to know Puppy was a gift from God to help her along the road. I believe that dogs are angels that God sends to care for and protect us as we walk this life and face challenges. The look of a dog's eyes speaks to us in ways words cannot even touch. I see God in Milo, our present resident canine angel (a.k.a. Smilo - he actually smiles). Be open to the things God sends into your life. He knows what you need before you know. He always gives you what is best for you even though you may not like it. But remember, God has a plan!

Lord God, thank You for Your plan to bless us in all things. You refine us through trials but help us along the way. You send us what we will need to pass through the valley to the table You have prepared for us on the other side. Thank You that you send Your furry angels to walk with us and make the journey more pleasing. They show us what unconditional love really means. Help us to love like that. In Your name we pray! Amen!

# AUGUST 10   WHAT WILL YOU REAP
Encouragement

Galatians 6:7 (NKJV)

*7 Do not be deceived, God is not mocked; for whatever a man sows, that he will also reap.*

God will not be mocked! People think they can do things and get away with it if they are careful. When Adam and Eve sinned, they tried to hide from God. God is omniscient and omnipresent. You are not hiding from Him. Even though He asked "Adam, where are you?"; He knew. He also knew what they had done.

What goes around comes around is the worldly expression. Ephesians says you will reap what you sow. With that in mind, shouldn't you sow good things? The golden rule says "do unto others as you would have them do unto you." Isn't that a good way to live your life? What about this sow to the flesh vs. to the Spirit? There is a difference between worldly and Spiritual things. Being in the flesh is our sinful nature with greed and selfishness leading the charge. Being in the Spirit is working in the way God calls us to go. It is doing things according to God's will. Being in God's will is always the best for us as it leads us closer to Him. God has blessings He desires to pour into your life. Living in the Spirit will release those blessings. What do you want to reap? Are you interested in corruption or everlasting life? Remain in the Spirit and reap the benefits. God has more blessings than you can ask for or imagine waiting for you when you walk with Him! It is the best way to go.

Today, as you go through the world, spread goodness, kindness, gentleness, self-control and patience. Greet people with a smile. Learn your server's name and use it when you thank them. Notice people and make them feel important. Ask how people are doing and really listen to the answer. You could be part of someone else's miracle. How will you find out if you don't pay attention? Go out to be a blessing. If someone doesn't have a smile, give them one of yours. That is living in the Spirit. That is loving God's creation. That is sowing in the Spirit and the benefits you will reap will last forever.

Lord, we want to live a life that will bring glory to You. Many will mock us for following You. Strengthen us that we may walk in Your ways no matter what the world thinks. Help us to sow seeds of grace, compassion and love so that we may reap the same. Pour out Your blessings upon us. Draw us closer to You that we may live with You forever. In Your name we pray! Amen!

# AUGUST 11 FLOWERS IN GOD'S GARDEN
Faith

Mark 4:3-9 (NKJV)The Parable of the Sower

[3] "Listen! Behold, a sower went out to sow. [4] And it happened, as he sowed, that some seed fell by the wayside; and the birds of the air came and devoured it. [5] Some fell on stony ground, where it did not have much earth; and immediately it sprang up because it had no depth of earth. [6] But when the sun was up it was scorched, and because it had no root it withered away. [7] And some seed fell among thorns; and the thorns grew up and choked it, and it yielded no crop. [8] But other seed fell on good ground and yielded a crop that sprang up, increased and produced: some thirtyfold, some sixty, and some a hundred." [9] And He said to them, "He who has ears to hear, let him hear!"

Our Lord calls us to plant seeds. These are the seeds of the Gospel. It is our job to plant, to water and to fertilize but it is God, by His Holy Spirit, the gives the increase. It is He who makes them grow.

The parable of the sower speaks about sharing the good news with people. Some will listen and some won't but we are called to share. I take that call seriously. I try to spread the good news wherever I go. Sometimes, I think I spend too much time with others and not enough looking after my own.

I was looking at my garden. It is a sad state of affairs. There are weeds everywhere. I look around and see other people's gardens and lawns and they are neat and well-trimmed. I know we are not supposed to compare ourselves to others but it is human nature. Then I got to thinking. I spend time on things that matter more to me and to Him. Instead of hours in the garden, I am investing in what's better.

VBS Sports Camp happened a few weeks ago and I spent the week with 122 kids and 100+ teenage volunteers. I was there in the morning to greet them and hung out encouraging them all through the day. I spent time with the teen leaders helping them navigate through challenges they had not faced before. With a little coaching, they did very well. I could have worked in my garden pulling weeds. My house would look better now.

Then it hit me! I am not tending my garden. I am tending God's garden. If I pull weeds in my garden, they will return in a week. If I plant seeds in God's garden, they will bloom into eternity. So it's My Garden vs. God's garden. Which should I choose? Thursday at VBS is commitment day. That is the day when we ask the kids if they want to enter into a relationship with Jesus Christ. During Bible time, the Gospel Message is presented and the kids are asked if they want to accept Jesus as their friend and invite Him into their hearts. It was my privilege to speak with the second and third graders and pray with those who decided to accept the invitation. Sixteen kids stood up to go with us to learn more and pray to receive Jesus. All sixteen prayed the prayer that day. I guess you could say there were sixteen new flowers in God's garden. These flowers can go on to change the world for the better. I made an investment that will pay dividends for the Kingdom into eternity. The weeds will always be there. But the Angels are singing for the sixteen. And who knows that those sixteen will not remember their time at VBS when they met their Lord and take vacation time to participate at VBS in the future. Then they too will add flowers to God's garden. It may yield a hundred-fold. Praise God! So, today, why not go and plant seeds in God's garden yourself? The growth may amaze you.

Lord, thank You for the honor of sharing You with others. Thank You for the opportunity to serve the kids and lead them to know You. You call us to make disciples. Give us the words we need to say and the opportunity. Open hearts and minds to hear the message. Draw people to You. The heavens declare Your glory. Help us to do the same and share that glory with everyone we meet. In Your name we pray. For more insight, read Mark 4:1-20

## AUGUST 12   KEEP GOING
Grace and Mercy

Philippians 1:3-6 (NKJV)

*³ I thank my God upon every remembrance of you, ⁴ always in every prayer of mine making request for you all with joy, ⁵ for your fellowship in the gospel from the first day until now, ⁶ being confident of this very thing, that He who has begun a good work in you will complete it until the day of Jesus Christ;*

We all come up against challenges that are overwhelming and we are not sure how we will make it through. Or we don't feel we have what it takes to accomplish something. We are walking through the valley of the shadow of death. It seems as darkness is closing in around us. But the key is walking *through* the valley. There is a table prepared for us on the other side if we keep walking. Don't stop here!

In his letter to the Church at Philippi, Paul writes words of thanks and praise about his flock there. They have been faithful thus far. He is concerned that they are having a hard time and losing faith. Jesus said in John 16:33 *"³³ These things I have spoken to you, that in Me you may have peace. In the world you will have tribulation; but be of good cheer, I have overcome the world."* In this world you will have trouble. He told them flat out. However, He told them He had overcome the world by His cross. And He did that for you and me. You may struggle but we already know the final outcome. You win because you are on God's team. Have confidence and fight the good fight. He who begun a good work in you will complete it.

What is the good work He has begun in you? In Galatians 5, we are told of these fruits. *"²² But the fruit of the Spirit is love, joy, peace, patience, kindness, goodness, faithfulness, ²³ gentleness, self-control."* All of these have been placed in us. You are God's Masterpiece created in His image and likeness. You are holy, righteous and redeemed by the blood of the Lamb. You are anointed. You are empowered. You are highly favored. You are guided by His Spirit. With all that behind you, this should be an awesome day for you. You are a child of the King. Put your shoulders back. Raise your head up high and go out and show the world what it looks like to follow a Risen Lord today!

Each day, when I awake, I have to make the choice to get out of bed as do you. Some days, I do not want to get up. Voices tell me nothing good is going to come out of today. But God's voice tells me this is the day the Lord has made. I choose to rejoice and be glad in it. You have a choice. Will you get up and do everything as if unto the Lord or will you listen to the negative voices which say you'll never accomplish your dream? What choice will you make? Remember who loves you and what He has placed inside you! You have everything you need. The dream in your heart is from Him. Go live the dream! Be who God calls you to be and let Him finish the work He has begun in you.

Thank You Father that you have created us to be who You decided we should be. Thank you for all the gifts and talents you have given us. Help us to use what You have given us to Your glory to complete the work You have begun in us today. In your name we pray! Amen!

From Greater by MercyMe: There'll be days I lose the battle Grace says that it doesn't matter
Cause the cross already won the war I am learning to run freely Understanding just how he sees me
And it makes me love him more and more.

## AUGUST 13   MASTERPIECE
Faith

Ephesians 2:10 (NIV)
*10 For we are God's handiwork, created in Christ Jesus to do good works, which God prepared in advance for us to do.*

God created you in His image and likeness. What does it mean to be in the likeness of God? Much of it is to be like God; to have some of His attributes. In fact, you were given the seeds of most of God's attributes. You were made to be in your place and time. You were given the gifts and talents you would need to run the race set out before you. You are one of a kind. As Zig Ziglar would say, "You were designed for accomplishment, engineered for success and endowed with the seeds of greatness." You are God's Masterpiece.

With all that going for me, you say, how come I am not more successful? How do you define success? Is it all about the money? Is "show me the money" your catch phrase? Success is different things to different people. God has a plan for you. Maybe money was not the dominant idea in His plan. He knows what you need better than you do. He has laid out a race for you that is specific to the gifts and talents He built into you. Will you use those gifts? How will you run that race and will you finish strong?

Also, we were created to do good works. The Bible says you will know them by their fruit (Matt 7:16). You can tell a lot about a person by looking at the work they do. What is the quality of the work? What kind of work is it? Do they volunteer a lot? God has ordained work for us to do. Doing this work will bring personal satisfaction. When I finish a project or solve a challenge, it makes me feel really good. Isn't it interesting to know that God planned these projects for us in advance? It is all part of His plan to highlight the gifts He has placed within you. You are one of a kind. You are amazing. You are God's handiwork and He made you perfect for His plan. You are His Masterpiece. Work within God's plan by asking to do His will. Ask His Spirit to lead you in the race He set out before you from the beginning of the world!

Father God, we thank You that You have a plan for our lives. It is good to know that You care so much that You establish the work of our hands. Thank You for the gifts and talents to accomplish Your plan. Bring us to where You would have us be so we can carry out the race that will take us closer to You and bless one another. Help us to achieve our destiny which will be our praise to You! In Your name we pray!

# AUGUST 14   CAN YOU HANDLE THE TRUTH
## Grace and Mercy

2 Timothy 3:16-17 (NIV)
*16 All Scripture is God-breathed and is useful for teaching, rebuking, correcting and training in righteousness, 17 so that the servant of God may be thoroughly equipped for every good work.*

Scripture is the only standard by which we should live. Some say that truth is relative. Does that mean that it depends on the situation? Is it OK for me to kill someone if they cut me off in traffic? Is gravity relative in different places here on earth? How can truth be relative? I need to know right from wrong and truth from lies. What standard should I use as a guideline? Should our government be the source of truth? Actually, it should but it isn't.

Paul tells us that all Scripture is God breathed. That means it is the Word of God recorded by approximately 40 men of diverse backgrounds over 1500 years. Paul's assertion is it was dictated or revealed by God to these men making it His Word. I heard it said that Bible stands for Basic Instructions Before Leaving Earth. Pilate asked "what is truth?" For me, the Bible is the source of truth. Many say it is just a nice history book. While archeology and science have been able to prove much of the Bible, I take God at His Word. Many, like atheist and author Lee Strobel, set out to disprove the Bible and ended up coming to faith in Christ through their efforts. God loves doubters. Just ask Thomas. They found the information compelling. When I read the New Testament, I realized what all the Old Testament prophecies were about. I came to Christ May 31, 1998 because of my research. Also, I was working with a Christian Youth Group and learned things from them. Paul goes on to list the benefits of Scripture. I like to use it to teach. There is only one perfect person in the Bible and they hung Him on a tree. The rest of us all had flaws but God showed us how He can use those flaws for our good and to bring glory to Himself. Adam was weak, Eve was gullible, Abraham lied, Moses stuttered, Aaron worshipped idols, Jonah was disobedient, David was a murderer and fornicator, Isaiah was afraid, Peter betrayed Jesus, and Lazarus was dead. And these are all heroes of the Bible. If you were going to write a book of fiction, would you include these characters? Probably not.

What is the good news? The good news is this. The Bible is a story of love, compassion and grace. God loves you and, through these stories, demonstrates how that love plays out. He shows you His grace given to people who are no better than you. If they received His grace, so can you. The Bible tells you that you are fearfully and wonderfully made. It says you are awesome! There are promises in there that still apply to you. Hebrews 4 (NIV) says *"Therefore, since the promise of entering his rest [heaven] still stands, let us be careful that none of you be found to have fallen short of it."* Pastor Joel Osteen opens his services with this statement. "This is my Bible. I am what it says I am. I have what it says I have. I can do what it says I can do..." You have the same Bible. Believe what it says about you and live accordingly. You are a child of God. As heir to the Kingdom, live boldly in love today!

Holy Spirit, help us to live boldly in You today! Remind us who we are in You and guide us as You would have us live. By Your power, help us to love one another as You have loved us. Help us to live in and share Your Truth. In Jesus name we pray! Amen!

# AUGUST 15    ONLY YOU
## Grace and Mercy

Isaiah 64:4-6 (NKJV)

*⁴ For since the beginning of the world Men have not heard nor perceived by the ear, Nor has the eye seen any God besides You, Who acts for the one who waits for Him. ⁵ You meet him who rejoices and does righteousness, Who remembers You in Your ways. You are indeed angry, for we have sinned— In these ways we continue; And we need to be saved.⁶ But we are all like an unclean thing, And all our righteousnesses are like filthy rags; We all fade as a leaf, And our iniquities, like the wind, Have taken us away.*

Who is like our Lord; righteous and Holy? You pour out Your favor upon Your own. You act *for* us! We cannot even fathom the height, width and depth of Your love and character. There is none beside You. Awesome in power and righteousness. To whom else can we go as Yours are the words of eternal life.

Which path do you follow? Are you familiar enough with God's way to know the path He has ordained for you? Do you seek His counsel to decipher the way you should go? When you walk the road God has chosen for you, He will make your paths straight. In the center of His will are peace, grace and love. God intentionally acts for your benefit. He cares for His own. Are you His own?

We get to choose our way. God created us and gave us free will. We can choose to love Him or not. Choosing to love and follow Him means He will act for you. When I was younger, I felt a lack of support as if I didn't measure up to the standards. Because of that, I think I over compensated acting as if I was better that I actually was. Then, I did not realize that every good thing comes from God. I thought it was all up to me. At fourteen, I claimed to have reached the apex of perfection. That was what I needed to do to boost my ego. I was unaware that, apart from God, we can do nothing. Now, I understand who I am. My righteousness is like filthy rags. But I also understand whose I am. In Him, I am holy, righteous and redeemed. Jesus covers me in His righteousness as a garment by the sacrifice of His life for mine. He died that I may live! And what a life it is. Old Bob was in charge. If it was to be, it was up to me. New Bob is along for the most glorious ride. I have a life of peace, joy, grace and compassion. There are still challenges along the way though.

Some years ago, as a devotional introduction to a Church meeting, we broke down into pairs and were to ask each other this question several times trying to draw out the deeper meaning. Our question was "What would it grieve you to have to give up to follow Christ?" I was the one to ask my partner the question first. She gave a long list of things like home, education and other things. I had a chance to think about this while it was her turn. By the time my turn came, I had clarity. The Spirit had spoken to me. There was nothing I would grieve because everything I have is from Him. He gave me every good thing in my life. You see, even when I was not fully aware of God, His hand was still on me and in my life! My God was acting *for* me. He always has and I see that when I look back. Looking forward is scary. But when you look back and see all the things He has already done for you in the past, it gives you courage and assurance that He walks with you and cares for you. You can walk boldly into the future, knowing the Creator of the universe goes before you making the crooked places straight and acting in your best interest in every situation whether you see Him or not.

Lord God, thank You that You act for the one who waits for You! Let us be those who love and serve You. May we walk with You as You lead us in the path You have ordained us to walk. Let us know You are with us when we are frightened. Guide us with Your righteous right hand. Help us to bring glory and honor to Your holy name we pray. Amen!

## AUGUST 16    BE POSITIVE AND ENCOURAGING

Encouragement

Hebrews 3:12-13 (NIV)

*¹² See to it, brothers and sisters, that none of you has a sinful, unbelieving heart that turns away from the living God.¹³ But encourage one another daily, as long as it is called "Today," so that none of you may be hardened by sin's deceitfulness.*

We are told to encourage one another. Why? Do you think people need encouragement? I do! In fact, that is why I began writing Encouragement Daily. Our world is a dark place. The adversary goes around causing confusion and doubt everywhere he can. He tries to distract us from all the good things God intends for us. That distraction leads to separation from God. That separation is called sin.

The world constantly hammers us with negative thoughts saying we cannot do things. If we listen to the negative voices, we will be held back from the destiny God has planned for us. What we believe will affect any outcome we may have. Whether you think you can or you think you can't, either way you are right. I have worked with foster children and youth groups and seen this in real life. One young man says "I cannot do this." He clouds up and frustration abounds to where he is ready to throw things away. We need a time out to chase away the negative mindset.

How can you chase away the negativity? With our young man, I know he can do it because he has done it before. But he focuses on his failures rather than his successes. First, hugs and consolation are in order. That is the beginning of the time out. We remind him of our love for him first. Sometimes, a little tickling is involved to change the mood. A child's laughter cheers any room. Then, we check the history. Have you ever done this before? How did it come out? You were able to do it then? "You helped me." He says. Don't you think I would help you again? If you did it before, why would you think you cannot do it again? We are all just children of all ages. We think we cannot do something. We get scared. We withdraw. God, our Father, has to ask the same questions. "But you helped me." we say. Then why wouldn't God help us again. All we need do is ask. Do you ask God for help? Do you listen for His answer or do you try to go it on your own? Going it alone is never fun. Sometimes, God puts other people in your life to help you with things as well. Sometimes you just need encouragement. That is true for others. They may need a kind word from you.

Today, encourage one another. That way, you will overcome the schemes of the adversary that are trying to discourage you. Discourage means without courage. You have courage. It was built into you. Don't let doubt separate you from your destiny. And don't let doubt happen to your friends. Encourage them. Encourage each other today!

Lord, thank You that You have given us everything we need to become who You designed us to be. We are Your children and we get scared. Comfort us on the road and let us walk with You! In Your name we pray.

## AUGUST 17    PRAISEWORTHY
Attitude

Philippians 4 (NKJV) Selected Verses
*¹Therefore, my beloved and longed-for brethren, my joy and crown, so stand fast in the Lord,....⁸ Finally, brethren, whatever things are true, whatever things are noble, whatever things are just, whatever things are pure, whatever things are lovely, whatever things are of good report, if there is any virtue and if there is anything praiseworthy—meditate on these things. ⁹ The things which you learned and received and heard and saw in me, these do, and the God of peace will be with you.*

To what are you listening? Are you listening to the daily news reports? If you listen to network news, you are getting more than your share of discouragement. We've been conditioned to believe that "no news is good news." That is more relevant to today than it seems. Our network news people tell us the most sensational headlines with the "story at eleven!" Facts and information are not needed. Just give us flash. There hasn't been a journalist since Walter Cronkite or Huntley & Brinkley. The worse the story, the more excited they are to promote it to us. If we listen to all this negative input all the time, what kind of disposition will we develop?

Paul had a better idea. He tells us to concentrate on better things. The mind takes in what you allow. If you allow negative input, you will develop a negative attitude. Why not allow positive input? Why not focus on the good things rather than just the bad. Become a Good Finder. We know that God works all things together for the good of those who love Him. Don't let the network news determine what goes into your mind. You bring about what you think about. What do you want to allow to go into your mind?

Also consider what comes out of your mouth. Do you speak what is praiseworthy? The world tears us down. Why not work toward building one another up as we are advised here. Use your words to build and promote others. As you go through your day, look for the good things that are happening and call them to people's attention. Praise people who are doing a good job. Activity that is praised will be repeated. Praise the activity you would like to have performed more often. Do this especially in young people. Set an example of how to praise and how to live. They are watching. What world do we want to pass to the next generation? Should it be a world of rudeness and self-absorption or a world of respect and common courtesy? You decide! Are you showing the example you wish to have followed by others? Paul suggests it be praiseworthy. Is your behavior praiseworthy? It is your choice. Decide for praiseworthy today and God will be with you!

Hello Lord! Thank You for giving us Paul's example of how to live. Paul learned from You how we should live. Help us to look for the good in all situations and praise that good. Teach us to focus outside of ourselves. Help us to live in a praiseworthy manner and encourage others to do the same by our example. In Your name we pray! Amen!

# AUGUST 18    A NEW HEART
Grace and Mercy

Ezekiel 36:24-27 (NKJV)
*24 For I will take you from among the nations, gather you out of all countries, and bring you into your own land. 25 Then I will sprinkle clean water on you, and you shall be clean; I will cleanse you from all your filthiness and from all your idols. 26 I will give you a new heart and put a new spirit within you; I will take the heart of stone out of your flesh and give you a heart of flesh. 27 I will put My Spirit within you and cause you to walk in My statutes, and you will keep My judgments and do them.*

The Lord is speaking to the Nation of Israel through Ezekiel telling them of the good plans He has for them. Israel was scattered among the nations because of their disobedience but God plans to bring them back to Him. He goes further to tell them He will give them new hearts and cause them to walk with Him. They will follow His ways because He will be within them. With God's Holy Spirit leading from the inside, the Israelites will walk with their God. Not only that, He will cause them to follow His commands. Oh, if that were possible for us. It is if we will listen. God still calls us today.

Romans 3:23 says "*...all have sinned and fallen short of the glory of God.*" Not one beside Christ is worthy of salvation. Romans 6:23 (NKJV) says *23 For the wages of sin is death, but the gift of God is eternal life in Christ Jesus our Lord.* What we deserve is death, not life. But instead, God offers us eternal life through Jesus. The clean water He says He will sprinkle on us to cleanse us is Baptism into Christ. Once in Christ, we are new creations. We will have a new heart. We will be transformed.

Transformation is different for different people. I had a friend who was addicted to illegal drugs. His life was not going well when he came to know the Lord. His transformation was instant. He was immediately freed from his drug addiction. I, on the other hand always had God in my life. There was no sudden change. Christ entered my life slowly, subtly but steadily. I have more peace. I am more patient. He calls me to walk with Him by guiding me through His Holy Spirit. I become aware of things through His leading. I know things I did not know before as they are revealed to me.

Do you feel you have strayed too far for Him to redeem you? We go astray by our own choosing. But God always has a plan for our return. He loves us that much. No matter how far you have strayed, God still loves you and has made a way back possible for you. He will gather you from all the world and bring you back to Him. And He will live within you to guide you in the way that is best for you. He loves you so much, He will always welcome you with open arms.

Thank You Lord that You always make a way for us to return to You. Thank You that You wash us clean and give us a new heart; a heart that loves You. Gather us to Yourself and let us live in Your grace forever. In Your name we pray!

# AUGUST 19   WAG YOUR TAIL AND NOT YOUR TONGUE
Relationships

Galatians 5:14-15 (NKJV)
*14 For all the law is fulfilled in one word, even in this: "You shall love your neighbor as yourself." 15 But if you bite and devour one another, beware lest you be consumed by one another!*

Many people have a critical spirit. They are always complaining or criticizing someone or something. Being around a person like that is depressing. According to them, there is nothing good around. It can really bring you down! Anyone who criticizes another is damaging their spirit.

In Galatians, Paul reminds us we are to love our neighbor as ourselves. We are to care for others and nurture each other. He warns us not to devour one another. Have you ever listened to a negative person talk about an opportunity? They dissect it, tearing it all apart with all the reasons why it will not work out. It is no wonder they don't realize their dreams. How about you? Do you look for the reasons why *or the* reasons why not? What you seek is what you will find.

There is a saying which goes "Dog got to be man's best friend by wagging its tail and not its tongue." When you come home, your dog is always happy to see you. Our dog, Milo, smiles when we come in the door and the tail is going crazy wagging. He is excited to see us and we are excited to be home with him. What if people were to show that kind of excitement toward each other? Would this be a better world? Would we not use angry words toward one another? Could we refrain from biting each other's head off? Try it! The next encounter you have where a person is cranky, try smiling at them. Refuse to get in a bad mood just because they are. They may have had an awful day. Tell them you are happy to see them. Ask them to tell you about their day and listen intently. There may be nothing you can do to help. Listening may be enough. Once they have been heard, you can work toward a better future since you cannot change the past.

We all get in bad moods. Is that where you want to stay? I am trying a little experiment. I have resolved I want to say yes more often. My background leads me to "no" too often. When asked a question, I pause and think. How can I say yes? What will it take? The other day, our 8-year old wanted to know about winding the clocks and how clocks work. I stopped to consider how I could say yes. I got the step stool out, lifted him up on it and taught him how to wind a clock. I will be showing him how a clock works soon. What if I said no? He would not have learned anything and neither of us would be very happy. Why not promote happiness? Wag your tail (symbolically) instead of your tongue and say yes!

Father, we thank You for all the blessings You put in our lives. Help us to recognize each person and situation for the blessing they really are. Lead us to speak peace and love into the lives of others. Teach us to love our neighbors as our selves. Oh yes, remind us we are also to treat ourselves well. Let us not use our mouth to bite but to smile! In Your name we pray. Amen!

# AUGUST 20  WHO ARE YOU IN CHRIST

### Grace and Mercy

You are awesome! You are made in the image and likeness of God. You can do all things through Him who gives you strength. Pastor Joel Osteen's Church has an opening statement for their worship services. It says "This is my Bible. I am what it says I am! I have what it says I have! I can do what it says I can do!" Have you read your Bible recently? Did you take note of all the things it says about you? Here is a short list of things the Bible says about you provided by Pastor Joyce Meyers Ministries. There are more! Just thought you would like to know.

I am complete in Him Who is the Head of all principality and power (Colossians 2:10).

I am alive with Christ (Ephesians 2:5).

I am free from the law of sin and death (Romans 8:2).

I am greatly loved by God (Romans 1:7; Ephesians 2:4; Colossians 3:12; 1 Thessalonians 1:4).

I am far from oppression, and fear does not come near me (Isaiah 54:14).

I am born of God, and the evil one does not touch me (1 John 5:18).

It is not I who live, but Christ lives in me (Galatians 2:20).

I am holy and without blame before Him in love (Ephesians 1:4; 1 Peter 1:16).

I have the mind of Christ (1 Corinthians 2:16; Philippians 2:5).

I have the peace of God that passes all understanding (Philippians 4:7).

I have the Greater One living in me; greater is He Who is in me than he who is in the world (1 John 4:4).

I have no lack for my God supplies all my need according to His riches in glory by Christ Jesus (Philippians 4:19).

I can do all things through Christ Jesus (Philippians 4:13).

I am God's child for I am born again of the incorruptible seed of the Word of God, which lives and abides forever (1 Peter 1:23).

I am God's workmanship, created in Christ unto good works (Ephesians 2:10).

I am a new creature in Christ (2 Corinthians 5:17).

I am a doer of the Word and blessed in my actions (James 1:22,25).

I am a joint-heir with Christ (Romans 8:17).

I am more than a conqueror through Him Who loves me (Romans 8:37).

I am an overcomer by the blood of the Lamb and the word of my testimony (Revelation 12:11).

I am part of a chosen generation, a royal priesthood, a holy nation, a purchased people (1 Peter 2:9).

I am the temple of the Holy Spirit; I am not my own (1 Corinthians 6:19).

I am the head and not the tail; I am above only and not beneath (Deuteronomy 28:13).

I am the light of the world (Matthew 5:14).

I am His elect, full of mercy, kindness, humility, and longsuffering (Romans 8:33; Colossians 3:12).

I am redeemed from the curse of sin, sickness, and poverty (Deuteronomy 28:15-68; Galatians 3:13).

I am firmly rooted, built up, established in my faith and overflowing with gratitude (Colossians 2:7).

I am healed by the stripes of Jesus (Isaiah 53:5; 1 Peter 2:24).

I am raised up with Christ and seated in heavenly places (Ephesians 2:6; Colossians 2:12).

I am submitted to God, and the devil flees from me because I resist him in the Name of Jesus (James 4:7).

There are more statements in the Bible about you. You are fearfully and wonderfully made. God designed you for great things. He put His spirit in you and ordained the race you are to run. Too often, we forget who we were created to be. Perhaps you can print this list and put it up somewhere where you will see it each morning. After having read it, can you go out and live according to what the Lord says about you in His book? He loves you and has already blessed you beyond measure!

Father, thank You that You bless us daily and have designed us for greatness in You. Lead us in the race You have chosen for us and take us to the destiny You have established. We are Your workmanship created in Christ unto good works. Remind us You walk with us and bless us each step of the way. In Your name we pray! Amen!

## AUGUST 21   THERE'S STILL A CHANCE

Support

Hebrews 4:1-3 (NKJV)

*¹Therefore, since a promise remains of entering His rest, let us fear lest any of you seem to have come short of it. ² For indeed the gospel was preached to us as well as to them; but the word which they heard did not profit them, not being mixed with faith in those who heard it. ³ For we who have believed do enter that rest*

According to Hebrews, the promise of entering God's rest *still* remains. What is God's rest? It is several things. To rest in someone means to believe in them. To rest may mean relaxation. Entering God's rest implies entering the Promised Land as well. God's rest is also entering into Christ. All of these things are significant. It takes faith which is belief and trust to enter that rest as well.

In these times as in Bible times, people say God is no longer active in His creation. That He has withdrawn from us and no longer cares about the world. Hebrews reminds us the Promise remains to all who believe and desire to follow Him. Following Jesus is the way to enter God's rest. The Promise still stands as it did then! And that promise is given to *you*! What will you do with it? Will you accept the gift of God's rest in Him? Or will you be like those to whom the author writes in his time who heard the message but were skeptical and cynical and did not believe the offer? Throughout the Bible, God reminds us of His promises. He made the Promise to Abraham, repeated it to Isaac and then told Jacob. He does not go back on His word. And His promise does not depend on our ability. It is God who extends the offer completely on His own (Genesis 15). All we need do is believe and accept. It may sound too good but it is true!

Many heard the offer but did not believe. It sounds too good to be true. The Apostles gave their lives to accept the promise. Would anyone risk their lives for a lie? Would you? *"Today, when you hear God's Promise, open your heart and mind to the offer He still makes to you. For the promise is to you and to your children, and to all who are afar off, as many as the Lord our God will call."* (Acts 2:39 NKJV). God has made you "an offer you shouldn't refuse" (but you can) as an heir to the Kingdom. Straighten out your crown, adjust your robe and start living within the promise of His rest. You didn't earn it; it is His gift to you! Live within His blessings.

Lord God, thank You for Your rest in so many ways. You provide us a place to live, peace in You in which to live, a Sabbath to worship You and life eternal to be spent with You. Help us to hear and accept the message. Lead us to others who need to hear Your word and give us the words to speak. Our faith feels so small and weak. Increase our faith Lord. Open all our hearts and minds to Your Son. In Your name we pray!

# AUGUST 22 RETURN TO ME AND I WILL RETURN TO YOU
## Grace and Mercy

Zechariah 1:3 (NKJV)

³ *Therefore say to them, 'Thus says the* LORD *of hosts: "Return to Me," says the* LORD *of hosts,*
*"and I will return to you," says the* LORD *of hosts.*

Zechariah had returned from Babylon to Judah and preached to the Children of Israel about the returning to a relationship with the Lord. They were supposed to rebuild the temple but progress had halted for about ten years. Things were not going so well for them. They were in captivity for 70 years in Babylon but King Darius allowed them to go back home. God had said He would gather His people from all the nations of the world and He did. His promises always come true.

The people had wandered away from God and His ways. They worshiped idols and took on the customs of the other people around them. Therefore, God allowed the Babylonians to conquer Israel and take the people of Israel captive and deport them to Babylon. God tells us to follow His ways and all will go well with us. When we choose our own path, bad things happen. If we stray, God will allow us to suffer the consequences. When we repent from sin, He will redeem us. He is always close by should we decide we want to walk with Him. He will extend His hand and lead us in His ways.

My friend Mark has an interesting way of explaining this phenomenon. Mark says when you stand up and decide how you are going to handle a situation; God sits down and lets you take it; consequences and all. When you figure out that it is beyond you and sit down (sometimes in defeat), God stands up and says "I've got this!" Who do you think can handle things better? Why not ask for guidance from the beginning and listen to what the Holy Spirit tells you? If you walk in God's ways, He will say "I've got this!" When you stray and realize you aren't going the right way, call out to Him. He hears you. He is there waiting. He loves you and will take care of you. He always does. Return to Him and He will return to you! Better yet, why not walk with Him always. That way, you won't need to return. And your path will be a lot smoother.

Father God, we admit we tend to stray. You have blessed us with so many talents that we begin to think we can do things on our own. We tend to forget about Your ways. By Your Spirit, remind us of our need to work with You to accomplish the great things You have ordained for us. Lead us in Your ways which will take us to our destiny. In Your name we pray! Amen!

# AUGUST 23   ARE YOU GOING TO OR *BEING* THE CHURCH
Relationships

James 2:14-27 (NKJV) Selected
*¹⁴ What does it profit, my brethren, if someone says he has faith but does not have works? Can faith save him? ¹⁵ If a brother or sister is naked and destitute of daily food, ¹⁶ and one of you says to them, "Depart in peace, be warmed and filled," but you do not give them the things which are needed for the body, what does it profit? ¹⁷ Thus also faith by itself, if it does not have works, is dead.... ²⁷ Pure and undefiled religion before God and the Father is this: to visit orphans and widows in their trouble, and to keep oneself unspotted from the world.*

What does it mean to *be* the Church? What actually is the Church anyway? How do you know which you are? Are you checking off a box of something you heard it is good to do? The Church is actually defined as the Body of Christ. In Jesus time, it was the people who professed their faith in Him and followed His teachings. They did not have a set meeting place or building. Some met in homes. They were a group of like-minded individuals. Acts 2:42 says *"They devoted themselves to the apostle's teaching and to the fellowship, to the breaking of bread and to prayer."* So, from the beginning, it was about relationships with God and each other. They shared what they had as anyone had need. This was not about spending precisely one hour on a Sunday morning on your way to somewhere else. This was not about being upset if the sermon ran twenty-*one* minutes. It was about loving God and loving each other.

Jesus said He came that we might have life abundantly. He asked us to love each other as He had loved us. He set the example. Are we doing that? The Good Samaritan did.

All through the New Testament, we are told that faith is the only way to God through Jesus. Now James tells us that faith alone is not enough or so it would appear. Is this a contradiction as many say are in the Bible? Not really! Works are evidence of true faith. If you truly believe in Christ, you will do what He asks. You will love one another as He loved you. You will not leave people destitute. You will take care of widows and orphans. You will do these things out of the overflow of blessings your faith has brought you. And what blessings will faith in Christ bring?

Acts 2:44-47 (NKJV) says *"⁴⁴ Now all who believed were together, and had all things in common, ⁴⁵ and sold their possessions and goods, and divided them among all, as anyone had need. ⁴⁶ So continuing daily with one accord in the temple, and breaking bread from house to house, they ate their food with gladness and simplicity of heart, ⁴⁷ praising God and having favor with all the people. And the Lord added to the church daily those who were being saved."* Sounds like a pretty good life to me! The rewards were gladness and simplicity of heart, and having favor with all the people. Faith brings you the fruit of the Spirit of love, joy, peace, patience, kindness, goodness, faithfulness, gentleness, self-control (Galatians 5:22-23). These are quite some blessings and they are yours for the asking. Put your faith and trust in Jesus and He will give you these gifts.

Are you *being* the Church? Are you building relationships and loving one another as He loves us? Will you go out today to intentionally build a relationship or two? Look for someone you don't know or get to know someone better. Ask about them and really listen. You will discover we have more similarities than differences. Go out and live as Jesus lived; love as Jesus loved and *be* the Church today! In Jesus name I pray for you!

# AUGUST 24    WHY WON'T YOU ANSWER MY PRAYERS
Faith

John 14:13-14 (NKJV)

*13 And whatever you ask in My name, that I will do, that the Father may be glorified in the Son.*
*14 If you ask anything in My name, I will do it.*

God says whatever you ask in His name, He will do, doesn't He? Why didn't He answer my prayer? Are you sure you heard Him? There are three possibilities: Yes, No or Wait. He may have said no. He may want you to wait until His timing is right. There may be others involved in your dream. Jesus tells us the Father is glorified in the Son when He answers your prayers. Sounds to me like God really wants to bless you!

There are a few things to consider here. One key phrase is "ask in *My* name..." What does that mean? If you ask something in Jesus name, does that mean according to His plan and purpose? Most likely yes. Also, there is something called intercessory prayer where you pray for the needs of others. Usually, when you pray for others, it is good to ask that God's will be done. That would be in His name.

We don't always know what is best for us. Be careful what you wish for, you just might get it. We ask for a promotion when God wants us to leave that company and go somewhere else. We ask for no traffic when God wants to delay us so will avoid an accident. We ask for more income when God knows it we lead us away from Him. We ask for our Pastor to stay when God wants us to go to another Church. We don't always know what is best for us. In many cases, God loves you too much to say yes to that prayer. God has a plan to bless and prosper you. It is like a tapestry interwoven with the lives of others. The Creator sees the front side with all the beauty. The created only sees the hanging threads and all the chaos. You have no way of knowing the pattern God is weaving. But He does. Trust Him. He can take your seemingly broken life and make it beautiful. Give Him the chance. Be patient and stay in faith! He wants what is best for you!

Lord God, thank You that You know what is best for us and You bring that about in Your plan. Teach us to ask for things in Your name. Let Your Spirit guide us daily toward our destiny. Help us to ask for things in Your name. In Your name we pray!

## AUGUST 25   WRAPPED IN RIGHTEOUSNESS
Faith

Isaiah 61:10 (NKJV)

*[10] I will greatly rejoice in the LORD, My soul shall be joyful in my God; For He has clothed me with the garments of salvation, He has covered me with the robe of righteousness, As a bridegroom decks himself with ornaments, And as a bride adorns herself with her jewels.*

Isaiah was fully aware he did not have righteousness on his own. Neither do we. But God clothed him in the garment of salvation. God offers that Garment to you; to me!

John 19:23 (NKJV) *says[23] Then the soldiers, when they had crucified Jesus, took His garments and made four parts, to each soldier a part, and also the tunic. Now the tunic was without seam, woven from the top in one piece.* I believe the garment, the tunic, they removed from Jesus at the cross was the robe of righteousness. Now that garment is available to you and me. Jesus provided us with the covering that allows us to come before the Father in righteousness. The price He paid for us to stand before the Father was high. Jesus gave His all for us. He gave the ultimate sacrifice that we might be called children of God. And that is what we are.

Are you a follower of Jesus? If so, He offers you His Garment of righteousness. If not, why not? With this garment, all of the bad things you have ever done are covered. Knowing that, how should you live? You are justified. That is "just as if you never sinned". Should you stand tall? Should you be bold? Because of this garment, you are holy, righteous and redeemed! *For God so loved you that He gave His one and only Son, that whoever believes in him shall not perish but have eternal life* (John 3:16). He did that for you and you are covered in the blood which this garment symbolizes. This love for you is beyond comprehension. But it is real and it is true. Live as one who is redeemed. Love others and tell them of God's love for them. His love is what clothes you. Know you are wrapped in righteousness!

Lord, we cannot fully comprehend all You have done for us. Amazing grace, how can it be, that You my God would die for me. Help us to accept that grace and begin to understand all we mean to You. Let us focus on You and become more like You. Help us to live as redeemed in You. In Your name we pray!

# AUGUST 26   HEAD TO HEART TO HEAD
Faith

Deuteronomy 8:2 (NKJV)
*"You shall remember all the way which the LORD your God has led you in the wilderness these forty years, that He might humble you, testing you, to know what was in your heart, whether you would keep His commandments or not.*

Remembering all the ways in which the Lord led you is knowledge of the facts. Facts alone do not constitute faith. Hebrews 11 tells us *"Now faith is the substance of things hoped for, the evidence of things not seen. ² For by it the elders obtained a good testimony."* Faith is believing with your heart. It is knowing in your gut even without facts to back up the feeling.

I took a course a number of years ago called Evangelism Explosion. Their teaching was that head knowledge of Christ alone was not enough. You needed to have Christ in your heart. I understood that concept. You see, I knew about Jesus. I knew He was a good man. I knew the stories about things He did. But I did not believe He was the Son of God nor that He did those things for *me*. When you have Christ in your heart, you just know things. And you know that you know that you know. It is a feeling. There is certainty. I did the studies. I learned the Bible verses. I invited Jesus into my heart to abide with me. He has been my faithful Friend for more than seventeen years. It brings me to tears when I ponder Him laying down His life for me, His friend. I now have Him in my heart.

Here is my dilemma. I was able to move Christ from my head the eighteen inches to my heart. I love Him. I believe in Him. He has my faith and trust in almost every area of my life. There is one challenge. I don't always believe He will do things for me. I guess I doubt His love for me. Who am I the He is mindful of me (Psalm 8:4)? I doubt that I am worthy of being a Child of God. Although Christ resides in my heart now, I do not have a full understanding of who He is to me and who I am to Him. I lack head knowledge. I cannot comprehend all I can do in Christ for His glory. I let the enemy distract me from the power I have received. How about you? Are you falling short of the destiny put in you by Christ?

God needs to be in every part of us. He moves from head to heart as your faith grows. Your faith can also help share Him with your head. He needs to be in both places for you to fully achieve all He has set out for you to do in His name. I am not sure how to make that happen yet and so I will pray for me and for you. I think this will take some knee walking like my friend Andy says. Here goes!

Lord, here is Your servant needing Your guidance. I have You in my heart. The evidence of that is Your fruit overflows from me to those around me. I know You are in there. And yet I struggle with letting go and letting You control every part of my life. The accuser tells me I am not good enough. Help me to listen to the voice of the Shepherd. I know Your voice. Help me to listen to the voice of truth alone. Father, I pray for those who will read this message. I pray that You will guide them and love them as You have loved me. Let them hear Your voice as well. Clarify their thinking to focus on You and ignore the lies that they are not worthy. They are Your children and heirs to the Kingdom. Please remind them of Your love for them. Help us all to come to full head knowledge of all we mean to You. In Jesus glorious name I pray! Amen!

Prayer for God's Guidance Anonymous www.beliefnet.com

God be in my head, and in my understanding;

God be in mine eyes, and in my looking;

God be in my mouth, and in my speaking;

God be in my heart, and in my thinking;

God be at mine end, and at my departing.

# AUGUST 27    I HATE THIS JOB
## Attitude

Colossians 3:23 (NKJV)
*23 And whatever you do, do it heartily, as to the Lord and not to men,*

Many people don't like their jobs. Zig Ziglar told a story about a woman with whom he met that hated her job and wanted help finding another position. He asked her to make a list of all the things she liked about the job and she said there was nothing she liked. He wanted to get her to look for the good. He asked if they paid her for working there. She said yes. "Don't you like being paid for working?" he asked. There was something about the job that she did like. On further discovery, she listed 23 things she liked. The job wasn't so bad after all. After reviewing the list daily for a time, when they next met, she told Zig "you can't believe how much those people have changed!" What about your job?

Colossians tells us to work as if unto the Lord. That we should put our best into everything we do. Attitude makes the difference. How you approach something determines the outcome. Do you look for the good in every situation? Do you see things through the eyes of faith? Are you believing for blessing?

Don't like your Job? Change it. Work as if unto the Lord. If you don't like your boss, stop working for them. Go to work for the Lord instead. You don't have to change careers or employers. Just change for whom you work. Whatever you do, do it heartily as to the Lord and not to men. Psalm 90:17 (NKJV) says *17 And let the beauty of the LORD our God be upon us, And establish the work of our hands for us; Yes, establish the work of our hands.* Wouldn't the One who establishes the work of our hands for us give us wonderful things to do? Aren't they a part of His plan? God's plan is to prosper you and not to harm you. A plan to give you hope and a future (Jeremiah 29:11). You are where you are for a purpose that is good for you and the Kingdom. Why not discover that purpose and work for your good? In the process, you will achieve what God destined for you. You will be running the race He set out before you. Why not be the winner of that race? Run your own race and have a marvelous time on the journey. But keep your eye on the prize of the Gospel. Remember, you run with purpose. And whatever you do, do it heartily, as to the Lord and not to men...

Lord, thank You that You have given us gifts and talents to use in our vocation for a purpose. Lead us where You would have us go and to the people to whom You wish to speak through us. If it is words we need to say, give us those words. If not, let our lives be the example You want us to set. Let us be a blessing to someone today. And bless us in that process. In Jesus name I pray for you all (y'all)! Amen!

## AUGUST 28   ARE YOU CLOSE

Relationships

Psalm 138:6 (NKJV)

⁶ *Though the* LORD *is on high, Yet He regards the lowly; But the proud He knows from afar.*

How does God view you? Does He know you from afar or are you in a relationship? God and I are on a first name basis. I call Him God and He calls me Bob. However, I do most of the talking. I'm sure that doesn't surprise you.

Who are we that God is mindful of us? We are His children, His beloved. He says you are His friend, you are justified and redeemed, an heir to the Kingdom, you have wisdom, that His Holy Spirit dwells within you, and that you have been chosen and set apart. You have a lot going for you. These are all the things He sees in you if you follow Him. But what if you are proud and arrogant? He remains distant. He will not draw close to you and pour out His blessings.

I have come to a place in my life where I realize that relationships are the most important thing of all. Without relationship, nothing else matters. God gave us the Ten Commandments to teach us about relationships with Him and others. How are you managing those relationships? Sure, you probably do well with those you know and love. But how about building relationships with people who are different than you? Yesterday, I was at a Prayer Revival meeting. One of the Pastors there spoke of his difficulty in building relationships with different cultures and people not like him. He mentioned that, sometimes, he does not even see those that are different from Him. We are all in that boat. I passed several homeless people on the way to the meeting. I am not sure what to do with them. Do I ignore them? Do I stop and speak with them? Do I encourage them? How should this be handled? Didn't Jesus say that whatever I do for the least of these, I do for Him? Is this the way to draw close to God? Maybe.

If God regards the lowly, shouldn't I? Every person wants and needs to know they matter. Can you show they matter to you in some way? Learn people's names. Really see them when you pass. Meet their eyes. Smile! Let them know you see them and they matter. On the way back from the meeting, I stopped to speak with a homeless mother and her kids. I cannot solve their homelessness but I can show the love of God. We are commanded to love one another as Jesus loved us. That is a tall order. Start somewhere. Notice people. Speak with them. Use encouraging words. Let them know that God cares and so do you. I pray this for you in Jesus name!

# AUGUST 29  BLESSED TO BE A BLESSING
Relationships

John 15:5-8 (NKJV)

*⁵ "I am the vine, you are the branches. He who abides in Me, and I in him, bears much fruit; for without Me you can do nothing. ⁶ If anyone does not abide in Me, he is cast out as a branch and is withered; and they gather them and throw them into the fire, and they are burned. ⁷ If you abide in Me, and My words abide in you, you will ask what you desire, and it shall be done for you. ⁸ By this My Father is glorified, that you bear much fruit; so you will be My disciples.*

It is all about relationships. Our relationship with Christ is the most important. Without that relationship, we can do nothing. God is so concerned about relationships He gave us the Ten Commandments which tell us how to relate to Him and each other. We must stay connected.

Jesus uses an analogy to explain how we need to remain connected to Him. When we do, we receive the nourishment needed to bear fruit just as a branch needs to be connected to the vine that supports it. Jesus is our support. He is the source of all good things. When we are separated from Him, we wither and die off. When we remain in Him, we will bear much fruit. That fruit is love, joy, peace, patience, kindness, goodness, faithfulness, gentleness and self-control from Galatians 5:22-23. Isn't that the kind of fruit you want to bear? How do we do that? By remaining in Jesus.

To remain in Jesus is to keep Him in the foreground of your mind. It means you ask and answer the question "what would Jesus do?" If you take the time to think about His ways, you will improve your life because you will be walking in those ways. Now I know we don't always do what Jesus would do. I know I am not the Son of God and do not have His strength to always do the right thing. But God is not looking for perfection. He is looking for someone who is trying to follow Him. He is looking for those who hold Him in their hearts. He is looking for *you*! Even a little faith in Jesus will turn you, however slowly, in His direction.

I have several friends that remind me of this process today. They walk with the Lord and follow His ways. Are they perfect in that walk? No! But, as I said, the Lord is not looking for perfection. My one friend is a Pastor. He lives a life that shows what it means to follow a Risen Lord. He welcomes people and loves them. He was listening when Jesus said love your neighbor as yourself. The others are a husband and wife team. They heard the part about caring for widows and orphans (God wants us to care for everyone). They are always aware of the needs of people around them. A kind word here, and invitation there and comfort and support for those around them. They abide in the Lord and he has caused much fruit to come forth from them. The seeds they have planted have blessed many and brought much glory to God. Many different positive Ministries have been started by these two to the blessing of many. God is glorified when we do things for others. He is certainly glorified in them. And they have been such a blessing to me.

How should you live your life? You should remain in Jesus and His ways. There are many more examples of people who remain in Him and are a blessing to those around them. Shouldn't you live that way? What stands between you and a blessed life and a life of blessing? If you are anything like me, all that gets in the way is yourself. Step outside yourself today! God has untold blessings stored up for you. They are already on the shelf with your name on them. He has peace for you. He has joy for you. Do you want them? Then abide in Him and watch Him bring these out of His storehouse and bestow them upon you. May the Lord bless you richly today!

May $^{24}$ *"The Lord bless you and keep you;*
$^{25}$ *The Lord make His face shine upon you, And be gracious to you;*
$^{26}$ *The Lord lift up His countenance upon you, And give you peace."'* Numbers 6:24-26 (NKJV) Amen!

## AUGUST 30   HAPPY HOUR
Prayer

Psalm 139:17-19 (NKJV)
*17 How precious also are Your thoughts to me, O God! How great is the sum of them!*
*18 If I should count them, they would be more in number than the sand; When I awake, I am still*
*with You. 19 Oh, that You would slay the wicked, O God!*
*Depart from me, therefore, you bloodthirsty men.*

What does Happy Hour mean to you? Happy Hour has a special connotation in our culture. It is late afternoon/early evening time in a bar or restaurant where they have reduced price drinks and food. It is a way that the hospitality industry markets to draw people in to their establishments. But for me, it has a completely different meaning.

Sometimes, at night when I am going to bed, I check the settings on my opportunity clock. It has two wakeup settings. The second one is always set to 7 am. I don't always set the first one which is usually 6 am or earlier. Many times, I will ask the Lord to wake me if He wants to talk. Often, I wake out of a sound sleep at 5 on the dot. It is the Lord calling. I know He wants time with me because He woke me just as I asked Him to do. Psalm 63:6 (NKJV) says *6 When I remember You on my bed, I meditate on You in the night watches.* I pray before I close my eyes and wake up often with a song of praise or a Psalm on my lips. He is with me. My family members are not morning people. Our house is quiet early in the morning. I have my place on the couch where I sit and open my Bible. I read Our Daily Bread, a Psalm and then begin my prayers. This is a time of peace for me. It is God's Rest! He calls me to Him. I am not good at being quiet so this is a special time for me with the Lord. This is the Happy Hour I look forward to attending.

How about you? What does Happy Hour mean to you? What is the happiest hour of your day? Are you spending time with your Lord? He is willing and waiting. All you need do is ask Him to wake you. Your eyes will just open and you will be wide awake. Find your way to your prayer spot or try several places out to see what works best for you. Spending time alone with the Lord will be your happiest hour too! Just try it! It will renew, refresh and redeem you. God can give you a sense of peace you will not find anywhere else. Just spend some time with Him. He will remind you that you are His and you are fearfully and wonderfully made because He is your Creator. You are His and He loves you. This quiet time will allow you to learn all the wonderful things He has in store for you. It will give you a chance to learn which path He wants you to follow.

Good morning Lord! Thank you for this day and every day. Please call me to time spent with You. We need You in our lives to love, lead and guide us to the destiny You have prepared for us. Quiet our hearts and connect them to You. When we abide in You, we are at our best! Hold us close and speak to us through Your still small voice. Give us ears to hear and open our heart to Your leading that we may walk with you. In Jesus name we pray.

# AUGUST 31   HE IS WITH YOU
Encouragement

Jeremiah 15:20 (ESV)
*And I will make you to this people [Judah] a fortified wall of bronze; they will fight against you, but they shall not prevail over you, for I am with you to save you and deliver you, declares the Lord.*

God is speaking to Jeremiah about himself. Jeremiah has just asked God why his own life is so difficult. Sound familiar? In prayer, Jeremiah has complained to God he feels forsaken. And God answers him by telling Jeremiah that God will strengthen him, save and deliver him. Even though the situation looks bleak, God is still working for the good of those who love Him. He did not rebuke Jeremiah for his doubt but reassured him of success in his ministry.

Many people wonder where God is in the difficult times of their lives. How could He let this happen? Why did God take away my loved one? Why did this person commit this horrible act? There are many other questions. My question to you is how do you know it was God who did this? There is evil in the world. There is greed. There is jealousy. God gave mankind free will to choose which path they would walk. Many choose evil. Jeremiah 17:9 says *"the heart is deceitful above all things and beyond cure."* It leads us to choose bad things. But when we allow Jesus into our hearts, His light and glory push out the deceit. Through Him, we can become the person we were designed to be. You were designed for accomplishment, engineered for success and endowed with the seeds of greatness! God tells us, in this verse from Jeremiah He will be with us to save and deliver us. He will keep us from the evil that lurks all around. His light can dispel the darkness.

How are you doing in the battle of good vs. evil? Do you prevail in good? Are you trying to win in your own power? Many try that and fail. The key is to accept the Promises of God. This one is that He will always be with you and you will prevail. He promises to deliver you out of the hand of evil. You mean that much to Him that He will fight for you! You really can't do it on your own. But you and God become a majority. When you remain in Him, He will deliver you! Walk with Him today. Ask for His protection. Moreover, ask for His direction and guidance into His ways. Ask Him into your heart to drive out the darkness and replace it with His glorious light. And then, let that light shine out to others to brighten their lives. One tiny candle in a dark room pushes back the darkness. *Be* that light today. In Jesus name I pray for you! Amen!

## SEPTEMBER 1   KEEP THE DREAM ALIVE
Attitude

Psalm 37:4 (NKJV)

*4 Delight yourself also in the LORD, And He shall give you the desires of your heart.*

Does this verse mean that God will give you whatever you desire? At first glance, it looks like God will give you what you desire. However, it means something much different. If you follow the Lord, He will determine what is good for you and place those dreams in your heart. He will give you the dreams that will bless you and take you closer to Him.

With that in mind, it becomes clear your dreams come from God. God has given you your imagination and creativity. He has a destiny planned for you and He wants you to reach it. What are your dreams? What are the secret petitions of your heart? Are you keeping them alive? They are not just your dreams but His too. They are given to you by God. They are part of His plan. His plan is to prosper you; a plan to give you hope and a future. What steps are you taking daily to keep the dream alive?

If dreams are from God, then He wants us to succeed in those dreams. What stands between you and success? Have you prayed? God is for you in this since He planted that dream. With Him on your side, what will you accomplish? This is no longer you working alone. The Creator of the universe will help if you would just ask! Go ahead. Ask Him. He is longing to help. He waits for you to say something and He will bring His blessings to you to make the dream a reality. What have you been believing for? What are the secret petitions of your heart? You may not see a way but God has a way. Keep the dream alive. Bring it out of the closet, dust it off and get to work. Pray about it and see if God will not open doors you thought would never open. He will bring people across your path that can help. He will make a way. Stay in faith and believe. The dream is about to come true. This is your time.

Father, we thank You that You give us dreams. You created us to be creative and to be good stewards of Your creation. Strengthen us in the resolve needed to take the steps to bring our dreams to fruition. Each of these dreams is from You. Bless us in them and make a way for us to glorify You with their accomplishment. In Your name we pray!

## SEPTEMBER 2   WHAT DO YOU SEE
### Attitude

Isaiah 58:10 (NKJV)
*10 If you extend your soul to the hungry And satisfy the afflicted soul,*
*Then your light shall dawn in the darkness, And your darkness shall be as the noonday.*

Do you see widows and orphans? James 1:27 (NKJV)says *27 Pure and undefiled religion before God and the Father is this: to visit orphans and widows in their trouble, and to keep oneself unspotted from the world.* Do you see other people that need your healing touch, your kind words and maybe some help? I was challenged the other day by a Pastor I know who said that he (and many others including me) did not always see those in need around him. There is a song by Brandon Heath that asks Jesus to give us his eyes to see. We all need that ability.

I went to San Francisco a number of years back for a conference. During one of the evenings, I went downtown to a gathering. As I parked my car on the street, I saw a man, apparently homeless, sleeping in a doorway. Actually, I heard him before I saw him. He spoke and offered to watch my car for me. I thought that was caring of him. I decided to be nice to him. I saw a tavern nearby and headed over there to order a hamburger deluxe to go. I returned to the man with what I thought was a nice gesture. To my chagrin, the man rebuked me for not asking him what he wanted. He was right about that. I did not ask him what he wanted. I thought anyone would like a hamburger. In fact, I was offended that he rebuked me. I said that I would take the hamburger and eat it myself if he didn't want it. He decided to keep it. I walked away confused and angry. I did not understand. I was not aware of the needs of that man. There was a lot I did not understand! Was this my thanks for caring? Now I am really confused. I guess that's why you leave these things to social services agencies. What did I know?

Since that time, I have read a book called *When Helping Hurts.* Now, I see people I did not see before and see them in a different light. I now know they are also children of God just like me. From it, I learned things about what people need. They need to be included in their help. They need to be consulted about their situation. They need to be valued! Maybe we could ask if and how we can help? Yes, we are supposed to help each other. But *asking* how we can help is the way to go. Jesus said to love one another. Perhaps He can show us how we can do that more effectively! Maybe we can see them through His eyes. Maybe then, our light will shine and bring glory to Him! It will also bring peace and comfort to us!

Thank You Jesus that you can open our eyes to what You see! Please open our eyes today to those in need of time, treasure or talent. There are wealthy people out there who need a kind word. There are poor people out there who need work. Everyone out there needs love. Help us to know what they need and provide what we can through You and in Your name. Let our light, which comes from You, shine to dispel the darkness. In Your name we pray! Amen!

# SEPTEMBER 3   UNMERITED FAVOR

Grace and Mercy

James 4:6 (NKJV)
*⁶ But He gives more grace. Therefore, He says: "God resists the proud, But gives grace to the humble."*

Grace is unmerited favor. You don't deserve it; you can never earn it and you can never pay the giver back. It is a gift given you because the Giver loves you and wants you to have the gift. The Gift of Grace goes so far beyond anything we can ask or imagine that it is hard to describe. Grace includes righteousness as well.

God gives us His grace in many situations. When we face something that is beyond us, God provides what is needed. You do all you can and God will do what you can't. When you live in His will, believing and trusting in Him, He will work all things out for your good. He gives more grace as needed. Remember, it is not for anything you have done. It is because of His mercy and compassion toward you. It is not of yourself. Humility is knowing that you don't deserve the gift.

Sometimes, when I hear a song or read something about the extent to which Christ went to redeem me, it moves me to tears. How could He do that for me? "Amazing Grace how can it be, that You my God would die for me" are the lyrics of a song. I don't deserve it, I can never earn it, I can never pay Him back, or can I?

In the parable of the Good Samaritan, the Good Samaritan had mercy on his neighbor. Jesus tells us to love our neighbor as our self. He says "go and do likewise". The Good Samaritan showed mercy. In Matthew 25:40, Jesus also said *"⁴⁰ And the King will answer and say to them, 'Assuredly, I say to you, inasmuch as you did it to one of the least of these My brethren, you did it to Me.'"* You see, Jesus wants us to treat others with the grace and mercy He has given to us. That is the way to pay Him back. We are to share the gift He has given us, the gift of grace. Out of the overflow of the gifts He has given you, you can give to others. Jesus will be glorified through that act. So be gracious, compassionate and merciful to those you meet. Each person is God's creation; His masterpiece. Treat them as such. Value them. Give the grace you have received.

Lord, we can never thank You enough for Your gift of Grace! It is beyond our ability to place a value. Since it is priceless, help us to share what we are given with those in need. Thank You that You love us so much. Many are suffering with insecurity. Many don't feel they deserve anything good. Although we don't deserve grace in our deeds, You still offer it to all people. You are willing to bless anyone who comes to You with a contrite heart. Draw us to You and cover us with Your Grace and righteousness In Jesus name! Amen!

## SEPTEMBER 4    FAILURE IS NOT FINAL
Failure

Haggai 2:19 (NKJV)
*19 Is the seed still in the barn? As yet the vine, the fig tree, the pomegranate, and the olive tree have not yielded fruit. But from this day I will bless you.'"*

Failure to plant the seed has caused plants not to yield their fruit. In fact, the plants are not even growing. It is that way in life too. If you do not do what you are supposed to, there will be consequences. That is the bad news. But the good news is that you can have another chance. Failure is not final. It is a stepping stone to success. Each failure can teach us a lesson that we could not learn any other way. Or, at least, not as well.

As parents, sometimes we need to let our kids fail at something. I am not saying to let them go completely on their own. Pick certain things which are not fatal and let them try it on their own. If they fail, you can help them try again. You can encourage them. You can ask questions which will lead them to understand why it went the way it did. It can be a teachable moment. They can learn from their mistakes and do better next time. That was how my Dad did it. One of his lines was "you'll do better next time." That always taught me that there was hope. I could try again. But mostly, it taught me that failure was not fatal. My Dad still loved me. I was not perfect although, when I was a teenager, I thought I was! How little we know.

Encouragement can make a world of difference. Believing you can do something is the deciding factor in whether it gets done. Having someone else believe in you will *propel* you to greater heights than you knew possible. I knew my Dad believed in me. He quietly assured me that success was within my reach. It has been suggested that we should be both encourager and encouragee. Who encouraged you? Who are you encouraging?

Haggai goes on to tell us that God is with us. He says of God "...But from this day I will bless you." God is for you! My earthly father believed in me. Now I know my Heavenly Father believes in me too! He will bless me! And He will bless you! How will you, as someone who knows he or she is blessed, live this day? Will you be bold? Will you be excited and exciting? Will you share the Gift given you with others even in the workplace? The world is hungry for approval. They are hungry for love. They are hungry for hope. You have been blessed with all those and more! And if you have not had those blessings, you can be the one to begin the blessing. Will you share them with those you meet today in Jesus name? Please say yes and Amen!

# SEPTEMBER 5    I'M ALWAYS ON TIME
Faith

Habakkuk 2:3 (NKJV)

*3 For the vision is yet for an appointed time; But at the end it will speak, and it will not lie. Though it tarries, wait for it; Because it will surely come, It will not tarry.*

God's timing is perfect! It probably doesn't seem that way to most of us because it is not when we want things to happen. We cannot see the whole plan nor how things are shaping up. But God knows where all the pieces fit and in what order they need to be assembled. Therefore, we need to be patient and let things go according to God's plan and timing.

Habakkuk tells us of a vision of things to come. Its time has not as of yet arrived. All things work according to God's plan. God has everything arranged in the whole universe so all the pieces will fit at the appointed time. Don't try to run ahead of Him because it will not work out right.

One of my faults is being a control freak. I want to work out all the details according to my plan. I used to think I was in charge. Now, that seems humorous. I have a friend named Ed who has learned earlier than me God is the One with the plan. Ed and I planned to go to a Promise Keepers conference in Baltimore some years back. Ed has challenges walking and we needed to get handicapped seating. Because he has learned to go with God's plan, he does not concern himself with timing. I went to pick Ed up but he wasn't ready so we were late getting on the road. I was already beside myself because we would be *late*! It went from bad to worse. Our hotel room was no longer available when we arrived. I thought we would end up sleeping in the car. We did find a flea bag motel but the room was awful. Sleeping in the car would have been better. We got a late start in the morning too so we were late to the conference. The handicapped parking spaces were already taken. I dropped Ed off at the door and parked the car. When we got inside, we were told the handicapped seating was on the arena floor. By now, I am a wild man because my plan has not been followed. I am keenly aware that if we head down to the floor and the seats are all taken, there is no way Ed will be able to make it back up. My worst nightmares are staring me in the face. Meanwhile, Ed is saying things will all work out. I am ready to murder him.

We go down to the arena floor and there are no seats left! Now I am panicked. Ed is leaning against the railing at the edge of the floor to rest so he will be able to move somewhere else where we might find a seat. But God had another plan. Actually, God had His plan all along. As we are leaning against the rail trying to figure out what we can do, a man in the front row overhears our conversation. He probably also observed my agitation. He leans forward and asks us if we need seats. He saved a few too many because some of his friends are sitting somewhere else and he has two seats available on the front row. All that worry on my part and we just step into front row seats. Not only did we get great seats but the guy and his friends were wonderful to us. They welcomed us, included us in their group and made our day terrific. They were real Brothers in Christ to us.

All that worrying wasted! Worry is a waste of the imagination. It also showed a *lack of faith* on my part. Instead of trusting God, I wanted to manage things in my own power. God's plan is always better. I have learned to go with God. While I try to be on time if I have made an appointment, I now know God may change my plans to fit to His. It always works for my good. I have found myself in the right place at the right time when I relax and let Him lead. How about you? Are you trying to control things? I can tell you; it doesn't work. Relax, breathe deeply and go with God's timing and plan. It will be better than you can ask or imagine. It will be divine. I am now always on time. Maybe not my time; but on His time.

Father, thank You that You give me patience to wait on You. Thank You that You have taught me how to go with Your plan for my life. Teach us all to trust in You and follow Your lead. Help us to see that following You is always our best option. In Jesus name we pray! Amen!

# SEPTEMBER 6    PRAYER MATTERS
Prayer

2 Chronicles 7:14 (NKJV)

*14 if My people who are called by My name will humble themselves, and pray and seek My face, and turn from their wicked ways, then I will hear from heaven, and will forgive their sin and heal their land.*

When was the last time you called on the name of the Lord? Do you call Him when good things happen? Do you seek His face? Are you walking in His ways?

Ezra is the traditional author and it dates back to 430 BC. Ezra was a Priest of God Most High and is writing to Israel and Judah about unity of the nation. They have gone astray as a people and as a nation. When you stray from Truth, you lose your way and bad things happen. Sounds like our world of today. We have lost our way because we have wandered from God's truth.

One thing I have heard is that, if you don't know history, you will most likely repeat the same errors. The Bible is full of stories about people who have made bad choices and suffered the consequences. When they returned to God's ways, He forgave them and returned to blessing them. When will we ever learn?

Yesterday, we saw a movie called *War Room* in which an older lady befriends a younger woman and shares her faith with this wife and mother. The focus of the story is how prayer can restore things that you thought were lost. It is hard to pray for someone and stay angry with them. If you pour out your heart to God on behalf of a person, your feelings for them begin to improve. The older lady begins to mentor the young wife in the art of Spiritual Warfare and how prayer changes things. It does! It removes anger and bitterness. Your heart goes out to the object of your prayer. Try it and see for yourself. You cannot stay angry with someone for whom your earnestly pray.

What would it look like if God were to heal your land? Is the inside of your house a war zone? Are you at odds with neighbors or friends or family or spouse? Have you tried Prayer? It works! Ezra tells us that God will hear our prayers from Heaven and He will forgive our sin and heal our land. Does your land need healing? Would you like peace in your home? What things about your spouse upset you the most? What if you were to pray for peace and blessing to cover them daily? Would your attitude toward them improve? If your attitude was that of peace, love and blessing, would they notice a change? So maybe, you could start by praying for yourself and your attitude. Ask God to change you. Ask Him to give you more patience and compassion. Whatever the need, just talk to Him. Prayer is not some special art you learn in Seminary. It is simply a conversation with God. He knows your thoughts. He just wants to hear your requests. Speak to the Lord. Ask Him to help you pray. Ask Him to change you and remove the things that displease Him and you. He is listening and will heal your land, your home, your family and you! Just ask Him!

Father, thank You that You are always listening for our prayers. Help us to come to you with our requests. Sometimes, we don't even know for what we should pray but

Your Spirit will intercede for us and give us what we need. Remind us that You are willing to forgive our sins and heal us from the consequences. You are our perfect Heavenly Father who dearly loves His children and wants what is best for us. Teach us Your ways that we might walk in them and know You better. Heal our land! In Your name we pray! Amen!

# SEPTEMBER 7    UNDER NEW MANAGEMENT
## Quality of Life

Ephesians 4:20-32 (NKJV)

*²⁰ But you have not so learned Christ, ²¹ if indeed you have heard Him and have been taught by Him, as the truth is in Jesus: ²² that you put off, concerning your former conduct, the old man which grows corrupt according to the deceitful lusts, ²³ and be renewed in the spirit of your mind, ²⁴ and that you put on the new man which was created according to God, in true righteousness and holiness. ²⁵ Therefore, putting away lying, "Let each one of you speak truth with his neighbor," for we are members of one another. ²⁶ "Be angry, and do not sin": do not let the sun go down on your wrath, ²⁷ nor give place to the devil. ²⁸ Let him who stole steal no longer, but rather let him labor, working with his hands what is good, that he may have something to give him who has need. ²⁹ Let no corrupt word proceed out of your mouth, but what is good for necessary edification, that it may impart grace to the hearers. ³⁰ And do not grieve the Holy Spirit of God, by whom you were sealed for the day of redemption. ³¹ Let all bitterness, wrath, anger, clamor, and evil speaking be put away from you, with all malice. ³² And be kind to one another, tenderhearted, forgiving one another, even as God in Christ forgave you.*

Are you happy with the way your life is going? Is everything perfect in your relationships? Is there tranquility in your home? Most would say no! Who is leading in your life? Are you the one making all the decisions? If so, are you making the right ones? Many times, things go on in all aspects of our lives that are not what we desire for ourselves or our loved ones. Do you wonder why? Who is in charge in your life? How is that working out for you?

Paul is writing to the Church at Ephesus about how they are conducting their lives. It seems they are lying, stealing and doing all sorts of bad things. But there is a key phrase. Paul says "nor give place to the devil...." Who is in charge in your place? Have you made Jesus the Lord in every area of your life? If not, why not? Don't you think He can do a better job with your life than you are doing?

John 10:10-29 (NKJV) says *¹⁰ The thief does not come except to steal, and to kill, and to destroy. I have come that they may have life, and that they may have it more abundantly.* Do you want to live an abundant life? Sure, you do! Why not live a life of blessing? To do that, you are going to have to make some changes. You need a new management team. It is time to elect a new leader. It is time to turn the reins over to the Lord. Put up that famous sign that others display when someone new is in charge indicating that things are going to get better. Under New Management! The old has gone; the new has come! I am a new person and will live a new life in Christ.

Satan pack your bags and get out! You are no longer welcome here! We don't want any more of your lies and deceit. It is time for depression, anxiety, doubt and despair to hit the road with you. You have done enough damage to our lives and families. It is time for new management. It is time for us to follow the Son of God most High and to live according to His ways. It is time for the Holy Spirit to guide us in which way to go. Since Jesus already won the ultimate victory and offers that to us, today is the day we can change our focus and leadership to Him. Make that move! Put up the sign! Under New Management! Start living the abundant life today. In Jesus name! Amen!

# SEPTEMBER 8    NO NEED TO GO THROUGH IT ALONE

Relationships

Deuteronomy 31:8 (NKJV)

*⁸And the LORD, He is the One who goes before you. He will be with you, He will not leave you nor forsake you; do not fear nor be dismayed."*

Many times, we go through challenges thinking there is no one to help and we are completely on our own. When things get tough, others seem to disappear leaving us to fend for ourselves. But is that really the case? Are you really alone? Have you asked for help? I am weak in asking for help. Many times, I decide to do something without considering the schedules of those who could help. I don't like working alone yet I set things up so that is how it turns out. And then, I complain! But am I really alone? There is One who walks with me who is closer than a brother who will never leave nor forsake me.

God tells us in Deuteronomy that He goes before us. That means He paves the way for our journey. He will be with us. That means that He is inside us through His Holy Spirit. He promises to never leave nor forsake us. That means we can count on Him to give us what we need when we need it. It also means His hedge of protection surrounds us. God's promises are sure and He can be trusted. Therefore, we should not worry or fear because He will be our strength and shield! We can stand on His promises.

How are you doing at standing on His promises? Are you fearless? Do you walk as if you know God goes before you paving the way? Or are you like me, worrying all the time about how you will accomplish all that is on your plate? We tend to forget the Lord in our day to day activities. He can make things smooth for us in some cases and give us what strength we need in tougher situations. Yet we do not ask Him for either. What would life look like if we asked the Lord for guidance on which way we should go and what we should do? I am trying to pray about more things. Rather than going on my own instinct, I am asking Him if I should undertake a new challenge. When people ask me to participate in some ministry, I defer to prayer about what the Lord wants me to do. I think about the possibilities and then leave the decision for later after I have had a chance to give it to the Lord. He will let me know. If I have a sense of peace and excitement, He is telling me to go ahead. If I have doubts and questions, He is saying either wait or no. How do you handle the day to day things you face? Do you make decisions on your own or do you ask the Lord? Do you have discussions with your spouse asking for input? Do you have a Spiritual Accountability Partner? If you are alone, why are you alone? God said in Genesis 2:18 *"It is not good for the man to be alone."* If the Creator of the universe says it is not good for us to be alone, shouldn't we try to avoid it?

Why are you alone? Is it just your feeling or have you isolated yourself? Have you accepted the offers of others to help you? I have a friend whose husband, my best friend, went to be with the Lord in February. She reminds me that she appreciates all the help I give her but wants the opportunity to repay me by helping me. This is a foreign concept to me at this point but I am learning. I cannot do it alone. I need the Lord and I need those He has put in my life! What about you? Are you still trying to make it on your own? How is that working for you? Ecclesiastes 4:9 says *"Two are better than one, because they have a good return for their work...."* I have a saying which is "Two people working together can accomplish as much as five people working alone!" There is synergy which makes it all go better and smoother. Do you think that is what God meant when He said it is not good for the man to be alone? Why not do it God's way?

Thank You Father that You walk before us, beside us and with us through all the twists and turns of life. Help us to feel Your Presence at all times. Remind us of Your concern for us and that You will be our Helper even when it seems no one is around. Teach us to count on You and ask You for direction. Most importantly, give us the patience we need to wait for Your answer to our questions. In Jesus name we pray! Amen!

# SEPTEMBER 9 HOW WILL I GET THROUGH THIS
## Grief

Psalm 18:18-19, 25 (NKJV)

*<sup>18</sup> They confronted me in the day of my calamity, But the L*ord *was my support. <sup>19</sup> He also brought me out into a broad place; He delivered me because He delighted in me.... <sup>25</sup> With the merciful You will show Yourself merciful; With a blameless man You will show Yourself blameless;*

One thing is for sure! You cannot get through it alone. I don't know how people without faith get through a calamity. My strength comes from the Lord. I know He will work out all things for my good even when I cannot see a way. I have faced a lot of loss this year and it was not easy. January was skin cancer. February was my best friend Carmen going home to the Lord. March was the sale of my parent's home and disposal of its contents; seeing my Dad's chair go to the Lord's Closet. My friend from Church went to be with the Lord in his fifties. And on it went. Yet here I am. I will admit that losses can become cumulative. I am sad at times. The grief sneaks up on me from a movie, a song or who knows what else. I am honoring my grief! But the Lord is my support! It is my love for Him and His great love for me that sustains me.

David wrote this Psalm about his deliverance from King Saul who was trying to kill him. It looked like everything was against David and his death imminent. But because God was with David, God delivered him from the hand of Saul. David praises God for His mercy and support.

I praise God for the same. Without His support, how would I face these things? There are many kinds of loss. People moving away is a loss. Moving to another Church is a loss. Foster children returning to their parents is a biggie! All these things take their toll. Romans 8:28 says *"And we know that all things work together for good to those who love God, to those who are the called according to His purpose."* When you are in the middle of the storm, that is not so evident. There were a lot of storms this year. The only way to see the good is to look back. My cancer was completely removed. Carmen found the Lord before his passing. The burden of taking care of the house is gone. God has worked things for my good. He has shown Himself merciful to me. I wish I could say I am blameless but it is just not true. Even so, God shows Himself blameless and faithful to me. He is my strength and shield, an ever-present help in times of need. Thank You Lord for walking me through the valley of the shadow of death.

Father, I thank You that You walk with us throughout trials. Thank You that You never give us more than we can handle. I thank You that You have blessings in our future that will overshadow the trials we face. Your mercy is far greater than anything we face. In You, we have hope. In You, we are blessed. You are our support, our delight and our deliverer! All glory, laud and honor be to You our Lord and King. Amen!

## SEPTEMBER 10    POLITICALLY OR BIBLICALLY CORRECT; YOU DECIDE

Faith

1 Corinthians 1:20-25 (NKJV)

*20 Where is the wise? Where is the scribe? Where is the disputer of this age? Has not God made foolish the wisdom of this world? 21 For since, in the wisdom of God, the world through wisdom did not know God, it pleased God through the foolishness of the message preached to save those who believe. 22 For Jews request a sign, and Greeks seek after wisdom; 23 but we preach Christ crucified, to the Jews a stumbling block and to the Greeks foolishness, 24 but to those who are called, both Jews and Greeks, Christ the power of God and the wisdom of God. 25 Because the foolishness of God is wiser than men, and the weakness of God is stronger than men.*

In today's world, many want to be politically correct. They want to tell people what they think they want to hear. And be sure not to offend anyone. And truth; is there no right and wrong? People want to say there is no absolute truth. It is all relative to your situation. I don't know about you but I need absolute truth and that comes from God and His Word! It is a choice between God's wisdom and the wisdom of this world. I choose God's wisdom. The Gospel is offensive! It tells us the wisdom of this world is foolishness. It tells us to walk in God's ways.

What is wisdom? Who is wise? Is the person who wants to follow the ways of this world wise? Not according to Paul. It seems that God says the wisdom of this world is foolishness. The Good News is that faith alone is what is needed to enter into a relationship with God. But to the world, that was foolishness.

How about you? What is your source of wisdom? What is the source of your truth? Do you want to follow relative truth (opinion) which sways from moment to moment? Or would it be better to know for sure what the standards are? Is good enough really good enough? Children who are given standards and boundaries do better than those who have to keep searching for what is right. Now I am not saying that we should intentionally offend others but we should speak the truth in love. And it should be God's truth that we speak. When a person strays from God's Law, we need to gently draw them back to the truth. There is trouble on the road ahead for those who do not follow the ways of the Lord. Time and time again, He has proven that His ways are best for us and yet, we still stray. Shouldn't we share the truth now before people face the consequences? It will be less painful if we do. Don't let them walk the slippery slope.

Not offending anyone at all costs is not what is in their best interests nor yours. Telling people what they want to hear will not accomplish the plan God has for us. God has laid out for us the ways that are best for us to thrive. We were not meant to just get by. We were made to thrive and He has blessings for us. We need to walk in His ways for that to happen. Our Creator designed us for a specific purpose. He gave each person what they need to reach the destiny He ordained. You are already blessed but need to walk in the way set out for you. Will you walk in His ways today? Will you speak the truth in love? God's Word is truth!

Lord, thank You that You have given us Your truth in the form of Your Word. You still speak to us today through the Word if we will but listen and read. Let Your Spirit open our eyes to Your truth and Your ways. Help us to be Biblically correct and follow Your teachings. Lead us in the beautiful plan You have for each of us today. In Your name we pray!

# SEPTEMBER 11    AN HONOR TO SERVE
Grace and Mercy

Joshua 24:15 (NKJV)

*15 And if it seems evil to you to serve the LORD, choose for yourselves this day whom you will serve, whether the gods which your fathers served that were on the other side of the River, or the gods of the Amorites, in whose land you dwell. But as for me and my house, we will serve the LORD."*

It is an honor to serve the Lord. If you listen carefully, He will call you to tasks He wants you to do. I have been writing Encouragement Daily each day since January 1. Each day, the Lord gives me what He wants me to write. Several people have come to the Lord through these writings. It is my service to Him but is also His blessing to me.

Joshua was the assistant to Moses and the one God trusted to lead the Israelites into the Promised Land. This was at the end of his time and he was giving instructions to his successors. He showed them his level of commitment to the Lord our God had not subsided after all those years. He was inquiring of the Israelites what their level of commitment was at this point. They were about to rededicate themselves to the Lord. God had proved his faithfulness over the years by delivering Jericho and other places into their hands. It was evident that the Lord was on their side! Now Joshua wanted to know if all of Israel was willing to recommit to the Lord.

Walking with the Lord has always been a blessing for me. I chose, long ago, to serve the Lord. I have come to realize what an honor it is to do His will. He has been so good to me. I wonder if you realize how good He is to you? All through my life, I have felt the Lord with me. At all the darkest times, I always had the sense that I was not alone. That He was close by nudging me in a certain direction. My earthly parents reinforced His leading with the example they set. One of the callings of the Lord was to be an encourager. In the early 1990s, it was the joke around the office that I could come up with an explanation for anyone's bad behavior and find a reason why they should be forgiven and encouraged. I listen to the Lord and try to find a way to lead them to Him. I seem to always have been an evangelist even before I knew Christ personally. Since January, I have been called to speak encouragement through writing to "all nations" in God's name. I have a hard time expressing what a joy this has been for me!

Long ago, I chose to serve the Lord. He has heaped blessing upon blessing on to me since. What is even best is that He has taught me to recognize those blessings. You are a blessing to me. The feedback I have gotten from some has proven to me the fact that God is writing to you through me. The subjects have been just what people have needed to hear. I want you to know that God still speaks. He may not be parting the Red Sea but He still says the right words at the right time for the comfort of His own! Maybe you don't consider yourself His. That's OK! He waits patiently for you to recognize His love for you and His blessings upon you. Trials are the only thing that helps us to realize those blessings. I hope this blesses you today. The same God that Joshua served who blessed him and me is now blessing you. Open your eyes and see how He works His plan for your good. Looking back, I have been blessed to see how each trial lead me in a direction that ultimately was the best place for me. Do I have a supernatural gift for this or has God just allowed me to see things clearly? The God who blesses me blesses you also. He loves and cares for you. Please, open your eyes and your heart to the Lord. Choose this day whom you will serve! And serve Him with all your heart! As for me and my household, we will serve the Lord!

Thank You Lord that You honor me by allowing me to serve You. Thank You that You give me the words that help many people. Thank You that You show me the results of the things you call me to do. Help me to spread Your love to the world. In Jesus name I pray to Your glory and people's benefit. Amen!

## SEPTEMBER 12    WHAT IS MY PURPOSE
Faith

Exodus 9:16 (NIV)
*"But I have raised you up for this very purpose, that I might show you my power and that my name might be proclaimed in all the earth".*

I am a miracle. My Mother was told she would never have any more children. She had a difficult delivery with my older brother and it looked like the end of her child bearing years. Yet, here I am. In speaking with my Mother today, she told me that she was 3 ½ months pregnant before realizing what was happening. Obviously, the doctor was wrong. My Mom calls me the surprise.

September 12    What is My Purpose The Lord has a purpose for everyone in His plan and, therefore, calls us to be or do something in particular. It is part of our destiny to learn that purpose and live accordingly. You have been raised up for this very purpose. What is your purpose? It may not always be evident. There may be more than one purpose and you may go through life traveling different paths. It is the journey that matters.

I have walked many different paths in my life. Many times, I wonder what the Lord wants me to do. Always, He has wanted me to bring glory to Him. In different places and different times, He has led me to things which are part of His plan. I wonder if I heard Him right because it seems strange He would want certain things. But the reason is sometimes clear and sometimes illusive. Like me, you may be wondering who you are [in Him] and why you are here. Everyone wants to know their purpose and that they are here for a reason. They want to know they matter.

Many times, we don't see the obvious. I have a tendency to try to ignore God's call. How about you? Is there something that keeps coming up which you have tried to disregard? Is there something that won't go away? I have been called to several purposes it seems. Looking back, encouraging people has been a recurring theme. I see times where people are discouraged, unhappy and alone. God seems to have raised me up to notice their situation and reach out to them in His name. He has given me the ability to speak with people I do not know and plant seeds of hope to encourage them. He does similar things for you. You are special. You were designed for a purpose. You are here for a reason. You matter. Through you, God will make this world a better place. His power and glory will be displayed through the blessing that is you! What do you love to do and why? Could you have been raised up for this very purpose; to show God's name, power and purpose to a hurting world? Listen for your call and step up to your purpose.

Lord, You said You raised us up for a purpose! Reveal to us that purpose and lead us on the path that will help us fulfill that purpose. Through Your power, we can make this world a better place. Give us what we need to glorify You and bless people through Your holy name. In that Holy Name we pray! Amen!

# SEPTEMBER 13    SAFELY DELIVERED
Grace and Mercy

Psalm 34:7 (NKJV)

*⁷ The angel of the LORD encamps all around those who fear Him, And delivers them.*

Do you ever feel that there is a shield around you? Have you ever been in a situation which should not have turned out well but you came out just fine? It's almost like you are coated with Teflon. Nothing bad sticks to you. If only all your days could be like that. When I was twenty years old, I built fast cars. I had a Chevy Nova in which I put a tricked-out Corvette engine and I was taking on all comers in drag racing. It was fast and I was winning money! That is until I ran out of road. The road turned to the right and I didn't. I remember it like it was yesterday. My friend Howard was in the car with me as we ended up off roading at high speed. The car turned sideways and began to roll over in slow motion or so it seemed. I thought for sure I was about to buy the farm and I was taking Howard with me. This looked like the end of the road in more ways than one. Talk about fear.

Some people say they don't want God in their lives. The angel of the Lord encamps all around all those who fear him. The angel of the Lord is another name for God and the pre-incarnate Christ. Encamping around is creating a hedge of protection. And fear can also mean respect. And God delivers them! He delivered me. Considering the rate of speed we were traveling, serious injury should have resulted. It didn't. The car was barely damaged considering it ended up on its roof. Neither of us were hurt. I thought we were going to die. The Angel of the Lord was there on the road or lack thereof. He held out His hands and gently laid that car on its roof so softly that it was barely damaged and we were safe. I believe in miracles. I just witnessed how our Lord delivers us. Without Him, I would not be writing to you now.

I am not the only one around whom the Angel of the Lord encamps. He loves you and watches over you. All those times when it seems things are going wrong and you are running late, He is delivering you from trouble! How about that flat tire? Did that delay keep you out of an accident? There were many people who worked in the World Trade Center who were late that day for one reason or another. Do you think they were probably unhappy at that time? But the Angel of the Lord was there for those who fear Him. He will and does deliver you, too!

Thank You Lord that You encamp around each of us and put your hedge of protection around us. We know that You work all things for our good. Help us to be patient while You are working out things for our benefit. Thank You that You deliver us from harm many times when we don't ever realize there is a problem. Thank You that You hold us in the palm of Your hand as we go through our days. Thank you for Your blessings and Your deliverance. In Your name we pray.

# SEPTEMBER 14   IT'S ALL ABOUT ME, ISN'T IT
Relationships

Romans 12:3 (NKJV)

*3 For I say, through the grace given to me, to everyone who is among you, not to think of himself more highly than he ought to think, but to think soberly, as God has dealt to each one a measure of faith.*

You mean it's not all about me? I am not the most important person in the world? Our society teaches us to look out for ourselves and to take what we want before someone else does. We are to look out for number one. How well is that working for us as a society? How is it working for us as a world? If your favorite radio station is WIIFM (What's in it for me), you are a taker and the world owes you something in your opinion. Takers look out for their own interests at the expense of others. They want to get their fair share and, sometimes, their unfair share.

In the Book of Romans, Paul is trying to teach us to have a servant's heart. Jesus speaks many times and sets the example of loving and caring for others. A world of takers is a mean place. For people to prosper on the whole, we need to care for each other. If we think too highly of ourselves, we will not care about the needs and feelings of others. C.S. Lewis said, in Mere Christianity, "True humility is not thinking less of yourself; it is thinking of yourself less."

When we think of others and their needs, we step outside ourselves to where God wants us to be. We were not designed to be alone. With that in mind, caring for each other should be an integral part of our lives. I have always said I would want my child to be a waiter or waitress so they could gain an understanding of what it means to be a servant. It is a special thing to have a servant's heart. With it, you learn to recognize the needs of others and learn to meet those needs.

The other day, as I walked through the hallway at Church, I heard a woman working in the childcare area talk about the great smell of the coffee coming from Fellowship Hall. A man asked her if she would like him to get her some since she could not leave her post. That is what we are called to do. We are called to care for one another. When you focus on meeting the needs of others, God will meet your needs. This is also a business principle. Sales are based on finding a need and filling that need. It is all about meeting the needs of others. So maybe, your favorite radio station should be WIIFT (What's in it for them)? Maybe that is God's solution to our selfish world? Why not try it and see how that works for you? Some will take advantage. Some will be skeptical. But many will respond with kindness and appreciation and that is what our Creator desires.

Lord, thank You for the gifts of Your Bounty. Help us to be good stewards of what You have given. There is more than enough to go around if people will think of others and share. Lead us to those whom we can serve. Teach us Your ways that we might know You better. Your ways are to care for those who cannot care for themselves and to share with others as they have need. You have told us that in Your Word and set that example in Your life. We are supposed to follow You "with actions and in truth"

(1 John 3:18). Help us to follow Your teachings in the way we live our lives. In Jesus name we pray! Amen!

# SEPTEMBER 15    SILENCE

Prayer

Psalm 46:10 (NKJV)

[10] *Be still, and know that I am God; I will be exalted among the nations, I will be exalted in the earth!*

The Wizard of Oz demanded Silence. Do you suppose he needed time to think? Many of you know me personally so when I say I have trouble remaining silent, you get it. But I find I am not alone in this. Being quiet is difficult when our society prompts us to do something at every given moment. How many times have you looked at your phone today? Are you looking at it now? Why? What is wrong with being quiet long enough to hear the voice of God. Remember, His is a still small voice. You have to listen carefully. Sometimes, when we ride in the car, I will remain silent. Why speak when you have nothing to say? Isn't it good to be open to what the Spirit might say?

David tells us to be still in order to know He is God. God speaks to us in His still small voice. To know Him, you have to listen carefully. When you listen carefully, you will hear more than just the words. Listening also involves perceiving the Spirit. When you perceive Him, you understand His character which will explain why He should be exalted in the earth.

How do we come to a place where we can be still? It is difficult for me to quiet my soul. Nature abhors a vacuum and tries to fill it immediately. When I quiet my mind to listen, thoughts creep in to fill the void. When I try to think about God, other things creep in to my mind. Did I call this person? How will I write the next devotional? Will I have time to visit a sick friend? Meanwhile, I am not quietly listening for what God wants to tell me. How well does that work for you? Maybe I need more training.

What I find works better for me is speaking with God and laying whatever down at His feet and leaving it there. He will return it to me when He is ready through my subconscious mind. I don't know what to do but then, all of a sudden, here is the answer! I know where it came from. Everything I have is from Him. He has blessed me more than I could ask or imagine. He will do the same for you! Listen for those blessings.

What are the benefits of silence? It causes a feeling of peace for some. It creates an atmosphere in which God can communicate His will to us. It gives us a chance to use the gift of intellect God has given us. You already have everything you need to fulfill your destiny. You may not realize it though. When you are alone with your thoughts, God may reveal the answer to you and show you how you can accomplish what He has set before you. Someone said silence is golden. Could this be why? Could it be that your gifts will show themselves in the silence of your mind? For me, they appear during sleep. I wake up with an answer. To ponder a question is to try to know God better. Listen for Him today!

Speak Lord, for Your servants listen. Give us Your peace that will quiet our minds and open them to Your leading. Help us to recognize the times of delay as a time to meet with You. Let those meetings teach us Your ways that we might know You better.

Draw us close enough to You that we can hear Your still small voice and follow Your will for our lives. In Your name we pray. Amen!

## SEPTEMBER 16    I NEED A LAWYER
Grace and Mercy

1 John 2:1-2 (NKJV)
*¹My little children, these things I write to you, so that you may not sin. And if anyone sins, we have an Advocate with the Father, Jesus Christ the righteous. ²And He Himself is the propitiation for our sins, and not for ours only but also for the whole world.*

I don't always do the right thing. Sometimes, others fail and I need to hold them accountable. I get emotionally involved when my livelihood is at stake. It is the principle. I want them to pay! What is the job of a lawyer? Aren't they supposed to represent their client in the court making sure justice is served? But what if it is me who made the mistake? Do I want them to prosecute me?

We all sin. *All have sinned and fallen short of the glory of God (Romans 3:23).* But do we want justice or mercy. I guess it depends on whether we are plaintiff or defendant. I think I would want mercy for everyone at all times although there are some exceptions. John is writing to help us refrain from sin but there is a strong reminder included. If we do sin, and you know we will, our Advocate is Jesus. Jesus came to us to reveal God's mercy and grace. Jesus goes farther than that. It goes on to say that He is the propitiation for our sins. What does that mean? Merriam-Webster defines it as an atoning sacrifice. In other words, Jesus paid the price for our sin. Leviticus 17:11 says *"For the life of a creature is in the blood, and I have given it to you to make atonement for yourselves on the altar; it is the blood that makes atonement for one's life."* It is Jesus blood in exchange for your sin; His life for yours! The price was high! Would you be willing to pay that much?

When you hire a lawyer to go to court with you for a traffic violation, is he or she willing to pay the fine to redeem you? They are an advocate but not a redeemer. What do you want in your life? If the wages of sin is death, do you want an advocate or a Redeemer? Not a very difficult choice, is it? Jesus is your Advocate with a capital "A". And as if that wasn't good enough, it goes on to say He is the Advocate and Redeemer for us yesterday, today and for everyone who will ever need Him at some time in the future. That is incomprehensible! You mean that sin is covered from the distant past until eternity? Jesus says "I've got this!" And He does. He has got your back and your front and your side and all of you now and always. He loves you that much. He stretched out His arms on that cross and, like the child's game, said "I love you this much!"

How can I thank You enough for something I cannot even fully grasp? Lord, You are my Advocate when I don't deserve You. Why would You pay such a price for someone so unworthy? Is Your love so great that you wrap us in Your righteousness? Your love is beyond comprehension. Out of the overflow of the blessing You have poured out on us, help us to share that love with all. In Your Name we pray. Amen!

# SEPTEMBER 17    CAN YOU FOLLOW DIRECTIONS
Failure

Joshua 5:14 (NKJV)

¹⁴ *So He said, "No, but as Commander of the army of the LORD I have now come."*
*And Joshua fell on his face to the earth and worshiped, and said to Him, "What does my Lord say to His servant?"*

Are you able to follow directions? Do you even listen carefully enough to get them correct? Ask God, by His Holy Spirit, to guide you. It has been said there is an acronym for the Bible. It is Basic Instructions Before Leaving Earth. God's word gives us all the instructions we need.

I don't always listen well especially when it is God's still small voice. Most times, the Commander of the Army of the Lord does not come to me to tell me what the Lord wants. Can you imagine the image of an ancient warrior in bright raiment standing before you? It is usually much more subtle and easily missed. If the Commander was standing before me, I would know. But we have God's Word to guide us. The more I read the Bible, the more I learn about God's plan for our lives. Joshua inquired of the Commander what the Lord wants to say to him. We have it much easier. We can just read the book and know God's will for us. When we read the Bible, we should worship its Author as Joshua did. When we follow what God says to do, things always go better. Many people say they don't understand the Bible. I don't think it is the parts they don't understand that trouble them.

Psalm 90:17 says *"And let the beauty of the Lord our God be upon us, And establish the work of our hands for us; Yes, establish the work of our hands."* Colossians 3:23 says *"²³ And whatever you do, do it heartily, as to the Lord and not to men..."* God laid out plans that will be a benefit to the whole world. He has told us what we should do. Are we listening? Will we follow directions? What does the Lord say to His servants?

The Bible is full of stories that illustrate cause and effect. Actions are revealed and the result stated. These stories are examples of what it means to follow instructions. God shows the way we should go and why. Each time, there is a situation in which we can follow the lesson and not fall into the same trap. The accuser sets a trap for us regularly. You can avoid those traps by hiding God's Word in your heart and following its precepts. What do you think? Can and should you follow God's directions. He has proven His great love for you in the outcome of the stories of others. He can guide you today if you will listen and follow. Will you come to enjoy the blessing of obedience?

Good morning Lord! Thank You for Your love and Your Word that was meant for our good. Thank You that You teach us Your ways and guide us in the way we should go. By Your grace, You speak to us through Your Bible of things we have yet to learn. Help us to learn the lessons with as little pain as possible. May we follow You so the world may be blessed through us. And may we bring glory to You in that process. In Your name we pray!

# SEPTEMBER 18 EVERYONE WANTS A SAVIOR
## Quality of Life

Romans 10:9 (NKJV)

*⁹ that if you confess with your mouth the Lord Jesus and believe in your heart that God has raised Him from the dead, you will be saved.*

Everyone wants a Savior; How many want a Lord? What is a Lord? Merriam-Webster defines it as: one having power and authority over others: *a):* a ruler by hereditary right or preeminence to whom service and obedience are due; *b):* one of whom a fee or estate is held in feudal tenure; *c):* an owner of land or other real property. In other words, someone who is in charge. We don't want to admit someone else is in charge. Especially if someone wants to be in charge of *your* life.

In this passage in Romans, Paul makes clear that Jesus is both Lord and Savior. Both of those are in the same sentence and are inseparable. You cannot have one without the other. To confess and believe Him as Lord is the only way to be saved. It is a prerequisite. Allowing Jesus to ascend the throne of *your* life is the only way to be saved. That causes quite a dilemma for most of us.

You see, in today's culture, we are taught *we* are the most important thing. We are worth it according to advertisements. Madison Avenue plays to our lust and ego. We are constantly bombarded by narcissism. To get us to buy, they tell us it is all about us and our desires. Leading that life is very shallow and unsatisfying. It leaves a big hole in our soul which can only be filled by our Creator and Lord. Letting Christ be Lord means we take a back seat to Him allowing Him to rule our day-to-day activities and decisions. It is no longer all about us. It is now all about Him!

When you live your life showing what it means to follow a Risen Lord, the fruit of the Spirit becomes evident in your ways. Galatians 5:22-23 says *"²² But the fruit of the Spirit is love, joy, peace, patience, kindness, goodness, faithfulness, ²³ gentleness, self-control."* Are these the things that shine out in your life? When you are led by your Lord, these are the fruits which will be displayed.

How about you? We know you want a Savior. How about a Lord? How do you go about stepping down as the leader of your life and asking Jesus to step in as Lord? In Revelation 3:20, Jesus says *"Here I am! I stand at the door and knock. If anyone hears my voice and opens the door, I will come in and eat with that person, and they with me."* Jesus says He will come in if you open the door. Will you open the door? All you need do is ask Him to come in. Just have a conversation. It does not have to be fancy. Invite Him in today. When Jesus becomes your Lord, He also becomes your Savior! Open the door!

Lord, thank You for Your offer of Your grace. You are the One who will lead us to be our best. Please come into our lives and be our Lord. With You at the helm, right decisions will be made. Right actions will ensue. Help us to show the world what it means to follow our Risen Lord! In order for us to follow, we need to let You lead. Lead us Lord! Amen!

# SEPTEMBER 19    WHAT WILL YOU LEAVE BEHIND

Encouragement

2 Peter 1:12-15 (NKJV) Peter's Approaching Death

*¹² For this reason I will not be negligent to remind you always of these things, though you know and are established in the present truth. ¹³ Yes, I think it is right, as long as I am in this tent [body], to stir you up by reminding you, ¹⁴ knowing that shortly I must put off my tent, just as our Lord Jesus Christ showed me. ¹⁵ Moreover I will be careful to ensure that you always have a reminder of these things after my decease.*

As I get older and friends and family pass on, I am thinking more and more about what will happen after I am gone. I know I will not always be able to do the things I do. I have been given gifts and talents that have been good for helping others. Who will help them when I cannot?

Peter is approaching his death. He is concerned for the people he is leaving behind that they will be able to carry on with what he has taught them. He has already taught them much. He wants them to be reminded of his teachings and conduct themselves in the way.

What are you going to leave behind? How will you be remembered? Have you shared what you know? Have you invested in others with the gifts you have been given? It is said every person should have a Paul, a Barnabas and a Timothy. Paul is the one with the gifts. Barnabas is the encourager who will help them use the gifts. Timothy is the one we can teach what we have learned to share the gifts. Where are you in that process? Will you go to your grave with your music still in you or will you teach the song to others?

Getting back to my story, I have come to understand I want to share the song. If I teach others, we can sing together and there will be harmony. My personal Mission Statement was Glorify God, Build Relationships, Benefit People. What's yours? I recently added three more words. They are Teach, Encourage, Inspire! I want to leave a legacy. When my friend Ron went to be with the Lord, there were 500+ people at his Memorial. His son asked us questions about which of us had participated in activities like building things for people and helping others through what Ron taught? He asked how many had lived with his Father? Almost everyone stood up. I worked with Ron on a project. I went home the day of the Memorial and spoke with our son Clayton about how I wanted to teach him things. I want him to be able to not only take care of himself but to take care of others. Ron inspired me to do that. Who can you inspire? How can I inspire you? Are there things I can teach you? I try daily to encourage you. How am I doing?

Lord, thank You for the gifts You have given each of us. Help us to learn how to share what You have given us with others. Lead us to people who we can help in some way. Remind us of all You have given us and the value those gifts hold for others. Give us patience to teach others what You have taught us. In Jesus name we pray.

## SEPTEMBER 20 NEVERTHELESS
Faith

James 1:12 (NKJV) Loving God Under Trials
*¹²Blessed is the man who endures temptation; for when he has been approved, he will receive the crown of life which the Lord has promised to those who love Him.*

What does nevertheless mean? Merriam-Webster defines it this way: adverb: nevertheless: in spite of that; notwithstanding; all the same. Basically, in spite of what has been said, I will continue. "You'll never amount to anything!" Nevertheless, I will keep trying. It is all about faith and that faith may not be in the spiritual sense only. Hebrews 11:1 says (NKJV) *"Now faith is the substance of things hoped for, the evidence of things not seen."* It is a feeling of certainty without facts to back up the feeling. It is *knowing* in your heart. It is the ability to stay the course even when you are not sure of the outcome. How does a person do that? I know it has been difficult for me. Maybe, we need to listen for God's voice and encouragement?

My old Russian friend Wally faced many challenges but still managed to love and serve others. Where did he get this spirit? How did he keep on against the odds? Wally is a friend of my Father's with whom I apprenticed in my early teens. He is like a second Father to me! He taught me how to act and conduct myself in life as much as he taught me auto mechanics. Right and wrong and integrity were part of the course of study. Wally believes that the whole person matters. He also knows how to encourage people. He draws out seeds of greatness in many.

Wally told me of bad times in his life. He was drafted into the Russian Air Force, wounded and shot down over Germany. But he still knew there was a better life. He had a dream in his heart to go to America and he kept that vision in his sights. One of the words Wally always uses a lot in his conversation is nevertheless. He will tell you of a setback he faced but, nevertheless, he went on to accomplish some goal. He worked as a farmhand in rural Germany to support himself but remained focused on going to America. And eventually, the Visa came. He had a sponsor and was able to travel to the place of his dreams. He faced many hardships and lack but, nevertheless, he arrived in America! The dream came true!

Are you a "nevertheless" person? Will you keep on the path even when it seems things are against you? 1 Corinthians 9:24 (NKJV) says *"²⁴Do you not know that those who run in a race all run, but one receives the prize? Run in such a way that you may obtain it ..."* Have you run the race marked out for you in faith? There will always be trials. Trials are God's way of testing to see how bad you want something. How committed are you to running the race? Run your own race and run it with perseverance in faith as a victor, one who will receive the crown. For long ago, when He formed you, God put the Spirit of victory in you along with all the seeds of greatness. You are anointed, equipped and empowered to win the race God has marked out for you! The course is tough. Nevertheless, keep your eyes focused on Him, the Author and Finisher of your faith. And you will receive the victor's crown! God is rooting for you. Go!

Lord, I thank You for these people who listen to Your word through my writing. Thank You for their faith and their willingness to try one more time. Help them to shine Your light into the darkness. Each act of love, no matter how small, brightens our world. You have shown us the way. Please guide us so we can remain on the path that glorifies You, benefits others and will take us to the victor's crown. In Your name we pray. Amen!

# SEPTEMBER 21    WHAT ARE YOU WEARING
Redemption

Isaiah 64:6 (NKJV)
*⁶ But we are all like an unclean thing, And all our righteousnesses are like filthy rags;*
*We all fade as a leaf, And our iniquities, like the wind, Have taken us away.*

There is a commercial for an insurance company where the woman asks the insurance agent what he is wearing as if it is some seedy late-night phone call. But it is a valid question. What are you wearing when you come before the Creator of the Universe? Do you want to make a good impression? What will it take to impress God? Matthew 5:48 tells us to *"be perfect as our Heavenly Father is perfect."* I am not up to that standard. How about you?

In whose righteousness does God see you? Are you wearing your own garments? How do you think they look? Check it out in the mirror of your soul. Is this the impression you want to make? Isaiah tells us that all our righteousnesses are like filthy rags. I'm thinking that is not the look we were going for! Our sin has soiled our Sunday best. We have fallen in the mud and mire. We are a mess! All of us have sinned.

What do we do? Our clothes are soiled and we have no way to clean them on our own. But there is One who can clean those clothes. Isaiah 1:18 (NKJV) *says*[18] *"Come now, and let us reason together," Says the* LORD, *"Though your sins are like scarlet, They shall be as white as snow; Though they are red like crimson, They shall be as wool".* The Lord our God had and has a plan. He knew we would never be able to follow the Law, so He made a way from before the foundations of the world. And that way is Jesus. On our own, we fall short. But in the Garment of Righteousness He provides; we will be seen in a better light. Our garment is the garment of sin. His is the Robe of Righteousness.

As Jesus was heading to the Cross, the soldiers divided His garments among them. In John 19:23 (NKJV) it tells us *"*[23] *Then the soldiers, when they had crucified Jesus, took His garments and made four parts, to each soldier a part, and also the tunic. Now the tunic was without seam, woven from the top in one piece."* It was very unusual to have a one-piece garment. As He was going to the Cross where He would take on all the sins of the world, that one-piece tunic was removed from Him. It is my belief that garment was His Garment of Righteousness and, when it was removed from Him, it became available for us. We can now stand before the Father covered in Jesus righteousness. God sees us as holy, righteous and redeemed by the blood of the Lamb. What we cannot do on our own, God does for us. His plan of redemption is fulfilled.

Father, thank You that You made a way for us to return to You. You laid on Him the sins of us all so we can stand before You in righteousness that was given to us. Help us to rejoice in that and let the love You showed us be sent out through us to others. Let us freely give what You gave to us! In Your name we pray!

# SEPTEMBER 22    MUSIC REACHES PLACES IN THE SOUL WORDS CANNOT GO

Prayer/Praise

Psalms 98:4 (NKJV)
*Shout joyfully to the LORD, all the earth; Break forth and sing for joy and sing praises.*

I believe music is the voice of God. Music expresses emotions that words cannot touch. When people make music unto the Lord, it moves me. There are Hymns that I have trouble getting through because of the emotion. When they sing *Here I am Lord*, I am a basket case.

This was a Song of Praise that David wrote to bring glory to God. David had a heart for the Lord and wrote beautiful words of praise. It is called a Royal Psalm. We are supposed to sing praises to our Lord. For Him to be our Lord, we must choose to obey Him.

Our worship team brings tears to my eyes. The words of the songs they sing speak of the inconceivable grace and compassion of our God and Savior. They recount all the blessings He pours out on us. I know I am not worthy but His love says He gives them anyway. I spoke about the hymns. But there is other music that is sacred. For hundreds of years, the Church has commissioned artists to write sacred music to be used in Worship. People like Vivaldi (the Red Priest), Hayden, Bach, Mozart and others wrote music that is inspired by God. It is Him speaking to us without words. Recently, we had a husband and wife play piano and cello for the gathering music for the traditional service. Music like that opens passages to our hearts. I just close my eyes so I am not distracted and focus purely on the sound. It is glorious! It speaks to me in special ways. How about you? Do you hear God in music? Do you wake up in the morning with a song of praise in your heart and on your lips? I do! God speaks to me through music and he says I am blessed! And you can be blessed, too.

Lord, we thank you for Your gift of music to help us praise You. It is our reminder of Your glory and splendor. It speaks of Your Majesty. It connects us to You. Continue to bless and encourage the music makers as they inspire us in worship. Reveal to them the true value of their sacred calling. Help them to continue to bless us, bring joy to us and glorify You. In Your name we pray!

# SEPTEMBER 23   WHAT IF I FAIL
### Failure

Genesis 15 (NIV) Selected Verses
*After this, the word of the LORD came to Abram in a vision:*
*"Do not be afraid, Abram. I am your shield, your very great reward."....*
*⁶ Abram believed the LORD, and he credited it to him as righteousness.*
*⁷ He also said to him, "I am the LORD, who brought you out of Ur of the Chaldeans to give you this land to take possession of it."......⁹ So the LORD said to him, "Bring me a heifer, a goat and a ram, each three years old, along with a dove and a young pigeon."*
*¹⁰ Abram brought all these to him, cut them in two and arranged the halves opposite each other; the birds, however, he did not cut in half...... ¹² As the sun was setting, Abram fell into a deep sleep, and a thick and dreadful darkness came over him......¹⁷ When the sun had set and darkness had fallen, a smoking firepot with a blazing torch appeared and passed between the pieces. ¹⁸ On that day the LORD made a covenant with Abram*

God called Abraham out of Ur to go to a land God would show him and Abraham went. God credited Abraham's obedience to him as righteousness. God told him He would be his shield and great reward. And God made the Promise no matter what Abraham did. It was a unilateral promise. The smoking firepot and blazing torch passing through the pieces was God making the commitment. Abraham was asleep at the time. That was the way a covenant was made in those days. Both parties walking through the pieces was their commitment to the covenant. If they failed, they would become like the pieces. Since God walked through alone, He is the Promissory, the Maker of the Promise. The Promise does *not* depend at all on Abraham. Abraham made a lot of mistakes along the way but God's Promise still stands.

What about you? Have you made any mistakes? Are you afraid God will give up on you? Fat chance! God made the promise to Abraham, Isaac and Jacob. He repeated it to all three generations and told each generation the promise was to them and their descendants as well. We are their descendants. The Promise still stands.

Even if you fall short of the mark, as we all will, God is the Keeper of the Promise. He walked through the pieces so you don't have to! Have you failed? So what! Pick yourself up. Dust yourself off and try again. The Promise still stands!

Lord, You said that You will keep the promise. You said You are our shield and our great reward. You said You would never leave us nor forsake us and You never have. You are the Promise Keeper. We thank You that You are always with us as our Shield. Give us the strength to try again and again. In Your name we pray.

# SEPTEMBER 24    LORD, HEAR OUR PRAYER
Prayer/Praise

Isaiah 1:11-17 (NKJV) Selected Verses

[11] *"To what purpose is the multitude of your sacrifices to Me?" Says the* LORD. *"I have had enough of burnt offerings of rams.... I do not delight in the blood of bulls, Or of lambs or goats...."* [15] *When you spread out your hands, I will hide My eyes from you; Even though you make many prayers, I will not hear. Your hands are full of blood.*

[16] *"Wash yourselves, make yourselves clean; Put away the evil of your doings from before My eyes. Cease to do evil,* [17] *Learn to do good; Seek justice, Rebuke the oppressor; Defend the fatherless, Plead for the widow.*

What matters more, words or actions? Are you willing to write a check to a charity but unwilling to go to the food bank Saturday morning to give out food? Do you have more important things to do? Are you willing to give of yourself? Many are not. Do you follow the letter of the law or the Spirit of the Law? Which is the better path?

In Isaiah's time, People were just going through the motions as many are today. Solomon said there is nothing new under the sun. They made sacrifices as the Law required but the Lord knew they didn't really care. It was sort of like a child where the parent made them apologize. They said "sorry" but everyone knows their heart was not in it. The challenge with the sacrificial system is it makes people think they can pay for their mistakes with someone else's blood. What if, instead of sacrificing a goat, we never did the bad thing in the first place? What if we knew right from wrong in our hearts and asked God to help us always do right? Sounds like a dream, doesn't it? But that is exactly what God is asking of us. He wants us to let His Spirit guide us to right actions so we don't have to repent. He wants us to live with a contrite heart that looks to Him for the way. Instead of following the letter of the Law in our human strength, He wants to write His Law of mercy, grace and compassion on our hearts and lead us in His ways. If we live rightly, will God not throw open the floodgates of heaven and pour out blessings upon us?

What is God asking of us? Are we to be parents who give our children things but not our time and attention? Certainly not! It is not about checking off a box that says we did what was required. Do you want to be known as the person who does what they *have* to or one who makes things better? Do you brighten a room when you enter? Do people murmur, "there he/she is!" when you walk in a room? Are you shining God's light to those you meet? Why or why not? 1 Samuel 16:7 says (NIV) [7] *But the* LORD *said to Samuel, "Do not consider his appearance or his height, for I have rejected him. The* LORD *does not look at the things people look at. People look at the outward appearance, but the* LORD *looks at the heart."* What does He see in your heart? Why not, instead of sacrifices to atone for poor behavior, live rightly and care for those whom you meet? Share the Good News! Cease to do evil. Be a blessing to everyone you meet. Let our prayers be actions of mercy and compassion. And Lord, hear our prayer! In Jesus name! Amen!

# SEPTEMBER 25    BREAKTHROUGH MINDED
Attitude

Philippians 4:13 (NKJV)

*13 I can do all things through Christ who strengthens me.*

Whether you think you can, or you think you can't, either way you're right! How do you approach a situation? Is the glass half-full or half-empty? I have a hat that says "Attitude is Everything!" and it is right. I have done things that amaze me. I now know it was God who led me through those successes. Your Creator has already given you everything you need to reach your destiny. You may need to practice but, just know it is in there! Remember you are not doing things alone. Christ walks with you. In fact, He will carry you in the difficult times. When it seems no one cares, you are still in the palm of His hand. You are loved and cared for.

Paul wrote Philippians while under house arrest in Rome. In Chapter 4, he is giving them the pep talk of their lives while facing persecution for his faith. He tells them to focus on praiseworthy things and that he is content in his life. And he is content because he knows Christ walks with him through the valley. What about you? Does Christ walk with you? Ask Him and He will. Are you content in your circumstances? Do you rely on the Lord for your needs? What if you did? Would your life be better?

At times, when it looks the most difficult and discouraging, those are the times you are closest to your breakthrough. Remain breakthrough minded. Remember for whom you labor. He calls you to great things! How many people have failed because they gave up too soon? If they had tried just one more time. If they had remained in faith, knowing that Christ would give them the strength they needed, they would achieve their victory. Are you close to a breakthrough? Will you stay the course and cross the finish line of success? You have everything you need. Remain in faith and walk with Christ into your destiny! Never give up!

Lord, thank You that You give us the strength we need for each day. Thank You that You walk with us and guide us into our breakthroughs. Let us reason together and see how we can serve You! Keep our eyes focused on You where there are no shadows of doubt. Let Your Spirit remind us that You give us strength and we can do all things through You! In Your name we pray! Amen!

# SEPTEMBER 26   WHAT DOES JESUS CALL YOU

Relationships

Exodus 3:13-15 (NIV)

¹³ Moses said to God, "Suppose I go to the Israelites and say to them, 'The God of your fathers has sent me to you,' and they ask me, 'What is his name?' Then what shall I tell them?"
¹⁴ God said to Moses, "I AM WHO I AM. This is what you are to say to the Israelites: 'I AM has sent me to you.'" ¹⁵ God also said to Moses, "Say to the Israelites, 'The LORD, the God of your fathers—the God of Abraham, the God of Isaac and the God of Jacob—has sent me to you.'
"This is my name forever, the name you shall call me from generation to generation.

Moses was wandering in the desert when he saw the Burning Bush. He went to investigate why the bush was not consumed. God revealed Himself to Moses and they entered into a conversation. God told Moses to go to Pharaoh to get the Israelites freed. Moses was asking on whose authority should I demand their release. God told Moses "I AM WHO I AM." That is the Name by which the Lord wants to be known. That is the authority under which Moses was to demand the release of the Israelites. That is the authority under which we live.

You are called to make disciples of all nations by that same authority. By what name does Jesus call you? What do you call Him? *Como te llamas?* How do you call yourself? What's in a name? In Biblical times, a name was also a description. Abraham means father of many. Jacob means supplanter. Moses means Born of God. Jesus means to rescue or deliver. A name is very important. What does your name say about you?

When Jesus calls you to make disciples, what name does He use for you? Is it friend? Is it brother? Is it My Child? Is it Hey You? How close are you to Him? Does he know your name? If He did call, would you answer? When you answer, how do you call Him? Is it Lord, Savior, Friend or something else? Names are important. Jesus knows your name even if you don't know His.

Dr David Instone-Brewer said "Is a perfect sovereign one who forces us or *enables us*? We see God letting Moses refuse to be his spokesman and strengthening Pharaoh's resolve - i.e. he "hardens his heart". God's loves us enough to let us have responsible freedom, while finding another way to carry out his will."

Does Jesus demand that you make disciples or does He want you to share the grace He has given you? Does He need you to do it? If you don't participate, will His plan fail? If you call Him Lord or Friend, he wants you to share what He has given you. The name you use to address Jesus speaks about your relationship with Him. The name He uses when He speaks to you is even more important. What does Jesus call you? He calls you blessed. He calls you redeemed. He calls you loved. He calls you His!

Dear Lord, I pray that You call us Friends and that You make known to us all You have received from the Father. Write Your story on our hearts. Help us to know and love You as You love us. Include us in Your plan of revival and let us be Your hands and feet in this world. Help us to reach out to those on the fringe. May the sound of our names bring Your love, peace and grace to all Your children by letting us shine

Your light. When they hear our name, may they think of You. All glory laud and honor to You our Redeemer King! Amen!

# SEPTEMBER 27   WHAT'S YOUR DREAM

Encouragement

Genesis 37:18-20 (NIV)
*18 But they saw him in the distance, and before he reached them, they plotted to kill him.*
*19 "Here comes that dreamer!" they said to each other. 20 "Come now, let's kill him and throw him into one of these cisterns and say that a ferocious animal devoured him. Then we'll see what comes of his dreams."*

Not everyone will celebrate you when you have a dream. In fact, sometimes, those closest to you will be the ones who point out all the pitfalls of your idea and it can be discouraging. Sometimes, they will be jealous. But dreams are important. In South Pacific, the line is "you've got to have a dream if you're going to have a dream come true."

Joseph was the oldest son of Jacob's favorite wife Rachel. It was no secret he was the favorite son of the twelve. His coat of many colors was just one example of the favoritism Jacob showed. I'm sure there were plenty more. In his case, his brothers hated him enough to kill him. Why did they hate him so much? Because he had a dream and they were jealous! Joseph could have used a little more discretion about what he shared with his brothers.

Dreams are from God. In 1 Kings 3:5-15 (NKJV), God spoke to Solomon in a dream.
*5 At Gibeon the LORD appeared to Solomon in a dream by night; and God said, "Ask! What shall I give you?"* Dreams are visions of what God has in store for you. It is what He places in your heart. Nothing can thwart God's plan. Joseph's dream was he would be a ruler of a nation and others would bow down to him. It took thirteen years during which he endured hardship but God was still running His plan.

We had a Foster Son who had been criticized for his imagination and dreams. Educators told him he was a dreamer and his imagination kept him from grasping what was right in front of him. They did not understand he saw something much greater out in the distance. They were not able to see his vision and keep his attention. His dreams were about a vocation in digital media. They squashed those dreams. The imagination is a place where God can deposit seeds of His vision for your future. Edison dreamt of a light bulb. Ford dreamt of a wagon with its own power source. Of what do you dream? The imagination is the strongest nation in the world!

My friend Tony used to ask me "Now are you sure you want to do that?" That question made me think through the idea without discouraging me. It made me consider the pitfalls and figure ways around them. Do you encourage others to dream? Jules Verne dreamt of a vehicle that could travel under water. The writers of Dick Tracy dreamt of a communicator in a wristwatch. Were they just dreamers too? What would you attempt if you knew you could not fail? When others share their dreams with you, do you encourage them or are you a murderer? Dreams are from God! Help yourself and others to recognize them as gifts and nurture them. After all, Joseph became Ruler of Egypt just as God had said in his dreams.

You give us dreams of what we can become and for that we thank You Lord. We know dreams are from You and You give us everything we need to accomplish Your goals for us. Give us wisdom in choosing what to share and with whom. Help us to recognize the dream as precious and Your gift to us. If we can dream it, we can do it because You give us what we need. Let Your Spirit guide us in the path Your dream has set for us. Show us what will become of our dreams. In Your name we pray.

## SEPTEMBER 28    WHERE DO DREAMS COME FROM

Quality of Life

Psalm 37:3-4 (NKJV)
*³ Trust in the Lord, and do good; Dwell in the land, and feed on His faithfulness. ⁴ Delight yourself also in the Lord, And He shall give you the desires of your heart.*

Where do dreams come from? Is it just our own imagination that conjures up these visions? Or could it be they are on a much larger scale and part of God's plan for us? At first glance, it looks like God will give you what you dream about. I don't think that is the case. Jesus said in John 14:13 (NKJV) *¹³ And whatever you ask in My name, that I will do....* The key phrase is "in My name".

This verse tells us to trust in the Lord and do good. It says we can feed on His faithfulness. It tells us to delight in the Lord and He shall give us the desires of our heart. Initially, I thought that meant God would give us what we want. I know my heart desires things for my benefit. With that in mind, I could not make sense of this passage. The Holy Spirit has revealed more to me through my friend Kathy. She explained that God is not giving you what you want but, rather, placing in you the desire for what He wants you to have. God will instill a desire for things that align with His plan for your life.

It reminds me of the Zig Ziglar story about dieting. Zig tells of the doctor saying Zig was going to be able to eat anything he wanted on this diet. In fact, Dr. Cooper had prepared a list of what Zig was going to *want*. How about you? Has God prepared a list of what you are going to *want*? When you feed on His faithfulness, He is going to prepare a list of what you are going to want. He will give you the desires of your heart. Your wants will be in alignment with the good things God has planned for you. Remember, God has a plan for your life to prosper you and not harm you. He wants to give you hope and a future. He will make your dwelling place safe and feed you from His bounty. So, isn't it best to delight yourself in the Lord? Won't the dreams He places in your heart lead you to the destiny He has planned for you? Shouldn't you delight yourself in the Lord? If you do, you can feed on His faithfulness and be blessed.

Father, help us to delight ourselves in You. When we do, we know You will place dreams and plans in us that are for our good. Thank You that You are faithful and always lead us in paths of peace and righteousness. Thank you for giving us the dreams and desires of our hearts. Amen!

## SEPTEMBER 29    NEW DREAMS
Quality of Life

Psalm 27:14 (NIV)

*14 Wait for the Lord; be strong and take heart and wait for the Lord.*

"Setbacks have an upside; they fuel new dreams." These are the words of Dara Torres, a five-time Olympic swimmer who beat her own world record twenty-five years later. What enables a person to continue to strive for excellence year after year? How do they keep from getting discouraged in the face of setbacks? When things come against you, how do you remain on track? For me, it is very difficult.

This Psalm tells us to be patient. I am not. How can we remain patient when what we want is not happening? It tells us to be strong and take heart. To take heart means to remain in faith. The only way I know to do that is to remain focused on the Lord, the giver of our dreams. Dara Torres says setbacks fuel new dreams. I have come to a point in my Spiritual Journey that I ask what the setback is trying to teach me. Instead of being upset, I search for a lesson. Since I know God works all things for my good, what could this setback be trying to teach me? There is also another meaning to "wait" for the Lord. Just as in a waiter or waitress, waiting means serving. What if you lived your life in Service to the Lord? Do you think your motive would be purer if your purpose was to serve the Lord and those he loves?

Suppose you were living a life of service. If a door closed in your path, would it be a setback or could it be an indicator to change direction? Closed doors are not always a bad thing. Your dream was to go in a certain direction but opportunities do not come. We serve a good God. He is merciful and kind and gracious and compassionate. He loves you more than you can fathom! What if the path you are taking is riddled with pitfalls and God wants you to go another way? What if you misinterpreted the dream He gave you? God loves you too much to answer some of your prayers and dreams. He knows what is best for you. He won't give you anything less than His best! Be glad some of those doors closed. The saying is "be careful what you wish for; you just might get it." Let's ask God for what He wants for our lives and *wait* in His timing until He brings about the destiny He has planned. Be strong and take heart and wait for the Lord! I can't wait to see where He leads us!

Lord, show us Your plans for us today. You are awesome and Your plans for us are amazing. Help us to be patient when things don't go the way we think they should. Remind us of Your goodness and lead us where You would have us go. We know Your direction will take us by the best path. Give us strength to continue even in the face of opposition. Help us to keep our eyes on You. Build our faith in You so we can persevere. In the name of Father, Son and Holy Spirit we pray! Amen!

## SEPTEMBER 30    WHO ENCOURAGES YOU

Encouragement

Psalm 32:8 (NIV)

*I will instruct you and teach you in the way you should go; I will counsel you with my eye upon you.*

If He wants me to do it; He will guide me through it! Since God is the One who gives us our dreams, doesn't it make sense that He can and will guide us through? He knows what is best.

David tells us God will instruct and teach us in the way we should go. Does that presuppose we will listen? If we listen, God will give us counsel in the best path to take and how to go about reaching our destiny. He goes on to say He will keep his eye on you. God will watch out for you. He will protect you. He loves you!

Sometimes, God sends others to do His work and encourage you. There was a person in my life that encouraged me. It was my Grandmother Rose. She listened to my dreams and crazy ideas and asked me questions which made me think through the idea. Her questions made me think. If the idea was really crazy, I would figure that out on my own. However, if it was a great idea, these questions would help me clarify my thinking. The questions were not judgmental. They were thought-provoking. It was more like counseling. Everyone needs someone like that in their life. Someone who will listen.

Who encourages you? Many will tell you the idea is crazy; it is impossible. Don't share your ideas with people who will not celebrate you. You have to be careful with your ideas. Remember they are gifts from God. Treasure them. Do not risk their murder by negative people. Many, if not most, of the people around you are dream killers. Avoid them. Hang around with dream encouragers. Henry Ford would have given up if not for Thomas Edison's encouragement. Anyone can tell you why not. Associate with people who ask "how will you do that?" They are the ones who will encourage you, celebrate your success and cheer you on along the path. In fact, why not *be* an encourager to someone else today. Ask how they are doing. Give them an encouraging word. Spur them on to do great things. The world will be a better place if you do!

How will you encourage someone today? What questions will you ask? What words of encouragement will you offer? Will you be a *good finder* today? You can spread God's light of encouragement everywhere you go. It will make the day brighter for everyone including the one doing the encouragement. You can be the light! And that light can shine on God's above and beyond favor in the lives around you.

Thank You Lord for the encouragers! You said that You would counsel us and keep Your eye upon us. Be our guide today. Let Your Spirit shine out from us to encourage others. Instruct us in the way we should go and give us what we need to get there. In Your name we pray! Amen!

## OCTOBER 1    PRAYER IS A GIFT
Prayer/Praise

Luke 11:1 (NIV)
*¹ One day Jesus was praying in a certain place. When he finished, one of his disciples said to him, "Lord, teach us to pray, just as John taught his disciples."*

Not everyone knows how to pray. Jesus was connecting to His Father through prayer. He prayed often and long. His communication with His Father was extensive. How about your prayers? Do they help you focus on God? Jesus disciples asked, Lord, teach us to pray. Jesus gave them the outline of how to pray. It is not natural for everyone. Practice will help.

Last week, Pastor Don Feuerbach and I went to a Wells of Revival Meeting. On the way there, we discussed the agenda for the meeting. We discussed how the group prays for each other. Don said prayer is a gift. I never thought of it that way but he is right. I met a lady at the last Revival Meeting who was a Prayer Warrior. You could just see her dig deep into prayer. She was speaking with the Father, no doubt about that! It made me want to grow closer to the Lord. I admire her. Sometimes, I wish my family had that kind of connection with God. They wait for me to do the praying.

Not everyone knows how to pray. Don and I discussed the ability to verbalize our thoughts and concerns to God. Many are confused about how to begin. For me, it seems natural. It is like a conversation. I am on a first name basis with God. I call Him Lord and He calls me Bob. Once I begin praying out loud, the Spirit rises up inside me making my prayers more fervent and passionate. Romans 8:26 says *"In the same way, the Spirit helps us in our weakness. We do not know what we ought to pray for, but the Spirit himself intercedes for us through wordless groans."* Even if you don't know what you should pray for, God, through His Spirit, will help you. The Spirit will guide your prayers. That is my experience. I hear myself praying and I know the words are being given to me. Although Jesus taught us the basic outline for prayer, He did not just leave us there. His Spirit remains with us at all times. Prayer is just a conversation with God. If you will just indicate your desire to have a conversation, God will help you pray. He will listen and answer. You matter that much to Him. However, you might not like the answer. He will give you what you need, not necessarily what you want. You can rest in the idea of His good plan for you.

Don't know how to pray? Relax and let the Spirit guide you. Start in silent prayer. Start with praise. Tell God about His majesty. Let Him know you are sorry for your shortcomings. Move to gratitude. Thank God for all the wonderful things in your life. Once you are feeling the joy of communication with God, ask Him for what you need. Make your requests known to Him who loves and cares for you. That is the model Jesus gave you. It is called ACTS (Adoration, Confession, Thanksgiving, Supplication). Once you start, the Spirit will help. It is up to you to start! Go ahead. Even if it is just a groan. Speak to the Father. He is waiting for you!

You are awesome Father! We admit we do not spend enough time with You. Lack of time in prayer leads us astray. Father, thank You that You wait for us to pray.

Thank You that You always hear. Draw us closer to you. Help us with our prayers. Teach us to pray for each other. Teach us Your ways oh Lord that we might know You better. In Jesus name we pray! Amen!

## OCTOBER 2  JESUS PRAYED FOR YOU

Prayer/Praise

John 17:20-21 (NIV) Jesus Prays for All Believers

*20 "My prayer is not for them alone. I pray also for those who will believe in me through their message, 21 that all of them may be one, Father, just as you are in me and I am in you. May they also be in us so that the world may believe that you have sent me.*

Jesus prayed for you! Not just for His disciples; but for you! He knew, when He invested in them and planted the seeds, He was also investing in you. The Son of God knows the future. Jesus was about to go to the cross. After He prayed for Himself, He prayed for them and you. He was preparing Himself and His disciples for what came next.

Unity of believers is a theme that is throughout the New Testament. Jesus prays that His disciples will remain in the Father (remain faithful) just as He has remained in the Father. Are you one with them? That faith will be the indicator to a hurting world that God loves and cares for them.

I am one who believed in Jesus because of their message. Because one person shared the message of hope and salvation with another and another, through thousands of years, I was able to hear the story and accept God's grace. I write to you today because Jesus prayed for me and for you. When I read this chapter, it moves me to know my Lord cared enough to pray for me. More than two thousand years ago, Jesus knew I would come to Him through their message of love and grace. And the offer still stands today. He prays for you. Jesus is calling. He bids you come to Him. Get out of the boat and walk.  He asks you to be one with the Father. Will you answer the call? Will you hear His prayer? *"I pray also for those who will believe in me through their message, 21 that all of them may be one, Father, just as you are in me and I am in you."* Will you answer His prayer? Will you put your faith and trust in Him?

Lord, we hear Your prayer and we long to be one with You. Sometimes we are afraid of what will we have to give up to follow you. Draw us closer to you. Let Your Spirit open our minds and hearts to the love You so generously pour out on us. Help us to become and remain one with and in You showing the world what it means to follow a risen Lord. In Your name we pray just as Jesus did. Amen!

## OCTOBER 3    SHINE THE LIGHT OF YOUR GLORY
Grief

Isaiah 60:19-20 (NKJV) God the Glory of His People

*19 "The sun shall no longer be your light by day, Nor for brightness shall the moon give light to you; But the LORD will be to you an everlasting light, And your God your glory. 20 Your sun shall no longer go down, Nor shall your moon withdraw itself; For the LORD will be your everlasting light, And the days of your mourning shall be ended.*

Shine the light of Your Glory into the dark places of our souls and our world Lord. Our world is very dark. That is because of the darkness of sin. When Eve let the serpent convince her to disobey God, darkness entered and corrupted His perfect world. But even back then, God had a plan to redeem us and all creation with us. When He completes his plan, God will be the light of our world. Isaiah tells us the Lord will be to us an everlasting light. He goes on to tell us the days of our mourning shall end. I am ready for the mourning to be over.

Grief is what we feel toward many losses. Many of the things that happen in our day to day lives are losses. I am finding all these losses are adding up making for sad times. The news is bleak. The world is mean. They are killing each other. What do we have to look forward to? It can all be depressing. But when the outlook is not so good, we can try the up-look. It is always better.

Are you ever depressed? I know I can be. There are so many bad things you have to face that you cannot see a way around them. It looks hopeless. Well, it is not hopeless. In fact, it is quite the opposite. If you follow the Lord, He will be your everlasting light. Even though all have sinned and fall short of the glory of God, your redemption is assured since before time began. We know the end of the story. Today, you will be with Jesus in paradise. He goes to prepare a place for you and will return to take you to be with Him. Let Jesus be your anti-depressant. When the world looks bleak, the Lord will be your everlasting Light! And the days of your mourning shall end!

Lord, please shine Your light into the dark places of our souls and our world. Drive out the accuser who tells us it is hopeless. He is wrong. Our hope is in You Lord! You have redemption for us since the formation of the world. Draw us back to you, clothe us in Your righteousness and be our light. In Your name we pray!

## OCTOBER 4    A HUG FROM MY FRIEND
Grief

Isaiah 40:11 (NIV)
*11 He tends his flock like a shepherd: He gathers the lambs in his arms*
*and carries them close to his heart; he gently leads those that have young.*

When you are feeling bad, don't you wish someone would put their arm around you and tell you everything will be alright? It may not be the same but it will be alright. When we lose someone, things will never be the same. But we must go on. And with time, the pain of loss subsides and the memories of time spent together overshadows the loss somewhat. It is never easy and the pain will never completely go away.

Isaiah tells us how our Shepherd gathers His lambs in His arms. The lamb knows his master and settles when the master comes to their rescue and holds them in His arms. In the same way, when we face challenging times, being held in His arms would be wonderful.

I had an interesting experience tonight. My best friend went to be with the Lord early in 2015. I miss him a great deal. He was like a brother to me. His wife gave me his leather jacket over the summer. Tonight, was a little cool so it was the first time I wore it. We went to a gallery for an opening and the gallery owner asked if she could take my coat. I said no because I did not want to take it off. Since I knew it sounded strange, I decided to explain why I wanted to wear it to her. After hearing it was my friend's coat, she said "oh, you are getting a hug from your friend." She was right. Carmen's arms were around me symbolically through the coat. I am getting a hug from him even though I can no longer see him or talk with him. I am sitting here in my family room late this evening still wearing the coat. My son came home from work and wondered why I still have my coat on. I shared the story with him. Even though we no longer have a loved one here with us, they are still within us. Thank you, Chris, for this coat. I still feel his presence.

How about you? Have you had a loss that still hurts? Some people leave a room exactly like it was when a loved one passed. Others try to completely change the scene. Different things work for different people. I like the reminders of those who have gone before me. I have my Grandmother Stella's lucky hat and her cane. I have my father's fountain pen. And I wear Carmen's coat. All these are reminders of my loss but, more so, my gain in having them in my life at all. I choose to remember them fondly and rest in the knowledge I will see them again when I go to be with the Lord. For now, I will have to settle for the hug of this coat around me and the memories of our 58 long years of friendship. What a blessing. Who do you know that still loves you from afar? Rest in their love and the love of the Father who gathers you in His arms to spend eternity with Him and them. In God's name we pray! Amen!

# OCTOBER 5    LOVE LIKE JESUS LOVED

Love

Ephesians 4:32 (KJV)
*32 And be ye kind one to another, tenderhearted, forgiving one another, even as God for Christ's sake hath forgiven you.*

Jesus told us we are to love our neighbor as ourselves. How are you doing with that one? I am not doing so great. I have not yet learned to live as Jesus lived and love as Jesus loved. I fall short of that mark.

Paul tells us we are to be kind to each other and be forgiving as God has forgiven us. He tells us we are to be loving. God has shown us examples of what love really is.

How can we possibly love like Jesus loved? Is there any one of us who would willingly lay down their lives to redeem our friends let alone our neighbors? I don't know about you but I am sure I do not have what it takes. But I do have a good example to follow. I believe that setting your aim very high can lead to reaching much higher even if you don't make it all the way to your goal. Low expectations bring poor results. I have decided to follow Jesus example of how to love. I know I cannot make it to that level but even trying will yield high results. It is worth the try.

What does it mean to love like Jesus loved? Will you do what is best for others? Will you put the needs of others first? Will you do the right thing according to Jesus way? All of the above are required. So how do we get started? The first thing that is required is to know what Jesus would do. We can learn that from His word. He teaches us in the Bible how we should live. You will need to know what the Bible says though. And that means you may need to read it. There is great reward in knowing Scripture! You have strength on which to call when in times of trial. The Holy Spirit will teach you all things and remind you of what Jesus said. You have a guide. All you need do is set the goal and be willing. Attitude is everything! May your attitude reflect the will of Jesus. And may you live with abandon. The blessings God has for you if you seek Him are beyond measure. I pray those blessing for you in Jesus name!

# OCTOBER 6    FORGIVENESS IS AMAZING
Redemption

Luke 23:33-43 (NIV) Selected Verses

*33 When they came to the place called the Skull, they crucified him there, along with the criminals—one on his right, the other on his left. 34 Jesus said, "Father, forgive them, for they do not know what they are doing." And they divided up his clothes by casting lots....... 39 One of the criminals who hung there hurled insults at him: "Aren't you the Messiah? Save yourself and us!" 40 But the other criminal rebuked him. "Don't you fear God," he said, "since you are under the same sentence? 41 We are punished justly, for we are getting what our deeds deserve. But this man has done nothing wrong." 42 Then he said, "Jesus, remember me when you come into your kingdom." 43 Jesus answered him, "Truly I tell you, today you will be with me in paradise."*

How serious a crime can be forgiven? Are there people who have fallen too far for God to redeem and forgive them? Have you fallen too far? Do you feel you are not worthy of God's forgiveness? Many people feel that way. But God offers forgiveness anyway!

Jesus was on the cross in between two criminals. One of them was insulting Jesus while the other recognized who He was. This second criminal asked for Jesus forgiveness. Did he deserve it? Do we? The truth is no one deserves forgiveness. *"For all have sinned and fall short of the glory of God"* (Romans 3:23). But God does not rely on our performance. God's promise to Abraham was a unilateral promise. God was the One who made the promise. It does not depend on us. It is God's goodness alone that offers redemption.

There is the age-old struggle with worthiness. The accuser constantly chirps in your ear that "God will never forgive you. You blew it! He doesn't care about you anymore." The truth is He doesn't care about you any less either. God loves you! God knows all the mistakes you are going to make and He loves you anyway. As kids, we lie about what we have done to avoid punishment. I have always had an anger issue. I hit and cracked our shower door as a kid but never told that I did it. I think I was more than fifty years old when I told my Mom; when I finally admitted it. What a relief! I finally put that burden down. Even the thief on the cross would receive forgiveness by just asking in sincerity. Why not me? God could see what was in his heart. God saw he was truly sorry for his deeds. He did the same for me. God can do the same for you.

There is truly forgiveness for those who will seek God with a humble and contrite heart. He stands ready to redeem even the worst offender. *43 Jesus answered him, "Truly I tell you, today you will be with me in paradise."* In the hymn *To God be the Glory*, it says "The vilest offender who truly believes, That moment from Jesus a pardon receives." If the vilest offender can receive pardon, why not you? Go ahead and ask Him. He wants to forgive you. He is waiting for your return and offers you grace for now and always. His Son made the way for your forgiveness. Lord, forgive us! In Jesus name we pray.

## OCTOBER 7    WILL I SEE THE KINGDOM OF GOD
Faith

Luke 17:20-21 (NIV)

*20 Once, on being asked by the Pharisees when the kingdom of God would come, Jesus replied, "The coming of the kingdom of God is not something that can be observed, 21 nor will people say, 'Here it is,' or 'There it is,' because the kingdom of God is in your midst."*

There is always a lot of talk about the coming Kingdom of God. People speculate when it will arrive and where it will be. The Pharisees asked Jesus when it would come. Interestingly, He said it "is in your midst." What does that mean? How can the Kingdom be in our midst? Where is the Kingdom? The New King James Version says the Kingdom is within you. I believe that to be true.

The Kingdom is wherever God is because He is the King of Kings. Doesn't it make sense that, wherever God is, the Kingdom exists. 1 Corinthians 6:19-20 (NKJV) says *19 Or do you not know that your body is the temple of the Holy Spirit who is in you, whom you have from God, and you are not your own?* God, through His Spirit, lives inside you. Therefore, God's Kingdom is within you. In my case, my body is the temple of the Holy Spirit and the Tenant is *complaining*! He wants better accommodations.

The Kingdom of heaven is not only here right now but it is also within you! How do you like them apples? It has been here all along. I talked about hearing God's voice. To me, He said "Trust Me!" A friend from Church, Helen, said she heard God say "I am all around you." Linda heard "It will be OK." And, in fact, He is all around us. God is everywhere. When I put that together, it says "Trust me! I am all around you! It will be OK!" In trusting Him, it *will* all be OK.

Christ before me; Christ behind me; Christ beside me; Christ within me!

Lord, thank You that You reside within us leading us in Your ways. It is You that we desire! Be with us in all we do and help us to bring glory to Your Holy Name! Since You are in our midst, direct us in Your ways that we may live within the Kingdom right here, right now! In Your name we pray!

## OCTOBER 8    HOW DO I FILL THIS HOLE

### Grace and Mercy

John 14:6 (NKJV)

*⁶Jesus said to him, "I am the way, the truth, and the life. No one comes to the Father except through Me.*

Many are wandering around in this world feeling incomplete. There is something missing from their lives but they are not sure what it is. Many worry about what the future will hold. Worry turns to anxiety and that can make life miserable. Are you missing something?

Blaise Pascal, a fifteenth century French theological writer, said "There is a God shaped vacuum in the heart of every man which cannot be filled by any created thing, but only by God, the Creator, made known through Jesus."

Jesus told us He is the way and the truth and the life. He is that missing part. In the few verses before this, Jesus is telling us to *"not let your hearts be troubled."* He goes to prepare a place for us. And if He goes, He will return to take us to be with Him. The future is not uncertain for those who believe in Christ. The plan is clear. Jesus is the way of the future. He is faithful to His word. He will return for you.

We know that intellectually but we still doubt. Why? The evil one whispers in our ears. He says "you're not good enough. You have fallen too far to reach. He has forgotten you. You'll never find the way". Don't believe those lies! Thomas, the infamous doubter, said they did not know where Jesus was going so how could they know the way. Jesus summed it all up neatly. Jesus *is* the way! We don't need to know all the details. We only need to believe. We only need to put our faith and trust in Him. Once we do that, the hole in our heart is filled by the grace, mercy and compassion of the Lord Jesus. The Creator completes His created! He will fill the emptiness and cover the void. In the 1996 movie, *Jerry McGuire*, Tom cruise says to Dorothy "You complete me." That is his description of their love. Jesus love for you goes so far beyond that He laid down His life that you might have eternal life by the grace of His sacrifice. Jesus gift more than completes you. It fills the vacuum. It makes you perfect!

Thank you, Lord, that You fill the empty places in our souls that only You can fill. You created us with the place within where You would reside. You said Your grace is sufficient. Help us to know Your grace and live according to Your plan for our lives. Calm our hearts. Let the peace that passes understanding shine out from us to draw others to You. Remind us who we are and Whose we are. In Jesus name we pray!

# OCTOBER 9    IT IS OUR JOB TO LOVE
### Grace and Mercy

John 8:10-11 (NKJV)
*[10] When Jesus had raised Himself up and saw no one but the woman, He said to her, "Woman, where are those accusers of yours? Has no one condemned you?" [11] She said, "No one, Lord." And Jesus said to her, "Neither do I condemn you; go and sin no more."*

In this story, Jesus is confronted by the Pharisees about a woman caught in adultery. They are testing Him to see what He would do about her breaking the Law. They wanted to judge her, find her guilty and stone her to death for her violation. Jesus wanted to show love, mercy and grace. Would you have thrown a stone? Do people deserve a second chance to get it right?

There is already enough judgment in the world. I am always ready to comment on how someone should behave. My Brothers in Christ remind me it is easy to judge when we have not faced the challenge ourselves. Luke 19:10 (NKJV) says .... *"[10] for the Son of Man has come to seek and to save that which was lost."* Jesus came that He might get us back on track within the Spirit of the Law. These laws were designed to guide us in ways that would enhance our lives. They are all about building good relationships. They are about God's desire for us to live blessed lives. Exodus 20:12 (NKJV) says *[12] "Honor your father and your mother, that your days may be long upon the land which the* LORD *your God is giving you.* This commandment gives a reason for its purpose. It is given so you will benefit and live long.

The Pharisees were ready to stone this woman to death for her crime. By the way, where was the man with whom she had committed this act? How did Jesus prevent an angry mob which was also trying to discredit Him from stoning her? In the verses before these, Jesus said "Let any one of you who is without sin be the first to throw a stone at her." That leaves me out. I am in no position to judge. How about you? Are you going to throw a stone? I didn't think so! You see, none of us is without sin. That is a really sad state of affairs until you remember that Jesus came to seek and save that which was lost. He told us we are to forgive seventy times seven. The best part of the story is the forgiveness which God offers. That is why Jesus came!

There is one more really significant lesson here. After all the mob dropped their stones and walked away, Jesus asked where are those who condemned the lady? They all walked away because they were all sinners too! And Jesus said to her, "Neither do I condemn you; go and sin no more." The key phrase here is "go and sin no more". Forgiveness is available but it is for the purpose of repentance. It was not offered so you can continue to sin. To repent means to turn away from that sin and strive to do better. Yes, you may fail again. I do! But it gets better each time. If, in your heart, you are truly sorry and strive to do better, God will forgive you and help you on your path.

I am unworthy! But He offers forgiveness anyway! And I accept. Lord, I come to You just as I am and ask you to cleanse me and remake me as You desire. I pray also for those who will read this that you would show them Your mercy and grace. Show us all to go and do likewise. Help us to love rather than judge. In Your name we pray! Amen!

# OCTOBER 10   WHY WAS I BORN
Encouragement

Job 3 (NKJV)
*¹After this Job opened his mouth and cursed the day of his birth. ²And Job spoke, and said:*
*³ "May the day perish on which I was born, And the night in which it was said, 'A male child is conceived.'*

What is my purpose? Why was I called into being? How many people ask themselves that question every day? Do you know why you are here? Is it just by chance or is there a greater purpose and a master plan? I don't think it is an accident. I believe in the Creator and that He has a master plan. You are part of that plan. It may take a while but you will figure out what part you are supposed to play.

Job went through some awful trials in his life. Job lost everything that was dear to him. He lost all his family and possessions. He was under the impression that God had forsaken him and caused all these tragedies to fall on him. At that point, Job was at the end of his rope, so to speak. He cursed the day he was born. But Job did not curse God. In fact, Job still honored God. In Job 19:25, he said *"I know my Redeemer lives."* At the time, Job did not realize it was Satan who was causing him all the troubles.

I asked myself this same question. Why was I born? One day, as I was driving to visit my Mom, I had a revelation. My Mother had a difficult time with the birth of my older brother and the doctors told her she would never have any more children. It was impossible according to them. Almost three years later, the impossible showed up at Lenox Hill Hospital. I was the miracle that would never happen.  So now what? I was not supposed to be born according to the world but here I am. I was called into being for a purpose and now I have to figure out what that purpose is for my life. I have figured out it is my purpose to encourage people. Our world is a dark place. Many need encouragement. I also want to help more people build a relationship with God. I want to help build the Kingdom. That is why I began writing *Encouragement Daily*. I want to help others learn to better know and love God.

I found my purpose. How about you? Are you still seeking an answer? You are not alone. Why not look at your life. What do you do best? What gifts and talents have you been given? What makes you the happiest? What gets you really excited? Knowing that all your gifts are from God, you can begin to see a pattern. That pattern will lead you to your answer. Find out why God designed you the way He did. It was no accident! You are special! You were born for a reason. Even if you were unplanned by your parents, God sent you for a reason and a purpose. You belong here. Use your gifts to make a difference and be a blessing to others. You can do it!

Thank You Lord for the unique combination of gifts and talents you have given us. Help us to use them for Your purpose and glory. Reveal to us that we were fearfully and wonderfully made and designed for accomplishment, engineered for success and endowed with the seeds of greatness. Lead us in the direction of our destiny. In Your name we pray!

## OCTOBER 11    WATCH WHAT YOU SAY

Encouragement

Leviticus 19:14 (NKJV)

*14 You shall not curse the deaf, nor put a stumbling block before the blind, but shall fear your God: I am the LORD.*

Thou shalt not curse a deaf man? Why not? He cannot hear you. What difference will it make? You can say whatever you want and it will not make a difference to him. Go ahead and say what you want to say, right? Well, maybe not. You see, words take on a life of their own once spoken. The deaf man won't be hurt by those words but those who hear them may. Those words will affect the speaker. So what do you say to yourself? What words do you speak? Who is listening? Words of bitterness are like acid in a vessel. They eat their way out destroying the vessel.

What does your vessel contain? Is it acidic? Do the words you say reflect a bitterness inside? If you speak positive, encouraging words, your life will become positive and encouraging. Your words will prophecy your life. God said to Ezekiel to prophecy to the dry bones and they came to life (Ezekiel 37). To prophecy meant to speak to them. God called the world into existence with His words. Words are powerful. What words will you use?

You can use your words and actions to help people or to hurt them. The choice is yours! Many people chose to hurt others as a way to boost their own ego. They may figure if they cannot get ahead, why should they help others? God's economy is different. When you go out of your way to bless someone, God will bless you.

Also, it says you shall fear the Lord your God. To fear means to respect. Respecting means to walk in His ways and do His will. Do you walk in God's way? He tells you to love others as yourself. He tells you to honor others. He tells you to hold others in higher esteem than yourself and to serve them. Would cursing them be walking in His ways? Shower others with words of kindness, humility and patience. Help people to think "I like me best when I am with you!" And do it in all sincerity. Be a blessing rather than a curse. See how life will improve!

Today, I tell you that you are Holy, Righteous and Redeemed. You are a blessing. You are fearfully and wonderfully made in the image and likeness of God. Live as a follower of the Lord God Almighty.

Father, help us to be a blessing to those we meet. Help us to share Your kindness, mercy and grace with all those we encounter along life's highway. Help us to be kind to the grumpy and friendly to the lonely. Give us the words to speak that people need to hear. May the words of our mouths and the meditation of our hearts be pleasing in Your sight, O Lord, our Rock and our Redeemer! Amen!

## OCTOBER 12   YOU ARE SPECIAL
Encouragement

Colossians 3:12-14 (NKJV)
*12 Therefore, as the elect of God, holy and beloved, put on tender mercies, kindness, humility, meekness, longsuffering; 13 bearing with one another, and forgiving one another, if anyone has a complaint against another; even as Christ forgave you, so you also must do. 14 But above all these things put on love, which is the bond of perfection.*

You are special! You were made in God's image and likeness. You are a child of God. You are holy, righteous and redeemed by the Blood of the Lamb and the power of the Holy Spirit. You were chosen by God to do special things God chose in advance for you to do. You *are* special!

In Colossians, Paul tells them all of the things God has said about them and you. You are the elect of God. As such, you are to be kind to one another and be forgiving. But most of all, you are to be loving. Paul calls this the bond of perfection. 1 Peter 4:8 (NKJV) says *8 And above all things have fervent love for one another, for "love will cover a multitude of sins."* Even special people sin.

What makes you special? Firstly, there has never been or ever will be a person just like you. Even if you are an identical twin, there is still something unique about you. I had twin girls in my Sunday school class years ago. One had a little birthmark on her neck that told me who she was. They were amazed that I always could tell them apart. I never revealed my secret. Secondly, you were fearfully and wonderfully made. There was a plan from before the foundations of the world. You are no accident! You are here for a reason! Thirdly, you were made in the image and likeness of God. That means you are *like* God. You were created with seeds of greatness inside. Sure, you don't measure up to the perfection of the Lord but you have been given what you need to become what He calls you to be. That alone is awesome!

There is a destiny for you to attain. There is a race for you to run. You were designed and created to be you. You are special. Why not run your own race and be the best you that you can be? Instead of trying to be someone else and do what you think they would do, why not be who you are? God loves you as you. He created you with the gifts and talents you have. Why try to be someone else? Bloom where you are planted and be who you are. He already approves you. Why not approve yourself?

Father, thank You that You created each of us in a way that we fit into Your plan. Help us to recognize our place and use the special gifts You have given us for the race we are to run. Guide us along the path and show us the benefits of our efforts so we may live encouraged and fulfilled. Reveal Your blessings to us. May we live Your plan for us in a way that brings You glory. In Your name we pray!

# OCTOBER 13 THAT'S NOT MY JOB
## Attitude

Ephesians 2:10 (NKJV)

*[10] For we are His workmanship, created in Christ Jesus for good works, which God prepared beforehand that we should walk in them.*

Who determines what is and is not your job? It seems as that may have been determined by the Creator of the universe. How do you think you should be doing your job? Ephesians tells us God prepared us for good works of His choosing. He created us to do things in His name and by His design.

So how should you do your work? Should you do whatever is required of you? Should you go out of your way to take care of things that need doing? Should you work as if unto the Lord?

I have a friend who runs an outsourced Human Resources company. He taught me valuable information. He taught me we hire for skills and we fire for behavior or attitude. Attitude is everything. How someone approaches their work is very important. Skills can be taught but attitude is ingrained in a person. How you approach your work matters more than the work to be done.

Your job is to serve the needs of the people in any way necessary. To begin with, everything is your job. I would ask you to do everything necessary to improve service to others or clients of any business. In your personal life, work to the best of your ability. Build relationships! Go out of your way to make things right. Take ownership for the cleanliness of the area and do anything else that will improve the customer experience. Work as if everything is a testament to its creator and yours! The work of your hands was ordained. You were given the gifts needed to accomplish your mission. It is an honor to have things you can do. Smile. Be pleasant and welcoming. You never know who you will meet and what their need might be. If they don't have a smile, give them one of yours. You were created for good works and to be a blessing to others. You are awesome! Be a blessing today!

Lord, thank You for the work of our hands. Thank You for the satisfaction that comes from a job well done. Help us to know what You want us to do and give us the strength to accomplish the tasks. Let our work be a blessing to others and a testament to You. In Your name we pray! Amen!

# OCTOBER 14    SEND ME    IN-REACH VS. OUTREACH
Redemption

Isaiah 6:8 (NKJV)

*8 Also I heard the voice of the Lord, saying: "Whom shall I send, And who will go for Us?" Then I said, "Here am I! Send me."*

What is the difference between a disciple and an Apostle? A disciple is one who follows a leader and teacher. An Apostle is one sent out to blaze a trail and be followed. Are we following the Great Commission and making disciples of all nations? Are we content to remain inside the walls of our Church and the safety of others who hold the same philosophy and belief?

Isaiah heard the Lord's call. God spoke to Isaiah and asked who would take the Message to His people. Isaiah stood up and said "Here am I! Send me." That took courage. The Message was one of repentance. No one wants to hear they have done wrong and must turn away from their sin. Isaiah would not be popular. Are you concerned about your popularity or God's message? Help us to hear the Lord's call,

I belong to a men's ministry group in our Church called Every Man a Warrior. We have been through the Resolution Course and signed a document that says we will be the Spiritual Leaders in our homes and our world. This group has been meeting weekly for more than three years to spur each other on. As it is said, iron sharpens iron. We are there to support and encourage one another to do good works which God has prepared for us. This is a group of committed disciples. But the question has come up on occasion about whether we are supporting ourselves alone or are we called to take the good news out to others. There are those in the seats at our Church who may not be sure why they are there. We were asleep at the wheel ourselves until God called us to task. Now that we are called, it is time to meet each man in our Church, face to face, and share the call of Christ. Once that is done, we are to reach out into the world at large. Do you hear the Call?

We are disciples of the Lord. It is time for the disciples to be sent out. It is time for God's disciples to become God's Apostles. It is time to go past the boundaries and safety of our small group and share God's Message with *all nations*. It is time to go out. It is time to be the "Sent Ones" of God. It is time for revival in the Somerset Hills, NJ and surrounding communities and it starts with each of us. You are being called. Do you hear God's voice? He has already given you everything you need to take His message of mercy, grace and salvation to a hurting world. Will you answer that call? Will you sign the Resolution and live your life in a way that brings glory to God? Only you can decide. Are you ready to be sent? I am! Will you join me in asking the Lord what He would have us do next? Let me know. Together, we can make a difference for the Lord.

Lord, we are Your disciples. Let us hear Your call and answer it in faith with enthusiasm. We know You live in us to guide and strengthen us. Give us courage to go and make disciples for You. Thank You that Your love extends mercy and grace to all who would take hold of Your promise. We don't deserve Your gifts but we gladly accept them. Send us! In Your name we pray! Amen!

## OCTOBER 15    YOU ARE A BLESSING

Redemption

Genesis 12:1-3 (NKJV)
*Now the LORD had said to Abram: "Get out of your country, From your family And from your father's house, To a land that I will show you.*
*² I will make you a great nation; I will bless you And make your name great; And you shall be a blessing. ³ I will bless those who bless you, And I will curse him who curses you; And in you all the families of the earth shall be blessed."*

I will make you a blessing. That is what God said. Exactly when would that occur? I purport it already has. In fact, you were a blessing before you were even born.

God was speaking to Abram [Abraham] asking him to leave his father's house and go to his Father's House; the Promised Land. God told Abram that, if he would do what God was asking, God would bless him and make his name great! And God is faithful. He always keeps His promises. We speak of Abram still today. But the best part of it all is the final promise. And *in you* all the families of the earth shall be blessed. You and I are still blessed today through Abram.

Getting back to you, you are a blessing because God said He would bless all the families of the earth through you, a descendant of Abraham. You were and are blessed so you can be a blessing to others. God also said He would protect you. He will curse those who curse you. It is like walking along with the armies of the Lord in tow. You think you are the one making things happen. All the while, the Lord was paving the way. It reminds me of the picture of the cat looking in the mirror and seeing a Lion. The Lion of Judah is in your mirror. He is in you. No matter what comes against you, greater is he who is in you than he who is in the world. You are blessed and you are a blessing!

Thank You Father that You have blessed us beyond anything we could ask or imagine. You are so good to us it is hard to comprehend. Help us to be such a blessing that people will want to know how and why. Give us the words we need so we can tell them about You. Allow us to lead them to You. In Your name we pray!

Psalm 19:14 (NKJV) *¹⁴ Let the words of my mouth and the meditation of my heart Be acceptable in Your sight, O LORD, my strength and my Redeemer.*

# OCTOBER 16   MY MIND IS A SCARY PLACE
Encouragement

Daniel 7:15-16 (NKJV)
*15 "I, Daniel, was grieved in my spirit within my body, and the visions of my head troubled me.*
*16 I came near to one of those who stood by, and asked him the truth of all this. So he told me and made known to me the interpretation of these things.*

I am a visual person. As such, ideas (most times given to me) appear in a flash in my mind's eye. I need to record it and act quickly or the idea may be lost forever. With that in mind, sometimes, I move too fast for those around me. It causes stress for others and me. I see the whole thing including outcome while others are still trying to understand the concept. It causes confusion for them and leads me to get discouraged and give up. I am asking God to prevent that now. I am asking for patience to hang in there. Do you give up too soon? Are you afraid others will reject your ideas?

Daniel spoke about how the visions troubled him. He went on to say he asked for an interpretation so he could understand the meaning of the vision. I sometimes don't understand the visions either. God may only reveal a portion of the dream now. He will explain things when the time is right. His timing is perfect. You may have to wait.

Get in God's timing. Just because He gives you a dream doesn't mean you have to share it right now. Maybe He has just planted a seed which He will help to grow later. Be watchful for other things that fit with the dream. Over the years, I have been given many ideas which I thought were great. One thing was a Motorhome equipped with a network and 12 laptops for doing computer training. The confused look on people's faces makes it obvious the timing was not right. They were not ready. God gave me the vision but it did not work in His timing. At that point, I did not understand He had a time for everything. I worked my own plan. Now I know His plan is better and I am open to His timing.

Be careful with whom you share your dreams. Only share with someone you know will encourage. Figure out who the encouragers are and only go to them with your dreams and visions. Sometimes, those closest to you will offer the least support. "That will never work" has sidetracked some of the greatest dreams of all times. But God's plan will not be thwarted. If He gives you an idea and you don't run with it, He will give it to someone else instead. Dreams are from God. Never give up on them! He gives them to you to take you places you never even imagined. He gives you all you need to accomplish them even if that means bringing someone into your life. Be open-minded. The mind is like an umbrella; it only works when it is open. These dreams can be the seeds of greatness God planted in you to bring you to your destiny! Follow your dreams.

Thank you, Father, for dreams. They are gifts from You. Guide us in Your timing as You go before us paving the way. Teach us to trust Your leading. Help us to stay the course and accomplish all You have destined for us. In Your name we pray! Amen!

## OCTOBER 17   WHAT NOW

Support

Psalm 121:3-8 (NKJV)

³ *He will not allow your foot to be moved; He who keeps you will not slumber.* ⁴ *Behold, He who keeps Israel Shall neither slumber nor sleep.* ⁵ *The LORD is your keeper; The LORD is your shade at your right hand.* ⁶ *The sun shall not strike you by day, Nor the moon by night.* ⁷ *The LORD shall preserve you from all evil; He shall preserve your soul.* ⁸ *The LORD shall preserve your going out and your coming in From this time forth, and even forevermore.*

People, in general, don't like change. Life gets uncertain when there are changes. Sometimes, we lose a job or the company changes the way they do things and we are in a different position. We may get a promotion. Uncertainty causes stress. What will I do now? How will this affect my life? Will I be able to manage this new responsibility, this new job? Many times, it is a double-edged sword. We are excited about new possibilities but wondering how we will handle these things.

Psalm 121 gives us a sense of assurance. We are reminded that He [who created the universe] will not allow our foot to be moved. In fact, He who keeps you will not slumber nor sleep but will remain watchful over you. We are told the Lord is our Keeper! With Him watching over you, all will be well. It may not seem good at the time but you have nothing to fear. He shall preserve your soul now and forevermore. Wow! That is exciting.

So why worry? What do you face today? Are things in your life changing? Have you been at a position for a long time and now, you are going to have to do something else? Are you starting a new position? It is scary until you remember He that watches over you neither slumbers nor sleeps. He preserves you in your going out and your coming in always. Change does not equal fear!

The accuser says:

> This new position will be terrible.
> It won't work out well.
> You might be out of a job.
> You will lose income.
> What will I do?

The Creator of the universe says:

> I am your Keeper
> I am your Shade
> I will preserve you from evil
> I will preserve your soul
> I will be with you always

To whom shall you listen? The great I Am! The Lord tells us He will prevail. If you read His Book, you know He is faithful. He has always kept His promises in the past. He will keep them now and in the future. His promises are that He will protect and preserve you. Believe Him! He has given you more than enough proof. Never mind being stressed. Remember, *stressed* is just *desserts* spelled backwards! Which do you choose; stressed or desserts? God prevails in the end. Isn't that where the desserts are usually served? Know that you are blessed and highly favored.

Lord, You said that You would neither slumber nor sleep in Your quest to protect and preserve us. You promised to be our Keeper, our Shade, our Strength and our Shield. Your promises have always been true. Help us to remember those promises as we walk through the valley of change. Give us Your peace in every situation. The peace that comes from knowing You are our Keeper. In Your name we pray! Amen!

## OCTOBER 18    GOD IS WITH YOU

Encouragement

Genesis 39:20-23 (NKJV)

*20 Then Joseph's master [Potiphar] took him and put him into the prison, a place where the king's prisoners were confined. And he was there in the prison. 21 But the LORD was with Joseph and showed him mercy, and He gave him favor in the sight of the keeper of the prison. 22 And the keeper of the prison committed to Joseph's hand all the prisoners who were in the prison; whatever they did there, it was his doing. 23 The keeper of the prison did not look into anything that was under Joseph's authority, because the LORD was with him; and whatever he did, the LORD made it prosper.*

Have you ever had a really bad day? How about a bad week? Many feel the world is against them. Everything is going wrong. Whatever they touch turns bad. The outlook sometimes becomes hopeless or so it seems. You are never alone. Even when everything seems negative, God is still with you. That is Joseph's story. Everything that could go wrong, did!

Joseph was having a really hard time. His brothers sold him into slavery. As a slave in Potiphar's house, he rose to distinction. He got thrown in prison because of a lie. He distinguished himself there too and rose to a leadership position. No matter how bad it seemed, Joseph always rose to the top. It was because the Lord was with him. The Lord made everything Joseph did prosper. But look at the story. It was not all good. There were plenty of obstacles in the journey. He was sold into slavery. Have you ever become a slave? I didn't think so.

So why is God telling us this story? He wants you to know *"In the world you will have tribulation; but be of good cheer, I have overcome the world."* (John 16:33 NKJV). Your God is with you too! Many things may come against you. This world is a dark place. But the Lord has overcome the world on your behalf. He will make you prosper, too, if you will walk in His ways. He knows what is best for you anyway. Why not follow His lead? The Bible does not tell cute stories of blessed people. It tells of the faults of mankind and how God's grace can overcome them. His grace is sufficient for His power is made perfect in our weakness. You may feel weak today. You may wonder how you will face another day. God is the answer. Don't attempt it in your own power. Lean on the Lord and let Him be your strength and shield. He is with you!

Thank You Lord that You are our all in all. You said You would never leave or forsake us. Even in the worst of times, Your presence can make everything alright. As You did for Joseph, walk with us today and every day so that we may rise to the top. And let people notice our blessings which you give and ask us why we prosper. Then, give us the words we need to tell them about and give the glory to You. In Your name we pray! Amen!

## OCTOBER 19    I NEED HELP
Failure

Matthew 5:48 (NKJV)
*⁴⁸ Therefore you shall be perfect, just as your Father in heaven is perfect.*

Do you think perfection is possible for human beings? We all have a desire to be perfect. Only One was perfect and they hung Him on a tree. Is perfection really the goal? For me, it is not possible. I am a bit of an obsessive compulsive but perfection is way out of my league.

Jesus was teaching people to love their enemies. I have enough trouble loving my friends. Jesus was telling us about what it takes to get into Heaven. Perfection is one of the ways. *He* is the other. I'm going with Jesus. What about you? Can you do it on your own? I don't think anyone can.

The other day, I saw a segment on Dr. Oz about suicide among college students. It seems as many kids go off to college thinking they are invincible as they have been the best in their high school. Now, they are among the best of the best and they are not happy. In fact, depression and despair usually sets in. Their concepts of being the best are destroyed. It is good to praise and encourage but do we go too far? If we give everyone trophies for showing up, are we setting the right example? You learn to appreciate that for which you work hard.

On Dr. Oz I saw something called the Duck Syndrome. It is something where the duck seems serene on the surface but they are furiously paddling underneath the water trying to stay afloat. This was an example of what it might be like for our kids and ourselves. We don't want anyone to know we are struggling because that might make us look weak. Are you able to ask for help? Do you try to do everything on your own? Would asking for help to learn be showing weakness? Could our kids or friends be quiet on the surface and frantic underneath? When you ask how someone is doing, really listen. Then ask a follow-up question. Many people are wearing their Church Face. If you notice a change in their behavior, ask deeper questions. Show your interest, not curiosity. Tell them you are there for them! There are always warning signs. Tell stories of struggles you have faced and how you managed. Tell them who helped you. Make asking for help easy.

We had a foster child visit for a weekend. He likes to build things but can be easily frustrated if there is a challenge. He will say he "cannot do it" and give up. I asked him if he had ever built anything like it before and he said yes. But he said that I helped him with that one. I asked if he thought I would help him again. In fact, I said I would help if he just asked me. I set up the expectancy that I would help if he would ask. That left room for him to do things on his own and ask when it got too difficult. We need to teach, inspire and encourage others. Go as far as you can on your own but know I stand ready, willing and able to help when you need it. Just like your Heavenly Father, I love you and want the best for you and will come to your aid. You are never alone! You are never in a situation where there is no way out. God always makes a way! It might not be clear to you at that moment. No matter what your age, there are those who care for you and will help if you just ask. Behold, He who keeps Israel [and you are his descendant] shall neither slumber nor sleep. He watches over you directly and through His angels, your parents and friends. Reach out! There are many who will give you aid. You are not alone!

Father, You knew we could not be perfect, so You made a way for us to do our best but come to You when we fail. Failure is not final. It is just a stepping stone to success. Remind us to turn to You. Show us what You would have us do with the gifts You have given. Uphold us when we don't achieve what we think is Your will. Encourage us to try again or try something different. Lead us in the way we should go. Write Your story on our hearts. In Your name we pray! Amen!

# OCTOBER 20  A SONG IN MY HEART

Prayer/Praise

Isaiah 12:1-3 (NIV)

*In that day you will say: "I will praise you, LORD. Although you were angry with me, your anger has turned away and you have comforted me. ² Surely God is my salvation; I will trust and not be afraid. The LORD, the LORD himself, is my strength and my defense; he has become my salvation." ³ With joy you will draw water from the wells of salvation.*

Sing to the Lord! Sometimes, I wake up in the morning with a song in my heart and on my lips. I listen to Star99.1, our local Christian radio station, and I love the songs. For me, one is better than the next. They each touch me and make me want to praise the Lord. They are reminders of all He has done for me.

Isaiah tells us we will praise the Lord. Even though we go astray, the Lord still loves us and has become our Salvation. We can trust in Him. No matter what, He is our strength and defense. We drink from wells of salvation. No wonder we can sing praises to the Lord! Look at what He has done for us. After all the things we have done poorly, He still loves us.

There is nothing like love to put a song in your heart. Knowing what God has planned for you and that He loves you is reason to sing. Is there a song in your heart? Are you feeling God's love for you? Is He your strength and defense? The offer is you may draw water from the wells of salvation with joy. Are you doing that? Is there joy in your life? It is available to you. God offers you comfort. You are holy, righteous and redeemed all by His grace alone. You have done nothing to earn your status. It is a marvelous gift from your Creator; the One who loves you!

Knowing all God has done for you should make you want to break out in song. This is such good news that you could stand on a street corner and burst into song. So why don't you? Because it would be weird, that's why. However, you could have a smile on your face and a song in your heart. Your attitude could be so good that people you meet would wonder why you are so happy. You have a lot to be happy about. Is your wonderful attitude contagious? Do people encounter you and long for what you have? Do you bring light into any room you enter? Why not share the comfort you draw from the wells of salvation the Lord has given you?

Lord, You are our comfort and strength and have become our Salvation. Thank You that Your anger lasts only a short while but Your love goes on forever! You said we can trust You and not be afraid. The world is a scary place and it terrifies us at times. Comfort us as You promised. Help us to stand firm in our faith and Your love. In Jesus name we pray! Amen!

## OCTOBER 21    WHAT WILL BE THE OUTCOME
Attitude

Job 3:25-26 (NKJV)
²⁵ For the thing I greatly feared has come upon me, And what I dreaded has happened to me.
²⁶ I am not at ease, nor am I quiet; I have no rest, for trouble comes."

That which I have feared has come upon me. After all, you bring about what you think about. If you focus on something, you move in that direction. When you are driving, if you focus on a pothole, you will hit it. On what do you think you should focus?

Job tells us about his story. He had fears and because he focused on them, they came to pass. He tells us what the outcome will be. Can we learn from his experience? I think we can.

In my work with computers, I face a lot of challenges. I come across new issues at every turn. When I think about how difficult it will be to solve, it will be difficult. I have overcome great challenges when I remember that God has given me gifts and talents to do the things He has called me to do. Philippians 4:13 (NKJV) says "¹³ I can do all things through Christ who strengthens me." Attitude is everything. Where we put our focus will determine the outcome. Whether you think you can or you think you can't, either way you are right. Look to the One who gives you the gifts and you will do fine.

So how will things turn out? Will you succeed or fail? That battle is fought inside your mind. You have already been endowed with the seeds of greatness and all the things you need to succeed. If you can keep your mind positive and remain in faith, you will come out great. When negative thoughts enter your mind, reject them. Throw them out. Fix your mind on that which is positive and rewarding. Yes, bad things can and will happen. If you remain in faith and believe that God is on your side, you will do great things in His name. And remember to give thanks for the gifts He has given you. Give glory to God for He gave you the gifts, talents and opportunity. Go out there and win for the Lord! In Jesus name we pray!

## OCTOBER 22    LET ME PRAY FOR YOU

Prayer/Praise

Luke 22:32 (NKJV)

*But I have prayed for you [Simon], that your faith should not fail; and when you have returned to Me, strengthen your brethren.*

Prayer is the most powerful tool in our arsenal. We overlook this opportunity to speak with God and ask His guidance. Jesus did it. Prayer is the source of our strength. It also involves active listening.

Luke tells us of Jesus' conversation with Peter in which He tells Peter that Satan wanted to tempt him and lead him astray. Luke goes on to tell us that Jesus prayed for Peter's faith. The One who created the universe took the time out to pray for Peter. Jesus also prayed for all of us who would believe in Him through the disciple's teachings in John 17:20. If Jesus thought prayer was that important that He prayed for others, don't you think we should do the same?

I believe prayer is very powerful and I have always offered to pray for people. It surprises some and delights others. Years ago, I was at a client's office and the owner called me into his office to talk. It didn't sound good. He seemed upset. I thought he was unhappy with my work. When we sat down, he was vague about what was on his mind. Finally, I asked him to tell me what was troubling him. He told me his wife needed open heart surgery in the next few days and he was worried. He said something curious. After all his dancing around the issue, he said he knew I was "connected". Much to my surprise, he wanted me to pray for them. I had never kept my faith a secret but this was a twist. I asked for him to ask his wife to join us and I prayed for both of them. The surgery went well! After that, others in the same office came to me with their prayer requests. The whole atmosphere in that office improved. Prayer changes things! P.U.S.H. (Pray Until Something Happens)!

Because I believe so strongly in the power of intercessory prayer, I regularly pray for others. If someone has a challenge, I take the time to pray for them right away. I have also been known to write prayers for people and send it to them. This gives them a chance to read the prayers again when they feel the need. Prayer is powerful. Go ahead, speak with God. He awaits your call. And He *will* answer.

Thank You Father that You love us enough to wait for us to call. You said You would listen and answer if we call out to You. Thank you that You pour out Your blessing upon us daily. Quiet our souls so we can enjoy that quiet time with You. Thank you, Jesus, that You pray for us. May our prayers strengthen our brothers and sisters. Help us to pray for each other and bring glory to You through our prayers. Amen!

# OCTOBER 23   JUST DO IT

Love

James 2:17 (NKJV)

*17 Thus also faith by itself, if it does not have works, is dead.*

Do we pray too long and not act? When is the best time to take action? Do we already know what we should do from Scripture but keep praying because we want a different answer? In many cases, we know what we should do.

James called us out two thousand years ago. He said our faith would be demonstrated by the works we undertake. If you are truly a person of faith, God has already taught you what steps to take. If not, now is the time to learn. You might say you are new in your faith. Perhaps someone will buy that story. In John 13:34-35 Jesus said (NKJV) *"34 A new commandment I give to you, that you love one another; as I have loved you, that you also love one another. 35 By this all will know that you are My disciples, if you have love for one another."* How are you showing that love? I hope it is more than just prayer. I have said prayer is very powerful which is true. But sometimes, God wants you to do more than just pray. Sometimes, He wants you to feed them. Sometimes, you may have to shovel the snow or rake the leaves. The Lord has given you gifts and talents that He wants you to use for your benefit and the benefit of others. Will you use them?

It has been said that your life may be the only Bible some people ever get to read. When they are reading your life, what are they receiving? Are the things you are doing comforting others? Do you shine your light into the dark places? Is the world better for you having walked through it? I know that, at times, I wonder if I can make a difference. I think about a situation where I could offer a kind word but it may be awkward. Sometimes, I let the opportunity go by. Usually, right after missing a chance, I regret not taking the opportunity. Zig Ziglar said you can say I wish I had or I'm glad I did. I want to be the one who said I'm glad I did! How about you? Will you go through life wishing you had? Sometimes, you can recover the opportunity. If it is not complimenting someone you know, you can call them or take some other action. I urge you to go ahead and take the shot. Let people know they matter. Let them know you are the kind of person who cares. Show them the love God has placed within you. You are magnificent. Share those gifts with those around you. Shine your light! Take action, for faith without works is dead.

Lord God, You said we should love one another as You have loved us. We are not capable of such a selfless love. But help us to love the best we can. You have shown us what real love looks like. Help us to live like that. Change our hearts by Your grace! And let evidence of that grace flow to those we meet by and for You. In Your name we pray!

## OCTOBER 24   GIVE US STRENGTH TO CONTINUE
Support

1 Kings 19:7-9 (NKJV)

*⁷And the angel of the LORD came back the second time, and touched him, and said, "Arise and eat, because the journey is too great for you." ⁸So he arose, and ate and drank; and he went in the strength of that food forty days and forty nights as far as Horeb, the mountain of God. ⁹And there he went into a cave, and spent the night in that place; and behold, the word of the LORD came to him, and He said to him, "What are you doing here, Elijah?"*

You don't have to be strong all the time. Even people of faith have their down times. Elijah had just come off of a big victory against the 450 prophets of Baal where the Lord Our God had defeated them through him. But, like most of us after a big win, we draw back in fear. We worry we will never be able to do that again. We wonder if we are worthy to succeed. For various reasons, we tend to think this was a fluke and will never be seen again.

Elijah was exhausted! He stood strong for the Lord and spoke the words God had given him to Ahab the king. The King of Kings had sent Elijah to rebuke Ahab and his evil practices. Elijah used up the strength the Lord had given him. It says "And the angel of the Lord came back the second time...." It was probably the Lord Himself who came to comfort Elijah. After all, Elijah was obedient to the Lord and did all he was asked. Now God Himself came to attend to His servant. He loves us that much that He would come to our aid. After all, He sent Jesus.

Many prophets needed to rest and be refreshed and God does that for them. The Lord takes care of His own. In fact, He offers the status of His Child of God to anyone who invites Him into their heart. We may think we do not have prophets today so the Lord does not need to take care of them. That is not true. Our Pastors and those who work to build the Kingdom are the Prophets of today. It's Pastor Appreciation month. Are you supporting your Pastor? Day in and day out, they attend to their flock. They listen to all our troubles. They encourage us with words from the Lord through Scripture. They counsel us through our difficulties. They comfort us in our loss. Who is looking after them? Is it you? Do you tell them how much you appreciate them and all they do? Do you tell them how much you enjoyed the message they shared? What steps do you take to encourage them? Just like Elijah, they have their down times. They can become overwhelmed. Exhaustion can set in after a big campaign or project. When it does, will you be there to listen to them? Will you share words of encouragement? Sunday is coming! Tell them how much they mean to you. Tell them how their leading helps in your life. Encourage them as you want to be encouraged. You can be the Lord's hands and feet coming to care for His Prophets! Bring them refreshment and encourage them on their journey of service!

Thank You Lord that You care for us so much that You are willing to come to us with Your comfort. Give us courage to continue in our walk with You. Help us to hear Your whisper of comfort at our down times. Let us remember Your Word to encourage us so we can encourage others. In Your name we pray!

# OCTOBER 25    TO DREAM THE IMPOSSIBLE DREAM
Faith

Ephesians 3:20 (NKJV)
²⁰ *Now to Him who is able to do exceedingly abundantly above all that we ask or think, according to the power that works in us,*

Dreams are from God. He plants ideas in your head to get you to your destiny. Many people ignore the big dreams for fear they may not succeed. People might think the idea is crazy. That's true! But if the dream keeps coming back after you try several times to ignore it, it may be from God. If it is, there is no way to ignore it. He will keep bringing it back time and time again. It will be like someone tapping on the window to be let in that never stops tapping. It can be annoying!

Ephesians 3:20 says *"More than you can ask or imagine."* The dreams God gives are above and beyond anything you could have thought of yourself. It looks impossible. In the natural, it probably is impossible. But we serve a supernatural God and with God, all things are possible. He can open doors and make a way where it looks like there is no way. One touch of His favor and all of the obstacles in your path can disappear. He will bring people and resources to you that will help you accomplish the dream. When Noah built the ark, he did not collect all the animals. The Lord caused all the animals to come to the ark and enter two by two. When God gives the dream and you obey, He makes all things possible. Some of those dreams could be to help others; to do justly, to love mercy and to walk humbly with your God. You never know what the dream will be.

What is your dream? Are you like Don Quixote tilting at windmills but all the while knowing what is right in your heart? Joseph's dream was that he would rule a nation although he did not know the "why?". Is it a big enough dream for God to enter in with you? If the dream is too small, there is no room for God. He is a gentleman and will not barge into your life. You need to dream the impossible dream; the big dream! Something so spectacular that when you accomplish it, everyone will know that God was with you and blessed you and your dream. God *is* with you! Remember, good things take time. Keep the dream alive in your heart.

Thank You Lord for the dreams that You give us. You said that You would be with us through all things. Help us to walk in Your ways. Speak to us in dreams. Show us the destiny You have planned for us and lead us in that direction. In Your name we pray! Amen!

## OCTOBER 26   JOY WILL COME IN THE MORNING
Failure

### Psalm 30:5 (NKJV)
*5 For His anger is but for a moment, His favor is for life;*
*Weeping may endure for a night, But joy comes in the morning.*

What frightens you? What makes you sad? Is it overwhelming? Many times, things look way worse than they are and we cannot see a way through. Sometimes, the losses are great and we become discouraged. There are times when no one seems to care. I think that could be worst of all. Those are the times that grieve the Holy Spirit! Have you done something wrong? Are you afraid God will never forgive you? Not to worry! You are not the first and you will not be the last.

Psalm 30 tells us God can and will become angry with you. It goes on to say that His anger is but for a moment and His favor is for life. You may be sad at the moment when facing the consequences of your choice but, this too shall pass. Tomorrow is another day and the sunrise can bring new joy of living. Things look scary in the dark but the dawn brings now hope and joy.

It also means He will not stay angry. I think it is more like disappointment than anger. He is disappointed that you made that poor choice and did not follow His advice. He has given you all you need to know in His Word. Have you hidden His word in your heart that you might not sin against Him? A sin against God is suffering for you. He leads you in the way that is best for you. Will you follow?

At times, everything may seem like it is against you. The news is bad. The economy is deteriorating. People are apathetic to our situation. Everyone seems to only care about themselves. Our world is a dark place. It seems as you are fighting on every front! When the outlook is not so good, try the up-look. It is always better. How you approach the situation really matters. Attitude is everything. As believers, we need to remember that war has already been won at the Cross and we are on the winning team. We have won the World Series! Yes, there are still battles that we face but we know the outcome. It is like watching a recorded sports event where you know your team won. You are able to watch the plays without a worry. That is the way God wants you to live! Don't worry! Just live and enjoy the plays. You know the destination already. Now just enjoy the ride.

Father we thank You that You have already won the war for us and that all we need to do is follow Your lead. You have given us all we need to live blessed and fulfilled. Teach us Your ways that we might live in the great joy You bring each morning. In Jesus name we pray! Amen!

# OCTOBER 27    I'M OUTTA HERE
Relationships

Galatians 2:20 (NKJV)

*20 I have been crucified with Christ; it is no longer I who live, but Christ lives in me; and the life which I now live in the flesh I live by faith in the Son of God, who loved me and gave Himself for me.*

Years ago, I was a different person. My level of tolerance was lower. I was more demanding and lacked patience. I wanted it done right and now! If things did not go my way, I would leave. Things have changed. I realize now that my way is not the best way. God's way is best. I am not in charge. I need to wait for His timing.

Galatians 2:20 speaks of a drastic change. What has happened is that those who are in Christ have crucified their old selves and allowed their new self, which resembles Christ, to come to the forefront. Instead of self-interest, we try to look out for the welfare of others. The Son of God loves us so much that He gave Himself up for us so we could be transformed and have sin removed. Sin is what causes the darkness in our souls to foster greed, selfishness and lust. That causes everything to be about us and what we want and need. Well it's not about you. It's about Him!

I recently went to a meeting where I was asked to venture an opinion on a policy that was being developed for the organization. We read the draft and were asked to send comments to the team that was working on the development. Since I have experience in the area the policy was covering, I shared my opinion and said I would do some research and forward the comments. The next day, I wrote a brief e-mail outlining what I felt would be needed hoping to get into more details and a conversation with the team. I got back an e-mail which I felt criticized me for venturing my opinion. The old me was the first to respond. I thought to myself I did not need this noise. I have valuable experience to share but if they don't want to hear it, I will take my bat and ball and go home.

Fortunately, the Holy Spirit now resides within me. He said just put it aside for now and think about how you want to handle things. Is that really what the e-mail meant? Could there be a misunderstanding? Is giving up going to benefit the people we want to serve? You see, my old self had the tendency to give up too soon. At the least resistance, I would walk away. You cannot grow the Kingdom by giving up! What is the objective and how can I move in that direction? The objective was to develop a great policy that would work for all concerned. To do that, I have to hang in there and ask the team members questions so I can better understand their position. From there, I can offer the knowledge the Spirit gives me and build a relationship that will grow the Kingdom. It is built one relationship at a time. I wrote back that there might be a misunderstanding and I would like to have a conversation rather than e-mail so we can build a spirit of cooperation and serve others through our work.

Christ is changing me from the inside out. I am different. He is making me better. He is removing all those rough edges; the pride, the anger, the attitude and replacing them with humility and a spirit of cooperation. He can do that for you. I have learned

387

relationships are the most important thing. Growing together with my brothers and sisters in Christ is what God calls us to do. It is how we can build the Kingdom. When non-believers see your actions, what do they see? Are you setting the example God wants you to set? Would they say to themselves "I want to live like that"? You can put off the old self and put on the new. If you are crucified with Christ, you lose the old self but He gives you a glorious new self a little bit at a time. You will notice you are more peaceful. You have more hope. You will develop a sense of joy. Things will go wrong but you won't get upset. What has happened? The Spirit has come to live in you and make you new. You will now live by faith. You understand God is directing your life and it all becomes easier. Follow His lead. Be at peace.

I can't believe You gave Yourself up for us; for me! Who are we that You are mindful of us? Why do You care so much? Help us to live lives worthy of the sacrifice You made for us. Change us Lord by Your Spirit which now lives inside us. Let us live lives of faith in You. In Your name we pray!

# OCTOBER 28    THE LIGHT OF THE WORLD
Encouragement

Matthew 5:14-16 (NKJV)

*14 "You are the light of the world. A city that is set on a hill cannot be hidden. 15 Nor do they light a lamp and put it under a basket, but on a lampstand, and it gives light to all who are in the house. 16 Let your light so shine before men, that they may see your good works and glorify your Father in heaven.*

The light of the world is in you. Jesus said so! He has just finished teaching the crowds from the hillside about how to live your life His way. This was known as the Beatitudes. When you do it His way, it all works out for the best. But what if you live your life as He guides and you keep it all to yourself? What if you don't shine the light Jesus has given you? It is from Him you know. The light.

In these verses, Jesus is telling us to show our light. He explains we cannot really hide our light nor should we want to hide it. He tells us to put the light up on a stand so it will benefit all who are in the house. I think He was referring to the house of the Lord. You are of the House of the Lord. The light will benefit you, too. But Jesus tells us to shine that light so others will see. Do you think He wants your light to attract people?

How do you live your life? What does it mean to shine that light? Could a smile be shining light? When you do things for others, you are shining. Go ahead and give out smiles. Let your face glow with the glory of the Lord that is in you. Listen to people. Ask how they are and listen to their answer. People are walking around discouraged. Encourage them. When you walk in a room, light it up with your whole demeanor. Leave every place you go brighter than you found it. Do good deeds that the Lord sent you to do long in advance. Visit a sick person. Pray for the weary. Make a difference. Invest in people. The benefits are amazing.

When you shine your light into the dark places, you drive out the darkness. You dispel discouragement and create hope. The world needs hope. We all need something to look forward to on a daily basis. This positive attitude will also make *your* day go better. Live with a sense of joy that excites. Make people wonder what you are up to! Joy is contagious. Go ahead and spread it around and see how things improve. The situation may not change but, when attitudes are good, you will more easily get through any challenge. You have already been given everything you need to succeed. Now, shine your light!

Thank You Lord that You are the light of the world. You have given that light to us. Help us to shine light into all the dark places and dispel darkness and despair. You said we are the light of the world. Thank you that You have given us Your light. Help us to do good works that bring you glory. In Your name we pray! Amen!

## OCTOBER 29    DO YOU CELEBRATE YOURSELF
Attitude

Romans 14:19 (NKJV)
*¹⁹ Therefore let us pursue the things which make for peace and the things by which one may edify another.*

What is all this talk about edifying one another? Or is there enough talk that builds people up. I will go even further. I would proffer that you should be building yourself up as well. Too many of us doubt our worth and don't accomplish what we were destined to do. We were made for so much more than our current state.

Paul tells us to seek peace. How can we do that? One way is by looking at others with the intention to find the best in them. It is said "seek and you shall find." What is it you seek? Do you look for the good in others? Zig Ziglar said "the best way to get a chip off someone's shoulder is to let them take a bow." If you compliment another in sincerity, how will that make them feel? It will build up a relationship. Even if you don't like someone, you can show respect and admiration for things they have done.

We have a tendency to look at that need to be appreciated but overlook our accomplishments. We have a full inventory of our shortcomings but few keep a list of the good things we have done. Why not start a Wins list? The other day, I was at breakfast with a friend. He shared a story of his niece being offered a new job within her company. Her reputation for good work had preceded her. She was not doing well in her current position because of the down economy and the market segment she currently supported. She saw it as her fault. This other Director saw her abilities and assets. She only saw her shortcomings. Our culture looks at the negatives. Let us be counter cultural and seek the good!

Today, I am asking you to look for the good in yourself and others. Focus on what you have and not what you lack. You have been given gifts and talents. Use them! You bring about what you think about. Think about good things. Philippians 4:8 says
*"⁸ Finally, brethren, whatever things are true, whatever things are noble, whatever things are just, whatever things are pure, whatever things are lovely, whatever things are of good report, if there is any virtue and if there is anything praiseworthy—meditate on these things."*
Meditate on these things is what you are asked to do. Look for the good. Use your talents to God's glory. When you work in your areas of strength, things will go well. Sure, there are times when God will put you in situations of challenge to grow your gifts. These may be gifts you do not realize you have. He knows what He is doing. Look at it as an opportunity to learn something new. See yourself as capable of accomplishing a new goal. And when you do, celebrate yourself and all God has called you to and given you!

Father, You said we can do all things through You because You give us strength. You said You would never leave nor forsake us. Be with us today as we face new things and help us to accomplish old things as well. Remind us we can bring glory to You through the work of our hands. Help us to see all we are in You. Give us confidence that You have created us in Your image for a specific purpose which You will bring to fruition. In Your name we pray! Amen!

## OCTOBER 30   MY FAITH IS WEAK
Prayer/Praise

Luke 22:31-32 (NKJV)

*31 And the Lord said, "Simon, Simon! Indeed, Satan has asked for you, that he may sift you as wheat. 32 But I have prayed for you, that your faith should not fail; and when you have returned to Me, strengthen your brethren."*

Do you feel like you are always under a dark cloud? Are the challenges you face daunting? At every turn, there is another obstacle for you to overcome. And, at this point, you are growing weary. How can you face another challenge? Haven't the ones before been enough? Don't I deserve a break? Come on God, help me out here, will ya?

Not everything that comes against you is from God. Sure, He will use it to refine you. He will turn it into something good for you but it may not have been Him who sent it in the first place. When Jesus had been baptized by John, the heavens opened and God said Jesus was His son. Right after that, Jesus was led into the wilderness to be tempted by Satan. Jesus passed the test. Will you?

1 Corinthians 10:13 says *"13 No temptation has overtaken you except such as is common to man; but God is faithful, who will not allow you to be tempted beyond what you are able, but with the temptation will also make the way of escape, that you may be able to bear it".*

Temptation is from the evil one who is trying to separate you from the Lord. You have a choice. You can listen to the accuser or the Truth of God. When presented with situations, you can ask what Jesus would have you do. It is all revealed in His Word. But what if you are a new believer and you don't know what is in His Word? Pray for help from the Holy Spirit. Ask a faithful believer to help and pray for you. Your conscience is from the Lord. You know what you should do and what you should not do. Temptations are *common to mankind*. Everyone has them. It is best to avoid a tempting situation. If you have a drinking problem, do not apply for a job in a bar. Instead, ask God for a better opportunity. Ask Him to give you what He wants you to have. Are you weak in your faith? That's OK! God is strong and will come to you aid if you just ask. Go ahead! Ask Him! He will hear and answer. And don't be afraid to lean on your praying friends and family for support. They love you and will hold you up in prayer. And *when you have returned* [to your faith], strengthen your brethren. He expects you to persevere and to be an example to others. You can do this!

So, should you take an opportunity that is presented just because you need that job? Is it God's will and desire for your life? Maybe it is just a temptation from you know who. There is a way out. Look for it! I have learned to stop and look. I don't move too quickly. I ask God what He wants and go with Him. Shouldn't you?

Father, I thank You that You hear our prayers and answer our call. You want what is best for us. Help us to be strong and courageous and wait upon You for our answers. Silence the voice of the accuser Lord. Give us discernment to hear Your voice alone and act upon Your Word. We need Your Spirit to help us know You. Walk with us today and every day. In Jesus name we pray! Amen!

## OCTOBER 31   THE VALUE OF A FRIEND
Relationships

Ecclesiastes 4:9-12 (NKJV)

*9 Two are better than one, Because they have a good reward for their labor.*
*10 For if they fall, one will lift up his companion. But woe to him who is alone when he falls, For he has no one to help him up. 11 Again, if two lie down together, they will keep warm; But how can one be warm alone? 12 Though one may be overpowered by another, two can withstand him. And a threefold cord is not quickly broken.*

Do you have a friend on whom you can count? I do! I have several. In this world of people who ask how you are but don't listen for the answer, it is rare to have such a friend who will help you with something. Our culture teaches we are self-made and independent. That may be true to an extent but we were designed to live in community. God said, *"It is not good for the man to be alone...."* Our Creator designed us to be with others for support, companionship and working together. My expression is two people working together can accomplish as much as five people working alone.

Solomon was considered the wisest man in the world. He said two are better than one *because* they have a good reward for their labor. He goes on to tell us two can help each other, stay warm and protect each other. That is quite a benefit for all concerned. You see, our Creator knows what He is doing. It is a great design! But why does Solomon say a *threefold* cord is not easily broken?

I have such a friend. The other day, I started a project that is definitely a two-person job. I was doing a network wiring job where we needed to remove and replace a whole bunch of wire. I asked my friend Fred if he could help. Of course, he said yes. There are many in my life who rely on me to help them but are always too busy when I am the one in need. Fred makes time for me. We scheduled for 8 to 1 but the job wasn't completed by 1 so Fred stayed. It is great to spend time with him. He isn't watching the clock looking for the end of his commitment. He is truly there to help. And help he does! Working together makes the day go smoother and makes it a lot more fun. Fred is pretty quiet but when he speaks it is either wise or funny. We laugh together. Fred lifts me up professionally, spiritually and emotionally, too. It was a great day. I am sitting here thinking we should spend more time together because it would be good for both of us. Fred is my Brother in Christ.

Solomon said a *threefold* cord is not easily broken. He only mentions two people in the previous verses. Why a threefold cord now? I believe that the Creator always planned and has worked with His creation. When these two companions work together, God enters into that relationship with them becoming the third cord. Jesus said that whenever two or more are gathered in His name, He is right there with them. Working together is being gathered in His name. Ephesians 2:10 says *"10 For we are His workmanship, created in Christ Jesus for good works, which God prepared beforehand that we should walk in them."* God planned these works for us to do. Why not walk in them with Him?

Father, You established the work of our hands. Isn't it right for us to do them as if unto You? Lead us to the works You prepared in advance for us to do and gather us to the people with whom we should work. I thank You for my companions including my Brother in Christ, Fred. Please give others such a friend that their lives can be blessed too! In Your name I pray!

## NOVEMBER 1    GOD IS IN THE RESTORATION BUSINESS
Faith

Luke 8:43-44 (NKJV)

*⁴³ Now a woman, having a flow of blood for twelve years, who had spent all her livelihood on physicians and could not be healed by any, ⁴⁴ came from behind and touched the border of His garment. And immediately her flow of blood stopped.*

This woman had been to every doctor and place trying to find a cure for her bleeding. So far, nothing had worked. Was Jesus her last resort? What did she think He could do for her? Had she heard of others being healed? I don't know what she was thinking other than getting to Jesus. She was focused! And touch Him she did.

Luke tells us this woman had the issue for twelve years and no one was able to heal her. She did not even speak with Him. All she did was touch His garment and she was healed. The chapter goes on to say *⁴⁵ And Jesus said, "Who touched Me?" ... ⁴⁶ But Jesus said, "Somebody touched Me, for I perceived power going out from Me." ⁴⁷ Now when the woman saw that she was not hidden, she came trembling; and falling down before Him, she declared to Him in the presence of all the people the reason she had touched Him and how she was healed immediately. ⁴⁸ And He said to her, "Daughter, be of good cheer; your faith has made you well. Go in peace."*

She was healed! You see, God is in the Restoration Business. They did not have a conversation. There was no discussion of her needs. In fact, all she did was believe Jesus would heal her and touch His garment. All it took was a touch. And Jesus knew power had gone out from Him through that touch. Do you think He felt her touch His cloak? Probably not. But He knew. The Creator of the universe knew in advance she would try to touch Him. If healing can come from just touching Him, what would happen if you got to know Him and He touched you? What would a full relationship with Jesus yield? Would it bring peace? Would it bring courage? Would it bring strength? All that and more! Why try to do this all on your own when Living Water and all the benefits of Christ are yours for the asking? Jesus is willing.

What is going on in your life? Are you in need of some kind of healing? God is willing and able to heal you no matter what the affliction. He is waiting to hear from you. Or, all you need do is draw close and reach out and touch Him. He is still there within reach. Put out your hand and see if He will not still heal you today.

Lord, thank You that You are still in the Restoration business. We come to you in our brokenness and You calm and heal us. You said You would always be with us. Help us to know You are there and feel Your Presence. Walk with us as we struggle and show us Your ways. Remind us You still offer us Your awesome power. You offer restoration. Give us the courage to reach out our hands to You!

Be of good cheer and go in peace. Your God loves you! Amen!

# NOVEMBER 2  MERCY DOESN'T MAKE SENSE
Grace

Psalm 51:1-2 (NKJV)
*Have mercy upon me, O God, According to Your lovingkindness;*
*According to the multitude of Your tender mercies, Blot out my transgressions. ² Wash me*
*thoroughly from my iniquity, And cleanse me from my sin.*

Why should God have mercy on any of us? All of us have sinned and fallen short of the glory of God. He has absolutely no reason to grant us grace. There is nothing we can do to earn it or deserve it yet He gives us grace and mercy daily.

David asked God for mercy according to God's goodness and not on his own merit. David knew he did not deserve mercy but he still asked. David knew the goodness of the Lord. The Lord is willing to accept our confession and restore us. It is not dependent on our merit but upon His grace.

Grace and mercy do not make sense. We will just fail again. Why bother forgiving and restoring us? He does it because He came to seek and save the lost. We are lost. The human heart is deceitful. Jeremiah 17:9 says ⁹ *"The heart is deceitful above all things, And desperately wicked; Who can know it?".* But God knows it. Yet He still sees the good He planted in each of us and works daily to grow those seeds. Your Creator put seeds of greatness in you and wants them to blossom. Therefore, He makes you over through His grace. When you fall short of the mark, He picks you up and dusts you off and helps you to try again. My Dad used to say "you'll do better next time!" That is just like our Heavenly Father. He knows you will do better next time. That is why He restores you. He *wants* you to succeed. He knew from the beginning that we would need work. He was prepared!

So why does He give us so many chances? Because He loves us! We are His handiwork made in His image and likeness. His mercy and loving kindness surround us. His grace is sufficient for His power is made perfect in our weakness. He overlooks our imperfections and leads us in His ways. And each time we try, we get a little better. He wants you to do justice and love mercy and walk humbly with Him. Will you try again to walk in His ways?

Mercy doesn't make sense. We do not get what we deserve. We deserve punishment but He gives grace. All our righteousness is like filthy rags (Isaiah 64:6) in light of God's perfection. Yet He still cares for us. There are some mysteries we cannot understand. Love and mercy are among those. They are God's free gift. Will you accept the gift? Will you extend to others what has been given to you? In Jesus name I pray for and with you! Amen!

# NOVEMBER 3    ATTITUDE IS EVERYTHING
Attitude

Ephesians 4:2-5 (ESV)
*With all humility and gentleness, with patience, bearing with one another in love, eager to maintain the unity of the Spirit in the bond of peace. There is one body and one Spirit—just as you were called to the one hope that belongs to your call— one Lord, one faith, one baptism,*

I have a hat that says "Attitude is Everything!" I believe that to be the case. I would rather hire a waiter or waitress with a good attitude and teach them the skills they would need than hire someone for their skills whose attitude sucks. It is said everyone brightens a room: some by entering and some by leaving. Which are you?

Paul tells us we should live with humility and gentleness. He adds patience and love to the mix. With those four characteristics at the forefront of our demeanor, it should be a great day. Unity seems to be a recurring theme in God's desire for us. Our attitude toward one another will either create unity or discord. Which would be a better way to live?

Are you eager to maintain unity of the Spirit? Do you consider the needs of others above your own? Are you patient and kind? Do you look out for yourself first at the expense of others? Since most of us need to work to maintain our lives, would a good atmosphere at work benefit all concerned? Ephesians 6:7 (NIV) says *"7 Serve wholeheartedly, as if you were serving the Lord, not people,..."* An attitude of service will create a positive atmosphere. You can make a difference.

A friend helped me the other day because he wanted to help. I had a job to do which required two people. I did not have to constantly tell him what needed to be done. He went looking for a way to make a difference. His attitude was to help Bob. And help he did. The day went quickly. The job got done and we had fun. It could not have been better. Skills can be taught. Attitude is part of our character. How you approach a task makes all the difference in the world. Do you *have* to do it or do you *get* to do it? Be thankful that you have the ability. Many do not! God has blessed you with the chance to enjoy a sense of accomplishment. Let an attitude of gratitude flavor everything you do!

*A willing Spirit changes the drudgery of duty into a labor of love.* David Roper

Father thank You that You give us the chance to glorify You through the work of our hands. Help us see joy in every opportunity. Open our hearts and minds to Your will for our lives so we see each task as a way to glorify Your holy name. Grant us humility and the gift of service to others. In Your name we pray! Amen!

# NOVEMBER 4   BUSINESS IS PERSONAL
Attitude

Leviticus 19:13 (NKJV)
<sup></sup> *13 'You shall not cheat your neighbor, nor rob him. The wages of him who is hired shall not remain with you all night until morning.*

Some people say Business is Business. Is that their way of saying they can set their values aside in order to complete a transaction at any cost? People use the excuse that business is business to justify actions they take which they know are not the best.

In the book of Leviticus, God tells us not to cheat our neighbor. Also, we are to pay wages promptly. The Lord wants us to do justly. Getting ahead at someone else's expense violates God's will.

Can you separate your personal values from your business values? Is it OK to do whatever it takes to make a buck? Would you want someone to lose their ethics when they are waiting on you? As a follower of Jesus, I try to live by His Word and treat others like I want to be treated. Years ago, I decided I wanted to take my beliefs and values into the business world with me and live like Jesus taught me to live. Many in the world do not want to hear the truth even if it is spoken in love.

My friend Jon teaches a seminar called Business is Personal. He, like me, figured out we cannot be one kind of person and a different kind of business person. When you stick by your values, given you by God, you act in a truthful and consistent manner. It takes time but people learn they can trust you. Will you be perfect? Absolutely not! But you can accept responsibility and make good on your shortcomings. The other day, I worked on a network wiring project. I goofed and drilled a hole through the neighbor's wall. They were gone for the day so I could not tell them but I was returning the next day and would let them know then. When I came in, they had discovered the hole. I told them it was my fault and I would take care of it. I think they were shocked that I took responsibility. Tomorrow, I will be patching their wall. I will make things right. That is what the Lord asks of us. He asks us to do justly, to love mercy and to walk humbly with our God. The neighbor is entitled to be made whole by my repair of their wall. My values demand it. Now, I will do it! It's my reputation on the line. You see, business is personal. Oh yeah, you can be sure they will brag to their friends about this crazy guy who drilled a hole in their wall but then came back to make things right. I might even get a referral out of it. Do not cheat your neighbor and take care of things promptly. It will give you peace and a good reputation. Proverbs 22:1 (NKJV) says *"A good name is to be chosen rather than great riches, Loving favor rather than silver and gold."* It tells people who you are and whose you are. You gain that reputation by following God's word which will never lead you astray.

Lord, thank You that You lead us in Your ways and help us live honorable lives. Help us to bring the values You taught us into our everyday business and all of life. Teach us how to love our neighbors and respect everyone. In Your name we pray! Amen!

# NOVEMBER 5 WHO IS THIS GUY
Faith

Luke 24:32 (ESV)
*They said to each other, "Did not our hearts burn within us while he talked to us on the road, while he opened to us the Scriptures?"*

Sometimes, we meet people and there is something special about them. We can't explain it but they have a quality that is different. There is a glow about them. It is like they have a power within that is finding its way out. What do you think is the source of their power? Is it their own or does it come from beyond them? Usually, people who have a glow have Christ inside and He is radiating out.

In Luke 24, two of the disciples were walking on the road to Emmaus when they encountered Jesus. They did not recognize Him but they sensed something special. Their "hearts burned within them." What can make your heart burn within you? Only the power of Christ!

As I walk the Spiritual Journey with my Lord, I have become more passionate about Him. When I think about all He has done for me, my heart *burns* within me. Any time I get to talk about Him, something wells up inside me. Words come to me that inspire me and others. These words are not my own. I don't always recognize them. They are inspired and are given to me. When I get to pray publicly, words are given me that I might fearlessly proclaim the Gospel! Power comes into and through me. His power.

As you walk on the road, are you meeting people who inspire you? Do you recognize a certain glow that comes from them? Are you the one who inspires others? You have seeds of greatness within you! I believe both things should occur. Iron sharpens iron. We were not meant to live and work alone. We were designed to live in community because we can encourage each other. The disciples only recognized Jesus and His inspiration after He broke the bread when He left them. I am asking you to be more aware of His presence in your life. He promised He would never leave nor forsake you. He is fully present in your life. Our chief purpose in life is to glorify God and enjoy Him forever. You must recognize He is there in order to enjoy Him. He is with you in all you do; good and bad. When the Lord walks with you on the road, you will have a true companion and your heart will *burn* within you!

Lord, help us to fan the flames that burn within us for You! You inspire passion, love, kindness, justice and mercy. By Your grace, let us live lives that glorify you. Let us come into and remain in Your presence that we may enjoy You each day. Inspire us through Your Word. Remain close to us so we can feel and enjoy Your presence. In Jesus name we pray!

# NOVEMBER 6   ALWAYS LOOK FORWARD
## Quality of Life

Philippians 3:12-14 (NKJV) Pressing Toward the Goal

*12 Not that I have already attained, or am already perfected; but I press on, that I may lay hold of that for which Christ Jesus has also laid hold of me. 13 Brethren, I do not count myself to have apprehended; but one thing I do, forgetting those things which are behind and reaching forward to those things which are ahead, 14 I press on toward the goal to win the prize for which God has called me heavenward in Christ Jesus.*

There are many people in life who are always looking back. If only I had...I could have...I should have... Zig Ziglar said you can say "I wish I had or I'm glad I did!" Which one of those do you want to be? When you get to the end of your earthly life, do you want to be full of regret? I don't! I want to have said what I really wanted to say and have done what God calls me to do. I tell people I love them. Nursing homes are filled with people who live in regret and bitterness. I don't want to be one of them. How about you?

The Apostle Paul knows he is not perfect. In fact, he realizes how flawed he is but thanks God for His grace. In his past, he persecuted God's people and rejected Christ. That could have been his definition; a man against God. But Christ appeared to him on the road to Damascus and his life was changed forever. Not only that, your life and my life are changed. Paul teaches us to let go of the past and press on toward the goal. Christ is that prize. He waits for you. Reach forward for the prize!

You cannot change the past. We have all made mistakes. The secret is to use the mistakes to learn for the next opportunity. Why not think about how Jesus would want you to handle something and strive to do it His way in the future. You are a Child of the King. Why not live in a way to bring Him glory? I know, you have this worthiness thing going on! That comes from the evil one. Drop that at the foot of the Cross and live as God intended. You are anointed, empowered, holy, righteous, redeemed, triumphant and victorious! Why not live that way? You say I don't feel victorious. Are you living by your feelings and what people say about you? Why not take a look in His best-selling book and see what He says about you? It is all in there. You are fearfully and wonderfully made! God says so. You are an heir to the throne. Reach up and adjust your crown.

2 Corinthians 5:17 (NKJV) says *"17 Therefore, if anyone is in Christ, he is a new creation; old things have passed away; behold, all things have become new."*

Stop living in the past. What does God call you to do today? How can you encourage others and bring glory to God? You cannot encourage another without some of that spilling over onto you. You will be blessed by being a blessing! Today is a new day. Be so positive and encouraging that it will make people wonder what you are up to! Keep them guessing as to your motive. God, you and I know it is to bring glory to Him and Him to them! The future awaits! Press on!

Father, we thank You that You give us grace to let go of the past and reach toward the future. Forgive our past mistakes and guide us in the way You would have us go.

Help us to lay down the burdens that keep us from doing Your will. Empower us to build others up. Show us the blessing that comes with doing Your will. In Jesus name we pray! Amen!

# NOVEMBER 7   I'M NOT READY
Faith

Exodus 4:10-16 Selected (NIV)

*¹⁰ Moses said to the LORD, "Pardon your servant, Lord. I have never been eloquent, neither in the past nor since you have spoken to your servant. I am slow of speech and tongue." ¹¹ The LORD said to him, "Who gave human beings their mouths? Who makes them deaf or mute? Who gives them sight or makes them blind? Is it not I, the LORD? ¹² Now go; I will help you speak and will teach you what to say." ¹³ But Moses said, "Pardon your servant, Lord. Please send someone else." ¹⁴ Then the LORD's anger burned against Moses and he said, "What about your brother, Aaron the Levite?... ¹⁶ He will speak to the people for you, and it will be as if he were your mouth and as if you were God to him."*

How many of us think we are not ready to do things? God promised to never leave nor forsake you. If He called you to something for which He had not prepared you, it would be leaving you alone. Since we know His word is true, that cannot happen so He has already prepared you whether you know it or not.

Moses spoke with God directly. God told him to go to Pharaoh and demand the release of the Israelite people. Moses decided to offer excuses instead. He told God he was not prepared to speak on God's behalf and asked God to send someone else. But God doesn't take no for an answer. God said He would help Moses speak and teach him what to say. God always prepares you!

Years ago, I asked my men's group one time "What would you do if someone was asking questions about Christ and it seemed they wanted to establish a relationship with Him?" One of the guys said "I would go get the Pastor." The great Commission calls us to make disciples of all nations. It does not say go get the Pastor. Shouldn't you be prepared to answer the questions and lead them to Christ?

You are probably thinking you are not prepared. Your story is the most powerful testimony anyone could have. You don't need to practice some fancy dialogue about how people can learn about and accept Jesus. Just tell about how He has made a difference in your life. What is new? What is different? How does this relationship make your life better? Are you calmer and more peaceful? What was your life like before Jesus came into your heart? What difference did He make? That is all anyone needs to know.

My short story is simple. I was riding along in my car thinking about a situation at work that I felt I could not do and trying to figure out a way to tell my boss why not. All of a sudden, I heard myself say it is not the Christian thing to do. At the time, I was not a Christian. So why was this reason revealed to me? Because God had a plan. Right then I knew that Jesus was knocking at the door to my heart asking to be let in and I had to decide. I opened the door but not without apprehension. What would this mean in my life? What would change? How would I tell my Jewish family? That was nineteen + years ago and it has been a fantastic ride ever since. That's my story and I am sticking to it!

Jesus is mine and I am His. That wasn't so hard! I am a new creation in Him. Most notably, I am losing the need to argue. I am learning to live for God and those God loves. Isn't that reason enough to allow Him in to your heart? Jesus is knocking. Go ahead, open the door! And when others ask about your peace and joy, tell them your story.

Lord, thank You for knocking at the door of our hearts. Give us the courage to open the door. Let Your Spirit remind us that You never leave nor forsake us. Knowing that, reassure us that You have already given us everything we need to accomplish whatever You ask of us. No more excuses! Lead us to the people to whom You wish to speak today and give us the words they need to hear. Help us to draw people to You! In Jesus name we pray! Amen!

# NOVEMBER 8   WHY DO I WRITE THESE

Encouragement

Romans 15:4 (NIV)

*"For everything that was written in the past was written to teach us, so that through endurance and the encouragement of the Scriptures we might have hope."*

Why am I writing this? I want you to be encouraged. I have been inspired to do so! Our world is a dark place and evil abounds. Negativity is everywhere and people are losing hope. The suicide rate is up. Drug addiction is rampant. People are losing jobs and not being able to find another. Things are not looking good. I write because there are too many people unhappy and unfulfilled. Are you one of them? Walk with me as we learn, together, how much we are loved and how wonderfully we were made! Our hope is in the Lord!

The Scriptures were given to teach us the best way to go and to encourage us. A lot of bad things happen in the Bible but a lot of good endings are brought out of those things. God wants us to know that bad things will happen to good people. But He also wants us to know He will use them for our good. He shows us He is able to make it all right in the end. Most importantly, He has already won the victory over sin and death for us through His Son. We are victorious through Jesus. There is hope!

I wanted to encourage you at a time when many need encouragement. In this world you will have trouble but, fear not because Jesus has overcome the world. No matter the situation, God has a plan for your good. If you will be patient and remain in faith, He will work out His plan. When it looks like there is no way out, God will make a way for you. He loves you that much.

I am in the same boat as you. I get discouraged. When I write down these thoughts which are given me, it helps me clarify my thinking. I am reminded of who I am and whose I am and what He wants for and from me and you. If you are like me (and you probably are), you are too critical of yourself. You have a tendency to forget your successes and amplify your shortcomings. Well be encouraged! As Ethel Waters said; "God don't make no junk"! You are fearfully and wonderfully made. I hope these help you live with abandon and be a light in this dark world. Let me know how you do. I know you will do marvelous things.

This, however, is a daunting endeavor. I feel the call but I am not always sure I am up to the task. I doubt myself. Pray for me also, that whenever I write, words may be given me that I might fearlessly proclaim the Gospel. Pray that I might be equipped, strengthened and empowered to run this race and manage to accomplish the task to which I am being called. Let me know if and how these words are helping you. Let me know how I can pray for you. God loves you and so do I! Be blessed!

# NOVEMBER 9   MY HELP COMES FROM YOU
### Grace and Mercy

Psalm 121:1-2 (NKJV)
*I will lift up my eyes to the hills— From whence comes my help?*
*² My help comes from the LORD, Who made heaven and earth.*

Do you think you can do things alone? Our culture teaches us we are independent but I doubt that. I used to think I could do things in my own power. With that came the responsibility of success or failure. It was all on me. I have come to lean on the Lord instead. With Him, all things are possible.

David told us where to look for our help. He knew the Lord was with him and would help him. We need to understand that truth. The One who made heaven and earth is poised, ready and willing to help us in whatever we need. All He asks is that we call on Him.

I need to learn lessons from David and rely more on the Lord than myself. I have a friend who has muscular dystrophy. She is a great example of how to live by faith. In fact, watching how she lives by faith inspires me to do better. She requires help with many things which she cannot do on her own. She has learned to rely on others and her faith. She is having surgery to help with some issues. Her life will be in the hands of doctors and nurses and her caregivers once again. The level of trust involved in this surgery is immense. I am not sure I am up to that level but she is. She inspires me!

What is your challenge? To whom do you look for encouragement and inspiration? Do you know someone of immense faith? Don't get me wrong. Even with strong faith, things seem scary. Doubt can creep in at any time. But when you look into the Light of our Lord, shadows disappear. Where will you focus your eyes? Focus on the light and darkness will run and hide. You can be held in the palms of His hands and carried through the valley. Put your faith and trust in the Lord and He will carry you through!

Lord, thanks that we can trust You to carry us when we cannot carry ourselves. You promised that You would never leave nor forsake us and you never have. Even when the clouds gather, those who wait on You can see the calm that comes after the storm. Carry us through the storms of life safely under Your wings. In Jesus name we pray! Amen!

# NOVEMBER 10    GREAT SCOTT
Encouragement


Proverbs 17:17 (NIV)

*A friend loves at all times, and a brother is born for adversity.*

I had a friend who was a great Scott. He was Bernard Scott and he had a way of making people feel important and loved. Many people are your friend when things are going well but few show up when it is time to move your office. But then, there was Bernard. Not only did he show up once, he came in a few times before we actually moved to help pack.

When I was in the process of setting up that office in 2008 Bernard visited and help me with wiring the place. On his own, he went to purchase a bottle of honey because he knew I like honey with my tea. I still have that bottle from 2008. Each morning, when I put honey in my tea, I remember Bernard Scott.

*The Adventures of Superman* was a TV show that ran from 1952-1958. Perry White, editor of the Dailey Planet, used to say "Great Scott!" as an explanation of exclamation. It was an apt description of Bernard. He was a great man because he modeled the life of Christ. He was always there to lend a hand and to encourage people. Bernard always had a kind word for those he met. We broke bread together often. I always felt better about myself when I spent time with Bernard. He was special.

Bernard was not successful as the world measures success. There was no write-up in *People* magazine or large foundation named after him but there should be. He modeled the life we are supposed to live. He treated people well and made them feel important. I want to be more like that. It is hard to follow Jesus. That is why I am so glad Jesus decided to guide Bernard and put him in my life to show what following a risen Lord looks like.

I have a voicemail I have saved for years. It is from Bernard asking me to give him a call. In the message, he did not even mention he was in the hospital. He just asked for a call back. Bernard had advanced stage cancer by then. But he just wanted to speak with his friend. I got to visit with him a few times. The cancer was getting the best of him. He was in and out of consciousness. One of our mutual friends suggested reading the Bible to him as he slept which I did. It was getting dark and Bernard was not responding so I decided to head out for the day. As I got to the door in the dark, I heard his voice say "I love you Bob!" I responded and told him I loved him too! That was the last time I saw my friend. They moved him to hospice and he passed the next day. But I know this. I will see him again! If ever there was a Mansion built in Heaven for one of Jesus followers, it was built for Bernard. Well done thou good and faithful servant! Save me a spot. We will break bread together again.

Lord, thank you for the life of Bernard Scott and the example and encouragement he was to me and so many others. He lived the life You desire for us. He was a true Brother in Christ sharing Your love. Thank you for putting him in my life and allowing me to be a part of his. Remind us, by Your Holy Spirit, of all those people in our lives who have been a blessing to us. Help us to be a blessing to others in Your name. Amen!

## NOVEMBER 11   HOW SHALL WE LIVE
### Quality of Life

Acts 4:18-20 (NKJV)

*18 So they called them and commanded them not to speak at all nor teach in the name of Jesus. 19 But Peter and John answered and said to them, "Whether it is right in the sight of God to listen to you more than to God, you judge. 20 For we cannot but speak the things which we have seen and heard."*

How then, shall we live? Who should we follow? What is the best course of action to take?

I don't think it is what people don't know that scares them; it is what they do know that really scares them. When you know about God and what He requires of you, you realize you should live for Him. I care what God thinks of my actions. I'm sure not everyone likes the things I do.

Peter and John had been arrested for speaking in the name of Jesus. The Sanhedrin was grilling them about their teaching trying to get them to stop spreading the good news. But Peter and John had seen too much. They walked by Jesus side. The learned from the Master Himself. They were witnesses to His love. There was no way they could keep quiet.

Those two were exposed to how life was supposed to be lived. They knew how God had designed the world to be because He sent His Son to set the example. Not only that, He left us a book with details too!

The world tells us to look out for number one. But God's ways are totally different. His ways are counter intuitive. They don't even make sense to our way of thinking. *Greater love has no one than this, that He would lay down His life for His friends* (John 15:13). God's way is to take care of others. To love and care for other people. The fruit of the Spirit is love, joy, peace, patience, kindness, goodness, faithfulness, gentleness, and self-control. These are how we should live. How are you doing in that department? I know I am falling short of the mark. But I also know that we can ask the Lord for help through His Spirit and He will help us. You are not alone. He will help you. You know how you are supposed to live. What stands between you and living that way? Invite the Spirit to guide you into all truth and you will receive the help you need to live a life that pleases God. And part of that life is to share the good news that has been given to you. God's love is like radiant diamonds bursting inside us, that we cannot contain. Peter and John could not hold it back. Let it out! Show others the beauty and love God has planted inside you. That is how we should live!

Father, thank You that You have planted the fruit of the Spirit within us. Help us to shine that light out to the world in Your name. Multiply our efforts. Bless our works. By Your Spirit, lead us in the way we should go and teach us how we should live. In Your name we pray! Amen!

# NOVEMBER 12    CAN I REALLY MAKE A DIFFERENCE
Faith

Psalms 96:3 (NKJV)

*"Declare His glory among the nations, His wonders among all peoples."*

Many of us go through life wondering if we can make a difference. Have you ever felt helpless? Do you think you shouldn't bother because "what difference will it make?" I am here to tell you every person makes a difference. Before the foundation of the world, God knew you would be here in this time and place and He has a plan for you. You are not here by chance.

This Psalm tells us to declare His glory to everyone. We are to share the good news about God to all people and all nations. Does that mean we are to get a soap box and stand out on street corners preaching? I'm not sure that would be the most effective method. When Jean and I were in New Orleans, there was a guy on the corner on a milk crate wearing an umbrella hat preaching to passers-by without a lot of success. Sometimes, the best way to share the good news is without words. Sometimes, your actions can speak louder than words. Are you kind and considerate to all those you meet?

I worked for a corporation about 20 years ago that made software we sold to Real Estate agents. We attended national and regional conventions and trade shows presenting our products. The meeting planner, Vicki, and I were both Christians and we lived our lives that way. At each show, there would be one night where the Exec VP would have us all gather for a dinner together. In Las Vegas, Vicki and I were the last two to arrive for this dinner because we had closed down the show booth together. It was a buffet so we got in the line for food. When we arrived at the table, I noticed that no one was eating. I thought that strange. And then, I was given the answer. The Exec VP asked me if I would say grace for the group before we ate. I was pleasantly surprised and offered thanks. From that day on, each time we gathered for the company dinner, they all waited for grace. I have pondered that moment for a long time. What made them ask?

Vicki and I usually said grace by ourselves at the end of the table. Apparently, others were watching. We never said anything about our faith to others but they noticed. Something about the life we were living attracted others to want to know more. In fact, they asked us to say Grace for them. Are you living that kind of life? Do others watch you to see what it is like to follow a Risen Lord? Can you preach the Gospel without words? Yes, you can! In fact, that is what I am calling you to do. Go out and live your life in a manner that makes others want the peace and joy you have. Your actions can and will make a difference. I have had clients ask me to pray for them when they faced surgery. You have the good news planted inside you. They will notice and they will ask. Be friendly and show the fruit of the Spirit which God has planted within you. Be a blessing to *all* you meet.

Father, thank You for all the gifts You have given us in our lives. The gifts of friends and family are incredible. Help us to shine Your light into the lives of everyone we meet. Lead us to the people who You know need that light. You are our strength and shield. Help us to declare Your Glory to *all* nations and *all* peoples. In Your name we pray! Amen!

# NOVEMBER 13   IS UN-FORGIVENESS BLOCKING YOU
Relationships

Ephesians 4:31 (NKJV)
*³¹ Let all bitterness, wrath, anger, clamor, and evil speaking be put away from you, with all malice.*

Sometimes, there seems to be something blocking you from achieving something you desire. You want something to work out but there are obstacles that keep arising. I had a bad day yesterday. That for which I prayed did not go my way. It left me wondering what God is doing. You think I would have learned that message.

Paul tells us to let go of all these bad things. When we harbor anger and bitterness, it clouds our whole life. My bitterness was in the form of un-forgiveness toward biological parents. Jean and I are Foster/Adoptive parents. As such, I become aware of some of the nasty deeds of biological parents. I have a great deal of difficulty forgiving them even though I Know God calls me to forgive. Jesus tells us in Matthew 6:15 (NKJV) *"¹⁵ But if you do not forgive men their trespasses, neither will your Father forgive your trespasses."* I know I am supposed to forgive but it is hard.

Yesterday was a hearing for a boy we are hoping to have come live with us and adopt if he becomes available. His Mom has done awful things in her life and it is making his life uncertain. We know about things she has done to other children as well and they are bad. Although we prayed for the outcome of Parental Termination of Rights, the Court declined that petition and offered the mom another 90-day extension. I was beside myself. From my point of view, it was all bad news. How could they give her more time when she has already been given more than the law allows? I was upset for the boy whose life will remain in limbo for three more months. I was disappointed for us because we want him here. He is a joy. What was the holdup? I have come to a place in my Spiritual journey where I ask God what He is trying to teach me in things. It seems God was asking me to let go of bitterness and rage!

I went to my Every Man a Warrior Men's Ministry meeting as usual. Only Mark was there when I arrived. That was probably God's design. I asked for a hug as I was having a bad day. As my Brothers in Christ do, he listened to my story. He was asking himself and me the same question. What was God's lesson in all this? Mark has been suggesting for a while I needed to pray for the mom. After all, she is a child of God. My un-forgiveness has prevented that so far. I knew he was right. By the Spirit, Mark explained to me the challenges the mom faced and the struggles she is going through in a way that made me realize she is doing what she can on her own. She needs the Lord to help her. It is my job to pray for *all* God's children of which she is one. I was finally ready to pray for her and asked Mark if we could pray right now. He agreed and we prayed for her to receive strength to overcome addiction and for strongholds to be broken. We prayed for her deliverance and restoration. We prayed the Lord would help her no matter the outcome. I was feeling relieved of the burden of anger I had been carrying for quite a while.

We were almost to the end of our prayer when my phone rang and the ringtone told me it was my wife Jean. Jean got additional information about the hearing. She found out that the Court decided to move him to our house in the meantime. Who says miracles don't still happen today? Although it is not the desired result according to my timetable, it is a step in the direction of stability for the boy. And remember, it is God's timetable that matters, not mine! Here is the kicker. It was like God was waiting for me to let go of the bitterness and He would make the call. The moment I released the anger and prayed for the mom; He made the call through Jean! It is astounding to me how quickly my prayers were answered. My prayers were for the mom, for the boy and for us. God heard our prayer and answered. He was there waiting for my change of heart and prayer. When I followed His will, He immediately answered.

What bitterness and rage are you carrying? Let go of all bitterness and rage! It poisons your heart and life. Forgiveness is most important. We need to pray for others for their restoration. We need to understand they may not be able to do what is right on their own. Let us ask the Lord to redeem them and help them to walk in His ways. Ask and you shall receive. I did!

Lord, you are an awesome God! You are always attentive to the needs of each of Your children. When You close doors, help us to understand it is for a reason. Even though we don't understand, help us to obey and wait for You to make things right. You said You would work all things for our good. Give us the patience to wait for Your perfect timing. In Your name we pray! Amen!

# NOVEMBER 14    CAN OR CAN'T - YOU DECIDE
Attitude

Philippians 4:13 (NKJV)
*13 I can do all things through Christ who strengthens me.*

Are you a can-do person? Attitude matters in all of life. Whether you think you can or you think you can't, either way you're right. How you approach any situation will influence the outcome. If you believe you can succeed, you will. It also helps when you realize the gifts and talents you have were given to you by your Creator. He also is willing to help you if you ask.

When you were created, the Lord gave you everything you would need to achieve your destiny. You may feel like you come up short but that is just not true. You are equipped, empowered and anointed for the life God chose for you. You have everything you need because one of the things you have is Him. No matter what you face, Christ, who is within you by His Spirit, can help and He is willing.

What is your situation? Are you a can or a can't? Can people don't waste time worrying about things that don't matter. They focus on solving the challenge. My friend Fred is a can-do person; a problem solver. He does not waste time on why it cannot happen. He finds ways to make things happen. Fred has faith he will be able to accomplish his goal because he does not work it alone. He knows the Lord God Almighty goes before him paving the way. I admire that quality and try to do the same. Fred is kind of quiet but there is an assurance built in that causes determination. And he uses that determination to help others. When Fred is involved, things get done.

What kind of person are you? Do you pray and ask God for His guidance and help? Do you approach a task with assurance and determination? Do you run the race with perseverance? Do you realize all the gifts and talents the Lord has given you? He has designed you to accomplish great things in life and given you the gifts you need to reach your destiny. What is stopping you? Don't you believe in yourself? Don't you believe Him? *Greater is He who is in you the he who is in the world* (1 John 4:4). You are accepted, chosen, equipped, favored, loved, redeemed and worthy all because God says so! It's in His Book. And He created you and knows that you are fearfully and wonderfully made.

So how should you handle a situation? Always approach with a can–do attitude and you will do well. If I get a "can't" on the phone, I hang up and call back even if I have to wait for another person. I am polite but I don't want to spend time with them. There is no sense wasting time with a can't. There is no sense being a can't! All things are possible with Christ. Believe!

Lord God, thank You that You go before us making crooked paths straight. When You give us challenges, it is to refine us and make us better. Thank You that You give us all the gifts and talents we will need to succeed in the race You lay out before us. Thank you that, because of Your design, we are well able to do all things set before us. In Your name we pray! Amen!

# NOVEMBER 15    GOD CHANGED MY NAME
Faith

Genesis 32:24-28 (NKJV) Wrestling with God

*24 Then Jacob was left alone; and a Man wrestled with him until the breaking of day. 25 Now when He [the Angel] saw that He did not prevail against him [Jacob], He touched the socket of his hip; and the socket of Jacob's hip was out of joint as He wrestled with him. 26 And He said, "Let Me go, for the day breaks." But he [Jacob] said, "I will not let You go unless You bless me!" 27 So He said to him, "What is your name?" He said, "Jacob." 28 And He said, "Your name shall no longer be called Jacob, but Israel; for you have struggled with God and with men, and have prevailed."*

What's in a name? Does what something is called really matter? What if your name meant supplanter or schemer or deceiver? Each time someone greets Jacob by name, they are saying liar, cheat, deceiver. Is that the way you would like to be greeted? Are you happy with who you are? Is God happy with who you have become?

God can change your name! He has done it for many. Jacob (deceiver) to Israel ("He who prevails with God,"); Abram (Noble father) to Abraham (Father of many), Simon (he has heard) to Peter (Rock). He did it for me too. Bob to Redeemed! Why? God may have wanted to indicate a change in the life of the person. Have you been changed? I have! Galatians 2:20 (NKJV) says *"20 I have been crucified with Christ; it is no longer I who live, but Christ lives in me; and the life which I now live in the flesh I live by faith in the Son of God, who loved me and gave Himself for me."* That is the life I want to live. I want to live by faith in the Son of God. Do you?

Jacob was known for manipulating things to suit his desire. He wanted to be blessed again. He tricked his brother Esau out of his birthright and his father-in-law Laban out of many sheep. It was the way he lived. His Mother was a part of the scheme. Her family used trickery in their ways. That method seems to be prevalent in today's world too. We see many who use trickery to get what they want. But is that the way God wants you to live? Why would God include a story of trickery in the Bible? Isn't the Bible supposed to show us how we *should* live and not how to get your way? God shows us there are no perfect people but He can redeem any situation. Even though Jacob was a deceiver, God could change him. And God did. He started by changing his name. From that day forward, Israel began to live a different and better life. Shortly after this, Jacob faced Esau after many years. Jacob, now called Israel, became humble and contrite toward the brother he had cheated. And God redeemed the situation and healed the relationship.

How about you? Are you living the life you desire? Is it what God designed for you? If not, you can turn to Him and He will change your name. By following God's ways, you can become the person He called and created you to be. He has already given you all you need to be that person. All you need do is ask Him. In Revelation 3:20, He says *"Here I stand at the door and knock. If anyone hears my voice and opens the door, I will come in and abide with them and they with me."* Do you hear him knocking? Will you open the door? He will come in and change your name and your life! He loves you so much that

He gave Himself up for you. Will you give yourself up for Him? It will be the best thing you ever did! Just ask!

Lord, thank You that You offer us a new name in You. Give us the courage to accept Your offer and be changed. We are afraid of what it all means. Offer us Your comfort and peace and draw us closer to you. Make us Your children. Jacob already did the wrestling for us. That is why You share the story. Help us to accept the reward and the new name in You! Amen!

# NOVEMBER 16    WHO IS TO BLAME
Grace and Mercy

Genesis 3:6-13 (NKJV)

*⁶ So when the woman saw that the tree was good for food, that it was pleasant to the eyes, and a tree desirable to make one wise, she took of its fruit and ate. She also gave to her husband with her, and he ate. ⁷ Then the eyes of both of them were opened, and they knew that they were naked; and they sewed fig leaves together and made themselves coverings. ⁸ And they heard the sound of the LORD God walking in the garden in the cool of the day, and Adam and his wife hid themselves from the presence of the LORD God among the trees of the garden. ⁹ Then the LORD God called to Adam and said to him, "Where are you?" ¹⁰ So he said, "I heard Your voice in the garden, and I was afraid because I was naked; and I hid myself." ¹¹ And He said, "Who told you that you were naked? Have you eaten from the tree of which I commanded you that you should not eat?" ¹² Then the man said, "The woman whom You gave to be with me, she gave me of the tree, and I ate." ¹³ And the LORD God said to the woman, "What is this you have done?" The woman said, "The serpent deceived me, and I ate."*

Who is to blame for all the things going on in our world? I'm sure it is not you. Someone else must be responsible for these bad things. No one wants to take responsibility these days. Everyone wants benefits without responsibility.

Eve was being tempted by the serpent to eat of the fruit. Adam was there with her. He knew they were not supposed to eat the fruit but he let the serpent talk Eve into it. Adam did nothing to uphold God's law nor help his wife according to the story. He allowed Eve to eat the fruit and he ate some himself. As soon they ate, their eyes were opened and they now knew good and evil. Actually, evil entered the world through their disobedience. The Lord asked what they had done. And, of course, they both passed the buck!

We are working on a relocation project. As is typical with moving phone lines, the receiving company did not take the number right away. The sending company did not check to confirm the transfer but just disconnected the number from their system cutting off the service on a fax line for a law firm. And it has been a nightmare ever since. The client wanted to know why this happened. I told him it was my fault for not confirming the transfer myself rather than allowing the companies to handle what they should be able to do on their own. Even an attorney was not sure what to do with the truth and someone who would take responsibility. Our team figured a way to fix the mess both companies made and we are getting things back on track. But that could not have been done if we spent our time trying to blame someone else. Instead, we focused on the solution and not excuses.

What about you? Are you willing to stand up and say it is my fault? Once blame is out of the way, a solution can be found. The Lord knew His creation would look to place blame. He knows how we are formed and that we want to pass the buck. At the foundations of the world, He decided to take the blame for all sin upon Himself to get blame out of the way. In so doing, he has allowed the focus to be on a solution. That solution is Him and His grace. *By Grace, you have been saved through faith and this is not from yourselves. It is the gift of God, not by works, lest anyone should boast* (Ephesians 2:8-9). While you are to blame for the things you do, God is willing to help you get past your shortcomings and restore you. Instead of hiding from God in your guilt, why not face up to the sin and accept His grace. It is better to face the music and put it behind you than to struggle with guilt for years. My Dad would say "You'll do better next time!" Your Heavenly Father loves you enough to remove your sin from you. Accept His grace and forgiveness and grow into who He designed you to be. Don't look for blame, look for and give grace.

Father, we thank You that You love us anyway! You know we sin yet You offer grace. Help us to face up to our shortcomings and learn to move past them into the center of Your love. By Your stripes we are healed. Remove our guilt and replace it with humility and a contrite heart so we can enjoy time with You. Help us to grow from each challenge to become the winners You designed us to be. In Your name we pray! Amen!

# NOVEMBER 17   WHAT SHALL I CALL YOU
## Faith

Romans 10:13 (NKJV)

[13] For "whoever calls on the name of the LORD shall be saved."

What are the names of Jesus? And by what name do you call Him? Do you call Him Lord? Do you call Him Savior? Do you call Him friend? What does He call you? There are many names by which Jesus is known and they range from meek to powerful. He was the Lamb of God as well as the Lion of Judah. Which name fits into your life?

What does it mean to call on the name of the Lord? It means to have a relationship. It means to know the Lord and to be known by Him. It means to put your faith and trust in Him. When you do, He will give you His grace. Christ offers you life everlasting to be spent in paradise with Him. That is what it means to be saved. Many do not like that term "saved". I wonder why? Is it not better than being lost?

You do not have to go through life alone. The One who created you is willing to walk along-side you and help you navigate this world and bring you to the next. He knew you before you knew yourself and offers justice, grace and mercy for the journey. Although there are bumps in the road, the Lord will guide you through. He loves you and cares for you. He will work all things for your good. Looking forward in this life, things appear tough. But looking back, you can see the hand of God guiding and protecting you on the journey. Is it not better to have a companion on the journey?

Ours is not to judge but to love. We are taught that we will be judged with the same measure that we judge others. I cannot stand on my own merits. I know who I am. I have seen some of my deeds. I would rather stand on the righteousness given me by Christ. He offers His righteousness to you as well. Will you take it? There is a judge whom we will all face. Do you want to face Him knowing He loves and cares for you or as a stranger? Do you call Him "Your Honor" or "Abba [Daddy]"? He came as the Lamb of God last time. He will return as the Lion of Judah. The offer is on the table. Take hold of Him who longs to take hold of you. *Choose this day whom you will serve...But as for me and my household, we will serve the Lord. (Joshua 24:15)*

Help us to serve You Lord because it is the best way for us to go! Service to You means love, joy, peace, patience, kindness, goodness, gentleness and self-control. We want to live like that. Teach us Your ways oh Lord that we might know You better. Help us to do justly and to love mercy and walk humbly with You. In Your name we pray! Amen!

## NOVEMBER 18    WHAT'S THAT IN YOUR EYE
Grace and Mercy

Luke 6:42 (NKJV)
*42 Or how can you say to your brother, 'Brother, let me remove the speck that is in your eye,' when you yourself do not see the plank that is in your own eye? Hypocrite! First remove the plank from your own eye, and then you will see clearly to remove the speck that is in your brother's eye.*

Isn't it easy for us to see the imperfections of others while, at the same time, overlooking our shortcomings? When we are calling attention to someone's faults, we are doing it for their own good. When they tell us about our shortcomings, they are being critical. It is hard to weigh the faults of others without putting our thumb on the scale.

Jesus is doing a whole theme on judging others where He tells us not to judge or we will be judged. There is only one Judge and it is not you or me. Our Judge is gracious, compassionate and forgiving. Not many of us can claim that status. He says "forgive and you will be forgiven." This verse tells us to not be a hypocrite, condemning others while we are also guilty. We all have sinned and fall short of the glory of God. There is none who is free of sin. Fortunately, there is One who is full of forgiveness and grace!

Since none of us are perfect, how can we live together in peace and harmony? The only way it will work is if we are forgiving and non-judgmental. I used to say "you don't know what they have been through." That is true. We do not understand what the other person is facing or what baggage they carry. You have not walked in their shoes and experienced the things they may have encountered. Many times, when people are mean to you and hurt you, it is because they are hurting. How will you handle that situation? Will you respond or react? Could you ask a question like "Have I done something to offend you?" What is the outcome you desire? Would you like to build up or tear down the relationship? If you take offense, you will tend to lash out in return. Their displeasure might have nothing to do with you. Would you like to retaliate or diffuse the situation? You are at a crossroads. Which way would you like to see it go? A kind word at that moment could change everything.

Romans 12:17-19 (NKJV) says "*17 Repay no one evil for evil. Have regard for good things in the sight of all men. 18 If it is possible, as much as depends on you, live peaceably with all men. 19 Beloved, do not avenge yourselves, but rather give place to wrath; for it is written, "Vengeance is Mine, I will repay," says the Lord.* What if you responded with kindness instead of reacting with more of the same? Would a relationship be possible? Would that person be in a better place after meeting you? Would you be reflecting the Lord and bringing Him glory? You know you would!

Since the seeds of love were planted in you, why not offer love in response? Anyone can give back the bitterness directed at them. You are mirroring what you received. But what if you changed things up? What if you stopped to realize that a person could be hurting and you offered healing and kindness instead? You have been in the place where they are. What if someone had offered kindness to you? Isn't that how you would have liked to be treated? The world would have been a better place. What do you see when you look at others? God looks at the heart. He sees their trouble and understands why they are acting as they are. Ask God to let you see others through His eyes. Realize you have been where they are and treat them as you would have liked to be treated. Turn things around for both of you!

Lord, please help me to clean my eyes so I can see others as You see them. Let me speak words of healing and love to those I meet. Help me to respond rather than react. May words of kindness and love pour forth when I speak. Help me to build up rather than tear down. In Your name we pray! Amen!

# NOVEMBER 19    YOU ARE THE PROMISE

Faith

Genesis 22:18 (NKJV)

*18 In your [Abraham] seed all the nations of the earth shall be blessed, because you have obeyed My voice."*

As a descendent of Abraham, not only are you blessed through him but you are a blessing to others. Obedience to God always brings blessings.

Abraham has just laid his only son Isaac on the altar and raised the knife to sacrifice him when the Lord stopped him. It was a test of Abraham's commitment. Abraham passed the test. And because of his obedience, God promised to bless Abraham, his descendants and *all the world* through him. So where does that leave us? If we are part of the world, we, too, are blessed. And out of the overflow of our blessings, we are to bless others.

Have you ever had a bad day? Does it seem like nothing is working in your favor? What if you took a few moments to consider that you were blessed to be a blessing? Firstly, you are blessed. God clearly tells us that "all the world" will be blessed through Abraham. That's you! Did you forget that? Abraham believed God and it was credited to him as righteousness. Therefore, God blessed him and his descendants and *all the world.* That includes creation as well. The Lord was so adamant about that He repeated the blessing to Isaac and Jacob. Through His Word, He reminds you too. You carry the Promise as well as the blessing. But you must believe that you have it for it to do you and others any good.

Too often, we let what is directly in front of us determine our mood. We get bogged down in a challenge and lose sight of the goal and finish line. We forget who we are and whose we are. You are a child of God! We forget the Lord God goes before us and walks with us. Would you stop to consider that for a moment? He said He would never leave you nor forsake you. With that in mind, what have you to fear? The challenge is keeping that in mind. Do you lose sight of the Lord? I do. When I get stressed by a challenge I face, many times I try to face it on my own. When I return to Him and ask for guidance, the stress leaves and the task moves ahead. Hebrews 12:2 says we should keep your eyes fixed on the author and perfecter of our faith. He promises to always be with you. He is the Promise and dwells within you!

Lord, thank You that You are always with us. When we turn to You, all things are possible. Lead us in Your path for our lives. Remind us we were blessed to be a blessing and we still carry the Promise You gave to Abraham. Help us to share that blessing with others today. In Your name we pray! Amen!

## NOVEMBER 20   IS JESUS YOUR LAST RESORT
Prayer

James 5:16 (NIV)

*16 Therefore confess your sins to each other and pray for each other so that you may be healed. The prayer of a righteous person is powerful and effective.*

Is Jesus your last resort? Do you try to do everything you can think of on your own and, when that is unsuccessful, turn to Jesus? What would it take to get you to Him sooner? Does prayer work anyway? Will He even listen to me? Let prayer be your first response, not your last resort.

James tells us to confess and pray. When we confess, we let go of the sin and the guilt it causes. Guilt is a heavy burden to carry. Our prayer should be for guidance that we will be led on a path that avoids future sin. James tells us the prayer of a righteous person is powerful and effective. Do you see yourself as righteous? Maybe that's the challenge.

Many of us don't think God will answer our prayers or that He even listens. That is just not true. God still answers prayers today. He answered mine last Thursday before I even finished praying. When I prayed for a situation offering forgiveness to someone, God answered by granting another prayer of mine. Even though we may not see ourselves as worthy, Jesus stands as our intercessor to the Father seeking our best solution. Hebrews 7:25 (NIV) says *"25 Therefore he is able to save completely those who come to God through him, because he always lives to intercede for them."* On your own, you may not be worthy but you are not on your own! Why wait so long to go to Him? He actually is there waiting for you when you pray.

Another way to make your prayer life more effective is to offer prayers of thanksgiving for all the good things that are in your life already. You have much to be thankful for so go to God with praise and thanksgiving. And it does not have to be fancy words. Just talk to Him. He loves you and wants to hear from you. He will answer your prayer. You may not like the answer but it will be what is best for you. God wants to bless you today. If you are not sure how to pray or what to ask for, that's OK. Ask Him! His Holy Spirit will help you in your prayers by guiding you. Don't wait! Keep God in the forefront of your life. Let Him be your guide and you will enjoy the journey. Jesus can be your guide rather than your last resort.

Lord, we thank You that You stand ready to intercede for us always. Remind us of Your presence helping us to come to You quickly. Help us build the habit of walking in Your ways. Keep us on the path You have designed for us. In Your name we pray! Amen!

# NOVEMBER 21    I AM YOURS AND YOU ARE MINE
## Redemption

Hosea 2:19-20 (NKJV)

¹⁹ *"I will betroth you to Me forever; Yes, I will betroth you to Me In righteousness and justice, In lovingkindness and mercy;* ²⁰ *I will betroth you to Me in faithfulness, And you shall know the* Lord.*"*

be·troth *verb dated*  enter into a formal agreement to marry.

Hosea is one of the Prophets of the Old Testament. He is speaking to Israel on behalf of God about their lack of faithfulness toward Him. God likens Israel's unfaithfulness to Him as that of a harlot. Yet He promises to be faithful to her no matter what. Although we cannot remain perfectly faithful in our relationship to Him, He still remains perfect in His faith to us! The Lord sets the example of faithfulness for us to follow. He will never leave nor forsake us. Never!

What does it mean to be faithful? *Merriam-Webster* says, "having or showing true and constant support or loyalty: deserving trust: keeping your promises or doing what you are supposed to do." On the receiving side, it means you know a person is there for you. Don't we all want to know that there is someone on whom we can rely totally? For the most part, people will let you down. If you are lucky (or blessed like me), you will find a few people who will be there for you even if they are not perfect. The Lord will be your perfect friend and you can always count on Him.

I have found someone on whom I can rely. In December 1972, I met the cutest little brunette. There was something special about her. She was and is charming and engaging. I asked her out for New Year's Eve. She was reluctant to go because she knew little about me but, after checking me out through my friends, she decided to go. That is a whole other story! Have you ever just known something was right? I did!

After New Year's, she went back to college and I missed her. I sent her a plane ticket to come home for Valentine's Day. This was the *one*. Nine months later, I was sure I wanted to spend my life with her so I asked her to marry me. As is typical of Jean, *she had to think about it*. I was a little disappointed at the time. I have since learned that Jean *always* thinks about things. The up side of that is that, once she makes a decision, it is for keeps. That was forty-plus years ago and she still keeps me. She is my faithful companion in sickness and in health, for richer or poorer, for better or worse. God has blessed us that the better has far outweighed the worse. We have been betrothed in righteousness and justice, in lovingkindness and mercy, and in faithfulness because we know and walk with the Lord. Last night at a concert, we were asked how we managed to remain married so long. I answered because we keep God at the center of our marriage. When we lost sight of Him, there were issues. As soon as our focus returned to the source of all good things, the marriage flourished. God said a man shall leave his father and his mother and shall cling to his wife. We cling to each other. That was His design. We trust Him! You can too! Look for the one God ordained for you and cherish them. Pay attention and He will let you know.

Lord, thank You for my Beloved! You knew and sent the one for me. Thank You that we can walk together with You and that You bless us in our marriage. Thank You that Jean came to the right decision. And thanks for putting in a good word for me! In Your name I pray!

# NOVEMBER 22    WHAT ARE YOU TRYING TO DO

Relationships

Galatians 1:10 (NIV)

*¹⁰ Am I now trying to win the approval of human beings, or of God? Or am I trying to please people? If I were still trying to please people, I would not be a servant of Christ.*

Are you one of those people who wants to be popular and fit in with everyone? Do you worry a lot about what others think of you? Do you try to please everybody by agreeing with them? When you do these things, what are you trying to accomplish?

Paul is writing to the Galatian Church about their straying from the Gospel and following other teachings. It could be about some teaching that followers had to become Jews first and then follow Christ. Either way, the teaching was contrary to what Christ taught Paul and he shared with them. Since Paul received direct revelation from Christ, his message was accurate and Christ's message was to be followed.

Years ago, I worked for a man who wanted to please everyone and be everyone's friend. He would agree with whomever he was speaking. That way, the conversation was always pleasant. He avoided confrontation at all costs. He would never disagree with someone or make a decision that was unpopular. That would cause conflict in his opinion. While he thought he was pleasing everyone it turned out he was pleasing no one; not even himself! He would never make a decision because someone would be unhappy. We were all unhappy in the end because nothing ever got done. Do you find yourself in that situation some times? Are you looking to please everyone? It does not work. Why not try to please the One who matters and let Him work all things for your good. Luke 10:41-42 (NKJV) says *"⁴¹ And Jesus answered and said to her, 'Martha, Martha, you are worried and troubled about many things. ⁴² But one thing is needed, and Mary has chosen that good part, which will not be taken away from her.'"* The one thing that is needed is to listen to Jesus and follow His teaching. Look to please the One that matters. When you please Him, everything else will fall into place.

Lord, we thank You that You have come to be our guide and will lead us through life. Help us to follow You daily and walk in Your ways. Remove from us the pride that makes us want to be liked by everyone and turn our hearts back to you. Let us be Your true and faithful servants, listening and following Your teachings. Write Your story on our hearts. In Your name we pray! Amen!

# NOVEMBER 23   A LITTLE CHILD SHALL LEAD THEM
## Relationships

Isaiah 11:1-6 (NKJV) Selected Verses
*There shall come forth a Rod from the stem of Jesse, And a Branch shall grow out of his roots.*
*[2] The Spirit of the LORD shall rest upon Him, The Spirit of wisdom and understanding, The Spirit of counsel and might, The Spirit of knowledge and of the fear of the LORD. [3] His delight is in the fear of the LORD, And He shall not judge by the sight of His eyes, Nor decide by the hearing of His ears; [4] But with righteousness He shall judge the poor,... [6] "The wolf also shall dwell with the lamb, The leopard shall lie down with the young goat, The calf and the young lion and the fatling together; And a little child shall lead them.*

Have you ever noticed that true and pure wisdom can come out of the mouth of a little child? When they suggest something, it is not polluted with their baggage or agenda. It is just an idea based on the facts presented at the time. They don't worry about what people will think. Some of the best ideas I have ever heard have come from a child. Do you listen to children? Will you heed their voice?

Isaiah is telling us about special children that will come from the line of Jesse. As is very often the case, the Bible is speaking outside of time because God is outside of time. He speaks of past, present and future all at the same time. This passage speaks of two children that I know of: King David and Jesus. In David's case, a young shepherd boy is chosen to be the next king of Israel. God would call David a man after His own heart. But the most important child would be Jesus, the descendant of David, the Eternal King and our Messiah. Both young people became renowned leaders.

A little child came to live with us on Friday! He is filled with childlike wonder and ideas. He speaks what is on his mind and it is pure and true. His conversation is not guarded and lined up with his personal agenda. He says what is on his mind. He asks for what he wants. Jesus said "you have not because you ask not." Adults don't ask because they are afraid of rejection. Kids will ask repeatedly until they get that for which they have asked! Our adult baggage can cause anxiety around an issue. We have ego and pride that we bring along to any discussion. Children just approach the situation with positive expectancy. They just ask with that cute little smile melting your heart and defenses all at the same time. I want to go with you. Stay here with me! Can I be baptized? Will you adopt me? Can I call you daddy? (Melt, melt, melted!) Children are closer to God because they have not yet built up pride, ego and defenses.

Do you answer or dismiss a child's question? When a child asks a simple question, it may not appear that simple to us adults. We go right to all the reasons why not. We think about permissions we will need. We think about the down side. But do we consider the up side? Instead of asking why; ask why not? From adults, it is easier to get forgiveness than permission. Have you taken time to consider the upside? If they go somewhere with you, you can have conversation. If you stay with them, you can make memories. If they ask to call you daddy, try not to cry! I have come to a place in my life where I have intentionally decided that I want to say yes. I pause to think (of the down side) and try to reason how and why I can say yes. Is there a compelling reason we should not move forward? Why not? If I say no, what opportunities will we miss? Do I want to build the relationship?

Another area in which a child can make an awesome difference is with teenagers. When you child becomes a teenager, they want to become independent so they no longer listen to you. Having a young child in the house who asks them questions leads them to truths they will not accept from you. It seems that the older we get, the less we want to listen. I have a challenge hearing out our teenager. I need to learn to be a better listener. Pray that we all can listen better and take our time to respond. And let a little child lead us all.

Father, thank You for the children of all ages You put in our lives. Help us to see the wisdom of the Spirit that you planted in everyone. Give us back our childlike wonder that we may see You through new eyes. Thank you for sending little children to lead us. In Your name we pray! Amen!

## NOVEMBER 24    PUSHING BACK THE DARKNESS

Encouragement

2 Corinthians 4:6 (NKJV)

*⁶ For it is the God who commanded light to shine out of darkness, who has shone in our hearts to give the light of the knowledge of the glory of God in the face of Jesus Christ.*

Would you agree this is a dark world? Almost everywhere you look, darkness pervades. People are out for themselves. Brutality is a daily occurrence. Could it get any worse? Some say these are the end times. But does it have to be this way? Is there something we can do to make a difference?

Paul is speaking to us about the sad state of affairs of the world in which he was living. Things have not gotten better. Paul reminds us we have the light of Christ in our hearts. We have been given what is needed to push back the darkness. God shone His light in our hearts. Paul reminds us there is always hope in Christ.

Have you ever sat in a totally darkened room? If you light just one candle, its light pierces through that darkness immediately penetrating the veil. That single candle pushes back the shadows and shows the room. So how does that pertain to the darkness of this world? You are that single candle. You have the power to overcome the darkness. What's more, you can join with others to shine your combined light. If we all shine God's light together, the world can be like the noonday sun. God has placed His light in your heart. You have everything you need to overcome evil with good. John 1:5 says (NKJV) *"⁵ And the light shines in the darkness, and the darkness did not comprehend it."* Darkness may not comprehend it but it sure is scared of the light! Evil flourishes in darkness. Light overcomes all of evil's schemes. You can make the difference. Stand up for God and show the world His ways are better. Be a light in this world.

You are the light! God has placed His light within you and calls you to shine that light into the dark places. Matthew 5: 14,16 says *"¹⁴ "You are the light of the world.........* *¹⁶ Let your light so shine before men, that they may see your good works and glorify your Father in heaven."* Each day, you come against darkness. You have a choice. You can choose to shine your light and dispel that darkness. Go ahead! Glorify your Heavenly Father by shining the light He has given you. Be the light!

Heavenly Father, You are the source of all light. You spoke light into being and placed it within us. Help us to shine Your light into the dark places in our world. Let the radiance of the face of Christ push back the darkness and the knowledge of the glory of God through Christ guide us daily. Help us to shine! In Your name we pray! Amen!

# NOVEMBER 25  ALLOW ME TO ENTER YOUR REST
## Quality of Life

Hebrews 4:9-11 (NKJV)
*⁹ There remains therefore a rest for the people of God. ¹⁰ For he who has entered His rest has himself also ceased from his works as God did from His. ¹¹ Let us therefore be diligent to enter that rest, lest anyone fall according to the same example of disobedience.*

How good are you at resting? In my case, resting is not my specialty. I want to rest but keep thinking about what I could be doing. The downside is I don't get the quiet time I would like to enjoy with God. When you are always busy, it is hard to hear God's still small voice. With all the chatter in my mind, it is hard to hear the whisper. God tells that we are to work six days and rest on the seventh just like He did. How are you and your Sabbath Rest?

Hebrews reminds us God's rest is still available to us today. The One who rested created that rest for us. As is the case in many places, the Bible often speaks on several planes at the same time. This rest is the Sabbath rest as well and our more permanent rest of heaven with God. Matthew Henry's Commentary says "This rest is, a rest of grace, and comfort, and holiness, in the gospel state. And a rest in glory, where the people of God shall enjoy the end of their faith, and the object of all their desires." We might also call it the Kingdom of Heaven.

Do you want to enjoy this rest? Is it still available to you? In our crazy world of constant communication and instant gratification, can we take the time to enter God's Rest? In Genesis 2:2, God tells us He had finished His work of creation and rested from His labors. It was His choice just as it is our choice today. You must be intentional about this rest. I choose to attend Church, do my Bible Study homework and visit my Mom on Sunday. Many times, we set up visits with friends too. I would like to spend more quiet time with God though. Silence is not my thing. In the movie, *War Room*, the main character has a prayer closet in her house where she goes to be alone with God. I intend to build one for myself. My seat on the couch is not private enough. I want a place where I can commune with God alone that does not have other distractions. What about you? What is your quiet place? Where can you go to speak with God but mostly go to listen?

Heavenly Father, we love You! It is clear that You love us. Help us to be with You more each day. You designed Your Rest for our benefit as a time of grace, comfort and holiness. Protect our schedules so we can share peaceful time with You. Renew us daily through Your Rest. Give us time to be quiet that we may hear Your voice. And when the time comes, may we enter Your Rest so we can glorify You and enjoy You forever. In Jesus name we pray! Amen!

# NOVEMBER 26   ATTITUDE OF GRATITUDE
## Attitude

Psalm 50:23 (NKJV)

²³ *Whoever offers praise glorifies Me; And to him who orders his conduct aright
I will show the salvation of God."*

How do you go through life? Are you happy or sad? Are you looking at what others have and wondering how you can get it for yourself? Do you let an attitude of gratitude flavor all you do? That way, everything will go better.

In this Psalm, God tells us praising glorifies Him. Gratitude is a form of praise. God tells us He will show us His salvation. His salvation means spending eternity with Him and that means everything. There is no better opportunity anywhere.

Life is too short to be living it grumpy! When you focus on what you don't have, you become bitter and angry. To be content with your situation gives you the chance to live in the moment and enjoy everything. You can see the little wonders of life and appreciate everyone and everything. In that frame of mind, you can overlook life's little annoyances and still enjoy things. Contentment does not mean resignation. It does not mean you don't try to improve your situation. It means being happy where you are in your God given journey. You are on your way to your destiny. Enjoy the journey.

In the USA, we celebrate a day of being thankful. It is a time to remember all we have been given. This includes those who are no longer here with us but have been in our lives. They are still a part of who and where we are today. We always celebrate at our house. There is always a seat at our table for those who may be alone. It is a time to count our blessings. I am blessed with a wonderful wife, with children, a great home, friends, health, great family, gifts and talents, deep faith and a Lord who loves me so much He gave Himself up for me! *Greater love has no one that this, than to lay down His life for His friends* (John 15:13). Oh, did I mention Jesus is my friend? And the really great news is He wants to be your friend too!

Are you happy where you are? Do you get real joy out of each day? If not, why not? There is joy, peace, patience, kindness, goodness, gentleness, faithfulness and self-control for those who invite Christ into their lives. He can change you from the inside out. You can begin to enjoy your life right where you are. You are surrounded with blessings right now. Open your eyes to your current blessings. Sure, there are still hurdles to climb. That's OK. You have what it takes even if you have to ask for help. Your help will come! May the God of all grace bless you beyond all you could ask or imagine this day and every day. He will never leave nor forsake you no matter what. He is your light no matter how deep the darkness seems. And He loves you so much! Whether you see it or not, you are blessed each and every day. Focus on Him and give thanks for He is good.

Father, thank You for everything. Even the bad things You use for our good. There has never been another like You who loves His children so much. Help us to feel that love each day. But moreover, help us to share that love with everyone we meet to let them know they are loved too! I pray each person would come to know Your love for them as I have. All glory laud and honor to You my Savior King! Amen!

## NOVEMBER 27    I FEEL LOST - WHAT ABOUT ME
### Quality of Life

Galatians 2:19-21 (NKJV)

*¹⁹ For I through the law died to the law that I might live to God. ²⁰ I have been crucified with Christ; it is no longer I who live, but Christ lives in me; and the life which I now live in the flesh I live by faith in the Son of God, who loved me and gave Himself for me. ²¹ I do not set aside the grace of God; for if righteousness comes through the law, then Christ died in vain."*

We all struggle with boundaries. If you don't set good boundaries, you can find yourself in a place of resentment. In fact, no matter what we have agreed to do, there comes a time of doubt. Why did I say I would do this? What was I thinking? We do not always realize the full extent of the commitment when we first agree. The life of service to others is usually difficult but always rewarding. When you live as God asks of you, He will always reward you.

Paul tells us how we are to live. Many were trying to live according to the letter of the law and not paying attention to the Spirit of the law. They did exactly what it said without concern for why it was written. Faith in the "why" of the law, which was faith in Christ, is how we should follow. Jesus summed that up when He said "love your neighbor as yourself." You should look out for the interests of others above your own so as to be generous. Only Christ was able to give Himself up for others. He literally died so you and I may fully live. Treat others like you would have them treat you. The only way to do that is to follow Jesus lead and to die to self. That is a tall order!

Have you ever been a caregiver? If you have children or an ill spouse or aging parents, you know what I mean. Do you feel overwhelmed by all you have to do and wonder how it will all get done? You probably wonder about any "me" time. When will that ever happen? You can get so caught up in your role that you lose yourself. So how do you draw boundary lines around caring? Can that be done? How do you specify how much you are going to care? This is really tough. And if you lose them, where does that leave you? These are very difficult questions. The thing to remember is you do not walk this path alone. Giving yourself up for others was the path that Christ walked for you and me and He went before us. He set the perfect example. He died to self and rose again to live for and in us. Would it not stand to reason that the One who raised Christ from the dead would protect, renew and restore us if we give ourselves up for another? By the grace of God, you will endure, be blessed and be a blessing! I don't know the answers but He does. Listen and follow His lead by faith and the Spirit.

Lord, thank You that You gave Yourself up for us. Who are we that You are mindful of us? You tell us we are your beloved children. As such, teach us how to share that love with others. Help us to give of ourselves freely knowing You will protect and restore us fully. Help us to live for You. Give us the strength to do what You would have us do.  May the love You poured out for us work through us allowing us to love others as You have loved. In Your name we pray! Amen!

# NOVEMBER 28    FOLLOW HIM AND BE BLESSED
Quality of Life

Deuteronomy 28:1-13 (NKJV) Selected Verses

*"Now it shall come to pass, if you diligently obey the voice of the LORD your God, to observe carefully all His commandments which I command you today, that the LORD your God will set you high above all nations of the earth. ²And all these blessings shall come upon you and overtake you, because you obey the voice of the LORD your God: ³ "Blessed shall you be in the city, and blessed shall you be in the country...... increase of your cattle and the offspring of your flocks. ⁶ "Blessed shall you be when you come in, and blessed shall you be when you go out. ⁷ "The LORD will cause your enemies who rise against you to be defeated before your face; they shall come out against you one way and flee before you seven ways. ⁸ "The LORD will command the blessing on you in your storehouses and in all to which you set your hand, and He will bless you in the land which the LORD your God is giving you....... ¹² The LORD will open to you His good treasure, the heavens, to give the rain to your land in its season, and to bless all the work of your hand. You shall lend to many nations, but you shall not borrow. ¹³And the LORD will make you the head and not the tail; you shall be above only, and not be beneath, if you heed the commandments of the LORD your God, which I [Moses] command you today, and are careful to observe them."*

Since He created everything, He knows how it all was made and the best way of doing things. When you do things God's way, it all works out well for you. In fact, you will be blessed if you follow His lead.

Moses spoke to the people of Israel telling them about all the blessing that were in store for them if they followed God's word written out for them in the Law. The Lord would set them high above all the nations and blessings would overtake them. The list of blessings is impressive. He also told them, in later verses, of the consequences of not following. The key point was to heed the commandments of the Lord and observe them. It is still the same for us today. God is waiting to pour out His blessings on us if we would but obey.

Do you want to live a life of blessing? Most do. Are you willing to learn and follow God's Word? Many say the Bible is irrelevant today. I do not agree. The Bible is all about relationships and nothing has changed in that area. Thousands of years ago, Cain killed able because he was jealous. We have jealousy today. The Bible speaks of how we should live. Since it was written by the Creator of the universe and everything in it, He knows what we need. He knows how we are formed. It is our Owner's Manual.

There is an impressive list of blessings in today's verses:

You will be blessed no matter where you are.

You enemies will be defeated before you.

You flocks will be increased.

You will be blessed at all times.

The Lord will bless all to which you set your hand.

The Lord will bless your land.

The Lord will open to you His good treasure.

The Lord will bless all the work of your hand.

You shall lend and not borrow.

You shall always be the head.

You shall always be above.

And there are more blessings in those verses. I would ask you to go and read it for yourself. In fact, why not copy it and put it up on your wall to help you remember all the Lord desires to do for you? He loves you that much. But what does He desire of you? He desires that you walk in His ways. That is not always easy. First, you will have to know His ways. To do that, you need to read His Word. While there are many warnings in the Bible, (Don't do this or that) there are incredible blessings written on the pages. These are promises and God is faithful. He will deliver! Do you want to be blessed? Do you have what it takes to follow? The even better news is that the Holy Spirit, which is in you, will remind you of all of God's ways and help you to walk in them if you are willing. Go ahead! Walk with the Lord. The rewards are beyond all you can ask or imagine.

Lord God, we desire to do Your will. There are those who would tempt us differently. By Your Spirit, remind us of all You offer and help us to walk with You in Your ways! In Your name we pray! Amen!

## NOVEMBER 29    PICK A FIGHT WITH THE CULTURE
Quality of Life

Romans 12:1-2 (NKJV)
*I beseech you therefore, brethren, by the mercies of God, that you present your bodies a living sacrifice, holy, acceptable to God, which is your reasonable service. ² And do not be conformed to this world, but be transformed by the renewing of your mind, that you may prove what is that good and acceptable and perfect will of God.*

God is not unclear about how He wants you to live! There is no ambiguity in His word. It is clear He does not want you to take on the ways of the world but, rather, to set an example for the world to follow. He wants you to reveal Him to them. He wants you to show the world how they should live. This will not be easy. Mark Twain once said "There is nothing more annoying than a good example!" You will be an irritation to the world at large when you walk with the Lord. Jesus tells you that the world will hate you. (Matthew 10:22)

Paul is begging us to live holy lives acceptable to God. He tells us that it is our service to the Lord. Paul clearly tells us to not follow the ways of the world but to be changed and renewed by following God's will. God's will for our lives is perfect.

We were chosen to reveal God to the rest of the world. That is only done by example because talk is cheap. Our example of right living is found in Christ alone. How can you live in the world and not be a part of it? The only way is to look to the One who is perfect in every way. He will transform you and renew your thinking enabling you to walk in His ways. You will be at odds with the world! The world says, go ahead, take what you want. You are worth it! The Lord tells you to look out for widows and orphans! It will be a battle. Zig Ziglar defined integrity as doing the right thing even when you think no one is watching. That is living in God's ways. Do you know what God expects of you? Are you willing and able to follow His will for your life?

I know I call these devotionals *Encouragement Daily*. And yet, I tell you the world is going to hate you. How encouraging is that? But here is the encouragement. There are over 400 uses of the words bless or blessing in the Bible. Each of those is tied to following the Lord. The world may hate you but God will love you. That alone, is worth everything! You are here to shine light into the darkness of the world. If you do, He will pour out so much blessing you will not have storehouses enough to hold it all! I beseech you. Walk in His ways and be blessed and be a blessing!

Lord, strengthen us to walk in Your ways. Let us shine Your light into this dark world so as to lead the lost to You. Use us to Your glory. Help us to endure the hatred of the world in order to receive the love and blessings of our Lord, Savior and Friend. In Your name we pray!

# NOVEMBER 30   KEEP YOUR KEY
## Grace and mercy

Joel 2:12-25 (NKJV) Selected Verses A Call to Repentance
*¹² "Now, therefore," says the LORD, "Turn to Me with all your heart, With fasting, with weeping, and with mourning." ¹³ So rend your heart, and not your garments; Return to the LORD your God, For He is gracious and merciful, Slow to anger, and of great kindness; And He relents from doing harm. ¹⁴ Who knows if He will turn and relent, And leave a blessing behind Him — ¹⁹ The LORD will answer and say to His people, "Behold, I will send you grain and new wine and oil, And you will be satisfied by them; I will no longer make you a reproach among the nations. ²⁵ "So I will restore to you the years that the swarming locust has eaten....*

We have strayed so far! The Lord has taught us how we are to live but each has turned to his own way. We do not walk in His ways yet we try to appear as if we do. We go to Church and sit to listen to the message but do we heed God's word? God is calling us to repentance. Our world has gone terribly wrong. We have the chance to change all that one person at a time.

The Prophet Joel tells the people of Judah (Israel's Southern Kingdom) where they have gone wrong. They, too, were about outside appearance rather than living rightly in their hearts. They would rend (or tear) their clothes to show repentance but there would be no change within their hearts. They were the same deceitful people inside. Joel calls out to us to return to the Lord who will restore His blessings upon us even making up for the punishment we received for our rebellion. He is that loving a God!

We, like ancient Israel have wandered away from the Lord. We look OK on the outside but our hearts are black with sin. All is not lost though. God will redeem if asked. Our Heavenly Father is gracious and merciful. He will restore us. I know this firsthand. He has always been with me.

My earthly Father was a model of my Heavenly Father for me as I grew up. My Dad was Fred and he was gracious, loving, merciful and compassionate too! Most of all, he was kind. You knew he loved you and wanted the best for you. He was sometimes disappointed but seldom angry. When I made mistakes, he would say "you'll do better next time." He was a man of few words. In case you are wondering, I take after my Mother in speaking as I am not of few words. One time, I had a battle with my Mom and decided to move out on my own. My Mother was upset. All my Dad said was keep your key. Only three little words. That was his way of saying I am always here for you. I don't want you to go but you can always come back. You will always be my son no matter where you go and I will always love you. You can go out into the world in strength when you have that ace up your sleeve. Not only was my Heavenly Father always with me but so was my earthly Father. I never did move out. My Dad got my Mother to apologize for her interference and promise to treat me as the adult I was at the time. I lived with my parents in mutual respect until I married Jean. I love my parents dearly and I am so blessed by them. Many are not that lucky.

In the same way, the Lord holds you in His heart and will restore you if you return to Him. You may have to face the consequences of your choices but He can redeem you and make you whole. No matter how far you have strayed, He can redeem you. Many people think they have wandered too far for the Lord to bring them back but that is just not true. There is no place His arm cannot reach. In the story from Joel, every living piece of vegetation had been devoured and the land was completely desolate. Yet the Lord said He would restore all that the locusts had eaten. Nothing is impossible with God. Return to the Lord. He is waiting for you with open arms!

Thank You Lord that You are gracious and merciful, slow to anger, and of great kindness. In Your mercy, lead us closer to You. Write Your story on our hearts. Help us to remain in You so we do not have to return. Let us walk with You and share Your love with all whom we meet. In Your name we pray. Amen!

# DECEMBER 1    WHAT DO YOU PERCEIVE
## Quality of Life

Luke 10:23-24 (NKJV)

²³ *Then He turned to His disciples and said privately, "Blessed are the eyes which see the things you see; ²⁴ for I tell you that many prophets and kings have desired to see what you see, and have not seen it, and to hear what you hear, and have not heard it."*

I see and hear things that amaze me. These are the things of God. I perceive in my Spirit things I cannot understand with my mind. I hear that which I write down and read the completed *Encouragement Daily* devotionals as if for the first time. The Holy Spirit speaks to me and through me and shows me things He wants me to see. It is outside of me, but I have learned to listen with my heart more than my senses.

Luke tells us Jesus told His disciples they could see with His eyes things that others would like to be able to see. Solomon asked for wisdom. Simon, the sorcerer (Acts 8:9-25) wanted to purchase this gift. When Jesus is in your heart, you see things differently. You see with your heart and His eyes and hear with His ears. Since I have been able to quiet my soul more, I am able to hear God's still small voice. I believe it started on my first trip to Honduras. There was a lot of noise in my life and mind. Part of the reason I wanted to go to Honduras was a change of scene to give me time away. I needed to draw closer to God. On that trip, He told me to "trust Him". I *heard* His voice. From that time on, I have been listening more closely. I am sure He was always speaking but now I am hearing and listening.

Do you hear God's still small voice? Do you see the things He wants you to see? Is your life guided by His Spirit? Jesus tells us we would be blessed by following God's desire for our lives. This is more of perception than hearing and seeing. Will you quiet your soul and perceive what the Lord is revealing to you? God speaks to all His creation. He is speaking to you! Listen with your heart and be willing to do what He calls you to do. You and the world will be blessed as a result.

Help us to hear You Lord! Take away the distractions and quiet our souls so we can hear You speak and see what You would reveal. Write Your word on our hearts. Give us all we need, including courage, to shine Your light into our dark world. In Your name we pray! Amen!

## DECEMBER 2     ONE DOOR CLOSES...

### Quality of Life

2 Timothy 1:15 (NKJV)

*¹⁵ This you know, that all those in Asia have turned away from me, among whom are Phygellus and Hermogenes.*

Are you kidding me? How could this happen? How could God allow such a thing? Those are the kind of things we think when we face a setback. It seems like a setback in our eyes because we cannot see the master plan. When one door closes, look around, because another door is opening. Do you see it?

Paul is telling Timothy the story of the challenges he is facing in Asia in his attempts to spread the Gospel. People have turned away from his message, but he remains in faith because he "...knows in whom he has believed...." He goes on to encourage Timothy to remain faithful to the Gospel even though it seems people will not accept it at the current time. His encouragement is also to us.

It is curious to me that the best thing in the world (everlasting life) offered at the best value in the world (free) would have to be "sold"! When offered freedom from sin and life everlasting in the presence of the Lord, people balked. They did not believe. Paul hit a roadblock. How was he able to remain faithful? Because he realized this was not the time or place for the message. God had another plan. God sent Paul to preach to the Gentiles in order to make His chosen people jealous so they would want the Good News. He has a plan.

How about your life? Is there something you keep trying without success? My former pastor described this phenomenon as beating your head against a wall. No matter how you try, you are just not making progress and it hurts. You are going against God's plan. When it is that difficult, it means He is wanting you to do it differently or maybe somewhere else. God did not want Paul to go into Asia at that time, so He closed that door. Paul went on to other places and was met with great success. He is the greatest missionary the world has ever known. What does God want from you? When one door closes, will you give up or will you look for the open door through which God wants you to walk today? He has a great plan for your life. Jeremiah 29:11 (NKJV) says *"¹¹ For I know the thoughts that I think toward you, says the* Lord, *thoughts of peace and not of evil, to give you a future and a hope."* Keep your eyes and ears and heart open for the will of the Lord for your life and you will never be disappointed!

Thank You Lord that You have a plan for our good. Lead us in Your ways that we might accomplish the work You set out for us. Take us to the places You ordain. Introduce us to those You would have us meet. Give us the words to speak that would draw them to You through us. In Your name we pray!

# DECEMBER 3  I LOVE YOU BUT....

Relationships

Romans 12:9-10 (ESV)
*Let love be genuine. Abhor what is evil; hold fast to what is good. Love one another with brotherly affection. Outdo one another in showing honor.*

I love you but vs. I love you and.... How many people love you, warts and all? Many people love you when you do what they like or when you help them with things. But when you need something, they are nowhere to be found. They love you if you do what they want. Their love is conditional. If you do this, I will love you. It seems controlling. What is their motive? What motivates you?

In Romans, Paul is teaching us about pure and unselfish love. He asks us to be authentic. He tells us to love in a way that is good for the other person. Your motive should be to do things that are for their good and not your own self-interest. How are you doing with that?

I have an acronym called RAM {Relationships Attitude Motive} by which I am trying to live with His help. I have come to realize relationships are above all other things. The attitude with which we approach something will determine the outcome. And our motive shows what is in our heart. Motive, then, shows who we really are. What motivates you? Do you use your love to manipulate others into doing what you want or are you looking out for them? If you are a spouse or parent, you know about doing things for the best interest of others. Shouldn't all of your life be lived for the good of others? Isn't that what God calls us to do? When a friend calls you at a low time in your life just to let you know they are there for you, how does that make you feel? Isn't that how you want to live also?

Jesus tells us to love our neighbor as ourselves. Are we doing that? Are you loving others back to health and wholeness? Is your motive right? Even strangers can use a kind word. Many people gossip about others which hurts their reputation. Try to avoid such talk. Stand up for others who may not be able to stand for themselves at this moment. Strengthen them so they can stand for themselves. Then they can pass it on to others later. You may not know what they are facing. There could be tragedy in their lives. They may feel unloved and of little value. All they need is a kind word and a smile from you to be able to go on! Will you give them love? It has been given to you. John 3:16 (NKJV) says *[16] For God so loved the world that He gave His only begotten Son, that whoever believes in Him should not perish but have everlasting life.* He loved you so much that He gave Himself up for you. Why not pass a portion of that love on to someone who needs it today?

1 John 4:19 (NKJV) says *"[19] We love Him because He first loved us."* Lord, teach us to love as You love. Help us to put others first. Give us a heart which loves others purely and unconditionally. Help us to love our enemies and the unlovable. In fact, help us to love the stranger. In so doing, help us to bring glory to Your holy name in which we pray. Amen!

# DECEMBER 4    YOU WANT ME TO PRAY FOR WHO
Prayer

Matthew 5:43-48 (NKJV) Love Your Enemies

43 *"You have heard that it was said, 'You shall love your neighbor and hate your enemy.'* 44 *But I say to you, love your enemies, bless those who curse you, do good to those who hate you, and pray for those who spitefully use you and persecute you,* 45 *that you may be sons of your Father in heaven; for He makes His sun rise on the evil and on the good, and sends rain on the just and on the unjust.* 46 *For if you love those who love you, what reward have you? Do not even the tax collectors do the same?* 47 *And if you greet your brethren only, what do you do more than others? Do not even the tax collectors do so?* 48 *Therefore you shall be perfect, just as your Father in heaven is perfect.*

Pray for your enemies. How can you pray for someone when the answer to that prayer would go against the desires of your heart? That is my challenge. While I don't really have enemies, there are a lot of people who do not share my values. I find myself at odds with them over our differences of opinion. I have a great deal of trouble with people who are not nice to children. My challenge is I need to pray for someone who has been cruel to several children.

Jesus is setting the standard way higher than I am able to reach on my own. He wants us to love our enemies. He asks us to pray for people who hate us. Does He really think I can do that? I am hoping He will help me because I cannot do it on my own. And on top of that, He wants me to be perfect. Yeah right! When I was fourteen, I had reached the apex of perfection. It has been all downhill from there.

So, I am supposed to pray for the person who has harmed others. I get that. But my prayers are supposed to be for their deliverance from addiction and their restoration. That is a good prayer. However, if my prayers are answered in a positive manner, I may lose what is of great value to me. I am praying against myself and my interests. It's like praying for someone else to win the race in which I am running. It seems so counter-intuitive. But that is God's way. He wants to see you will do that which seems too difficult in order to follow His lead. Since I know my desires are not pure, I pray that His will be done. His will is best for all because He will work everything out for the good of all. Yes, someone wins, and someone loses this particular challenge. But God can still work everything out for good.

Years ago, we had a foster child we wanted to adopt. He ended up going back to his father instead. We were very disappointed and grieved the loss. We had poured everything we had into him, but he did not stay. He still visits from time to time. The good news is all the seeds we planted in him are still there. Life may not be perfect, but he remembers the love and truth he learned years ago. He knows how life should be and can live that way when he gets out on his own. God's plan will not be thwarted! His word does not return to Him void. Keep on planting the seeds God gives you even if you cannot see the results. God will give an increase. His grace will manifest itself in each life you touch. It did for us. It will for you. Our foster son still visits and realizes all we have done with and for him. He is forever changed as are we.

Our God worked all things out for our good even if it wasn't our way. He will do the same for you.

Father God, we know Your plan is always for everyone's good. But even so, we have trouble with the twists and turns of life. We see things going badly. Show us Your long-term plan for our good. Keep us calm while You work out Your plan. Remind us of Your love so we can wait for Your redemption and grace. In Your name we pray! Amen!

# DECEMBER 5    SPEAK LORD, FOR YOUR SERVANT LISTENS
Faith

1 Samuel 3:7-11 (NIV)

*⁷Now Samuel did not yet know the LORD: The word of the LORD had not yet been revealed to him. ⁸A third time the LORD called, "Samuel!" And Samuel got up and went to Eli and said, "Here I am; you called me." Then Eli realized that the LORD was calling the boy. ⁹So Eli told Samuel, "Go and lie down, and if he calls you, say, 'Speak, LORD, for your servant is listening.'" So, Samuel went and lay down in his place. ¹⁰The LORD came and stood there, calling as at the other times, "Samuel! Samuel!" Then Samuel said, "Speak, for your servant is listening." ¹¹And the LORD said to Samuel: "See, I am about to do something in Israel that will make the ears of everyone who hears about it tingle.*

Does the Lord speak to you? Are you listening well-enough so you would know if He did? 1 Kings 19 says *"And after the fire came a gentle whisper."* That whisper was God speaking to Elijah. He also speaks to you. Did you hear it? He said He loves you. He said you mean everything to Him. He said He will always be with you. He said He has plans to prosper you.

Samuel was pledged to the Lord by his mother Hannah. He was an intern to Eli the Priest. The Lord decided to reveal Himself to Samuel and called to him. It was not a great profession of who God is but a still small voice. If God had shown up in all His Glory, Samuel would have been terrified. Instead, the fact is the Lord *"came and stood there"*. God revealed Himself to Samuel quietly because He had great plans for Samuel. The new thing He would do is to have Samuel anoint a poor shepherd boy, David, to be the next king of Israel. And through the line of David, the Christ would be born. But first, Samuel had to hear the call.

Do you hear God's call on your life? I have heard His voice a few times. It was a whisper. When I was in Honduras, He said "Trust Me!" My friend Helen heard "I am all around you." My friend Linda heard "It'll be OK." I put those together as "Trust Me! I am all around you. It'll be OK!" and try to live my life in peace believing in Him. He is my strength and shield.

Few people are willing to admit that God has spoken to them. They say they get strange looks from others if they mention the encounter. I have spoken with many privately who tell of hearing God. I plan to interview them and write a book about hearing God. Maybe, if we spent more time listening to Him, our world would be a brighter and safer place. Ask these questions of the Lord and see if He does not answer you. What would you have me do? To whom do You wish me to speak through me? How can I share Your love with others? Speak Lord, for Your servants listen!

Lord, speak to us Lord in our daily lives. Make Yourself known in all the small things we do. Guide us in the way we should go. Lead us to the people to whom You wish to speak through our lives today! In Your name we pray! Amen!

## DECEMBER 6    TIE IT ALL TOGETHER
Support

Psalm 32:8 (NIV)
*8 I will instruct you and teach you in the way you should go; I will counsel you with my loving eye on you.*

Teach, Inspire, Encourage (T.I.E.) is a phrase that came to me last year. God has revealed to me I personally will not be able to do all I have done in the past. That is true for each of us. It does not get better. He let me know He wants these things to continue so I have to teach others. I am an A+ personality. I want to do it *all*! Alas, I cannot. God has shown me I can make a bigger difference for His Kingdom by investing in others to multiply my efforts in what He calls me to do. In other words, don't be Chairperson of one committee but be an encourager to others so they will work on multiple committees. J. C. Penny said I would rather have a one percent stake in 100 people than a one hundred percent stake in one person. Encouraging others will yield greater return for Him and His Kingdom. My how things have changed.

The Lord is willing to teach you how. Many don't like these lessons because some include pain. If you would get the idea sooner, He may not have to take such drastic measures. The key phrase for me is "I will counsel you with my loving eye on you." God will love you through everything. It is all meant for your good. To be counseled requires listening though. He will speak if you will listen.

Many people today don't teach their kids things. I hear "It is easier to do it myself than waste time teaching them." If you go that route, your kids won't know anything. When you are no longer there to do things, they won't know how, and your skill and contribution will be lost. Have you ever wanted to ensure a great mission would continue? That will only happen if you encourage and inspire the next generation. And that is not only your kids. I am asking you to teach Sunday School, mentor a troubled teen, participate in Youth Group and Mission trips, shadow a child and be a role model. When you see a person off by themselves, invite them to sit with you! Early teenage years are awkward at best. Why not encourage a young person. I began writing these devotionals because I saw so much discouragement. How are you at loving your neighbor? All it takes is a smile!

Sometime, people won't teach coworkers what they know because they think they will lose their job. While that is possible, you can always find a better job. If you know what to do, you will always have a job. If you know why you do it, you will be in charge. Teach others. Build a team where everyone supports the others. Work together. It's more fun!

Follow His instructions and teach others. You will build relationships for the journey and walking with others is always better. But remember, He will keep His loving eye on you.

Lord God, Thank You that You teach us and keep Your loving eye on us. Instruct us in our path. Counsel us as to how You would have us live. In You, we are blessed. Amen!

# DECEMBER 7   DO YOU CELEBRATE YOURSELF
## Quality of Life

Psalm 139:14 (NIV)

[14] *I praise you because I am fearfully and wonderfully made; your works are wonderful, I know that full well.*

If you read through the Bible, you will see, time and time again, how awesome you are. God reveals part of His glory in and through you. You were made in His image and likeness. That means you are like God! Lakewood Church has a mantra which is "This is my Bible. I am what it says I am.  I have what it says I have. I can do what it says I can do...." Do you operate under that assumption? Imagine what your life would look like if you did?

In this Psalm, David tells us about ourselves as God sees us. Since we were created by God, we are wonderful. David knows that, but do we? He tells us we are fearfully and wonderfully made. Read all of Psalm 139 to find out how wonderful you really are in God's eyes. And it is His opinion that counts.

Do you celebrate yourself? Do you appreciate all God has done in you? Are you aware of the gifts and talents He has placed inside you for the benefit of the world? You were designed with excellence and given everything you need to accomplish your destiny. In so doing, you bring glory to God. When you minimize your talents, you are disrespecting the Giver of those talents. Why not approach every situation knowing the Lord has equipped you and you will work in His power to accomplish what He set out for you to do?

Praising God for what He has done in your life is key. Thank Him that He has given you what you need. Speak as if He has already accomplished what He set out to do in your life. Declare the victory in advance and victory you will have. You bring about what you think about. Celebrate yourself. God thought enough of you to create you. Get in agreement with Him. You are fearfully and wonderfully made. Be bold and do what He calls you to do. You will be victorious!

Thank You Lord that You have given us victory over the challenges we face. Thank You that we are fearfully and wonderfully made. Thank You that You have given us everything we need to live out the great plan You created for us. Thank You that You go before us preparing the way and making the crooked places straight. Thank You for being our help, our shield and our strength. In Your name we pray! Amen!

# DECEMBER 8   LIKE A BROTHER
Relationships

Proverbs 17:17 (NIV)
*A friend loves at all times, and a brother is born for a difficult time.*

A brother is someone who sticks with you in difficult times. Do you have a brother? I do! Over the years, David has been there for me as I have for him. We appreciate each other and know that we can rely on one another.

Proverbs tells us all kinds of wise things. This is just another example. It says you can count on your brother. There is a special bond between brothers. Even when they are not in the same place, they know there is someone else who shares their DNA. It defies explanation but there is a connection that exists at a cellular level that draws us to our brother.

There are many things I notice when I am with my brother. We fit together well. We have the same sense of humor. There is a certain feeling of teamwork when we work on a project. We know each other fully; likes and dislikes. We have the same history and know all the same people. It is a comfortable relationship. I don't have to pretend. I am who I am. It is a natural fit. You don't need to force things; they just go together. David and I share that bond. After all, he took care of me when I was a baby. We look very much the same although Dave doesn't think so. One Monday he called me. He asked where I had been over the weekend. I had just returned from Dallas. He turned to the person in his office and said "Yup, it was him." She said she had seen his double on the plane.

But what about brothers that were not raised together? Do they have that kind of bond? Yes, they do. The bond is part of their makeup. It goes beyond location. There are many stories of kids separated at birth that find out years later they have a sibling. They find an instant bond. Our boys met officially this past June after an almost eight-year separation. Brandon instantly took to Clayton although he never really knew him before. It is special to watch them together. There is a faint smile on Clayton's face that will not go away. Brandon is *his*! He has family now. Family is special. You love them warts and all because they are yours.

Today is special because it is Dave's birthday! I am glad he was born. He is *mine*! Take today to think about your siblings. Maybe give them a call. Marvel at the things that bind you together. They are beyond our understanding but true none the less. Thank the Sovereign Lord that He has placed you in a family and given you those who care about you. Perhaps you don't get along with your siblings. This might be a day to reach out to change all that. The Lord desires unity. Maybe you could change things today.

Thank You Lord for your design of the family. Thank You for placing us in groups that love each other and share common bonds. Help us to appreciate each other and draw closer to You in unity. You said it is not good for us to be alone. That is why you created marriage and families that come out of that marriage. Bless our families and give us Your peace. In Your name we pray! Amen!

## DECEMBER 9  ARE YOU A CHARACTER
Quality of Life

Proverbs 31:10-17 (NIV) Selected Verses

*¹⁰ A wife of noble character who can find? She is worth far more than rubies. ¹¹ Her husband has full confidence in her and lacks nothing of value. ¹² She brings him good, not harm, all the days of her life. ¹⁶ She considers a field and buys it; out of her earnings she plants a vineyard. ¹⁷ She sets about her work vigorously; her arms are strong for her tasks.*

I have been called a character, but do I display character? Many do not understand the value of character. The value of a person who is faithful and who will do what they say is above most things in life. In fact, I would rather have a person of character in my life than wealth. Solomon chose wisdom over wealth. I would choose character.

Proverbs speaks about a wife of noble character and how her worth is far more than rubies. Her husband has full confidence in her. She is a trusted life partner. My Sister-in-law is a wife of noble character. I have known Sandy for more than 50 years and she has always been a blessing to my brother. They have been married 48 years, raised two wonderful boys and now enjoy 6 grandchildren. Sandy invests a lot of time in her family. She spent a lot of time with her sons and it shows. They are raising great children of their own. You reap what you sow. If you sow character, that is what will result.

What example are you setting for those around you? Do you bring value to your relationships? Are you a person of character? You were created with all the seeds necessary to be the person God created you to be. God has written His word on our hearts so we can follow His wonderful ways. You have everything you need but it won't be easy. Do you want a life of integrity? Do you want to raise children of character? If so, you need to walk in God's ways. He is with you. All you need do is ask and He will help you. You are not alone in this quest.

Today is Sandy's birthday and a reminder of a woman of noble character. If she can do it, you can too! Walk with the Lord today and He will put a crown of righteousness on your head also!

Lord, thank You for women of character. Thank You that You are willing to walk with us all leading us in the way we should go. Help us to hear Your directions and follow. The world calls us astray. Draw us back to You. In Your name we pray! Amen!

# DECEMBER 10   WHAT IS YOUR GPS
## Quality of Life

Isaiah 30:21 (NKJV)

²¹ *Your ears shall hear a word behind you, saying, "This is the way, walk in it," Whenever you turn to the right hand Or whenever you turn to the left.*

What is your GPS; your God Positioning System? How do you know where God wants you to be? Do you listen for His voice guiding you? It is often hard to know what God wants for us. There are so many things that confront us today that we are not sure which way to go.

Isaiah tells us we will hear a word behind us indicating which way we should go. The Lord will guide you if you let Him.

My GPS is a woman's voice. She knows men don't ask for directions, so she tells me which way to go. She is very explicit in her instructions. She leaves nothing to chance. She even tells me how many more feet it is until I have to turn and which way. If I listen, I am able to get places I have never been before. I drive her crazy when I don't listen. "Make a U-turn if possible" is heard a lot in my car. I am difficult to manage. I always want to go my own way. I don't listen well. Someday, she is going to scream "You never listen to me!"

That is sort of how it is with me and God. He stands on my dashboard and sometimes my shoulder telling me which way I should go but I don't usually listen. I am getting better though. I have come to a place where I hear when He speaks. When I choose which direction, things are not always so good. When He chooses, things work out great. Do you listen to your GPS? God will tell you exactly which way to go either through His word or by His Holy Spirit. But you have to listen. Don't be like me and try to get there on your own. The road is bumpy. When you listen to the GPS, God goes before you paving the way. He will tell you which way to go if you will ask and then follow the directions. Will you listen? I pray you do.

Sovereign Lord be our GPS today! Direct us aright through Your own good counsel. Lead us in the path we should take. Teach us Your ways. Let us follow You that we may bring You glory. In Your name we pray! Amen!

# DECEMBER 11 AMAZING LOVE, HOW CAN IT BE

Grace and Mercy

Philippians 2:7-8 (NIV)
*7 rather, he made himself nothing by taking the very nature of a servant,*
*being made in human likeness. 8 And being found in appearance as a man,*
*he humbled himself by becoming obedient to death— even death on a cross!*

Who would do such a thing? Who would sacrifice themselves in a horrible way in place of another? You would have to be either crazy or divine. Which do you think it was?

Paul tells us about what steps Jesus took and how he humbled Himself to save us from our sins. He entered this world as a man, fully human, so he could experience all that we face to understand and set an example. He faced the most gruesome kind of death offering Himself as an atoning sacrifice for the sins we have and will commit. Incomprehensible!

Why would he do such a thing? John 3:16 says (NIV) *16 For God so loved the world that he gave his one and only Son, that whoever believes in him shall not perish but have eternal life.* He did all that because He loves you and He loves you more than you can grasp. He loves you enough to give up everything for you! He did this so you and I will not perish but have eternal life. Let that sink in for a moment. He gave Himself up for us. How will we live in response to that? With so much love poured into you, what will be our next steps? Will you look out for others? Jesus does not expect you to die on a cross, but He does expect you to care for other people. He does want you to be unselfish. He does want you to shine His light and share His love. *No greater love has anyone that this, that He would lay down His life for His friends* (John 15:13). He is our friend and so much more. I don't think I could lay down my life for another, but it sure makes me wonder who I am the Jesus would lay down His life for me. We are all that special.

Knowing you are that special, go out today and live a blessing life. Be a blessing to others. Be bold. Be brave. Be courageous. Smile at others. Show the world what it means to follow a Risen Lord! Shine His light into the dark places. Share the love given to you!

Lord God, thank You for Your gift of love. We don't deserve it, but You give it anyway. Help us not to keep it for ourselves but to freely share Your love with all we meet. Help us to love the difficult people. May we see them through Your eyes and reflect Your face to them. In Jesus name we pray! Amen!

# DECEMBER 12    THE EVENING NEWS
Faith

Psalm 37:1-4 (NKJV) The Heritage of the Righteous and the Calamity of the Wicked
*¹ Do not fret because of evildoers, Nor be envious of the workers of iniquity. ² For they shall soon be cut down like the grass, And wither as the green herb. ³ Trust in the LORD, and do good; Dwell in the land, and feed on His faithfulness. ⁴ Delight yourself also in the LORD, And He shall give you the desires of your heart.*

The Evening News is so discouraging. There is mostly hatred and violence and greed. It is so bad I try not to watch the news or read the paper. It just upsets me. I cannot change things. I have voted for who I thought would make it better, but the world is still a dark and dangerous place.

King David tells us not to worry about the evildoers and how they seem to prosper. He tells us they will soon perish. He goes on to remind us to trust in the Lord and walk in His ways. When we do, we can "Dwell in the land and feed on His faithfulness." Would you like to feed on His faithfulness?

A few days ago, I was at a meeting where the guys were talking about a shooting in San Bernardino which I knew nothing about. I am a little embarrassed that I am so ill-informed, but I get overwhelmed by the darkness and violence. The only way I can deal with all the bad is to not know. It makes me anxious and that is not right. I am a Christ-follower and I am supposed to trust in Him. Then why am I so anxious? What am I afraid of? Isn't His grace sufficient? Isn't He still on His throne? Yes, He is! But I still don't understand why He allows all this evil. How can I deal with it all? That is the point. It is not up to me or you! It is all up to Him.

As I have approached Christmas over the past years, I have been sad. I look at the condition of the world and I am embarrassed the Lord is coming, and I still haven't cleaned up my corner of the world. The Christmas Season held little joy for me because I had the wrong focus. I thought I was responsible for the world. How could I face Him and explain why things are so bad? I thought I had control. Finally, I realized it is my Father's World and I am not in control. What a relief! While I am responsible for what I do and how I act, the world is not my fault nor responsibility! When you think you are in control, it is a heavy burden. With great power comes great responsibility. I do not want either. I just want to walk with my Lord and do His will. He asks us to take care of widows and orphans and love others as He has loved us. I can try to do that! You can too! Are you walking around with the weight of the world on your shoulders? Isn't it a bit heavy? Why not lay it down at the foot of the cross and enjoy the beauty of the season when we remember how much He loves us? When you trust in the Lord, you will be able to feed on His faithfulness. He is with you always. Enjoy Him forever! The wicked will be cut down. Grace is coming for you!

Lord, help me to trust You and not lean on my own understanding. Teach me Your ways that I might walk in them. Help me to release control and reach for the joy of Your Salvation. Instead of the outlook, help me to focus on Your Up-look and fix my eyes on You. And, grant all these blessings to my friends as well. Come Lord Jesus, come! In Your name I pray! Amen!

# DECEMBER 13    WHO IS YOUR SUPERHERO

Redemption

Revelation 5:5 (NKJV)
*⁵ But one of the elders said to me, "Do not weep. Behold, the Lion of the tribe of Judah, the Root of David, has prevailed to open the scroll and to lose its seven seals."*

Who is your Superhero? Who do you know that has powers above and beyond that of mere mortals? The entertainment industry has no shortage of heroes they send our way with one more super than the next. But none of them are real. My hero is the Lion of Judah. Proverbs 30:30 ESV says *"The lion, which is mightiest among beasts and does not turn back before any;"* My hero is not afraid of sin or death or anything else in all creation. Exodus 14:14 (NKJV) says *"¹⁴ The LORD will fight for you, and you shall hold your peace."* He will be my vindicator.

Jesus has many names given Him throughout the Bible. Lion of Judah is just one. In Revelation, His return is described to us. Jesus first appearance was as the Lamb of God to take away the sins of the world. His return will be as the Lion of Judah to judge the world. Meek and mild will not be words used to describe Christ, the King of kings, this time. He will come in glory and majesty and power and will take unto Himself His own and destroy all evil. He will create a new world; a New Jerusalem as described when He opens the seals of judgment.

Yesterday, we went to a Christmas party run by Foster and Adoptive Family Services with our 8-year-old son. They had all types of activities there including face-painting. One child was Spiderman. Another girl was a fairy princess and there were many other characters like the Hulk. As I watched and enjoyed the playing, I was given the thought of who is my Superhero? I thought about who is the strongest, the most powerful, the one who can do anything. It is my Lord, the Lion of Judah! He holds the keys to hell and death and will remove both of them from His own.

Spiderman can bind things with his webs. The Lion can lose the bindings of sin. Superman has x-ray vision. The Lion sees all things; nothing is hidden from His eyes. The Hulk can move large things. The Lion created those things. Ironman can fly. The Lion of Judah is already everywhere and has no need to travel. Yup! My hero is better than them all. For my hero, while coming in power and glory, also comes in love. *For God so loved the world that He gave His one and only son, that whoever believes in him shall not perish but have eternal life* (John 3:16). What superhero has ever done that? He is coming! He that gave Himself up for you is coming! He that loves you more than life itself is coming. And He is looking for you. Do you perceive Him? Will you receive Him? Your Superhero is coming!

Lion of Judah, come to us and take us to Yourself! Be our Superhero. Remind us always of all You have done and will do for the love of Your children. May Your mercy always precede Your power. Thank You that Your love comes before Your justice. Come Lord Jesus to those who eagerly await You! And put sin and death under Your feet and away from our lives. Draw us to You! In Your name we pray! Amen!

## DECEMBER 14   EVERY DAY HEROES
Grace and Mercy

Romans 15:1-2 (NKJV) Bearing Others' Burdens

*¹ We then who are strong ought to bear with the scruples of the weak, and not to please ourselves. ² Let each of us please his neighbor for his good, leading to edification.*

Each and every day, people make choices. Some choose to do what is good for themselves while others choose to take care of others around them. Why do some look after others? What makes someone selfish? How are we supposed to live?

Paul tells us what God says about how to live. He tells us the strong are supposed to take care of the weak. Instead of looking after our own interests, we are supposed to please our neighbor for their good. He tells us it leads to edification.

Edification is building one another up. Have you built someone up today? TV shows us superheroes but what about the everyday heroes? What about the people who look after their neighbors daily? We don't see too much of that on the evening news, yet I know there are heroes all around. We have friends who have taken in foster children. Because of our friends, we decided to become Foster Parents. In fact, through Foster Parenting, we have met many incredible everyday heroes. There is a whole network of people we have met through Foster and Adoptive Family Services who look after the least of these every day. One thing is for sure. You find what you seek. If you listen to the news about bad things, that is what will fill your mind. Why not look for the real everyday heroes. There are many in the world around you who are looking out for others. Why not becomes one of them? In this season, many exhibit the Christmas Spirit. I ask you to live that Spirit all year long. Every day be a hero to someone! No matter how small you think the gesture might be, it can mean more than you will ever know to someone! It doesn't take much to be a hero. Give out smiles. Give out kind words. If appropriate, give out hugs! When someone is having a bad day, remind them God still loves them. Be someone's hero today. Do something for the benefit of another. You won't believe what it will do for your frame of mind too. Be a good finder and build others up. The rewards are incredible!

Sovereign Lord help us to live lives that build others up. You are our hero. By Your example, teach us how to be heroes to those who need reassurance. Let us follow Your lead and strengthen those whose faith is weaker. May our courage in our walk with You strengthen and encourage them and turn their hearts toward You. Grant that we might win some for the Kingdom. In Your name we pray! Amen!

## DECEMBER 15    LET'S SEE WHAT YOU CAN DO
Faith

Titus 3:5 (NKJV)
*⁵ not by works of righteousness which we have done, but according to His mercy He saved us, through the washing of regeneration and renewing of the Holy Spirit,*

Can you do things all on your own? Are you an independent person? Many people think they are self-made. They tend to think they are the captains of their own ship and it is all up to them. The older I get, the more I realize how little control I really have. I am much better off when I wait upon the Lord.

In Paul's letter to Titus it is not our works but His mercy that gives us our salvation. Further, we are saved by the washing of regeneration. We are renewed by the Holy Spirit who is constantly guiding us in our walk. When the Spirit guides us in the way we should go, it always goes better.

In our own strength and power, things are limited as to what we can do. When we open our hearts and minds to the Lord, He will give us all the wisdom and power and resources we need to reach the destiny He has planned for us. Mark 10:27 (NKJV) says *²⁷ But Jesus looked at them and said, "With men it is impossible, but not with God; for with God all things are possible."* So, do you want to do it on your own? Or would you like to go the easy way and walk with the Lord?

When I try to do things on my own, I stress over things and try to make everything perfect. And with that stress, there is anxiety. The journey is not enjoyable. When I relax and let Him lead, we go along without me worrying. I enjoy the ride. Don't you want to enjoy the ride? Then let Jesus be the captain of your ship. I was presenting a class at a national Real Estate convention. At the time, I thought I was in charge and I made things happen. I needed to eat quickly so I could get to my next class but couldn't find an open seat. A seat appeared next to a gentleman with whom I got a contract for training for the next two years. I thought it was luck but is appeared out of nowhere. Looking back, it was God's plan, not mine, that was in play that day. It was His grace that led the way.

Lord, please guide us in the ways You would have us go. Regenerate our minds in You. Help us to relax and be renewed by Your Spirit. Help us to trust Your leading. May we always be guided by Your Spirit and remain in Your grace. In Your name we pray. Amen!

# DECEMBER 16   WHAT DO YOU HAVE TO GIVE
Relationships

Matthew 12:34 (NKJV)

³⁴ *Brood of vipers! How can you, being evil, speak good things? For out of the abundance of the heart the mouth speaks.*

I would like to share a story that was sent to me which illustrates human nature, In Matthew 12, the Lord told us we can only produce something which matches that which is in our hearts; either good or bad. What is on the inside will determine what comes out.

Israel's Prime Minister, Benjamin Netanyahu, received an item from the leader of HAMAS. During the recent cease-fire, the leader of the Palestinian terrorist organization Hamas, Khaled Mashal, sent a "gift" in an elaborate box with a note. After having the box checked for safety reasons, Prime Minister Netanyahu opened the box and saw that the content was cow dung. He opened the note, handwritten in Arabic by Mr. Mashal, which said, "For you and the proud people of the Zionist Entity."

Mr. Netanyahu, who is literate in Arabic, pondered the note and decided how best to reciprocate. He quickly did so by sending the Hamas leader an equally handsome package, also containing a personal note. Mr. Mashal and the other leaders of Hamas were very surprised to receive the parcel and opened it, very carefully, similarly suspecting that it might contain a bomb. But to their surprise, they saw that it contained a tiny computer chip. The chip was rechargeable with solar energy, had a 1.8 terabyte memory, and could output a 3D hologram display capable of functioning in any type of cellular phone, tablet or laptop. It was one of the world's most advanced technologies, with a tiny label, stating this item was "Invented and produced in Israel."

Mr. Netanyahu's note, personally handwritten in Arabic, Hebrew, French, and English, stated very courteously... "Every leader can only give the best his people can produce."

What is it that you give to others? Is it your best? Do you praise others and build them up at every chance? Are you the type of person who brightens up every room you enter? Are others always glad to see you? Look into your heart and see what resides there. For out of the overflow of the heart the mouth speaks. If there is goodness within you, goodness will come out. Who are you on the inside? Are you setting the kind of example that you want others to follow? If not, why not? You have everything you need to become the person God created you to be. You are fearfully and wonderfully made. Are you using your gifts and talents to benefit others? When we treat others well, the world will become a better place. Each little gesture matters, make it a point this day to love the Lord Your God with all you are and love your neighbor as yourself. That means you need to love yourself as God already loves you. You are blessed to be a blessing!

Lord God, You placed every good thing inside us. Yet we often let our evil inclination rule our lives. By Your Spirit, let joy and blessings rule in our hearts and spill over into our whole lives. Teach us to be a blessing to every person we meet. Help us to share the love You gave us with all we meet showing them Your glory! Let us become the lights You created us to be. In Your name we pray! Amen!

# DECEMBER 17   DON'T BE AFRAID
Faith


John 14:1-3 (NKJV)
*"Let not your heart be troubled; you believe in God, believe also in Me.* [2] *In My Father's house are many mansions; if it were not so, I would have told you. I go to prepare a place for you.* [3] *And if I go and prepare a place for you, I will come again and receive you to Myself; that where I am, there you may be also.*

Are you afraid to die? Are you afraid to live? What do you think will happen when you leave this life? What will you leave behind? Paul says in 2 Corinthians 5:8; *"Absent from the body; present with the Lord."* Is that how you feel? If not, why not?

Jesus tells us to not be troubled. He wants us to believe in Him. He also tells us He is going ahead of us to prepare a place for us so we can be with Him. He further tells us He will return for us to take us unto Himself. It sounds pretty certain and wonderful to me! I know I will be with Him when I pass from this world. You can be sure also.

What about you? Where will you go at the end of this life? Have you believed in Jesus and are you going to be with Him when you pass from this world? Many people have doubts. They look at their lives and think they do not deserve Heaven. No one does and that is why it is a gift. After all, look at all the mistakes we have made along the way. We all have those things we have done that we regret, and God knew we would do them even before we were born. So, He made a way for us to be redeemed and justified back to Him even though we went astray. You see, He loves us that much that He wants us to be with Him where He is. Maybe you cannot understand how He could accomplish that because of our limited finite minds. God is infinite and can-do things we cannot grasp. He has done this for you and me.

This is a special time of year. Christmas was the day in which God stepped into time and entered our world physically. John 3:16 says *"[16] For God so loved the world that He gave His only begotten Son, that whoever believes in Him should not perish but have everlasting life."* God took on human form in the person of Jesus the Christ in order to present Himself as a living sacrifice, holy and pleasing to God, that you and I would be covered by the blood of that sacrifice. Every bad thing you have done past, present or future is covered by the perfect Blood of the Lamb. Jesus is the Lamb of God who takes away the sins of the *world* and He is coming! He is coming to take away your sin. He has overcome death all for you. No matter what happens, you are in His care. You are holy, righteous and redeemed! The burden has been lifted. Now go out and live in assurance that Jesus has established a place for you. And don't worry!

Well, what if I am at the end of my earthly journey and I have not lived in assurance? Now is the time to look at the offer again. God is the same yesterday, today and forever. His offer still stands. He told the thief on the cross "I tell you the truth, today you will be with Me in paradise." What about you? Will you listen to Christ's offer? It is still on the table. Reach out your hand to Him. He loves you and wants you to be with Him. When that day comes, remember the carpenter from Nazareth who has gone ahead and built a place for you in His Father's house. You know the way. He will be there to greet and guide you. You are His beloved child. Enter His house with joy and thanksgiving for it was built for you! He is coming! In Jesus the Christ's name I pray for you today! Amen!

## DECEMBER 18    I DON'T MEASURE UP
### Quality of Life

John 19:23-24 (NKJV)

23 Then the soldiers, when they had crucified Jesus, took His garments and made four parts, to each soldier a part, and also the tunic. Now the tunic was without seam, woven from the top in one piece. 24 They said therefore among themselves, "Let us not tear it, but cast lots for it, whose it shall be," that the Scripture might be fulfilled which says: "They divided My garments among them, And for My clothing they cast lots." Therefore, the soldiers did these things.

The world is a dark place because too many people do not feel they are worthy of God's grace and mercy. They go around trying to always do better and give 110% hoping to make up for the nagging empty part inside where worthiness should dwell. People work many hours extra to make a name for themselves. Yet nothing seems to fill the void!

John gives us an account of the crucifixion of Christ. The soldiers divided up Jesus garments among themselves as spoils. John describes the tunic "was without seams" which was unusual. It was a special garment. Since it was mentioned particularly in this account, there must have been much significance attached to it. The soldiers cast lots to see who would get the garment. I believe the lot fell to us instead. We are the big winners.

I believe that tunic was the Garment of Righteousness. The soldiers removed this garment from Jesus at the cross. There is no doubt that Jesus was righteous. As the Son of God, He was perfect. When He was placed on the cross and all the sin of the world was absorbed by Him, His righteousness was separated from Him as the garment was removed. I believe it was given to you and me through that garment. So, you are right! No, you don't measure up on your own. But you are not on your own. You are holy, righteous and redeemed because Christ's righteousness, symbolized by that tunic, has been given to you.

Now this is something too big for us to fully or even partially understand. How can we be perfect in God's sight and righteous before Him? It is a mystery. I certainly don't feel perfect. I am far from that. But we are covered in this Garment of Righteousness and God sees us through the eyes and filter of Christ. On our own merit, we cannot stand. But on Christ, the solid Rock, we can all stand. The anniversary of the birth of the One who came to perfect us all by His blood is rapidly approaching. Let us be joyful and accept the gift we were and are given. May Christ reside in our hearts and our heads richly this Christmas Season. In His name we pray! Amen!

# DECEMBER 19    EVERYONE WANTS A SAVIOR; HOW MANY WANT A LORD
### Quality of Life

Exodus 14:13-14 (ESV)

*13 And Moses said to the people, "Fear not, stand firm, and see the salvation of the LORD, which he will work for you today. For the Egyptians whom you see today, you shall never see again. 14 The LORD will fight for you, and you have only to be silent."*

When Jesus came along and offered Salvation to those who would believe, there were takers. As He entered Jerusalem on what would become Palm Sunday, the crowds were cheering. But many would fall away. John 6:60 (NKJV) says *"60 Therefore many of His disciples, when they heard this, said, "This is a hard saying; who can understand it?"* I don't think it was the part they did not understand that troubled them; it was the part they did understand. It was clear they would have to stop living for themselves and start walking in God's ways that was troubling.

Even Moses tied Salvation to accepting the Lord. Those words both appear in the same passage. Their redemption would come from Him. He would free them from their bondage in Egypt and, ultimately, their bondage to sin. The Israelites had already seen the Lord defeat the Egyptians. Moses told them "the Lord will fight for you while you keep silent." They did not have to do anything but watch and be delivered.

Does the Lord still fight for you today? Your Savior is coming. It is six days until Christmas, the anniversary of the Savior entering this world. Luke 2:11 says *"11 For there is born to you this day in the city of David a Savior, who is Christ the Lord."* He is your Lord as well as your Savior. So, what does it mean to acknowledge Jesus as your Lord? It means you need to follow His teachings. You are to love the Lord your God with all your heart and all your soul and all your mind and all your strength and love your neighbor as yourself. I think that is a tall order. Perhaps that is why some fall away. They may have thought they could not live up to the requirements. But the angel told the shepherds "I bring you good news of great joy that will be for *all* people." What is this good news? The good news is that Christ, the Savior is born unto you. And He brings help with Him. In John, the Lord *says 14 If you ask anything in My name, I will do it. 15 "If you love Me, keep My commandments. 16 And I will pray the Father, and He will give you another Helper, that He may abide with you forever— 17 the Spirit of truth."* Jesus was born into the world and changed things forever. He made a way for us all to return to the Father. But there was much more than meets the eye. He also brought the Helper which is His Holy Spirit to live inside all believers. You have the Spirit of the Lord within you who will give you all strength and power to keep His commandments. He gives you everything you need to hold Him up as Lord. Christ can now be your Savior and Lord! Remember, you were made in His image and likeness. You have what you need to follow your Lord. The world will be a better place when Jesus is your Lord!

Lord, You said You would do whatever we ask in Your name. For what shall we ask today? We ask Your Spirit help us love You and our neighbors. We ask You guide us in the ways we should go and lead us by Your Spirit. Teach us to ask in Your name and love as You love. In Your name we pray! Amen!

# DECEMBER 20   ANY EXCUSE FOR A PARTY

Love

2 Samuel 6:12-15 (NKJV)

*Now it was told King David, saying, "The LORD has blessed the house of Obed-edom and all that belongs to him, on account of the ark of God." David went and brought up the ark of God from the house of Obed-edom into the city of David with gladness. And so, it was, that when the bearers of the ark of the LORD had gone six paces, he sacrificed an ox and a fatling. And David was dancing before the LORD with all his might, and David was wearing a linen ephod.*

David knew how to celebrate! He was dancing before the Lord with all his might. He was excited because the Ark of the Covenant was being brought in to Bethlehem, the City of David. Some people criticized David because they thought his dancing was undignified. He was filled with joy to overflowing for God and it showed. There is no account of David acting this way in another circumstance. As humans, we tend to celebrate many things but overlook ourselves. Saint Augustine said, "Men go abroad to wonder at the heights of mountains, at the huge waves of the sea, at the long courses of the rivers, at the vast compass of the ocean, at the circular motions of the stars, and they pass by themselves without wondering." Do you celebrate yourself?

Last night, we were at a party of members and spouses of my Every Man a Warrior Men's Group celebrating each other. There is not enough celebration in our lives. When we accomplish a small step toward our goal, we need to recognize the accomplishment. Each course passed toward a college degree should be noted. Otherwise, the finish line can become too distant and out of sight. We may give up and that would be sad. We are supposed to build each other up in our lives. There was discussion of progress made in our families. There was fellowship. There was the sharing of the love of God between us all. There was generosity. Most of all, there was encouragement. Each person left the evening with joy and contentment. You could see it on their faces and feel it in the hugs! We did not dance but there certainly was a lot of building-up going on. So, what was our excuse for this party? The best excuse of all. We got together in the name of Christ because we are brothers and sisters in Christ. Christ is what we all have in common and His love permeated the whole evening. In light of the Christmas season, there was an easy excuse for a party, but you don't need an excuse. Gather together in His name and celebrate Him and each other all year every year. Do it every day in small ways as you can. Life will be so much more joyous this way.

*Those living in darkness have seen a great light.... For unto us a child is born.* (Isaiah 9) You are that Child Lord. And You gave Yourself to us completely. Words cannot express the joy and beauty of Your gift so let our actions show others how we love You and them. Help us to celebrate with all our might. You said You would write Your Law on our hearts. I ask You to manifest Your love there instead beyond what we can contain so it overflows to the world. Then they will know we are Yours! In Jesus name I pray! Amen!

# DECEMBER 21   LOVE HAS ALREADY WON
Love

John 16:33 (NKJV)

*33 These things I have spoken to you, that in Me you may have peace. In the world you will have tribulation; but be of good cheer, I have overcome the world."*

We face many troubles and tribulations these days as many have faced for centuries. Wherever you turn, there are challenges. The news reports are mostly bad. It seems very discouraging. It can be overwhelming. A friend shared an expression his brother uses. He says he is not overwhelmed but he certainly is whelmed! I am feeling whelmed! And I may be close to the border of overwhelmed today.

In John, Jesus is speaking to His disciples about the events about to take place. He is going to be crucified and they will be scattered. He is concerned for their safety and that they will remain faithful. He has warned them about all the things that will take place. Now, He tells them not to worry because this is all part of God's plan and it will all work out. Jesus has overcome the world. His love will triumph over evil!

Sometimes, we come to a place where things are crazy, and we don't know what to do. It seems there are no good choices. All the ideas we have present a down side we dislike. We are at a point where we don't even know for what we should pray. Romans 8:26 says *"Likewise the Spirit also helps in our weaknesses. For we do not know what we should pray for as we ought, but the Spirit Himself makes intercession for us with groanings which cannot be uttered."* At times, I am at the point I do not know for what to pray. Sometimes, situations come up I don't truly understand and with which I am not prepared to deal. Have you ever been in that type of place? Have you ever been in uncharted waters? It is scary. When you are in that place, the only thing that can get you through is your faith. He has gone before us making the crooked places straight and paving the way for us. So, even if you do not know how to pray or what to pray for, you can call on Him to lead you, guide you and make your way joyous. You see, Jesus has overcome the world for us.

Thank you, Jesus, for all You have done for us. You overcame sin. You overcame death. You overcame the world for us! We don't deserve it. We can never earn it. We can never pay you back. But we do accept your gifts gladly! Since You have overcome the world, could You help us to do the same as we want to walk with You. In Your name we pray! Amen!

# DECEMBER 22    BE KIND
Relationships

Ephesians 4:32 (KJV)
³² *And be ye kind one to another, tenderhearted, forgiving one another, even as God for Christ's sake hath forgiven you.*

We were watching a movie and I heard something. They said, "Life goes by quickly, but kindness lasts forever." That struck me! If everyone tried their best to be kind to others, wouldn't our world be a much better place.

Paul is writing to the Church at Ephesus telling them not to grieve the Spirit. He is telling them to remove anger and wrath and all things evil. He tells us we are to offer forgiveness as God has done for us. He asks us to be kind.

Did you know there is a website called www.randomactsofkindness.org? There are actually people who want to spread kindness throughout the world. Are they crazy? What kind of world would it be if people started being kind to one another? How would anyone be able to climb over the bodies of their competitors if they took the time out to be kind along the way? This is insane, or is it?

When your body is lowered into a grave, it doesn't matter how much money or success you had. But if you were kind to everyone you met along the way, even the unlovable ones, the blessings you leave behind will live on forever. You can give money but when you give your time, people know you really care. Kindness is a fruit of the Spirit. God also gave us six commandments about relationships to each other in Exodus 20. If you were kind to each other, would you do any of these bad things. Jesus said to love your neighbor as yourself. Do you think you would like kindness? The randomactsofkindness.org website goes on to say that kindness spreads. It makes everything around it better. In fact, you can sign up to be a RAKtivist (RandomActsofKindness) today. You can improve your health and well-being and that of others simply by being kind to one another. Why not give it a try?

Lord, your advice is always good and good for us. Help us to be a blessing through kindness to one another. You gave us the ultimate kindness by taking on Yourself all the sin of the world. Let us reflect Your beauty to others through kindness. In Your name we pray! Amen!

I borrowed this from an e-mail I received:

May your troubles be less, your blessings be more, and nothing but happiness come through your door. Merry Christmas! "In God I Trust!"

# DECEMBER 23    HE HAS PLANS FOR YOU
## Quality of Life

Isaiah 46:10 (NKJV)

*Declaring the end from the beginning, And from ancient times things that are not yet done,*
*Saying, 'My counsel shall stand, And I will do all My pleasure,'*

In his book, *Anointed for Business*, Ed Silvoso wrote "God's purpose for you is immutable, and you have the full power of Heaven at your disposal to fulfill it." He cites John 14:14 (ask anything in My name....) and Phil 4:13 (I can do all things....) as proof. Sometimes, I wonder what God's plan is for my life. Don't you? I feel a call to do more in the work of the Lord, but I am not sure that is what He wants. Does He want me to be a tentmaker like Paul and support my own ministry? Does He want me to give up business and work for Him full-time? From moment to moment, I waver back and forth.

Isaiah tells us God's purpose will be established, and He will accomplish all He plans. God had a plan for each of us from the beginning and from ancient time. Also, God will do new things that "have not been done"! He will bring about His plan. Nothing can thwart His purpose!

Are you going along with God's plan? Do you know what His plan is? Gaining clarity of the plan seems to be difficult. I have spent time in prayer but not enough. While He speaks to me audibly at times, things are not so clear at others. Have you ever been confused? I know I am. It is hard to have one foot in each world but, with God's help, it is possible.

Well Ed Silvoso tells us we can be in both worlds at the same time; both business and ministry. In fact, he suggests the best vehicle to take us to people who need the good news is the marketplace. There are those who say, "Leave the ministry to the professionals." From what I have seen, there are not enough professionals to comfort all those who are hurting. Each day, I come in contact with hurting people that need encouragement. Many will not meet a professional minister because they have been hurt by and now avoid the Church. Even the professionals don't always get it right. It is no coincidence Jesus said to "Love others as I have loved you." He did not teach that lesson to the Pharisees. He taught it to fisherman and many on the edge of society. After all, He came that we might have life and have it abundantly. He did not come to condemn us but to save us. Can you wrap your head around that? He loves you so much He wants to be with you and wants you with Him. Wow! The Creator of the universe wants to be with you!

So, what is His plan for us? It is hard to say. Each person has a different plan which God knew before the foundations of the world. But I can tell you this. It is a plan to prosper you and not to harm you. It is a plan to give you hope and a future. (Jeremiah 29:11) So be encouraged. His plan for you is awesome. Discovering that plan is part of your purpose. I wished I could say it was easy but it's not. However, nothing really worthwhile has ever been easy. But it certainly is worth the search. I am still looking for answers. I am on the journey. Will you join me? We can enjoy each other's company on the way.

Lord, thank You for Your awesome plans for us. You said that we could ask anything in Your name, and You will do it. You said we can do all things through You. You said You would renew our strength. You tell us over and over how much You care for us. Help us to hear Your blessings and accept them into our hearts. Silence the evil and let us hear Your voice clearly. Reveal Your plans for us to us. In Your name we pray! Amen!

# DECEMBER 24   THE GREATEST GIFT
Love

John 3:16-17 (NKJV)

*16 For God so loved the world that He gave His only begotten Son, that whoever believes in Him should not perish but have everlasting life. 17 For God did not send His Son into the world to condemn the world, but that the world through Him might be saved.*

John 3:16 is probably the most famous verse in the Bible and I have read it hundreds of times. There is something special about the Bible. It is a living, breathing document. It reveals to its reader what is supposed to be revealed at any given time. This most recent reading revealed John 3:17. *For God did not send His Son into the world to condemn the world, but that the world through Him might be saved.* Bam! The greatest gift ever given is given to save the world.

The Gospel in its entirety is summed up in these verses. Jesus was speaking to Nicodemus (a member of the Sanhedrin and a religious leader in Israel) and explaining to him why He came into the world. It was hard for Nicodemus to comprehend at that time, but God's full plan was revealed in these verses. What was not yet clear was Jesus would sacrifice Himself for the saving of the world. Jesus is the gift that keeps on giving.

So, what does this mean to us on Christmas Eve? Can we even fathom the immensity of what is about to happen? The Savior of the world is about to appear and enter the world as a helpless baby. Are we ready? Romans 8:1 (NKJV) says *"There is therefore now no condemnation to those who are in Christ Jesus, who do not walk according to the flesh, but according to the Spirit."* In light of this gift, how are we supposed to live? Are we supposed to do anything we want because it is all forgiven? Certainly not! In fact, it is quite the opposite. When we are in Christ, we are a new creation. When He is in us, the light of His goodness will overflow our hearts and spill out into the world. Jesus also told a woman to "go and sin no more." With the Holy Spirit guiding you, your best self will show through.

What does it mean to be "saved"? God is offering you, through the sacrifice of His Lamb [Jesus], forgiveness of sins and life everlasting to be spent with Him in paradise. It is quite an offer. How will you respond? It's not about gifts and parties. It is about love and relationships. The love of God, which is so great that He offered Himself as a sacrifice for you, is within you. He planted the seeds there. Nurture the seeds within yourself and let that love blossom to share with all the world! In Jesus name I pray! Amen!

# DECEMBER 25   CODE ENFORCEMENT

Grace and Mercy

Deuteronomy 28:1-4 (NKJV)

*"Now it shall come to pass, if you diligently obey the voice of the LORD your God, to observe carefully all His commandments which I command you today, that the LORD your God will set you high above all nations of the earth. ²And all these blessings shall come upon you and overtake you, because you obey the voice of the LORD your God: ³ "Blessed shall you be in the city, and blessed shall you be in the country. ⁴ "Blessed shall be the fruit of your body, the produce of your ground and the increase of your herds, the increase of your cattle and the offspring of your flocks.*

Why are there laws? Why does God give you rules and regulations to follow? Is He just mean and wants to control you? He does tell us that we are to obey carefully all of His commandments. And speaking of commandments, He didn't call them the Ten Suggestions. So, what are the consequences of not following His commandments? Better yet, what if we do follow carefully?

Moses is speaking to the Children of Israel toward the end of his time leading them. They have spent close to 40 years in the wilderness and are now preparing to enter the Promised Land. Moses wants to make sure they understand why they are to follow all of God's commandments. Most people fear punishment more than they enjoy benefit. In Deuteronomy 28, Moses gives them a whole list of benefits of following. There is an incredible list of blessings in this chapter. I suggest you go there and read the whole chapter for yourself. Mainly, you will be blessed everywhere you go! God *wants* to bless you. He wishes that none shall perish.

So why enforce rules? Do they really matter? Why would anyone make rules anyway? Could it be that rules are made to make things go well? For instance, a traffic light stops traffic at times letting others go. Without the stopping, traffic would be all snarled. So, God establishes rules to prevent bad things from happening. Society has followed God's lead to some extent. Rules and laws are created to help life go more safely and smoothly.

I recently moved a client's office to a new location. Part of the process was to install new network wiring for the computers. Building permits are required for this type of work. I had to get an electrical permit to have the wiring checked and a building permit to check the fireproofing around the connections. At first, I thought that was crazy; two permits. Others said the town was very difficult and gave everyone a hard time. But I thought about the process. Why did these things need to be inspected? Because faulty wiring and lack of fireproofing can cost lives in a fire. The reason for the Building Codes was to prevent loss of life in the event of a disaster. So, these rules or codes save lives. The Building Inspector said they need to make sure fire cannot penetrate the holes made for the wiring. That would keep fire from spreading and injuring people. That means it is a good thing when you see it in that light.

It is the same way with God's rules. When they are obeyed, people are protected. Things go better in relationships. God tells you to honor your Father and Mother so you may live long in the land.... This is the first command with a promise. God wants it all to go well with you. There are many laws and rules that God set out for us and they are all intended for our benefit. There are blessings in following them and curses in disobedience. But today is a special day! You see, God knew we could not always be obedient, so He made a way for us to be reconciled to Himself even when we go astray. He sent His Son, the Lord Jesus, to redeem us. For there is forgiveness! For unto us a child is born. Unto us, a Son is given. He is the Prince of Peace. May the Peace of Christ be with you today and every day! In His name I pray! Amen!

## DECEMBER 26    F.R.O.G.

Encouragement

Proverbs 3:5-6 (NKJV)

*⁵ Trust in the LORD with all your heart, and lean not on your own understanding; ⁶ In all your ways acknowledge Him, And He shall direct your paths.*

Do you Fully Rely On God (F.R.O.G.)? Trust is a hard thing to learn. It would seem there is no reason to believe anyone would come through on a promise made. Doubt sneaks in and convinces us it is unlikely they will do it so why believe? Trust usually has to be earned. When there is a consistent pattern of promises made and promises kept, we begin to trust.

In the Book of Proverbs, we are told to trust in the Lord with all our heart and not follow what we think is right. Like a good parent with full knowledge of a situation, the Lord knows the best course of action. He will lead you in ways that will build you up. History has proven His plan for you is one for your good.

How do we Fully Rely On God (F.R.O.G.)? God says, "I will never leave nor forsake you." Should we believe Him? What proof do we have? At bad times in our lives, don't we feel terribly alone? Was Jonah alone when swallowed by a great fish? Was Moses alone when the Red Sea was parted? Was David alone when he fought Goliath? In 1 Samuel 17, David explains why he is willing to face Goliath in battle. It says

*"³⁷ Moreover David said, "The LORD, who delivered me from the paw of the lion and from the paw of the bear, He will deliver me from the hand of this Philistine."" ...... ⁴⁵ Then David said to the Philistine, "You come to me with a sword, with a spear, and with a javelin. But I come to you in the name of the LORD of hosts, the God of the armies of Israel, whom you have defied. ⁴⁶ This day the LORD will deliver you into my hand, and I will strike you and take your head from you. And this day I will give the carcasses of the camp of the Philistines to the birds of the air and the wild beasts of the earth, that all the earth may know that there is a God in Israel. ⁴⁷ Then all this assembly shall know that the LORD does not save with sword and spear; for the battle is the LORD's, and He will give you into our hands." (1 Samuel 17 NKJV)* David trusted in the Lord. He knew Scripture and remembered all the times the Lord had saved others. He recounted all the times The Lord had saved him from the lion and the bear. David fully relied on God. That is why he was called a man after God's own heart! He had evidence enough to put his trust in the Lord. Beside the Bible, don't you have evidence also? I do! There were many times where things went in my favor that were inexplicable. Divine Providence guided me. The Glory of the Lord was upon me. There was no other explanation.

What does it mean to Fully Rely On God? Is it without doubt? Can we do it completely? Does it mean you are to sit back and wait while God does all the heavy lifting? In my experience, it is a process. I don't think I have ever fully relied on God yet, but I am working in that direction. I am learning to do what I can and when I have done all I think I can, to lay the outcome at the foot of the Cross. Some people call it "Let go and let God!". Each time you try to trust, it will get better. It is like the team-building exercise where you have to fall backwards into the arms of your teammates believing they will catch you. It is scary but you learn to trust. If you trust God for the small things, He will give you bigger and bigger things as your trust grows.

Jesus has come. He has been born. So far, He has appeared as a helpless baby, but He will grow in wisdom and stature and will offer Himself as your Savior. To be redeemed, you will have to trust Him. You have the gift of hindsight and the Bible. Hopefully, you know the whole story of His coming and sacrifice on your behalf. He has made the offer and will return to draw, to Himself, His own. Will you trust Him? Will you Fully Rely On God?

Lord Jesus, we want to trust you, but it is hard. The forces of this world throw up doubt in our path. Help us to keep our eyes focused on you. When we draw back in fear, send us Your Comforter to help us through. You said You would never leave nor forsake us. Remind us of Your presence in the midst of our trials. And then, remind us of all the blessings You have already poured out upon us and let us be grateful! In Your name we pray! Amen!

# DECEMBER 27 LOVE RIGHT THROUGH

Loneliness

James 1:12 (NIV)

*"Blessed is the one who perseveres under trial because, having stood the test, that person will receive the crown of life that the Lord has promised to those who love him."*

Life is tough! There are a lot of challenges and much pain. We lose friends and family along the way. We face trials and tribulations. It is easy to get discouraged and feel like giving up in the midst of the battle. But don't hide from the pain, love right through it. The things you face are there to make you stronger and refine you in ways that an easy life cannot. Trials are good for our character! I know you are already a character, but this will still help.

James tells us to be strong and persevere through the trials. He tells us a person will receive the crown of life. What is this crown of life? Jeremy Meyers (https://redeeminggod.com/what-is-the-crown-of-life/) tells us that The Crown of Life, however, is a reward for special acts of service and perseverance under trial. The Crown of Life is special reward for a special act of service and dedication to the King. It is not eternal life which is given to anyone who believes in Jesus.

There are all kinds of trials. People are entering and exiting your life, some by death. We think it was providential that someone from a long time ago re-enters our lives and we are joyful. Some people are in your life for a reason; some people are in your life for a season. It is good when some leave. It is devastating when others leave without reason. We thought they were going to be a blessing but that is not the way it turned out. The feeling of loss at this time of year can be overwhelming. There were empty seats at our Christmas table. Are you feeling the loss, too?

When loneliness or disaster strikes, which way do you run? Do you run to or away from God? Proverbs 18:10 says *"The name of the Lord is a strong tower; The righteous run to it and are safe."* Since God is love, wouldn't it be best to run to Him? Don't hide from the pain, love right through it. When you run to the Lord, He will receive you and give you all you need to stand firm in His love.

It is written that love never fails. Since God is love, He never fails you. Run to him for comfort and strength. He never slumbers nor sleeps. He is always there waiting for you to receive you and embrace you. Revel in that embrace! He will give you what you need to persevere. He will help you love right through!

How is it that you are always there for us Lord? Thank You that You give us what we need to stand firm in You. A mighty Fortress is our God. Run to Him for safety. He loves you and has your crown of life waiting. In His name we pray! Amen!

# DECEMBER 28   WHAT IF

Grace and Mercy

Luke 2:11-12 (NIV)

*¹¹ Today in the town of David a Savior has been born to you; he is the Messiah, the Lord.*
*¹² This will be a sign to you: You will find a baby wrapped in cloths and lying in a manger."*

Have you ever noticed the young children ask a lot of questions? We have a new foster son. He asks questions constantly. One of the biggest questions is "what if...?" What if the sun doesn't come up? What if it never rains? What if the other person doesn't like me? What if? What if? What if?

Luke told the story of the birth of Jesus. He told us that a Savior had been born in Bethlehem. And this child had been born to *us*! The Messiah, the Lord had come into this world to free us from sin and overcome death. Angels told the shepherds they would find this baby in a stable's feeding trough. How unlikely!

A few days ago, was the anniversary of the birth of Jesus, our Savior. My pastor in her message today asked "What if Jesus had not come?" That is a really tough what if question. What if Jesus had not come? Wasn't He the Savior of the world? Didn't He overcome sin and death all on our behalf? Where would we be without Him? We would still be facing sin and death. You see, Jesus took upon Himself all of the evil of this world so we would not have to carry it anymore. The Law pointed out our faults but only offered animal sacrifices as atonement. Those sacrifices had to be repeated each time we sin. Jesus was the perfect and complete sacrifice once, for all! That is why He is called our Savior. As He said, "It is finished." What if He had not come?

Do you run your life around "What if's"? Are you paralyzed by every situation worrying what might happen? Does fear grip you constantly waiting for the next disaster to happen? Is that the way you want to live? Fortunately, Jesus has come! He absorbed sin and tasted death on our behalf. There is nothing else you need do except put your faith and trust in Him. Will you? What if Jesus offered you forgiveness? What if He offered you grace? What if He offered you life eternal with Him in paradise? Well He did! Now what? Will you accept the offer? What if you accept His offer? Will your life be curtailed? Quite the contrary! With fear and anxiety removed, your life will be incredibly better! Accept His grace and live the abundant life He came to give you! In Jesus name I pray! Amen!

# DECEMBER 29    ARMED AND DANGEROUS

Prayer/Praise

Daniel 3:16-18 (NIV)

*¹⁶ Shadrach, Meshach and Abed-Nego replied to him, "King Nebuchadnezzar, we do not need to defend ourselves before you in this matter. ¹⁷ If we are thrown into the blazing furnace, the God we serve is able to deliver us from it, and he will deliver us from Your Majesty's hand. ¹⁸ But even if he does not, we want you to know, Your Majesty, that we will not serve your gods or worship the image of gold you have set up."*

I'm a dangerous man. I've got a Bible and I am not afraid to use it! I pray dangerous prayers. I will boldly pray for healing. Someone once said that my prayers are dangerous. What if I pray for healing and the person doesn't get well? What if I don't pray for their healing? Will that help them? If I pray for healing and their illness gets worse, am I a failure at praying?

Sometimes we pray for healing when God has a resurrection in mind. Their healing may not come in this life. Should I give in to the enemy and not pray at all? After all, what good will it do? The Scripture says the prayers of a righteous man avails much. Maybe I am not righteous enough? Maybe that is why God did not answer my prayer in the way I wanted. Or did He? You see, I usually add an addendum. Four words: *"Thy will be done!"* I believe God knows best! When I pray, I ask for what I think is best but know God's plan is really the way to go.

I have a friend with stage 4 cancer. He is a believer! The cancer is all over and spreading. I take him to some of his appointments and we speak frankly. What if he does not make it? Our conversation is about the truth. We plan for contingencies. Things are not looking good. But we do not speak as those who do not have hope. For I was not given a spirit of timidity but of boldness. I boldly ask for his healing. I am going to launch an all-out campaign of fervent prayer. I will P.U.S.H (Pray Until Something Happens)! It is my nature to push. So Lord, watch out. I am going to keep bugging you for the healing of my friend. I will pray without ceasing. Since I am righteous by the blood of the Lamb, I know You will hear and listen to those prayers. I will come into Your presence again and again with this petition. Please heal him! But even if You don't my hope is You alone. Shadrach, Meshach and Abed-nego were tested and replied to him, *"King Nebuchadnezzar, we do not need to defend ourselves before you in this matter. ¹⁷ If we are thrown into the blazing furnace, the God we serve is able to deliver us from it, and he will deliver us from Your Majesty's hand. ¹⁸ But even if he does not, we want you to know, Your Majesty, that we will not serve your gods or worship the image of gold you have set up."*

You see, I am not just a man of faith when things are going my way. I walk with my Lord wherever He leads. Good times and bad, Jesus is my Lord and Savior. It is all up to Him. He will deliver me. Who will deliver you?

Father, I thank you for each day and each person I meet. Your grace is unfathomable. Nevertheless, I come to Your throne boldly asking for more. I ask for the healing of my friend. I know You can do all things. As Your servant, I ask for this one thing. While I remain steadfast in my faith, I boldly pray for a healing now. In Jesus name I pray.

## DECEMBER 30    A PRISON OF REGRET

Failure

Luke 22:61-62 (NKJV)

*The Lord turned and looked at Peter. Then Peter remembered the word of the Lord, how He had told him, "Before a rooster crows, you will deny Me three times." So Peter went out and wept bitterly.*

Have you ever made a mistake? I mean a really bad one; the kind of mistake that could ruin everything. Something you think could damage your future. That is what happened to Peter. He thought it was all over.

Jesus had predicted that Peter would deny Him and that is exactly what happened. It's that whole Son of God thing. When Jesus was at the house of the High Priest being berated and falsely accused, Peter arrived. People recognized Peter as a disciple of Jesus, but he denied it three times out in the courtyard. Then he saw Jesus and remembered the prophecy. Then, the rooster crowed. Peter had told Jesus he would never deny Him and now he had three times. Peter wept bitterly.

Peter probably thought it was all over for him. He had betrayed the Christ and there was no turning back. What was he thinking? He had gone back on his word and doubts of his worthiness were creeping in. The accuser always uses doubt to get us off track. If he can distract us from the goal, he wins. Peter probably feels everything is lost at this point. He has denied the Lord. It cannot get any worse. But Jesus made another prophecy about Peter also. Jesus changed Simon's name to Peter and said "on this rock, I will build my Church" Peter means rock. Even though Jesus knew Peter would fail, He also knew Peter would come back stronger. There was redemption in the plan. The changing of Simon to Peter also indicated a new redeemed life. No matter how dark it looks, God still has a good plan for you. Have you failed more than once? Peter did! I sure do. Do you think you are beyond redemption? Are you carrying that heavy burden? Remember the thief on the cross beside Jesus? Jesus said that thief "would be with Him in paradise!" If Jesus can redeem the thief, He can redeem you. You may have lost the battle, but Jesus already won the war! Love wins!

What burdens are you carrying today? Do you feel you are beyond hope? Are you discouraged? It doesn't have to be that way. Every mistake you have ever made can be washed away and your life can take a whole new direction. In Christ, you can be made new. There is hope for you! Ask Him!

Lord, will You redeem us? You said we could be with You in paradise. You said You go to prepare a place for us. You said You would give us rest. We are in need of all these things. We are in need of You! Open our hearts and minds toward You and give us Your Salvation. As the year draws to a close and we make plans for the next one, help us include You in those plans. Walk with us and guide us where You would have us go. Bless us by Your Spirit and guide us into that good plan You have for us. In Your name we pray! Amen!

## DECEMBER 31   LOVE HAS ALREADY WON
Love

Romans 8:37–39 (NKJV)

*37 Yet in all these things we are more than conquerors through Him who loved us. 38 For I am persuaded that neither death nor life, nor angels nor principalities nor powers, nor things present nor things to come, 39 nor height nor depth, nor any other created thing, shall be able to separate us from the love of God which is in Christ Jesus our Lord.*

It is the end of another year! Was it good or bad for you? It was challenging for me. I lost my best friend and several others, went through skin cancer, and struggled through a few other challenges along the way. I am not complaining. The Lord has been with me every step of the way. I can feel Him. Don't get me wrong. I don't understand why Carmen died at 63 and I am suffering the loss. It ambushes me when I least expect it. Considering all the things life throws at us, it is easy to get discouraged. John 16:33b (NIV) says *33 "In this world you will have trouble. But take heart! I have overcome the world."* Jesus told us so we would know that we can too with His help!

In Romans, Paul tells us we are "more than conquerors" through Him who loved us. Fortunately, He still loves us and walks with us. Paul tells us nothing can separate us from the love of God through Christ. He gives a substantial list of things that can get in the way but with the Lord's help, we can overcome them all. Nothing can separate us from the love of God.

At this time of reflection of the past and anticipation of the future, we can have mixed emotions. Do we make New Year's Resolutions? I know it is good to have a plan but make sure you include the Lord in that plan. Leave Him room to guide you to your destiny. Many are concerned about the future. There are many bad things happening. There are wars and rumors of wars but there have always been those things. Yet the Lord is still on His throne. He can make all things new. When the world looks dark, it is time for you to shine the light God gave you. There, inside you, is the light of His Spirit. You can shine that light into the darkness and chase it away one person at a time. Love one another as God has loved us. Love never fails. As the New Year approaches, make a resolution to do random acts of kindness and spread the love of God, which He gave you, in this world and see what happens.

Lord, You said in 1 John 4:18 (NIV) *18 There is no fear in love. But perfect love drives out fear, because fear has to do with punishment.* The one who fears is not made perfect in love. Help us drive out fear with Your love both in ourselves and those we meet. Help us to anticipate the coming year with joy, knowing You have a great plan for us. Guide us in our making plans that will include Your will for us. Remind us that You walk with us every step of the way. And, in the times we are unable to take the next step, we can rest assured knowing that You will carry us. Thank You for Your faithfulness always. Mostly, thank You that You love us with an incredible love! In Your name we pray! Amen!

## AFTERWORD

Why does God love us so much? Because we are His beloved children. I want you to know the height, width and depth of the love the LORD has for you and to walk in that Grace. You are loved beyond anything you could ask or imagine and highly favored.

The Lord has been good to me. Encouragement Daily is all His doing. By His Spirit, I am able to share His Word with you in a way I hope will draw you closer to Him. I set out to encourage you! How did I do? Did I achieve the goal for which I was called write these?

While this was not easy, the rewards are incredible. I have led several people to Christ. I have heard from many people who said that each article was just what they needed at the time. That is proof that God's timing is perfect.

Please let me know how these devotionals have touched you and what I can do to further encourage you. Also, if there is a need that you have, let me know. It may help others as well. Your feedback is important to me. It gives me encouragement to continue and an idea of what you need.

There are additional devotionals on www.EncouragementDaily.us. I hope to be inspired to post more articles on the website. Write to me at bob@calldrbob.com and *let me remind you how much God loves you.*

In Him,

# "Dr. Bob"

Robert "Dr. Bob" Springer
225 Peachtree Drive
Rural Delivery #2
Basking Ridge, NJ 07920
908.625.8149
bob@calldrbob.com
www.EncouragementDaily.us

ABOUT THE AUTHOR

### *Robert H. "Dr. Bob" Springer Biography*

Bob was Born in NYC as a first-generation US Citizen to German Holocaust survivor parents, Fred and Trudy Springer. He moved to Fords, NJ, the suburbs, in the 1950's where he lived until marrying Jean. He met and befriended Carmen DiCanto in Kindergarten and they remained friends until his Carmen's home-going in 2015. Out of that friendship came a lifelong friendship with Christine, Carmen's wife and Bob and Jean's friend. Carmen and Bob raised a lot of hell before their wives entered the pictures and calmed them down.

Bob married Jean in June 1975 and moved to Basking Ridge. Life before Jean was pretty insignificant. Things happened but she made everything better.

Bob and Jean are proud Foster and Adoptive parents to Devon, Josh, John, Kiara, Clayton & Brandon. They have two sons – Clayton, who came to live with them in 2009 and is currently in Raritan Valley Community College and Brandon who joined the family in 2017. Brandon is in 5th grade.

Bob volunteered with Youth Group at Pluckemin Presbyterian Church in 1996 for a week. That lasted 7 years. It seems Youth Ministry was Bob's passion. In fact, the youth led him to Christ. He is an ardent and passionate follower of Jesus Christ since May 31, 1998.

Bob's career in education began in the US Army Reserve in 1975 when he became the Chief Instructor of the Motor Transport Operators Course at Fort Dix. He was awarded US Army Reserve Outstanding Instructor commendation at Annual Training in 1975. In the pursuit of excellence, Bob became a Certified Master Automobile Technician which is a certification he has held since 1977. With a strong background in service-related business, Bob has served people in many capacities.

Robert H. "Dr. Bob" Springer is a nationally known consultant, speaker and trainer who motivates audiences with an exciting blend of humor, animation and information bridging the gap between faith, technology and real-world business. He speaks your language! He has delivered messages on business and life and now, Spiritual disciplines.

He believes in the phrase "Learn from the mistakes of others." You don't have time to make them all yourself!

As a Microsoft Certified Professional and Small Business Specialist with over 40 years in business experience, He is uniquely qualified to address people from varied backgrounds in regard to life, business and technology. Bob started in small business in 1973, sales in 1990 and technology in 1995 after years of using technology as a hobby. He founded several companies dedicated to education, motivation and personal growth through technology. Bob serves to make people more efficient, effective and profitable.

*Things Bob has done:*

US Air Force Jet engine technician
Woodbridge Township Adult Education Instructor in auto mechanics
Strong background in service related business
Worked in Service & Inside Sales since 1970
Spent eight years in outside Sales
Small business owner for over forty years
Member of Lions International (service club that serves the visually impaired) since 1976 and entered into the Melvin Jones Fellowship (Founder of Lions International).
Worked with both micro & mainframe computers business applications since 1978
Joined with Action Leasing and Sales in 1992 as their VP of Sales and Marketing
Created and instituted a *TOP PRODUCER* computer training program in 1994
Presented seminars on how to automate your Real Estate business
Installed and serviced individual and networked computer systems since 1992
Volunteered as an instructor in Hunterdon County's Senior Citizen Computer education program
Formed *SPRINGER SYSTEMS* in 1995 to focus on computers in the Real Estate
Developed a one - one consulting program for Real Estate Agent development
Became a member of the Real Estate Educators Association in 1996
Became an Advisor for a Youth Outreach Program in July 1996
Formed an alliance with the Somerset County Board of REALTORS in 1996
Formed an alliance with the Mercer County Board of REALTORS in 1996
Formed an alliance with the Hunterdon County Board of REALTORS in 1996
Became an On-Line Agent Software Distributor and a Gold Reseller in February 1997
Joined Lincoln Technical Institute as Corporate Training Specialist in January 1998
Joined *MOORE* Data Management as Eastern Regional Sales Manager in Sept 1998
Became National Account Manager for Moore/VISTAinfo in August 1999
Reestablished *SPRINGER SYSTEMS* in August 2000 as a Manufacturers Rep
Developed the "No Fear Technology Boot Camp" to train the technologically challenged
Created a business consulting program to help small business grow using technology
Joined with MIMS™ Software to offer technology to Funeral Directors in July 2003
Youth Group Leader 1996-2004
Bible Study Fellowship 2001-2015
Church Elder at Christ Presbyterian Church 2009
Board Member of New City Kids Church 2003-2009
Board Member of Youth Empowerment Services in 2014

Bob has been on a continual program of self-improvement, studying books, tapes and attending seminars of some of the finest trainers available. These include but are not limited to Tom Hopkins, Zig Ziglar, Brian Tracy, Dr. Dennis Waitley, Floyd Wickman. Norman Vincent Peale, Roger Dawson, Og Mandino, Dave Ramsey, Dr. Nido

Qubein, Joel Osteen, Napoleon Hill, Mark Sanborn, Randy Schwan, Dr. Robert Schuller, Michael Gerber and Dale Carnegie, Joel Osteen and Joseph Prince.

### *Memberships:*

Interfaith Hospitality Network, Habitat for Humanity, Promise Keepers, Lions International Melvin Jones Fellowship, Associate Member of Union County Association of the Blind, Bible Study Fellowship, Real Estate Educators Association, National Institute for Automotive Service Excellence, Somerset Hills Business Network, Kingdom Chamber of Commerce, Honda Council of Sales Leadership, Every Man a Warrior Men's Ministry, Hearts for Honduras, Boy Scouts of America

.

# INDEX

### *Failure*

## *Faith*

| | | |
|---|---|---|
| January 8 | Run Your Race | Hebrews 12:1-3 |
| January 17 | Don't Worry, Be Happy! | Philippians 4:6-7 |
| January 18 | How's Your Faith? | Hebrews 11:1-6 |
| January 20 | The Devil Made Me Do It! | Luke 10:17-20 |
| January 21 | If God Be For Us.... | 2 Kings 6:16-18 |
| January 28 | Are You Listening? | 1 Kings 19:9-13 |
| February 1 | You Are Amazing! | Philippians 4:12b-13 |
| February 2 | Ask and You Shall Receive | James 4:1-3 |
| February 6 | Getting to Know You | 2 Timothy 3:16 |
| February 28 | How can I be Sure? | Isaiah 54:10 |
| February 29 | Take a Leap of Faith! | Hebrews 11:1-3 |
| March 1 | What, me worry? | Luke 12 (NIV) |
| March 3 | God Loves You | John 3:16 |
| March 10 | Live Confidently | Hebrews 13:5b |
| March 13 | Who Do You Say I Am | Matthew 16:13-18 |
| March 19 | He is Risen So We Can Rise | 1 Corinthians 15:3-4 |
| March 20 | Salvation is Here | 2 Corinthians 6:1-2 |
| March 23 | Who is This Man | John 1:29-31 |
| March 25 | How Can I Do This | Hebrews 2:17-18 |
| March 26 | Leave room for God | Numbers 14:39-45 |
| March 27 | One wish | Luke 18:35-43 |
| March 30 | Fan the Flames | Luke 24:13-35 |
| April 5 | It's Friday | Luke 24:1-12 |
| April 7 | Going Through It | Psalm 30:11-12 |
| April 8 | Stay the Course | Luke 18:1-8 |
| April 9 | I Am With You | Isaiah 41:10-11 |
| April 11 | If you Want to Walk | Matthew 14:25-33 |
| April 20 | You Are Chosen | Isaiah 49:6-7 |
| April 21 | The Bible is the Word | 2 Timothy 3:16-17 |
| April 25 | Send Us | Isaiah 6:8 (NKJV) |
| April 28 | Why Am I Here | Ephesians 2:8-10 |
| April 30 | Sing to Him Who Listens | Psalm 68:4 (NIV) |
| May 1 | Do the Impossible | Romans 8:31-32 |
| May 8 | Are You Looking For Jesus | Revelation 3:20 |
| May 14 | Undefeated | 1 Samuel 17:45-46 |
| May 16 | Is Jesus an Accessory | John14:12-14 |
| May 18 | Seeing is Believing | John 20:24-29 |
| May 22 | Your Dreams Are Not Dead | Numbers 17:7-8 |
| May 27 | Whom Shall We Follow | Acts 4:18-20 |
| May 31 | Your Will Be Done | Luke 22:42 |
| June 3 | Who do You Say I Am | Matthew 16:15-15 |

| | | |
|---|---|---|
| June 6 | I'm Not Sure I Can | Philippians 4:13 |
| June 7 | Because You Said So | Luke 5:3-5 |
| June 15 | You Will Prevail | Psalm 129 |
| June 27 | Just as I Am | Romans 8:1 |
| June 29 | Spread Your Wings | Isaiah 40:30-31 |
| July 6 | Singing the Blues | Psalm 30:11-12 |
| July 15 | All things Are Possible | Ezekiel 37:4-6 |
| July 24 | Who is in Your Heart | Ephesians 3:14-19 |
| July 25 | Thanks for Doubting | John 20:26-29 |
| August 7 | Unimpeachable | Acts 1:8 |
| August 9 | God's Timing is Perfect | Galatians 4:4 |
| August 11 | Flowers in God's Garden | Mark 4:3-9 |
| August 13 | Masterpiece | Ephesians 2:10 |
| August 24 | Why Won't You Answer | John 14:13-14 |
| August 25 | Wrapped in Righteousness | Isaiah 61:10 |
| August 26 | Head to Heart to Head | Deuteronomy 8:2 |
| September 5 | I'm always on time | Habakkuk 2:3 |
| September 10 | Politically or Biblically | 1 Corinthians 1:20-25 |
| September 12 | What is my purpose | Exodus 9:16 |
| September 20 | Nevertheless | James 1:12 |
| October 7 | Will I See the Kingdom | Luke 17:20-21 |
| October 25 | To Dream the Impossible Dream | Ephesians 3:20 |
| November 1 | God is in the Restoration Business | Luke 8:43-44 |
| November 5 | Who is This Guy | Luke 24:32 |
| November 7 | I'm Not Ready | Exodus 4:10-16 |
| November 12 | Can I Really Make a Difference | Psalms 96:3 |
| November 15 | God Changed My Name | Genesis 32:24-28 |
| November 17 | What Shall I Call You | Romans 10:13 |
| November 19 | You are the Promise | Genesis 22:18 |
| December 5 | Speak Lord, Your Servant Listens | 1 Samuel 3:7-11 |
| December 12 | The Evening News | Psalm 37:1-4 |
| December 15 | Let's See What You Can Do | Titus 3:5 |
| December 17 | Don't Be Afraid | John 14:1-3 |

## *Grace and Mercy*

| | | |
|---|---|---|
| January 14 | Are you different? | Matthew 5:17-18 |
| January 19 | Mindful of Grace | Jeremiah 31:33 |
| January 26 | Why Can't I Forgive Myself? | Leviticus 16 |
| February 3 | His Grace is Sufficient! | 2 Cor 12:7-10 |
| February 5 | Dying to Self | John 12:24 |
| February 14 | Who Loves You? | 1 Cor 13:1-13 |
| February 18 | Who is the Guy | Mark 1:40-45 |
| February 19 | I Know What You Mean | Hebrews 4:15-16 |

## *Quality of Life*

### Redemption

### Relationships

### *Support*